The Fence

THE FENCE
In the Shadow of Two Worlds

DARRELL J. STEFFENSMEIER

ROWMAN & LITTLEFIELD
PUBLISHERS

for
Erin, daughter and friend

ROWMAN & LITTLEFIELD

Published in the United States of America in 1986
by Rowman & Littlefield, Publishers
(a division of Littlefield, Adams & Company)
81 Adams Drive, Totowa, New Jersey 07512

Library of Congress Cataloging-in-Publication Data
Steffensmeier, Darrell J., 1942–
  The fence.

  Bibliography: p. 287
  Includes index.
  1. Receiving stolen goods—United States. I. Title.
HV6658.S72   1986   364.1'62   85–23752
ISBN 0–8476–7494–0
ISBN 0–8476–7495–9 (pbk.)

86 87 88 / 10 9 8 7 6 5 4 3 2 1
Printed in the United States of America

Contents

Acknowledgments

I am grateful to many people who have contributed to this document in one way or another. I thank the scholars who read parts or all of the manuscript: Emilie Allan, Gilbert Geis, Don Gibbons, Gary Faulkner, Miles Harer, Carl Klockars, Roland Pellegrin, Don Shoemaker, Lisa Sherlock, R. H. Steffensmeier, Robert Terry, and several anonymous reviewers.

For help with the typing I want to thank Barbara Harry, Susan Mann, Rita Kline, Debbie Shade, and Betsy Will. Thanks, too, to Glenn and Claire Krieder for much needed help with the university computing and word processing system. I am particularly grateful to Barbara Johnson for superb transcribing of tapes and field notes, to Barbara Minard for consistently fine editing, and to Mary Simmons of Rowman & Littlefield for her final editing touches. I also want to thank several research assistants who provided invaluable help in so many ways: Jane Boehm, John Kokenda, Kim Law, Mary Petruska, Peggy Phelps, and Carol Williams.

In addition, I wish to thank Frank Clemente, who used his position as chairman of the sociology department at Pennsylvania State University to foster efforts such as this, both through personal encouragement and some financial assistance. The Liberal Arts Research Office at Penn State also provided some financial assistance, for which I am grateful. I also thank the Pennsylvania State University for providing a sabbatical leave that enabled me to complete much of the field interviewing for the study.

Very special thanks are due to the many "informants" who made this document possible. I offer here confidential acknowledgment to Bogart, Chubby, Cecil, Dorothy, Larry, Mickey, Rocky, Squirrel, Steelbeams, and Tommy as well as to two very special couples: Jesse and Bernice, John and Clare. Some others who participated but preferred no public acknowledgment, not even a confidential one, to them I simply say "thanks."

Most important, of course, is Sam himself. This book uses him as an exemplar of a kind, but in many ways he was a collaborator as well. He taught me much, for which I am grateful.

Thanks, too, to Renée, for putting up with it all, and for much listening. I appreciate her confidence in this venture.

And, a giant thank you to Erin who wished her Daddy didn't have to make so many out-of-town trips to see "bad" people and who greeted him so enthusiastically when he returned. This book is dedicated to her.

Chapter 1

Introduction

Sam Goodman

This book is about the world of the "fence"—the dealer in stolen goods. It is based on the experiences of "Sam Goodman" (the pseudonym of a real fence) and on the observations of persons who did business with him; it is a study of how crime is woven into the fabric of society, of how thieves and fences rely on all of us "law abiding citizens." It is, in effect, an analysis of contemporary society, since the fence and his social world are a reflection of the state of the larger society.

I first met Sam Goodman, a white male, nearing sixty years of age, through the recommendation of several burglars I had been interviewing as part of a research project on the topic of female criminality. "Talk to Sam," they advised, "He's an 'old head,' knows his way around if anybody does." I did interview Sam—in January of 1980 in the Midstate Penitentiary where he was serving a three year prison term for receiving stolen property. During this interview, in questioning Sam about the types of crimes women commit and the criminal roles they play, I found my interest shifting to questions about Sam himself, his life and his colorful criminal career. And hence this book was born. Since then, I have regularly interviewed and studied Sam, even after his release from prison in the summer of 1981 and on into the present period.

At the time of his arrest on charges of receiving stolen goods, which led to his incarceration at Midstate Prison, Sam was probably the best-known fence in the city (hereafter American City) where he practiced his illegal trade. Here Sam drifted into fencing on a part-time basis in the early nineteen-sixties and then graduated to a large-scale dealership during the late sixties and mid-seventies. (Sam describes his criminal career as well as his eventual drift into fencing in chapter 3, Getting Into Business.)

At present, Sam has settled in a mid-sized city about eighty miles from American City where he has reestablished himself as a legitimate dealer in secondhand goods and antiques. He has not completely abandoned the fencing, but it is small-scale compared to what it once was. Very recently, indeed in the spring of 1984, Sam again was arrested for receiving stolen goods, prompting this response:

▶ The charges are gonna be dropped. My lawyer is handling that. But it is costing me a pretty penny. Really, this is it. I'm gonna pack it in for good, go strictly legit. The dealing I'm doing now is nickel and dime anyway, not like it was in American City. See, I don't have the contacts here, and, with my record, there are too many hassles. ◀

Whether Sam will really "pack it in," remains to be seen, since he cautiously vouchsafed similar intentions to reform during his imprisonment at Midstate. At that time, Sam told me:

▶ My aim when I get out is to pack in the fencing altogether. Open up a little secondhand shop but run it strictly legit 'cause I always made good money from just the legit side. That's not a hundred percent, now, 'cause you never know what you can fall into, how you'll respond on the outside. But I am going to get away from American City, too many temptations. I'm gonna open up elsewhere. ◀

Because Sam's career as a fence was in fullest bloom in the early and mid-seventies, the book focuses more on the conditions of that time period. Furthermore, because Sam has not completely abandoned fencing and because he maintains contacts with thieves and fences and, hence, has access to current activities, I use the present tense in presenting my analysis while maintaining the past tense when quoting from Sam's personal account.

In order not to endanger my security, Sam's security, and the security of others, I have changed the names, dates, and certain details so that neither Sam nor his associates can be identified by what is written here. I have also rearranged the order of many of Sam's statements and have edited his prose to remove the false starts and repetitions common to speech, but annoying in print.

Also, I have "cleaned up" Sam's language in the document, with the exception of chapter 3 in which Sam offers a firsthand account of the events, people, and turning points that shaped his life and his eventual drift into fencing. I also leave intact the language of Sam's associates whose comments I occasionally footnote in the document. The flatness of perspective in writing style that is evident in my analysis juxtaposes the colorful comments of Sam and his associates, so that the book is an engaging as well as informative document.

The Approach

I approach Sam's dealership in stolen goods and describe his fencing involvement as akin to that of any legitimate occupation or business. There are, after all, many similarities between a legitimate business and a fencing business—the incomes of both depend on the scope of operations and the operator's skill at marketing; both need people who can be trusted, people who can remain loyal, people who can keep secrets or at least are discreet about what they say, people who are on time, and people who are dependable.

At the same time, I approach Sam's trade in stolen goods as an *illegal* business, as a business having an *underworld* side to it. Unlike the honest businessman, the fence has to avoid the arm of the law, so that the essential characteristics of any criminal career or an illegal occupation are similar to, yet in other ways profoundly different from, the characteristics of any legitimate career, business, or type of work. Unlike the legitimate entrepreneur, the would-be fence must deal with at least two major threats. One is the threat of arrest and imprisonment—the fence is subject to sanctioning by the authorities. The second is the threat from other criminals who may betray one another to social control agents, blackmail each other, cheat in their dealings, or attack one another. Criminals lack the institutional supports available to respectable people: they cannot turn to social control agents to enforce their rules and mediate their disputes, and they must do without many of the protections that the law provides.

These two conditions—the dangers posed by officials and by deviant associates—provide the would-be fence with the situational problems to which the organization and culture of a fencing operation must adapt. First, the fence faces the problem of acquiring the skills and qualifications for undertaking a fencing business. These are not available through conventional channels, such as schools or books, but are mainly acquired through illicit and cumulative criminal experience.

Second, the fence confronts the problem of establishing safe and predictable relationships in a hazardous environment where there are special impediments to mutual trust and communication. Not only must he worry about the dangers posed by officials but deviant associates may also jeopardize his security or well-being. The fence's trade partners also experience these dangers, so that both sides will attempt to neutralize the law and its agents and to regulate their relationships with one another, such as by concealing their operations and by restricting their dealings to those who can be trusted.

Third, the fence faces the problem of gaining satisfaction from dealing in stolen goods in the face of high risks and a hostile environment. The rewards of fencing, such as money or excitement, must compensate for time and effort as well as for the risks of sanctions and exploitation.

Fourth, the fence encounters the problem of rationale—how to look at, justify, make sense of, and refer to his particular world. That is, he must contend with the invidious moral evaluation and the "put down" that society evinces toward those engaged in behavior which is illegal, immoral, and disapproved.

This does not mean that Sam and his deviant associates inhabit a social and physical world strictly separate from the rest of society. They walk the same streets, dine in the same restaurants, and send their children to the same schools. Indeed, as in Sam's case, most fences also run legitimate businesses. Nonetheless, it is also true that those regularly involved in illegal activities form a subculture that is distinct from the society in which it is embedded. Merchants and businessmen who are not fences are unlikely to know anything about the relationship between "Fat Tony" and "The Iceman" or to include among their regular contacts persons who can obtain a stolen gun or false identification papers if needed.

The underworld is not a mythical notion. Broadly, it refers to the culture, setting, or social organization associated with criminal activities and more general rule-violating behavior. It consists of a heterogeneous set of persons, organizations, and relations, a system of informal unity and reciprocity. Burglary crews, auto thieves, gamblers, drug dealers, fences, illicit gun dealers, forgers, the syndicates, and corrupt police all have actual and potential relationships with one another that are different from those they have with people not in the underworld. These individuals and groups form a kind of "loosely coupled system"—in the sense of being linked to one another and to crime activities, responsive to one another while still maintaining independent identities and some evidence of physical and logical separateness.

The embedment of a fencing business in the setting and culture of the underworld permeates Sam's experience as a dealer in stolen goods. The themes of trust, safety, reputation, and toughness shape Sam's perception of the reality of fencing and color the language he uses to portray it.

Corroboration and Generalizability

A case study of this kind raises two questions: Whether the subject is telling the truth, and whether what he tells, or what we learn from him, can be generalized to similarly situated persons or involvements.

Consequently, I have sought in several ways to cross check what Sam told me, and also to supplement his experiences. This process, in my view, not only has attested to the overall veracity of Sam's account but has demonstrated that what is written here about him and his methods of doing business is applicable to other fences—in particular, to the generalist dealer who operates fairly openly and is known to be a fence among thieves and police. (See chapter 2 for a description of the kind of fence Sam represents.) This does not mean that all fences run a fencing business exactly as Sam did, nor that they got into fencing by the same paths as did Sam. Rather, the legal and economic obstacles faced by Sam are faced by other dealers, and the contingencies for meeting these obstacles are as operative for fences as a whole as they were for Sam (See discussion in chapter 13). So too, Sam's moral stance towards dealing in stolen goods, together with the rewards and risks of a fencing involvement, are shared by other fences. And the skills Sam possessed or acquired are the trademark of fences more generally.

First, the interview format itself provided a cross check of what Sam told me. Talking about his fencing involvement at different intervals, allowed me to compare what he told me the second, third, or fourth time with what he had told me five or six months earlier. Since many of these conversations were routinely tape-recorded, it was easy to check for discrepancies. In fact, I found only the most minor discrepancies. The tape-recording also helped ensure that I have not added phrases and sentences to Sam's discourse which he did not actually say. And Sam has read over this document to further ensure that any particular phrase is his and not mine. Nonetheless, even a transcribed recording may not always adequately convey what Sam meant because he accompanies what he says with gestures, facial expressions, and changes in voice tone which are fully a part of the words he uses.

Second, I had access to documents which corroborated Sam's testimony. These included newspaper articles, court records, and miscellaneous personal doucments which Sam himself showed me, such as letters, sales receipts, and advertisements.

Third, in addition to interviewing Sam about his business and watching him work at it, I was able to interview or to meet with, in a casual way, many persons who had contact with him or know about him: thieves, customers, other dealers, friends, and police. Sam freely allowed me to talk to anyone I desired, and frequently assisted me in making the initial contact. With their agreement, I provide footnoted comments from some of Sam's associates about his character and about his fencing business, that includes: *Steelbeams*—an established burglar and truck hijacker; *Rocky*—a young burglar and one of Sam's "regulars"; *Mickey*—a general thief who occasionally sold to Sam; *Tommy*—a truck driver who "dropped off" overload items at Sam's store or at a prearranged setting: *Chubbie*—a hanger-on who spent much of his free time at Sam's store; and *Jesse*— Sam's one-time burglary partner and crusty friend. As the comments of Steelbeams, Rocky, Mickey, and Tommy are flattering toward Sam— from whose perspective Sam was a "good offman"—Jesse's comments about Sam's success as a dealer in stolen goods are sobering.[1]

Fourth, I have discussed the ideas and themes of this book with a number of police and legal officials, several of whom have read and commented on parts of the manuscript. And I have discussed some of these matters with several other fences that I met in the course of this study.

---

1. Besides "fence," some burglars/thieves use the expression "offman" to mean: someone by whom the thief is able to unload or "get off" the stolen goods in his possession. Of his part, Sam observes:

"The cops and some of the thieves would call me a fence. Or some thieves will say offman. Not you truck driver or employee thief, now. They might say fence, but not offman 'cause that is more thieves' slang.

Myself? A businessman and somebody who bought hot goods is how I thought of myself. As a dealer, too, I guess. Fence is used but not that much. Doing this book is how I got to feel easy calling myself a fence or saying so-and-so is a fence. I mean, you sure as fuck don't go around telling people: I'm a fence! So I didn't think of myself that way."

The information from these sources is reflected in my commentary and analysis, so that this document goes considerably beyond the ordinary case study.

Fifth, Sam's descriptions are consistent with the firsthand testimony about fences available in the biographies and autobiographies of thieves. His descriptions are also consistent with the more systematic research about fences which has relied on police and other criminal justice records — including Jerome Hall's classic chapter on "Receiving Stolen Property" in his work *Theft, Law, and Society* (1935), and Roselius and associates' early 1970s study of some aspects of how fences market stolen goods in *The Design of Anti-Fencing Strategies* (1975).[2] And Sam's descriptions square with the only other two fences whose lives have been studied in detail. The one is the eighteenth-century fence, Jonathan Wild, without doubt the most powerful and prominent fence in history. The other is the modern-day fence, "Vincent Swaggi" (an alias), whose life and fencing career is chronicled in Carl Klockars's *The Professional Fence* (1974).[3]

---

2. A recent work by Marilyn Walsh, *The Fence: A New Look at Property Theft* (1977), also provides some useful information but the study has some serious shortcomings such as (1) an inexact and misleading definition of "professional fence" (2) a narrow conception of "thieves" that overlooks truck drivers, platform workers, and employee thieves as major suppliers of stolen merchandise (3) a description of the traffic in stolen property that ignores the role of complicitous authorities in large-scale fencing operations. These shortcomings partly reflect Walsh's use of data from police files, so that she was limited both by the confines of "officially known cases" and by the need to secure their cooperation just to get access to the files. But the shortcomings also reflect a correctional perspective in the book's focus, to show the manner in which the fence "affords aid . . . furnishes incentives . . . provides a market . . . and organizes and finances" the traffic in stolen property. In this sense, Walsh's "new look" is really a quite "old" one, what Stuart Henry in *The Hidden Economy* (1978) argues is a centuries-old trend by many crime commentators to transform the fence into the "Mr. Big of Property Crime" for purposes of prodding the law and public policy towards a more serious enforcement effort.

More discussion of the Walsh work is provided in Appendix 1. (There is also an occasional footnote in the text that concerns the Walsh report.) Appendix 1 includes a general survey of images of the fence's role in property theft as portrayed in the socio-legal writings on fencing. The appendix is intended as background reading for the book as a whole.

3. The first fence about whom there is any detailed information is Mary Firth, alias Moll Cutpurse, an outrageous woman who dressed in men's clothes and claimed she was the first woman to smoke tobacco. A pickpocket turned fence, Moll ran a thriving business in London in the 1620s and 1630s restoring stolen property to its rightful owners, and, at the same time, currying the favor of the authorities. Ronald Fuller, in *The Beggars' Brotherhood* (1936:184) describes Moll as follows: "In her diary she points out that the world is made up of Cheaters and Cheatees, and decides that she may as well belong to the more profitable company of the two . . . She established a kind of Clearing House for stolen goods next

Jonathan Wild

Jonathan Wild, perhaps the most powerful criminal in recorded history, dominated the London underworld from roughly 1714 until his hanging in 1725 and, according to Daniel Defoe, employed some seven thousand thieves. Wild's career captured the imagination of pamphleteers of his age who peddled biographies of him before and after his death, while historians have recorded Wild's exploits in numerous monographs. Immortalized in John Gay's *The Beggar's Opera* (1728) and Henry Fielding's *The Life of Mr. Jonathan Wild The Great* (1743), Wild enjoys a literary legacy second only to that of Charles Dickens' Fagin, a character based on the nineteenth-century London fence, Ikey Solomon.

Wild's gambit was to advertise in the papers that he was a "thief-taker" —someone who specialized in capturing thieves and restoring stolen goods to their proper owners. The fee which he received from property owners was considerably better than the amount the thief would get from a normal fence, so both Wild and the thief made a good profit. Because of Wild's prices, thieves began doing business with him in large numbers and his competing fences suffered. In order to make good the claim of "thief-taking," Wild had to, on occasion, turn a thief over to the authorities. At the peak of his power in 1724, he nearly ruled the London underworld (e.g., he had destroyed the major gangs in London, save his own) and knew more about what was happening in it than all of the law enforcement bodies in Great Britain combined. The historian Luke Owen Pike summarizes the situation thus:

> "In the republic of the thieves' guild Jonathan Wild became as it were a dictator; but like many of the great men of the middle ages, he owed his greatness to double-dealing. From small beginnings he became in London at least, the receiver-in-chief of all stolen goods. He acquired and maintained this position by the persistent application of two simple principles; he did his best to aid the law in convicting all those misdoers who would not recognize his authority, and he did his best to repair the losses of all who had been plundered and who took him into their confidences. By degrees he set up an office for the recovery of missing property, at which the government must, for a time, have connived. Here the robbed sought an audience of the only man who could promise them restitution; here the robbers congregated like workmen at a workshop, to receive the pay for the work they had done. (Pike, *A History of Crime in England*, 1876:256)"

door to the Globe Tavern in Fleet Street. Here thieves brought their booty and here too owners came to recover them, Moll and the Cutpurses sharing the rewards of the spoils. She thus not only gathered a knowledge of the underworld as wide and as exact as Jonathan Wild's, but became the acknowledged head of a great gang of bullying cheats and robbers. 'The Boyes,' she called them. They would obey her slightest wish, and followed her like a bodyguard as she paced down Fleet Street in top-boots, puffing at her long pipe and swinging her sabre."

Wild was successful because he was a believable thief-taker to honest people, and a believable crook to his thieving associates. His downfall came in 1725 when he tried to bring some thieves to justice and they, in turn, accused him of being a fence. His reputation suffered, and soon the story of double-dealing unfolded. He was sentenced to death and hanged.

Vincent Swaggi

The other fence who has been intensively studied is the modern-day fence, Vincent Swaggi, who at the time of Klockars' study had been operating for over 20 years (from roughly the early fifties to the early seventies) at buying and selling stolen goods. In the first part of the book Klockars details the career of Jonathan Wild and describes how Vincent got into fencing. In the remainder of the book, Klockars presents the practices and procedures of fencing, how the fence "wheels and deals", and the fence's "apologia pro vita"—the rationale that Vincent used to justify his fencing involvement.

At the book's end, Klockars outlines his theory of becoming a fence, which goes as follows. Such a person must be energetic, ingenious, capable of making sound decisions, quite personable. A modest amount of money, the opportunity to buy stolen property, and the willingness to do so are the necessary conditions. Once these factors are present, the would-be fence must learn how to buy and not be cheated. Next, he must learn how to distribute his product(s). He may do so on a face-to-face basis, selling his goods on the street; or he may set up his own place of business (as Vincent did). The successful fence must handle the classic problems of capital, supply, demand, and distribution. Finally, he must develop a style of presentation that will avoid the likelihood of being arrested.

Significance of Study of Sam Goodman

The present document builds on Klockars' study to provide a more comprehensive treatment than is available in the literature of how the fence goes about the business of dealing and how he involves others in his illegal trade. The detailed coverage is partly due to the freedom Sam gave me, not only to write what I wanted but to interview others and to collect information as I pleased. Indeed, many of the anecdotal events recounted in the document first came to my attention from interviews with associates of Sam. Klockars' work, on the other hand, is an edited case study:

"Some aspects of Vincent's methods of doing business have been omitted, because Vincent considered that a detailed description of them might endanger his security or the security of others. He offered me the choice of an edited account or no account at all, and I chose the former. (Klockars, *The Professional Fence*, p. 2)"

What, in particular, Klockars is unable to reveal was Vincent Swaggi's role as a police informer, a fact that provides an intriguing link between the two studies. One of my contacts is a retired FBI agent (hereafter called Agent Bogart) whose law enforcement career spanned the fencing career of the real Vincent Swaggi, in the same city where Vincent practiced his fencing trade. Agent Bogart not only knew and investigated Vincent, but used him as an informant from the late fifties almost until the fence's death in 1976. Bogart, in fact, has in his possession today a copy of *The Professional Fence*, proudly given to him by Vincent and personally autographed in Vincent's real name. Because of Agent Bogart's knowledge about fencing and because of his relationship with Vincent Swaggi, I provide footnoted comments from Agent Bogart in the text to compare Vincent and Sam's methods and to illustrate the complexities of fencing.[4]

The Fence: One Kind of Trafficker In Stolen Goods

There are many paths that stolen property may take from thieves to eventual customers. The shortest is from the thief himself as the ultimate consumer, using what he steals. In other cases, the thief or his agent may sell to friends or neighbors, or he may peddle his stolen wares at auctions or flea markets. Yet other paths are more complicated, involving the thief and dabbling "middlemen" who buy and sell stolen property under the cover of a bar, a luncheonette, or an auto service station with the encouragement, if not the active participation, of the proprietor. Another path may involve the thief pawning his takings to ordinary shopkeepers who are not in the business of dealing in stolen merchandise, which they purchase "as if" it were legitimate stock and sell it to unsuspecting customers. Still other paths are both more sophisticated and require more skill on the part of the successful dealer, as when the thief sells stolen property to a "fence" who markets it to other secondary purchasers (e.g., legitimate merchants, private collectors) in what may be both local and out-of-state

---

4. For those not familiar with Klockars's work, Vincent's and Sam's methods of running a fencing business are similar in some ways yet different in other ways. Both were generalist fences (i.e., a dealer who will buy almost anything), although Sam was a specialist dealer in the early stages of his fencing career. Both had a speciality line within their generalist trade—Vincent in clothes and furs, Sam in furniture and antiques. Both purchased stolen goods from a wide variety of thieves and suppliers—burglars, drug addict thieves, shoplifters, dockworkers, shipping clerks, and truck drivers. But Vincent's trade was more skewed towards the drug addict thief while Sam's was skewed towards the ordinary burglar. And both Vincent and Sam received "slack" from the authorities, but in somewhat differing ways. Interestingly, the overlap and differences between Sam and Vincent have a parallel in American City where Sam can be compared to Louie Zarelli (an alias), a local fence who Sam frequently mentions in the text as Sam's way both of explaining his own dealership in stolen property and of puffing up, perhaps, his own cleverness and moral integrity.

outlets. More so than other traffickers in stolen goods, it is clear that certain fences have handled enormous quantities of stolen property over many years.

The rise of large-scale fences who buy and sell stolen goods to consumers or to secondary purchasers parallels the industrialization of society. Thieving has ancient origins—even in the simplest of societies, if there is property, people steal from each other. But prior to the Industrial Revolution, few thieves made a living out of stealing and most theft was committed for immediate consumption by the thieves and their accomplices rather than for redistribution in the marketplace. Society's small population and technological inability to mass-produce identical goods precluded the possibility of fencing stolen goods on a large scale. There were too few buyers, and highly individualized property owned on a limited scale could be easily identified. The unprecedented economic and demographic growth of eighteenth century Europe, however, dramatically changed the nature, the abundance, and the distribution of property. The growth of mass-produced and mass-owned consumer goods, of which there is little chance of being traced or recognized by the owner, paved the way for "receivers" who on a large scale buy stolen property to resell it, often at a distance or after a time has elapsed, for a handsome profit.

The development of this specialized role of the receiver, who buys and sells stolen goods and who acts as a ready market enabling thieves to convert goods into unidentifiable cash, was an escalating feature of the eighteenth century underworld. Indeed, the cant expression "fence" first begins to appear in the slang of thieves during this period and was common underworld slang all over Europe and America by the end of the eighteenth century. It derives from the middle English word meaning "defense."

Legislation criminalizing fencing activities and the receiving of stolen property also emerged at this time. The 1827 English statute—"a person receiving stolen property knowing the same to be stolen is deemed guilty of a felony"—is the prototype of subsequent American law. The exact wording may vary from one state to another, but the basic elements of the crime—"buying or receiving," "stolen property," and "knowing it be stolen"—have remained essentially intact.[5]

Many jurists and commentators have criticized the language of the receiving law as being so broad that it does little more than exempt the "innocent" purchaser of stolen goods from prosecution. Not only large-scale dealers in stolen goods (e.g., a fence like Sam), but many other persons qualify as criminal receivers: persons who buy stolen property for their own use (a housewife, for example, who buys stolen groceries from a neighborhood thief); persons who gain temporary custody of stolen property (a thief's girlfriend who wears a stolen string of pearls or a friend who temporarily hides loot for a thief); and persons who occasionally buy and

---

5. See the appendix for a discussion of the origins of, and problems with, modern-day law on receiving stolen property.

sell stolen property (the jeweler, for example, who buys stolen jewelry when the safe opportunity presents itself and sells it to unsuspecting customers). Even the thief can be charged with criminal receiving since by his theft, he possesses or conceals stolen property. (In fact, the large majority of those arrested and convicted for criminal receiving are thieves, especially burglars.)

To push for reform of the receiving law and to distinguish *true* fences from other criminal receivers, Jerome Hall, in the 1930s, delineated what he called the "professional receiver" or "dealer". The law, Hall proposed, does not recognize that those who receive stolen property are of three types: *The Lay Receiver*—"one who knowingly buys stolen property for his own consumption," *The Occasional Receiver*—"one who buys stolen property for resale but very infrequently," *The Professional Receiver*— "the dealer in stolen goods."[6]

By this typology Hall intended to show how the legal concept of "receiver" distorts a proper portrait of the traffic in stolen property by ignoring many relevant activities in its distribution: intent, skills, scale of operations, and the receiver's relationship to thieves and customers. The law emphasizes the receiving of stolen goods, whereas the most salient characteristic of the professional receiver is his delivery and distribution of stolen goods after they have been received. He is a *dealer* in stolen goods. Varieties of criminal receivers may shade one into another, Hall pointed out, but the fence or dealer's "activities are entirely different from those of the lay or the occasional receiver. [The fence's] behavior is persistent and complex. For the prospective thief, he is a reliable market, known in advance to be available" (Hall, 1952: 155).

Hall's redefinition of the professional receiver as a dealer and his break with the traditional legal image of the receiver is elaborated on by Klockars in his 1974 study, *The Professional Fence*. Klockars, however, dropped the legal term *receiver* altogether and made use of the term *fence*, a concept meaningful in the vocabulary of the underworld for centuries, and he also made explicit that the fence is a *public* figure. That is, he has "acquired a reputation as a dealer in stolen property among law breakers, law enforcers, and others acquainted with the criminal community" (Klockars, 1974:172).

It is Hall's notion of "dealer" and Klockars's conception of "fence" that describes the kind of trafficker in stolen goods that Sam Goodman represents.

Objectives

Among my objectives in preparing this document, I wanted not only to contribute to the sparse literature on fencing but to add to the developing

---

6. See the appendix for a discussion of the use (mainly misuse) of the designation "professional criminal" in both the popular and scientific writings on crime.

body of writings in criminology which describe what criminals do, their methods of operation, careers, lifestyles, and their relationships with each other as well as with law-abiding citizens. These writings, along with this document, help to rectify the popular but inaccurate conception of crime which has so retarded its study—that of crime as an isolated act committed, without regard to the perpetrator's relationship with other people, groups, and organizations.

Second, I sought to redress a major shortcoming not only in the study of criminal careers but in the study of legitimate work and business careers as well where the significance of skills, rewards, and connections is commonly recognized but where in fact such matters are dealt with in sketchy fashion.

But above all, I intended this document to be an in-depth, inside look at a modern dealer in stolen goods and the world in which he conducts his business. To convey this, each chapter addresses a separate issue, yet still is an integral part of the document as a whole. Agent Bogart, after reading a draft of the document, gave this evaluation: "Somebody (e.g., the courts) ought to keep it from being published. It's a manual, a handbook, on how to be a fence—everything you ever wanted to know about fencing." Half serious, half tongue-in-cheek, this comment ought not to be taken literally: this book, nor any book for that matter, will not show someone how to become a successful fence. Rather, Bogart's reaction is, I think, a testimonial to the document as a thorough account of how the dealer goes about the business of fencing stolen goods, and of the meaning of a fencing career.

Chapter 2

Sam's Place Among Fences

Fence: One Type of Criminal Receiver

While varieties of criminal receivers may overlap, the fence is here defined as someone who purchases stolen goods both on a regular basis, and for resale. He is above all a *reliable outlet for prospective thieves*. The critical features of this definition are that the fence has *direct* contact with thieves, he buys and resells stolen goods *regularly and persistently*, in so doing, he becomes a *public* dealer—recognized as a fence by thieves, the police, and others acquainted with the criminal community.[1]

This definition of the fence is consistent with the firsthand writings on the trade in stolen goods. It is the meaning of fence which has been part of the cant of thieves for at least two centuries, and which survives today both in Sam's vocabulary and in the language of the underworld as a whole.

Fence Deals Directly With Thieves

The fence is a middleman, a *layer in between* the thief and the buyer. This means, in particular, that the fence is distinguished from the merchant, the businessman, or the wholesaler who buys stolen goods from true fences and then resells the goods to his legitimate customers. These "*business buyers*," as they are better called, do not deal directly with thieves, and their involvement in the larger distribution of stolen goods is marginal in comparison with that of fences like Sam.[2]

---

1. This conception of fence derives mainly from Hall's meaning of "professional dealer" and Klockars' definition of "professional fence", as reviewed in chapter 1. See the appendix for a detailed treatment.

2. A partial exception to the stipulation of dealing directly with thieves if the criminal receiver, frequently a person with syndicate ties, who regularly buys stolen merchandise from fences like Sam and who then sells or redistributes it to other outlets where the merchandise is sold to the consuming public. Such a re-

▶ To my thinking, the merchant or storeowner who buys from a dealer like me, they ain't fences. 'Cause they're not dealing with both ends. There's always a layer between them and the thief. Their chances of taking any heat from the cops or having any hassles is very little. To me, they're businessmen looking for the easy buck. They buy what they can get cheap and only if it's what they're covered on—what they can mix in with their legit business. ◀

Fence Buys and Sells Stolen Goods Regularly

The fence buys and sells stolen goods regularly and has been doing so for a sustained period of time. His trading in stolen goods is a systematic rather than a situational or occasional involvement. He is, in the vocabulary of thieves, "an offman"—a ready-made market for getting rid of stolen goods which thieves can rely on. This does not so much mean that a fence will buy from every thief he encounters, but rather that he is a reliable outlet for a particular subset of thieves.

▶ Say, you run a store and a couple of your cousins are into burglary. You buy from them once in awhile, put the stuff on your shelves and sell it to your store customers. To me that ain't fencing.

Even your burglar, especially your good burglar, may do a little fencing. Sometimes a lot. Take Jesse, he already has handled stuff for

---

ceiver is a *distributor* of stolen property and if he meets the other two criteria described next, qualifies as a "fence" in Sam's view: "Well, you ask about Angelo [a local syndicate figure]. In my book, he's a fence even though he don't deal direct with thieves; now, at one time he did—in fact, I sold to Angelo when I was clipping [as a burglar]. Now, Angelo only deals with a couple of fences like me. He always wants that layer-in-between. Like the cigarettes, sugar, and liquor I handled—went right to Angelo 'cause he's got the connections for unloading those things."

So-called "master fences"—those who deal with thieves and purchasers indirectly, neither seeing nor touching the stolen merchandise—may qualify as true fences. But Sam doubts if such fences, in fact, exist apart from a fence like himself or an Angelo who on occasion may act as a "go-between" or a "broker" arranging for the distribution of stolen goods without ever touching them. "I already have had somebody contact me, saying if I run across such and such, they could help me find an outlet. This is one kind of 'contact man' and I needed that like a hole in the head 'cause all you're doing is cutting the profit one more time. What you do have sometimes, is someone like Angelo or Louie [another large fence in American City], handling, say, a load of warm stuff without ever putting their hands on it, even seeing it. Like on the liquor, I would call Angelo and he would tell me where to drop it and the person on that end would take care of it. Or, say a thief contacted Louie and said he had a load of tires; well, Louie had some good contacts with a couple of auctions, and he may arrange for the thief to run the load to his auction contact. Now, this would be just an on-and-off thing 'cause you want to see what you're buying and [keep in mind that] Louie is dealing regularly with this and other thieves too."

burglars—for a cut or just buy and then sell to one of his outlets.
'Cause Jesse has a lotta connections.

Same with some of your truck drivers who will know other truckers or guys that work in warehouses or on the docks. So he opens up
a shop of some kind, really just for a front. Peddles the stuff for
maybe three, six months, then pulls back 'cause it will get too risky
once he gets known.

It's more an all-the-time thing. Different thieves got to know you
will take whatever it is you're handling. When a thief says, so-and-so
is my "offman," he means he can count on unloading what he steals;
he doesn't have to go peddling 'cause the fence will handle it.

Some of the burglars I dealt with were hitting something fierce,
bringing stuff in sometimes four and five times a week. Unless it was
clothes or something "off the wall," they knew I would handle whatever they brought. Same with a couple of good safemen: if they run
across a good antique, they'd grab it 'cause they knew they could unload with me. Now, a lot of your dealers are really nickel and dime,
their buying is off and on. The thief can't depend on them. ◀

Fence Is A "Public" Dealer

The fence is a *"public"* dealer; he has acquired a reputation as a fence
among thieves, the police, and others acquainted with the criminal community. Becoming known as a fence is not necessarily a successful dealer's
own idea, but rather an almost sure fire outgrowth of dealing directly and
regularly with thieves. Not only will thieves know the fence, many customers also will, and because of bargain prices, they will suspect that
goods are stolen, and eventually the police will also know.

The circumstances a fence finds himself in and the kinds of thieves he
does business with will influence his chances of becoming known. The
specialist, say in jewelry, who buys only from a small clientele of established thieves, may manage to keep his fencing secret in comparison to
the secondhand merchant who buys whatever comes his way from a variety of thief-types. Also, the merchant or private collector who deals only
with a small number of thieves over his entire career may never be discovered. In such cases it is better to consider him a private buyer for
those thieves, perhaps successful on his own terms, rather than a fence as
defined here.

▶ This will depend on what kind of thief you're dealing with, how often you're buying, how big you are, how wide open, too. Say you just
buy from a handful of very good thieves, then you can maybe keep
from being known, really known. Know what I mean? Like the one
lawyer in town, buys jewelry and coins from a few good burglars.
He's not very known and the few that really know will turn their
heads anyway.

But that kind of fence is very rare, if you want to call him a fence.

What it comes right down to, it is hard to be a fence without the police knowing. Fucking hard. Say a shoplifter gets picked up, and the
cops hit on him, "Where'd you get rid of the stuff. Tell us that, and
we'll let you go." They're gonna come up with a name, so the chances
of being known is very high. ◀

Fencing As A Criminal Career

Taken together, these criteria help to distinguish Sam and dealers like
him from those criminal receivers whose dealing in stolen goods is not so
much a career line as it is episodic, situational, or opportunistic. While
numerous individuals may buy and sell stolen goods on a part-time basis,
taking opportunities as they present themselves, fencing stolen goods on
a regular and sustained basis requires much skill, time, planning, and organization. Fences like Sam don't so much capitalize on opportunities to
buy stolen goods when legal and reputational risks are low, as they actively exploit their environment and create and control their opportunities. They explicitly intend to deal in stolen goods and approach their
environment with an attitude that presupposes its susceptibility to manip-
ulation.

Viewed this way, fencing is much more than the simple act of buying
and selling stolen goods for money. It is a way of life, and anyone becoming involved is forced to come to terms with the other people associated
with a trade in stolen goods. This means that to survive and succeed as a
fence involves (a) partaking successfully in dual worlds of commerce—the
respectable world in which he provides legitimate goods, and the criminal
world in which he disposes of stolen goods; and (b) managing to avoid the
possible negative effects of one's illegal trade. Not only must fences re-
cruit thieves, develop outlets, and manage potential threats from both the
police and criminal predators, but they are also faced with concerns such
as managing identities with families, children, and themselves, and fitting
into both the underworld and legitimate society. Consequently, fencing
very much involves the whole person. For those who pursue it, fencing
tends to be the primary occupation from which they extract a living income and at which they spend the bulk of their time. Sam summarizes his
meaning of "fence."

▶ To me, a fence is a person dealing in hot things. But there has to be
turnover, too; not just the nickel and dime stuff and more than five
times a year, say. Take Bill Toscano, or Joe Toscano his dad. Ran little secondhand shops, and they'd buy off and on from the walk-ins,
off the street. Now in the cops' eyesight, they probably would be
fences but not in my eyesight. Not enough turnover. The cops are
very loose with that term.

This is a funny story about a guy we call Calvary Harry—fell into a
shitload of World War II guns one time, that were hot as hell. Harry

wasn't a fence at all, but a half-assed hustler and gambler. That's how he got the guns, from a couple of guys in a crap game who ran short of money and unloaded the guns on Harry. Now Harry can't sell the guns cause they're too hot. So he finds an old garage, holds them. In the meantime the cops hear about this 'cause, really, by now the whole fucking world just about knows. They find the guns but could never pin it on Harry. But Harry was the biggest laugh in town, and that's where he got the name "Calvary Harry," on account of getting taken on those fucking guns. In the cops' eyesight, this made Harry a big fence, and they would always preach that. Fuck, he was shit. That was the only hot stuff I ever heard he bought, and he couldn't unload it. And afterward, Harry was so leery it never entered his mind to fuck with the hot stuff again.

I don't know what you'd call people like Bill or Joe Toscano, not fences. Sure as hell, not Calvary Harry. In my eyesight, you become a fence when you more or less do it for a living or, say, when you're pulling in enough to make a living off the hot stuff. ◀

For ease of exposition, the adjective "professional" can describe the kind of dealer in stolen goods that Sam represents, if that term is used restrictively. Sam is frequently characterized as a "professional criminal" by many of the police and media people who know him. Yet, one hesitates to use the expression "professional" for several reasons. First, many crime writers and law enforcement officials use the term as an attention-grabber, and label as "professional" virtually any dealer, thief, or underworld figure without regard for the offender's skill level or scale of criminal activity. Second, notions like career, status, rationality, skill, which the word professional connotes, already inhere in the concept of fence as used in the underworld. Third, the expression "professional fence" is not part of Sam's vocabulary.

▶ Thieves and dealers don't talk that way, don't use the word professional. Except maybe to say, so-and-so's an old pro, he's been around a long time, but even that is used very seldom. It's the cops that use it, to blow themselves up, make themselves look good—so-and-so's a "professional" thief when in fact the guy's an asshole, a real bum. And you see it used in the papers and on TV, but it ain't that way at all. See, a couple of the cops called me that—"a professional criminal"—but I never thought of myself that way 'cause it's really a foreign word. Know what I mean? In my eye, the only ones that you might call professional would be those that are high up in the rackets, say in the Mafia, 'cause they have always made their living from crime and are at the top of the crime world, you might say. But the word just ain't used.[3] ◀

---

3. Agent Bogart, an FBI agent who spent his career investigating fencing in Mid-City (alias) and who intimately knew Vincent Swaggi (alias), the subject of Carl Klockars' *The Professional Fence*, agrees with Sam: "If we picked up a bur-

There is no way of knowing at present what proportion of the traffic in stolen property passes through "professional" fences. Not all stolen goods are fenced: some thieves keep the goods or sell them directly to a customer who plans to use them. In other cases, thieves may "peddle" their stolen wares on streetcorners, in bars, or at flea markets. Also, there is an almost ubiquitous "amateur trade" involving employees who pilfer and then sell the stolen merchandise to friends, neighbors, co-workers, and schoolmates under the cover of friendly or neighborly privacy.[4] In addition, there is the casual or occasional trading of the ordinary shopkeeper who does not make a business of dealing in stolen goods, but buys stolen merchandise when the opportunity presents itself, perhaps places it on the shelves next to his legitimate stock, and sells it to the next customer who comes through the door.

It is safe to assume, nonetheless, that fences like Sam get their share of minor thefts and employee pilferage, but that they, in particular, are the characteristic outlets of property stolen by career-oriented and professional thieves; that is, they are the major outlets for thefts involving moderate to large quantities of merchandise and they also handle a sizable proportion of high value, but small quantity, thefts.[5]

▶ There's a lot of stuff that doesn't go through dealers like me. You wouldn't believe the peddling that goes on, the different ways it is done. Your ordinary thieves and good burglars will mostly unload their stuff with regular dealers, but your good burglar will have private people he can sell to, too.[6] ◀

---

glar, say, and we'd ask: 'Do you know so-and-so?' They might say, 'Yeh, he's a hijacker, a big burglar, he's a professional thief.' But amongst themselves, no, they would brag about the jobs they pulled, but they wouldn't talk that way. They did this talking to us, 'cause they knew we talked that way. Really that term [professional thief] is used mainly by district attorneys, U.S. attorneys, and law enforcement officers. It's a short statement that burglary or crime is this guy's occupation, what he does for a living, and is probably making a lot more than you and me."

4. The best treatment of the "amateur" trade in stolen goods is provided by Stuart Henry in *The Hidden Economy* (1978). See also Klockars (1974:163–164) for a description of some paths by which stolen goods pass from thieves to eventual consumers.

5. Peter Bell (1983:789) proposes that "the well-organized fence, master of the nation's burgeoning market for stolen goods . . . inspires 95 percent or more of the theft in America." Bell provides no justification for how he arrived at this figure, and I am not aware of any such calculations being available in the literature. Rather it is not known at present, nor can it be even roughly estimated, what proportion of stolen property fences like Sam handle or what *is* the fence's role in the overall flow of stolen property from thieves to eventual consumers.

6. Jesse, Sam's former burglar partner and close friend, points out: "Many times the real good thief who is stealing the top dollar stuff will be selling to a lawyer, a contractor, or somebody like that. These people may have the contacts to unload, so they will buy—but it has to be very worth while 'cause they ain't gonna

To further clarify Sam's place in the larger trade in stolen goods, additional lines can be drawn which link him to other fences and which distinguish him from other, unlike, types. Specifically, fences can be arrayed along several dimensions relative to the kind of cover used to conceal their fencing trade, to the scale of their fencing operation, and to their relationship to the larger criminal community. Thus, Sam can be classified as a business fence, a partly covered fence, a generalist fence, and a fence with extensive affinity with the criminal community.[7]

Sam Is A "Business Fence"

All fences are by definition businessmen: they are middlemen in illegitimate commerce, providing goods and services to others, regardless of whether they operate from a legitimate business enterprise or rely solely on individual resources. If the latter, the trade in stolen goods is not linked to any legitimate work or business activity; often, the fencing is just one of several illicit pursuits, such as drug-dealing and loan-sharking. An example is the neighborhood connection who deals primarily with small amounts of property, with the stolen goods supplied by local thieves such as shoplifters or dishonest cargo company employees. Stolen goods may be hustled on the streets or they may be sold in living rooms, local bars, or garages. As the neighborhood connection acquires a reputation as a dealer in stolen property and as he develops a clientele of thieves, he may expand his operation by organizing thefts for customers or by working closely with other fences.

---

fuck with nickel-dime shit. They are known but not known. 'Cause the cops can only surmise but really don't know. Know what I mean. And the few cops that really know are just as fucking bad, may even be part of it. These kind of people are very protected, don't kid yourself. Take the lawyer in town—he ain't a fence like Louie or Sam but he's making a fucking lot of bread off the hot stuff. A fucking lot 'cause he's handling only the top dollar stuff."

Rocky, one of Sam's "regulars" and an established burglar in the area, notes: "You have a lot of private people that are buying from this or that thief, the better thief, now. If it's the right piece and the right thief, these people will buy. The ones I know, and from my buddies, too, it will usually be a lawyer or a jeweler. But it can be a contractor, an antique dealer, or maybe somebody that's connected with the family [Mafia]. We just call them private buyers 'cause they really ain't fences, know what I mean. But profit-wise this is very big."

John "Steelbeams" Willadson, a good safeman and hijacker who sold to Sam (and who was nicknamed "Steelbeams" because of the thick glasses he wore), adds: "For jewelry, coins, small antiques, and that, I'd say your better thieves will take some of that to dealers like Sam but most will go to private people who deal only with a thief they personally know, really trust. On truckloads and the general stuff, fences like Sam and Louie would get a fair share of that."

7. This classification draws heavily from Roselius and associates (1977) study of fencing and the scheme they use to distinguish among types of criminal receivers.

▶ The ones that operate without a legit business, to me, are in a different league. If they start handling much stuff, they will get popped 'cause they won't have the cover. In your bigger cities, now, you might find some that do well, say, in your black areas where they peddle on the streets or in the bars. They're more hustlers than anything; many times they're dealing in dope, in girls, too.

I never did much business with them. See, they will try to unload with dealers like me 'cause they ain't got outlets. If it was guns or a good antique I might take a shot. Otherwise I'd walk away. ◀

The overwhelming majority of fences, however, are simultaneously proprietors or operators of a legitimate business which provides a cover or front for the fencing. Businesses most often favored are those having a large cash flow (e.g., coin and gem shop, secondhand store, auction house, restaurant) and the flexibility to set one's own hours (salvage yard, bail-bonding). Two sets of books may be kept, one to inflate the amount of money actually made (especially for losing businesses) and another to launder fencing money through the legal business so that it can be turned into safely spendable income.

For some business fences, the trade in stolen goods is the major source of income and the central activity of their business portfolio. For others, fencing is either a lucrative sideline to their legitimate entrepreneurship or just one of a number of illicit enterprises they are involved in. Which part of the fence's business portfolio dominates or is more profitable—the legitimate or the illegitimate—may shift over time. Whatever the nature and profitability of these businesses, however, they tend to remain secondary in focus in that the individual's pivotal status and self-identification remains that of a dealer.

Sam is a business fence. He operates a secondhand and antique business which serves as a base of operations for his fencing activities. Sam not only models his trade in stolen goods after the normal procedures and conventions of the business world, but each trade shapes and is shaped by the resources and practices of the other.

▶ The two go hand in hand. The legit helps the illegit, and vice versa. It's covering your back, but more than that. It's overhead expenses and everything. What I had with the legit business, like the trucks and the warehouse, helped make the fencing go. And the money you make from one can help build up the other side. Same thing with the contacts—the one hand feeds the other.

Really, all of your fences pretty much have a legitimate business. It would be hard to be a fence and not have the legit side. And most of your dealers will make more from the fencing. That's why they're in it. But this depends on their legitimate holdings, what else they got their fingers into. Like the foundry guy I dealt with; he makes a killing from the legit side, but he was still making good money from the fencing. ◀

That fencing itself is a business and is typically linked to a legitimate business helps account for fences being older than is characteristic of most property offenders, particularly the thieves they purchase stolen goods from. The accumulation of experience, connections, and, perhaps, capital needed to run a fencing *business* are a function of age. Also, age-graded expectations make it difficult for the younger person to assume the role of businessman, primarily because the younger person is less able to inspire the confidence and trust necessary for exchange transactions and for making contacts.

▶ Your younger person isn't worldwise, is too half-assed to be a fence. He thinks he knows but he doesn't have the knowledge. Same as any business, you need the experience and the money to make money. The other thing is, people are less leery of an older person. In any business, the people have to have confidence in you and it's hard for your younger person to get that. Most of your fences are like your legit businessmen, are older, and most people feel more at ease doing business with an older person. Even your thieves which are mostly young would rather deal with an older person. You don't have kids running a fencing business, same as they don't run a legitimate one. ◀

Sam Is A Marginal Or Quasi-legitimate Businessman

While fences are typically businessmen who trade both illegitimately and legitimately, they may vary in the degree of respectability of their "legitimate" operations. Some fences operate establishments which are perceived by the community-at-large as strictly clean (e.g. restaurants, appliance stores); some fences operate businesses which are perceived as clean but somewhat suspect (e.g. taverns, auto parts shops, antique shops, and jewelry stores); and other fences operate what are viewed as quasi-legitimate or marginal businesses (e.g. pawnshops, coin and gem shops, secondhand discount stores, salvage companies, auction houses, and bail-bonding).[8]

---

8. Agent Bogart agrees. "I would say the majority of fences I ever knew ran secondhand shops, a foundry, a junk yard, a novelty shop, or a jewelry store." To this list, Jesse adds: "More than anybody, I think your fucking bondsman are fences—'cause they have contacts with thieves, and are in with the fucking cops and magistrates."

The firsthand studies of fences and the general surveys also document the considerable participation of fences in quasi-legitimate businesses and occupations. A representative view is Hall's observation: "that the business of dealing in stolen goods is closely interrelated with those of auctioneer, pawnbrokers, and dealers in second-hand goods who provide large outlets for the sale of stolen goods. These businesses are regulated, but in such a perfunctory manner that they continue to be active in both the receipt and the disposal of stolen property. There is very little regulation of transient vendors of jewelry or of smelters and refiners of precious metals." (Hall, 1952:162–63)

Additionally, some fences are more disreputable than others in that they come from thief or hustler backgrounds or have a fairly extensive affinity with the criminal community. For example, the fence may be an ex-thief or have ties with the local syndicate; indeed, it frequently happens that the fence is involved in the rackets (e.g., gambling, loan-sharking), with fencing being just one among a number of illicit pursuits. The skills and contacts acquired by racketeering may be highly conducive to running a fencing operation.

Sam is a marginal businessman in all three ways: he runs a quasi-legitimate business (is a dealer in secondhand goods); had a background in burglary before becoming a fence; and has extensive affinity with the local underworld (e.g., he knows the major thieves, socializes with local syndicate members).[9] Not all fences are as disreputable as Sam, but they typically are marginal in one sense or another. This does not mean they have extensive criminal records. In fact, most do not.[10]

▶ I can't speak for every fence, but the fences I knew pretty much had their fingers into different things, were clipping one way or another. Or they were connected, had ties. This was their background before they got into fencing. Now, that doesn't mean they did time 'cause most of them haven't. You'd find their records pretty clean. Some have been popped for this or that, but very few convictions. See, my record was mostly from the burglary. I was only convicted for the fencing this one time.

I wouldn't say that many fences had been burglars or thieves before, like it was for me. But most will be shady in one way or another. If not into crime, on the edge of it. Maybe their old man or an uncle

More recently, Vincent Teresa (*My Life In The Mafia*, 1973) provides an insider's view commenting: "discount store owners . . . would buy all you could get them, no questions asked, whether it was liquor, furs, television sets, appliances or shoes." (Teresa, 1973:113)

9. Vincent Swaggi was also a marginal businessman in a threefold fashion: he ran a novelty or general merchandise shop; had a background as a hustler or a swindler; and had extensive affinity with the underworld. According to Agent Bogart, not only did a number of retired thieves and "gangster" types regularly hang out at Vincent's store, but one of Vincent's daughters was married to a well-known burglar. And Bogart adds: "Sure Vincent had friends and associated with businessmen who were legit, but a lot of them weren't. The majority of those he was close to I would say were into one thing or another. His main buddies were a big Jewish dealer who ran a restaurant with a novelty shop tacked on, drove an old pick-up truck. And he was buddies with a guy [Sam Levin, alias] Klockars writes about in his book—a big, big wholesaler. They'd see each other every day. But this guy wasn't the upstanding businessman that Klockars paints him to be. The FBI had him tagged for being in on the bankruptcy frauds but we could never prove anything on him."

10. For more discussion of the character and backgrounds of fences, including an assessment of Walsh's description of the typical fence as "most respected businessmen," see the appendix.

was into fencing. Some of the main fences I knew were into gambling, counterfeiting, in the rackets, and different things that weren't aboveboard.[11] ◄

Sam Is A Partly-Covered Fence

Regardless of whether or not the stolen goods match the legitimate goods sold, a legitimate business always provides at least some commercial legitimacy and a cover for a fencing operation by providing a setting for the exchange of goods and services, for the comings and going of customers, for the transferral of merchandise, and the like. Nevertheless, business fences can be distinguished by how closely the stolen property corresponds to the legitimate goods sold, that is, whether the trade in stolen goods is *fully* covered, *partly covered*, or *noncovered* by the fence's legitimate business identity.

Fencing through noncovered fronts—where the illicit lines of goods are distinct from the legitimate commerce—tends to be small in scale. Typically these kinds of fences or criminal receivers are owners or operators of bars, restaurants, and similar businesses where knowledgeable contact with thieves may occur and where contacts with would-be customers and certain types of business arrangements are possible. Restaurants and bars, for example, may serve as social sanctuaries where burglars can meet or relax in familiar and relatively secure settings; the owners may, since they own businesses with normally variable employment pools, provide the thief with the employment he may need for parole. In addition, from information gleaned from their customers and patrons, the owners may sometimes give to burglars tips helpful to the commission of a crime. In these ways, contacts with other thieves might be generated and expanded through the grapevine. The stolen goods may be disposed of by selling them to a patron or business associate who is a proprietor of an unrelated business, or they may be peddled to a larger fence.

---

11. Agent Bogart comments: "I would say most of your fences started out like Vincent did—hustling on the street, and were swindlers, really. Very few would be into burglary before going into the fencing like your man, Sam. But some started out as truck drivers—that's how they got their contacts, from other drivers and guys working on the pier. They'd open up a store, and their buddies would drop stuff off." Agent Bogart adds: "The main Mafia people are not going to get their hands dirty with the fencing. They're making too much money off the gambling. We had taps on them for years and it [fencing] never came up. With the middle people, maybe, and the underlings, yes, but not your top guys."

Bogart's observation squares with the situation in American City where Angelo was a big fence in the sixties but drifted out of fencing as he became more heavily involved in gambling and as he secured a powerful position within the local syndicate. Louie, on the other hand, was only "connected" with the Mafia [not really "in" it as was Angelo] and remained a fence throughout both the sixties and the seventies.

▶ The only dealers I knew that weren't covered at all were ones working out of a bar or a restaurant. That's how they got their contacts, from thieves and maybe business people having a drink or stopping for dinner. The other thing is, the guy who runs a tavern, say, may not have the outlets to get rid of what he's covered on, like food or liquor, so he doesn't handle that 'cause he's leery of being set up or of having his place searched, and the cops find the stuff. But usually it's much better to be covered on what you handle.

All the ones I came across like this you could hardly call fences, 'cause they were so nickel-and-dime, and they would buy only if the coast was very clear. There were a couple that was unloading their stuff with me. I handled it 'cause they helped me out in other ways. I never seen this myself, but you do hear of places that is strictly a front—no legit business at all, to speak of, like maybe a little coin shop, or a corner bar or gas station, maybe even a flower shop. It would be a front, like what is sometimes used to cover a bookmaking or a gambling setup. I can't see how that kind of dealer can last, if he's handling much stuff, unless he has terrific outlets and has the cops in his pocket something fierce. ◀

By comparison, the fence who can mesh his stolen goods with legitimate ones—the fully or partly covered fence—is usually safer from law enforcement. Stolen goods can go undetected among legitimate items. There are, as well, other advantages to the fence who meshes an illegal with a legal inventory. He is able to fill out an otherwise legitimate product line through illegitimate sources; he has less need for special storage arrangments, such as a secret warehouse, since both products are identical; he does not require any special knowledge or schooling relative to the pricing and selling of products, and thereby reduces the financial risk involved.

Throughout most of his fencing career, Sam has operated as a *partly-covered* fence, more or less continuously adapting his legitimate business to an increasingly diversified trade in stolen goods.

▶ Most of the time, I was pretty well covered for what I handled. See, my legit business kept growing. It got to where I was handling antiques, furniture, carpeting, TVs, appliances, clocks, tires, almost anything but clothes.

Now, I always handled some stuff I wasn't covered on. I always handled guns. I handled a lot of food, sugar, liquor, and that. Different things would come up, like one time I handled a truckload of batteries. I wasn't covered on these. Most of your fences are covered more than I was. They stick to what they handle in their shop, except they might handle something like guns 'cause they are easy to get rid of. ◀

Sam Is A Generalist Fence

Fences also vary in terms of "product specialization"—the kinds of stolen goods they handle. At one pole is the generalist, a fence who will buy and sell virtually anything a thief offers. At the other pole is the specialist, who handles only certain kinds of goods such as auto parts or jewelry. Most fences are probably specialists in that they handle only one or a few product lines.

Early in his fencing career Sam tended to specialize, dealing mainly in stolen antiques, precious metals (e.g., silver or coins), and guns. With time, Sam became a generalist fence handling a variable assortment of products, although dealing in stolen antiques remained his major fencing line.[12]

▶ The first couple of years, I just dealt in guns and antiques; these were mostly small antique pieces like figurines, cut glass, and that. Once it got going, at one time or another, I think I dealt in almost any goddamn thing.

Now, I never handled clothes. Didn't have the knowledge. I had the outlets, but didn't know the prices. Your clothes is penny-ante anyway, unless you could get a truckload or, say, you were getting good furs. Another thing, the real valuable antique pieces that are worth a big, big dollar, or like high-class art pieces, I didn't handle that. Too much risk 'cause that stuff is very hard to unload. And what do I know about the art stuff? Nothing.

My main thing was always antiques and furniture and your household items, like appliances and TVs. I was content with that. But if you brought me shit wrapped in paper and I thought I could make a good dollar, I'd probably buy. ◀

On the one hand, Sam's shift from a specialist to a generalist fence was a function of greater capital and a growing knowledge of varied merchandise, which coincided with the expansion of a business in used furniture to a general merchandise dealership (in which he handled both new and used merchandise, as well as antiques). On the other hand, Sam's drift into the role of generalist fence was an outgrowth of mushrooming contacts with thieves as suppliers of stolen property and with business buyers and other secondary purchasers as outlets for reselling the stolen goods.

Suppliers: The Production of Stolen Goods

Fences vary not only in terms of the kinds of stolen property they handle, but also in the kinds of thieves and suppliers they purchase stolen goods from. At one pole are fences who deal only with established burglars or

---

12. Mickey, a smalltime thief in the area, comments: "You could always peddle some stuff at any of the secondhand places. But Sam and Louie were the main two outlets. No one came close to them. They would take almost anything but Louie wanted guns and Sam wanted antiques. That was their specialty."

Rocky comments: "Sam would buy just about anything, didn't matter. If it was a bottle cap, he'd take it. If he didn't want it, he would send us to someone who

some other subset of thieves. At the other pole is the more wide open
fence who buys stolen goods from virtually any thief, with "thief" used
very broadly here to refer not only to burglars, shoplifters, and drug-
addict thieves, but to truckdrivers, warehouse workers, salesmen, and the
like who steal or pilfer property from their places of employment.

▶ Once I started dealing with your ordinary thief, then what I handled went swoosh. See, your better thief is choosey about what he
takes. He ain't gonna carry a fucking sofa or TV out of a house. The
run-of-the-mill burglar and the shoplifter, your common thief, will
pretty much take what he runs across. Same thing with truck drivers,
or the guys that work in the warehouses or on the docks, they will
bring what they're hauling, could be almost any damn thing. But the
doper and the real asshole thieves are the worst, 'cause they will grab
anything. And you'd be surprised at what your Joe Citizen thief will
bring you. ◀

It is clear from Sam's comments that a fence's suppliers of stolen goods
are not limited to "thieves" as the word is used in common language. Sam
has bought stolen goods from three broad groupings of thieves—*criminal*
thieves, *employee* thieves, and *Joe Citizen* thieves. In describing these
three groupings, Sam's vocabulary and his method of distinguishing one
from the other is followed.

Criminal Thieves

Although Sam may sometimes use the designation "thief" quite broadly to
refer to anyone from whom he buys stolen goods, he usually restricts the
label to burglars, shoplifters, drug-addict thieves—that is, to thieves with
a strong affinity with the underworld and whose status and self-identity
tend to revolve around their criminal involvement. The latter are a large
and diversified group, so that Sam matter-of-factly makes additional distinctions among criminal thieves on the basis of their skill level and character. Sam's distinctions reveal the pecking order in the world of theft and
also suggest Sam's preferences regarding the types of thieves he desires to
do business with.

First, Sam broadly sets apart the "good thief" from the amateur or the
common thief. The latter are then further distinguished, with the "run-
of-the-mill" or the "in-between" thief, for example, set apart from the
"penny-ante" and the "walk-in" thief. Depending on the circumstance,
Sam attaches a variety of labels to the mix of in-between and penny-ante

---

would. But come in with a good antique, his fucking eyes would light up. His
main thing was antiques."

Chubbie, one of the hangers-on at Sam's store adds: "I seen stereo equipment,
guns, kitchen appliances, furniture, tools, some jewelry, 'lotta porcelain. I seen a
Chevy Station Wagon full of musical instruments one time. Sam would take almost anything. A very big variety of stuff."

thieves he bought stolen goods from (e.g., "ordinary" thief, "common" thief, "hustler" thief, "snatch-and-grab" thief, "bottom-barrel" thief, "doper" thief).

Sam's division between good thieves and penny-ante thieves is relatively sharp. Less sharp is the division between good thieves and in-between thieves, and between in-between thieves and penny-ante thieves. The distinctions Sam makes may sometimes shade one into another, but the meaning is usually clear in context.

Good Thieves

Good thieves tend to be in burglary or in related thefts such as truck hijacking and cartage theft,[13] tend to be specialists, and are generally older thieves (e.g., in their mid- to late twenties, or older). They are knowledgeable about merchandise, use extensive planning in executing a theft, tend to select targets of high value, view theft as a "business," have strategic connections, and have a reputation for personal integrity.

▶ There were always four or maybe five good burglary crews operating in the area. If this burglar or that crew packed it in, then someone else takes its place. Mostly, they were hitting safes and clipping houses for good antiques but they might knock off a truck, too, take the whole load. Usually they would give me a shot at it, but they had different places to unload. ◀

A subset of the "good" thief category is the "decent" or "pretty good" thief. He may be an older thief who hasn't quite achieved "good" thief status; or he may be a younger thief (early to mid-twenties) who is on the rise. While he may still commit "opportunistic" crimes, and volume rather than quality crimes, he also exercises planning, is making more connections, is acquiring a reputation for trustworthiness, and may hook up with a good thief on occasion. If he is working with a couple of other "pretty good" burglars, their crew may get to be known as a "good crew" and, by extension, so will one or more of its members.[14]

---

13. Agent Bogart clarifies the meaning of *hijacker*: "You'll hear people say, hijack a truck or refer to a hijacker. Well, unless it's taken by gunpoint or by force in some other way, it's not hijacked. It's just a stolen truck. But you hear burglars and cops talk about, 'Oh yeh, we hijacked this truck,' but they didn't actually hijack it. They found it on the street, broke into it or maybe backed the tractor onto their trailer, and drove it off. There was no gunpoint. Or many times they will have inside information, somebody working from within. Or they are hooked up with a regular driver who parks the truck where they can hit it. Very, very few of what are called 'hijackers' by your law enforcement people are true hijackers. Really, most truck hijackers are burglars. It's one kind of burglary."

14. Jessie comments: "Shit, Sam uses that word "good" too freely. Gets that from jail 'cause of the time he did. That is where the slang really comes from, from jail. Some of the ones he'd call good, if they wanna do a job with me, they can get fucked. There are very few good ones, and fewer now than ever."

In-between Thieves

The in-between thief—sometimes labeled as run-of-the-mill, so-so, ordinary, or regular—is usually a less skilled but highly active burglar who has established himself over the years, with the police and with the criminal community, as a consistent or known thief.[15] They tend to be younger than good thieves, usually in their late teens or early twenties (although they are not juveniles), prompting Sam to occasionally describe some of them as "kids." They commit volume rather than quality thefts, exercise less planning, and have less skill. Many of them use drugs (especially marijuana), but their drug usage is minimal while committing crimes. A sizable share of Sam's trade in stolen goods is with in-between burglars, and he often refers to them as "my regulars."

▶ I shot for the in-between thief, between the good burglar and the asshole thieves and the hustlers. I catered to the in-between burglar. They were my bread and butter, you might say. Some were pretty decent now. But most of them were so-so, and they'd always be that way. ◀

Penny-Ante and Walk-In Thieves

The penny-ante thief category includes a large grouping of "walk-in" thieves and hustler types who are active in theft in general, commit quantity rather than quality merchandise thefts, are of lesser skill, and are among the least trustworthy of thieves. Most shoplifters, a variety of hustler- and street-type thieves, and jack-of-all-trades offenders qualify as penny-ante thieves in Sam's view. In later years, especially as he acquired more of what he called "a license to operate," Sam is less selective about the thieves he deals with and is more willing to buy stolen goods from what he calls the "walk-in trade"—that mix of snatch-and-grab thieves who frequent or check out places like Sam's secondhand store for purposes of selling merchandise they have probably just stolen.

▶ Off and on I bought from the penny-ante thieves, the assholes, and the hustlers—the "walk-in" trade, you might say. They can be more trouble than they're worth 'cause there's more risk, and they bring you little stuff that ain't worth much. Except now and then they grab

---

Rocky adds: "There are some pretty good burglars and that out there. Maybe less than when Sam and Jesse were clipping 'cause now a lot of burglars are into drug dealing. The money is good in drugs, fucking good. The better burglar is wanted by the people bringing the stuff in, by the bigger drug people to work with them on account he's trusted and knows how to handle hisself. Is the layer-in-between they need."

15. Rocky maintains that the term "known burglar" is a law enforcement designation. "The cops use it all the time. Just means they know he's a burglar or was one in the past. If burglars use it among themselves, it means the guy ain't very good."

something good which you can get for an easy dollar, and make a good buck on. ◀

As detailed later, Sam prefers dealing with good burglars, does a thriving business with in-between thieves, and vacillates between periods of heavy and light trading with penny-ante and walk-in thieves. Furthermore, Sam is reluctant to do business with black thieves, female thieves, and doper thieves, because he sees them as untrustworthy, or because they tend to peddle low-value merchandise, or both. And Sam is least likely to buy stolen merchandise from "kids," juvenile thieves.

Dopers

Drug-addict thieves, those Sam calls "dopers" are very active thieves with variable skill levels whose planning of thefts depends on their pre-addiction experiences in theft and the nature of their habit. Dopers tend to be the least respected of thieves and are both a risk to do business with and a nuisance to have coming in and out of the store. Sam only sometimes buys from addict-thieves, mainly when the addict has something valuable that Sam hopes to buy cheaply, or when the addict is a thief Sam regularly dealt with prior to his addiction. Sam, a non-user, views drugs as antithetical to the tenets of good thievery.

▶ I didn't buy much from your dope heads. It's a fact that a doper can't be trusted. Will do anything for a fix, to get his dope. Now, some of them are good at stealing and can bring in good stuff. But mostly they're bringing petty shit, piece of this and piece of that. I shied away from their business 'cause it's too much hassle all around. In fact there were many times I more or less kicked their asses right out of the store. Chased them away. Once you let the dopers peddle their stuff, its like they're always there.[16] ◀

Black Thieves

Sam is also reluctant to trade with many of the local black and Puerto Rican thieves.

▶ I was always more leery of buying from blacks. To my thinking, your black thieves don't believe in trust like a lot of your white thieves do. See, your blacks are more into the hustling, more into the dirt, you might say. Hustling dope, women, and doing anything to make a buck. And I was always more leery that your black thief was a doper, into drugs. I didn't like that.

I've never known a black that was a good burglar, really good, you know. Now, I've bought from some blacks that were pretty decent

---

16. Chubbie notes: "Sam would buy from junkies he knew, like Lemont Dozier. But many times a junkie off the street, he'd turn away."

thieves, but really good, no. Most of your black thieves are penny-ante, bring you more junk than anything. Whatever they can grab.

In my legit business, now, it was a whole different thing. I dealt with your blacks and Puerto Ricans a lot. They were a main part of that side of it. But buying what's warm, where there's some risk involved, I was less likely to take a shot at it if the thief was black. I don't think I was prejudiced against blacks, like a lot of your white thieves and some of your dealers are. I don't know how to say it; I guess I just felt safer dealing with your white thief.[17] ◄

Female Thieves

That female thieves comprise a very small part of Sam's trade in stolen goods is partly a matter of numbers—there are far more male than female thieves, especially of the more career-oriented type. But there is, as well, a strong reluctance on Sam's part to deal with them.

► I didn't have much to do with your women thieves. I didn't trust them, that was part of it; but it was more that they are really, really penny-ante, bring you nothing but little shit. It ain't worth your time.

Now, there were a couple shoplifters that were prostitutes, too, that I did buy from. This was fairly regular, now, and they did bring me some pretty decent stuff. See, I would trust a prostitute more 'cause she's been through it, can handle the police and that.

The other thing is your female thieves are more likely to be on dope, or they're stealing for some guy, some asshole. I didn't like that. If she was stealing for her kids, or herself, then I'd help her out. Pay her a good price or I'd sell her very cheap what I had in my store. ◄

Juvenile Thieves

Buying stolen goods from "kids" or teenage thieves is especially risky, partly because they haven't been "tested" but mainly because buying from them may strongly arouse public and police hostility at a Fagin-like fence who is seen as duping or corrupting youth.

► I would never buy from kids, never. A kid cannot be trusted 'cause he hasn't been tested—as soon as the cops pick him up, his mouth will be running. You can get jammed up very easy, not just for receiving but for other bullshit charges, like corrupting a minor.

---

17. A black thief comments: "Maybe some of my brothers he didn't buy from but he did from me. Me and another black dude and a white dude was a team. Hitting motels was our specialty, for TVs and that. They were easy to rip off. All the stuff was going to Sam. Hit houses, too. Watch a place, somebody'd walk up and knock on the door. No answer, we'd hit it."

Now, Louie was different. Off and on he'd deal with kids, already has had them stealing cars and pulling other shit. To my thinking, this was dumb on Louie's part—'cause mostly what these kids steal is penny-ante, and in the long run it will hurt you 'cause the people really look down on that.[18] ◄

Employee Thieves

An assortment of employee thieves constitutes a second major source of stolen goods for Sam. These include truck drivers, deliverymen, dock-workers, shipping clerks, warehouse workers, and salesmen. While these tend to be one-time or occasional transactions, some develop into fairly stable arrangements. In some cases, in fact, this or that driver or ware-house thief is a "regular," a designation Sam attaches to that group of thieves from whom he consistently, and over a sustained period of time, has bought stolen goods. While most of the employee thieves have very little in the way of underworld affinity, some are ex-thieves or semi-re-tired burglars who now hold legitimate jobs, but more or less "moonlight" at theft as a spin-off of their legitimate employment.

► Here's the thing. Your public doesn't think this way. They have it, it's only your thieves, what they call "thieves," the burglars, the shoplifters, and the dopers that are bringing the hot stuff. But your regular guy that works in the store, drives a truck, works on the dock, can be a thief, too. I got a lot of stuff, some real good stuff, from your truck drivers, dockworkers, this or that salesman.[19] ◄

---

18. Jesse's reaction to Sam's claim that he never bought from young kids [juve-niles] is: "as a rule he wouldn't, I'll give him that. But, holy fuck, if it was some-thing worth a good dollar and he could get it cheap, he'd buy from a baby. Who in the fuck is he trying to kid."

Agent Bogart notes that "Vincent always claimed he won't buy from juveniles, but I believe if the right product came along at the right price, Vincent would grab it."

19. Jesse comments: "Believe it or not, but a lot of truck drivers, guys working at a warehouse, at the big truck terminal in town, would dump things off a Sam's. Without a doubt he got a lot of stuff from them. But I would say that guys hitting trucks—which is really your burglar—what is called hijacking, was bigger than anything else."

Agent Bogart states: "Vincent would buy from anybody, including truck driv-ers; whereas other fences would have just specific drivers they're buying from. Might have only five drivers working for them, and those drivers are tightly knit. It never went beyond the five drivers. Say the driver has a load, he'd come by and drop off eight cartons of what the guy's supposed to get, then give him another ten cartons. Two hours later he gets to the next stop, he calls his dispatcher and says I'm missing ten cartons coming here. It's not on the truck. He dropped them off at the fence two hours before."

The major writings on the traffic in stolen goods consistently report that ship-ping clerks, truck drivers, warehouse workers, and other apparently honest em-

Joe Citizen Thieves

A small part of Sam's trade comes from what Sam refers to as "Joe Citizen" thieves (or sometimes "Joe Blow" thieves). These are occasional thieves who run short of cash and steal something, perhaps the ownership of which is open to question, from someone with whom they have a friendly or intimate relationship.

▶ This was not a main thing, but different times I bought from your plain "Joe Citizen," your ordinary "Joe Blow." They're not really thieves, but they might clip if push comes to shove, know what I mean. Oftentimes, it would be an "alkie" who goes on a drinking binge, maybe ties one on for a couple of days, and runs out of money. Then, he clips a girlfriend or a relative or somebody he knows—usually it would be a piece of jewelry or maybe a good antique. Or maybe its a woman who is living with a guy, but she wants to split. Checks me out and sells the furniture and that in their apartment to me. For me, an easy dollar; for him, he's pissed. ◀

Other Dealers As Suppliers of Stolen Goods

A final and very substantial source of stolen goods for Sam is both part-time receivers and full-time fences, including a number of generalist fences like Sam.[20]

▶ A lot of the bigger dealers I was hooked up with, we bought from each other; many times it was more or less an exchange, a swap. You give me so much of that and I'll give you this. You could turn a good profit that way, without much risk.

---

ployees frequently sell pilfered goods to fences (see Colquhoun, 1800; Crapsey, 1871; Hall, 1952; and Klockars,1974. But see Walsh (1977) who does not list drivers and employee thieves as suppliers of stolen goods.)

20. By comparision to Vincent Swaggi, Sam did not receive stolen merchandise from "tailgaters", a thief-category prevalent in large cities (e.g, in Mid-City where Vincent operated) which are centers of wholesale and retail trade. Agent Bogart notes: "Vincent got a lot of stuff from guys who'd follow trucks around, wait for the driver to move the stuff to the tailgate and when he takes a couple of cartons into a store, the thief runs up and grabs a carton and heads down the street. A lot of these tailgaters were general thieves. The younger ones and the dopers would just walk on foot and hit a truck downtown. But some we considered professionals. They had their own vans and trucks. Were very planned. That's all they did for a living."

Nor did Sam receive illicit merchandise through bankruptcy frauds, as Vincent apparently did. Agent Bogart adds: "Another thing, Vincent for years was involved with bankruptcies. What happens is, somebody opens up a company, and he orders merchandise from different wholesalers, pays for it and establishes a credit record. Then he buys on credit maybe half million dollars worth of merchandise. Files bankruptcy and sells the stuff to guys like Vincent."

I also bought from the little dealers, you might say. Like, the other secondhand places, I might buy the antiques and that which came their way. Or, maybe a guy runs a tavern, he comes across some guns or a TV. If I knew him, I'd probably buy, more or less just to help him out, to let him unload. This didn't happen very often now. ◄

Obviously, the fence can only buy what the thief brings to him. Equally so, what the thief brings will depend a great deal on what the fence will take, and what the fence will take depends greatly on his outlets. The need to develop outlets will vary by type of fence and by the fence's legitimate holdings. For example, the specialist fence who handles jewelry, and perhaps owns a chain of jewelry stores, will have less need to develop outside outlets than a generalist fence or a fence with less comprehensive legitimate holdings.

Outlets: The Distribution of Stolen Goods

The paths by which the stolen goods purchased by Sam reach eventual consumers are both direct and indirect: direct, as when Sam resells the stolen merchandise to up-front customers in his store or to patrons of one of the many auctions that are within driving distance of American City; less direct, as when Sam channels the stolen goods to business buyers or to other dealers who then sell the goods directly to consumers or perhaps channel the goods along additional distribution paths.

Store and Auctions as Outlets

Secondhand stores and auctions are both exceptionally conducive settings for the trafficking in stolen goods. Both are more or less trading post environments, and their patrons frequently are in the market for bargains even when they benignly suspect that the merchandise in question is less than legitimate. For Sam, the auctions are an extension of both his legitimate and illegitimate portfolios. He not only peddles stolen goods at auctions but he buy and sells a large volume and assortment of legitimate merchandise.

Only so much in the way of stolen goods can be fenced or resold through one's store or nearby auctions. Stolen goods that are not covered by one's legitimate business identity, that are exceptionally warm, and that are in large quantities, are difficult and risky to fence through conveniently available legitimate channels. Unless the fence can develop other outlets, he is likely to remain a small-time generalist fence or to confine his fencing to one or a few product lines (e.g., the jeweler who fences stolen gems).

► You can unload only so much through your business or through the auctions, the local auctions I'm talking about. Now, if you're just buying jewelry and maybe have a couple of stores in different places, then maybe you could. But someone that is dealing direct with thieves and is buying pretty regular, especially if it's worth a good dollar, will need contacts with other jewelers or whatever. Or, say, you get a truckload of something, say it's whisky, what the hell you gonna do then? Or, if it's very, very "warm"—there's too much risk to run it through your store. Too much risk. Really, very few fences run that much through their own store. ◀

Therefore, establishing connections with business buyers and other fences as outlets for stolen goods is typically an important condition for running a successful fencing business.[21]

Business Buyers As Outlets

The designation "business buyer" refers to the retail merchant or the wholesaler who purchases stolen goods from dealers like Sam and then resells them to the consuming public as part of his legitimate stock. In comparison to fences, business buyers are *secondary purchasers* of stolen goods; they do not deal directly with thieves, and they generally resell the goods directly to the consuming public rather than redistribute them to other buyers. Business buyers typically are seen by business colleagues as respectable members of the business community. They usually are aware or, at least, can strongly surmise that the goods in question are illicit, frequently adopting a policy of "no questions asked."[22]

▶ I got rid of a lot of stuff, whole lot to your regular businessman, say, to a guy who runs a TV or appliance shop, or has a restaurant, or a wholesale business. I had different ones in American City and in other places, too. One would take this, the other would buy that. They were out to make an extra buck if there wasn't too much risk. They won't buy direct from the thief; it goes the other way, too: your thieves, and especially your better thief, won't deal with them.

---

21. Agent Bogart comments: "The bigger fences I knew were not running that much through their own legitimate business. Someone like Vincent, or your man, Sam, will rely mostly on other outlets. Vincent sold stuff to regular businessmen but an awful lot of his stuff he sold to other fences, and they sold a lotta stuff to him."

22. Agent Bogart maintains that some business buyers qualify as "true fences," even though they don't deal direct with thieves. "Take a guy who owns a couple of restaurants and, say, five, six times a year he buys a tractor trailer load of meat from someone like Vincent or your man Sam. That will add up to thousands of dollars a year, tax free, and if he does this over a number of years, more than a million dollars. By the law he's a fence 'cause he's receiving and selling stolen goods, and in my mind he is, too. Now in my twenty-seven years I knew maybe five or six that for sure would qualify. This isn't nickel and dime at all, 'cause probably forty, fifty percent of their business profits comes from deals like these. In my book, that's a fence."

Altogether now, I would say they were as big an outlet for me as anything. ◄

Other Fences As Outlets

Another major outlet for Sam is other dealers in stolen goods. These included both antique dealers specializing in the fencing of antiques, and generalist fences running a general merchandise business or perhaps operating an auction house. Some of these are local contacts but most are long-distance outlets; that is, they are located some distance from American City and, in fact, oftentimes are in another state. Frequently, these fence-fence linkages involve the reciprocal buying and selling of stolen goods.

► I had contacts with places more or less like mine: secondhand shops, auction houses, and that. These were mostly places out of the area, maybe in another state. With some of the dealers, they was getting warm stuff from me, and me from them. ◄

Private Collectors As Outlets

A final outlet for Sam is a small number of special customers who purchase specific kinds of stolen merchandise for their own use, for example, additions to a valued collection in coins or in guns. These transactions are infrequent, but tend to be fairly stable and lucrative arrangements.

► I had a few people that would just buy certain things, like coins or World War II guns. They would be interested anytime those things came my way. Might be a lawyer or maybe a judge who's into coins, or a cop who collects guns. Can be almost anybody, maybe a retired person who's into antiques. But mostly will be a professional person or a businessman 'cause it takes money to be a collector this way.[23] ◄

To this point, the focus has been on the kind of fence that Sam represents and on drawing lines which link him to others like him and distinguish him from other, unlike types. In the next chapter, strictly in his own words and without commentary on my part, Sam traces the turning points in his life and describes how he got to be a fence in the first place.

---

23. Sam in fact doesn't know if these private collectors, like the one lawyer in American City, resell the stolen property or not, but assumes they don't. But according to Jesse, "Sam doesn't know it but this lawyer has a contact elsewhere, in another state, for unloading the stuff. And the guy on the other end is very protected, too, so there is no worriment for anybody."

Chapter 3

Getting into Business

Looking back, I knew early that you have to look out for yourself.[1] I had to go hustle for myself all the way. If I wanted a bike, I had to go get it. My attitude was I'll go do it myself. I could pull my own way, I really didn't need anybody.

I think, too, I always had a little larceny in me. Looking for the buck. Way back when I was 14, 15 years old I was out for the buck. I don't know how to put this. I always thought I was sharper than the next guy as far as getting over. This goes back, Christ, even in grade school I was in different deals. I would always come out ahead. I just had a head for getting over.

Growing Up

My mother and my real dad split when I was about a year old. Never did know my real dad. My mom and I moved in with my grandparents, and my mom worked. Then she remarried when I was about seven but I was still spending most of my time at my grandparents 'cause we lived close by. If I wasn't home at night, my mom assumed I was at my grandparents. My stepfather and me weren't close at all. It wasn't that I disliked him, but I certainly wasn't in love with him, put it that way.

My grandparents mostly raised me. I remember most about them was that they were really tight with the money. Like the old Germans were.

---

1. This first-person account of Sam's life and criminal career up to the point when fencing becomes his main line of work was compiled from several interviews that were conducted in a number of settings (e.g., prison, bar, Sam's home, Sam's current place of business). Other works in the criminological literature which adopt a similar style include: Shaw (1930), Sutherland (1937), and Jackson (1969). As in the present chapter (and in the document as a whole), these works describe and analyze not only the actor (e.g., the burglar) but the action or the criminal activity (e.g., burglary).

They believed in work—I always helped out when I was there. No such thing as a free ride. They had a little farm on the edge of town. I had to get my chores done and stay out of trouble at school. If something happened at school, the people would notify my grandparents. They were good to me but as far as like a bicycle or BB gun, they never got me that. I got mine hustling, dealing, and trading. I would save a little money, put it away. Then I'd turn that money over, buy an old bike or an old car, fix it up, and trade for a better one. Jeez, from little on I was doing that.

I would say that by the time I was fifteen I was running my own life. I went to work full-time, right after I graduated from regular school [eighth grade], for a construction company. Turned most of my salary over to mom. Did this until I turned sixteen. I'm staying at my mom's most of the time now. But just to hang my hat. I was always on the go. I'd come to sleep and leave in the morning. I didn't see them hardly at all. All that I had was a bedroom.

I got my driver's license right after I turned sixteen. Right away, I bought a new car with money I had saved. It was a 1939 Lafayette Plymouth convertible. One helluva car. I wish I had it now. Be worth one helluva lot of money.

Uncle Howie

My Uncle Howie was a lot older, maybe fifteen years older than me. Nice looking guy. My stepfather's brother. He done time in Midstate Prison for a hot car. Was kind of a gambler, a hustler type. Liked the fast life. Was always out for chasing women, really liked the young stuff. I hooked him up with a lot of younger girls who were more my age. He was a lot of fun, lot of fun. It was a "live and learn" thing for me.

Howie was the one that took me to the whorehouse. I was hardly fifteen years old. That was my first experience with a woman, first time I got pussy. Boy oh boy! That was a helluva experience. See, my Uncle wanted me to fix him up with a neighbor girl that was really stacked. Big tits. Really stacked. So I got rapping with her and said my Uncle wants to meet you. So, she went out with him. I says to him, "Did you score, get into her pants," and all that shit? He said, "Yeh, it was good, real good." I said, "Hey, what can you do for me?" He says, "I'll get you something better."

So he picked me up and took me to Cloverdale, to a whorehouse there. Jesus Christ, I mean to tell you, that was something. It was the funniest goddam thing. You know how kids talk in school about sex and that shit. Try to figure out what's going on. This place was just a big room with maybe four or five beds in it, and had curtains in between the beds. So I got me a skinny one and I heard my Uncle say "Hold onto my ears, hold onto my ears." So, when we come out I says, "Were you eating that pussy." He said, "No." "Then why were you telling her to hang onto your ears?" He said, "That way she won't be going through my pockets." Evidently he had gotten rolled before. See, in there you didn't take your pants off. Just pulled them down, screw and then you leave. If she was holding onto his ears while he's screwing her, she couldn't be picking his pocket at the same time.

Crummy, goddam, it was crummy. Just a sheet in between the beds. I could hear him on the other side: "Hold onto my ears, hold onto my ears." It was like a jailhouse cot and that was it. It's a wonder I didn't get all kinds of diseases. Jesus Christ, I'll never forget her. That was a helluva one.

I think I was more advanced for my age than the girls were who were my age. A way lot more. I could get over on them. Get in their pants. Because I already went through it and they didn't. I knew what was happening, especially from running around with Howie. I don't think I was a ladies man, no way. But I've had some helluva experiences with women. And see, I always had a car and that made it easier to pick them up.

Working, trading cars, horsing around, hustling pussy—was the big thing in my life at that time. See, I always worked. I'm working six days a week and long hours, long days. After work, I would bum around, maybe go to the skating rink—which was known as a place for finding a woman. Were some that were really easy lays. The Williams sisters, three of them—Louise, Theresa, and the older one, used to call her Boots—were screwing anybody. Or I hanged around the gas station. There'd always be guys hanging there, maybe some girls too. The gas station crowd was an older crowd. When I was 15, 16 years old, they were maybe 2, 3 years older. Some of them like my Uncle Howie was a lot older.[2]

In many ways, though, I was a loner. I could meet people easy but I more wanted to go my own way. Looking back, I was mostly out to pick up a broad, get in her pants. That's about all I was. A lot of times I'd sleep in the car and go right to work.

"Popped" for Burglary

The first time I was really in trouble with the law was on a gas station burglary, with a guy named Ronnie. Before then, I really hadn't done nothing. Maybe some petty shit, kid's stuff,—like take apples from an orchard or take hubcaps. It was more a little hell raising.

Then this happened with Ronnie. I was just past seventeen. I met this Marge at the skating rink, had the rocks for her. Not love, but getting my rocks off. Ronnie was her first cousin, and he was staying with Marge's

---

2. The one-time owner of this gas station—a man who is now in his mid-seventies and who occasionally drops by to visit Sam—offered this anecdote. "Ask Sam about Mildred Streit sometime. Milly was sixteen, seventeen at the time. Was putting out for the guys that'd hang at the station. Doing it for nothing. So Sam gets her to charge—couple of candy bars or whatever—and he was lining guys up with her but keeping half for himself. He could come up with the damndest ways to make a buck."

parents. That's how I met him, and we horsed around together 'cause he was about my age. Just off and on, like when I would stay over at Marge's.

One evening, Ronnie and me is driving around. I goes into this place to get some gas. And Ronnie is looking over the place. When we're leaving, Ronnie says: "Hey wanna make some quick money? This place is a piece of cake. All you have to do is watch and be ready to take off with the car." I'm not sure those were his exact words but, anyways, I went along with the idea. So we hit the place later that same night, got maybe like thirty bucks. In the next month or so, we hit two more gas stations. They were penny-ante, too. Altogether I don't think we got more than seventy-five bucks.

Then I broke up with Marge, and Christ, it musta been a couple of months later, the cops come to where I'm working and arrest me. It turns out that they had popped Ronnie 'cause he had been clipping some other gas stations besides the ones with me. Somebody had spotted his car, that's how the police found him. But Ronnie, the cocksucker, cops out, and fingers me. Said he did different gas station jobs, like six of them altogether, and that I was with him.

It went to court and he testified against me, that the burglaries were my idea, and that I was in charge. I said I didn't know nothing about the burglaries. Plead not guilty. Ronnie got probation and I got sent to Morningdale, a reformatory for juveniles. To my thinking, the judge came down hard on me 'cause he saw me as a wiseass and cause nobody from my family showed up for the court hearings. See, Ronnie had his own attorney and his parents were always there. I was even in jail for two months before the trial while Ronnie was out on bail. The only person who ever showed up was Marge, and couple of the guys I sometimes ran with. Nobody from my family got involved at all. Didn't see nor hear a peep from any of them.

I was at Morningdale about eight months and then I got out. It wasn't too bad a place. In some ways it was more like being in school than in prison. You had to go to class and that. You didn't really have your real thieves and murderers. Mostly it was just wiseass kids. I wasn't what you would call jail-wise or nothing like that but I knew how to take care of myself. And, see, I had already been in jail about two months, and with older guys. Learned how to handle yourself. Like if they make cracks on you, say, yeh—you can get all you want, but you got to take what comes with it. That, and it don't take me long to make friends, you know. It never did.

The only trouble I had at Morningdale was some of the city kids razzed me as a "farmboy," as being from the "sticks," a "country hick." There was a lot of needling and that shit going on there. That was one reason I took up boxing. I was always pretty strong and with the boxing, I could handle myself pretty well, real well I would say. I wasn't one to pick fights, but I wouldn't be backing away either. The first few months there I got into a lot of fights. But afterwards I was left alone. The "jailbirds," the ones who done time before, were the worse for the needling shit, see if they can get to you, get under your skin.

After doing my bit at Morningdale, I stayed at my mom's place. I just came and went. It was altogether different. We would talk but there's no conversation. It was like nobody was there. I would stop by to see grandma and grampop, but it was like we didn't have anything to say. I could see the hurt in their eyes.

After-Work Burglary Clique: Initiation

First thing, I got my old job back, driving a tractor trailer truck for this construction company. This was pretty good money. Did this for a couple of years. Then I went to work at the big paper mill in the area. Worked the evening shift mostly.

That's when the burglary really started, with this group of guys, twelve to fourteen maybe, that I worked with. This went on for maybe two years before we all got popped. I really don't even know how it started. We'd go out after work, fuck around, drink beer, guys showing off to each other and one thing leads to something else. It started with little shit, like hubcaps or like wheels or tires, stuff like that. And it got bigger and bigger. If a guy needed a tire, couple of us would go out and get a tire. Might steal a car, take the tires off and then let the car sit. We'd laugh about it afterwards, bullshit about it at work. I don't think anybody thought about getting caught. It was more or less just going out for devilment, having some fun. But then later it got to be more for the money, too. It was a little bit of everything-burglaries, stealing cars, even a couple of gas station robberies. Mostly petty shit. More damage than anything else.

Then, a couple of 'em were caught in the act. See, it wouldn't be all twelve to fourteen guys breaking into an empty house. Maybe three or four one night and another two or three a different time. I don't know what really went down. But the ones caught started talking and the other guys are getting picked up, at work and that. I was about the last one to get picked up. Picked me up at work.

It went to trial and I plead not guilty. But several guys testified against me. That I was the ringleader, that it was my ideas all the time. I didn't think it was my idea. If there were a bunch of guys around and they'd say let's do this, I'd say, "Solid, let's go." Because I had been in jail, their lawyers were saying if we pin it on him, you'll be let off. See, I was the only one to have a record. I had a public defender for my lawyer and he knew what was going down but couldn't do nothing about it. And these guys confessed to all kinds of things, burglaries they didn't even do. Cleared the books for the cops. Tell me this and tell me that, we'll let you go. One of those deals.

I was the only one to do time. The rest all got probation. I think my having a record really worked against me. See, at that time having a juvenile record counted against you. It's different now. I was sentenced to one to two years in the county jail.

Escape From Prison—Life on the Run

I had been in jail about ten months when I broke this guy's jaw, this queer. This queer came into my cell. He wanted to blow me. I guess he was making the rounds. I told him to get the fuck out. Called him a fucking queer, shit like that.

Then later, when I walked out of my cell, he was waiting for me and hit me with a broom, with a deck brush, knocked me to my knees. Then we started fighting. It was him or me. I broke his jaw in three places. He was worked over pretty good.

They charged me with assault and all they had was a hearing and the judge gave me one to two years. There never was a trial. No questions were asked. Just bang, bang, two more years. That was the routine way at that time. You were just given more time. Now you got to have lawyers, a trial, and everything.

It was about a month later, after the court hearing, that my buddy O'Keefe got a bottle of vodka. Stole it from the warden's house. We drank that, took money out of the jail safe and then we took off in the warden's car. We both worked for the warden. O'Keefe was the houseboy and I more or less worked in the jail office. This warden was an old Dutchman, on the make all the time. Looking for something for nothing. Like, guys I knew from jail who were now out would bring me stuff—cigars, candy, hams, and that. I used to take the extra and give it to him. He ran a pretty loose operation. Like the safe was open during the day in the office. He was pretty slipshod, you know. We were drinking the vodka and we decided to take off. It was a spur of the moment thing. Stole the warden's car and took I believe $882 from the safe. We went a few blocks, hollered a cab and went to the next town, got different clothing at a secondhand shop. Called another cab and went to the next state, got a train and got off in Oceantown. The first night we had a good time. Girls and everything. After that we got jobs and O'Keefe went his way and I went mine.

It's hell being on the run. In the beginning you're always looking over your shoulder. But afterwards you get to feel you belong there. It's very hard to make it. I would say if you wouldn't need a clean social security card and you kept out of trouble, you could make it. Otherwise, your odds will run out on you. I lasted as long as I did by moving a lot and by getting tied up with women, mostly older women, like 35, 40 years old. I worked mostly at hospitals and places like that 'cause they ain't too careful about who they hire. I'd give them a phony name and turn in a false number to start with, and then I'd keep forgetting to bring in the card. When they would ask: "Yeh, I'll bring it in, I'll bring it in." Hold them off awhile and then I'd know the jig was up. I'd quit, get my last pay and move on.

I was always living with a lady when I was on the run. The only special attraction I had for the older ones was the money. See, they're out looking for a man so much that they don't ask that many questions. They might ask, did you have any luck getting a job today. That's about it. I would usually meet them at a bar, like a neighborhood bar, or maybe meet them at work. Most of the time it was just to find a place to eat and sleep, you know, but I hustled money off of some of them.

This one time, I'm brickcoating, and here comes this lady walking down the street. She was short and hefty, maybe thirty years old. I started bull-shitting her. My that's a fine looking ass, shit like that. She stopped and started talking and I asked her for her phone number and all that bullshit. I told the guy I was working with, I think I got a live one here. Gonna check it out. She would do anything. You name it, she done it. I used to pick her up at work and take her to the bank, you know, to deposit her paycheck and that. She'd give me maybe $35. It was comical as hell. Then I convinced her that we should buy a restaurant, get married, and I'd run the place. See, there was this greasy spoon place that I ate at quite a few times. So, I asked the owner if he wanted to make an easy $500 bucks. Just thought I'd take a chance. But I could tell he had been around. So, I told her about this place and told her we ought to buy it. I told her we would just have to put $5500 down but that the guy wanted it in cash. So, I took her to the place and the owner rapped with us, you know, said he wanted to get out of the business and how he thought I had the personal-ity to run a place like this. She went for it. She went to the bank and got the money. And swoosh, I was out of town.

The only crime I did was checks and one burglary. The first time I did checks I was living with Ann Sanders, a nurse. Lived in her house about two months. I took her checkbook and wrote out bad checks at different grocery stores and then took off. I'd buy like $40 worth of groceries and write the check for $150 to $200. This is a funny damn thing 'cause I had all these fucking groceries. So I just started giving the stuff away. It was right before Christmas and it was like I was playing Santa Claus. I'd say, "Miss, this is for Christmas." Load up her baby carriage with ham or whatever. I got a hell of a kick out of it. I wrote like thirty checks in one evening. Then got the hell out of town.

The burglary was in Oceantown. I was broke. I was in this little café, sitting in a booth, drinking a coke and eating a bowl of soup. I don't think I had but a couple of bucks in my pocket. This guy comes in and after a while comes over and asks if he can sit in the booth. We got to talking and he said he had a job to pull. Needed somebody to drop him off and watch. I didn't say anything at first. Thought he might be a cop when he first sat down. He asked me where I had done time—see, he could tell I was an ex-con. How, I don't know. I denied it. We kept rapping. Finally, I said all right. I watched him and he was cool. He picked me up that evening and I drove his convertible car. He knew what he was doing. I sat and watched. Told me to blow the horn in case anybody came. He wasn't in-side very long. Came out and gave me a handful of money, it was like close to $1600. He dropped me off and I never saw him again. That was it. That was really something. Flat broke and then this happens.

Being on the run, escaping from jail, changed things for me. I had to pull a lotta shit to make it. I went into conning, hustling, checks, a little bit of everything. I knew I had to keep running, and had to make money to keep running. And once I got into these things, you understand, there's excitement in it, a certain kick you get out of it. And I got more cockiness, that I could pull my weight at whatever came up. Gave me a lotta confidence in myself that I could do what I had to do, to survive.

Back To Prison

I was on the run about three years before I got popped. I had three different numbers in Midstate. I had a number for the warden's car and for the money in the jail safe. I had a number on the escape. I had to finish the old sentence and the one for the assault in the jail when I broke the queer's jaw. So, I ended up in penitentaries in Midstate for another six, seven years.

I always hung with the burglars and good con men when I was in the penitentiary. See, you have guys in for burglary, in for rape, in for murder, in for different things you know. You sure as hell don't hang with the rapists and baby molesters. You learn that right away. You pick your own group to hang with. Some guys you want nothing to do with. That's natural, same as in the public, on the outside. You're a college professor, right? You ain't gonna hang with no hippies, the long-hairs, you know. You are what you are, they are what they are. It's the same thing in jail.

The guys in for burglary would be talking, stories and that. You listen and raise your head up, that it sounds feasible. This was already at Morningdale. Then in the adult penitentiaries you would be meeting guys who were a whole lot better, say, at Highpoint. That's where the lifers and some good thieves were. A lot of safecrackers I met there. It sounded easy and it sounded good. Now, there wasn't that much talking, not that much. 'Cause as you get higher up, with the better criminal, you don't hear that much talking, that much bragging. But, in a way, I learned how to crack a safe at Highpoint, from hearing different ones talking about it. Main thing I got from the safecrackers and them was that crime was a business. I learnt that crime is a business.

Really, I met a lot of people, learned a lot of things in the penitentiary. I learned how to get over individuals, because at the time I was a merchant. A merchant in prison. And I learned how to hustle. I just took everything in. Listening, people would talk and I would listen to everything. Not so much how they do it, but whether they knew what they were talking about, whether they were bullshitters or not. Like two people having a conversation about busting a safe. I'd listen to this and then go into my cell and analyze what I heard. I was studying people, learning how to read people. And I think that was very helpful in terms of being a better thief and, down the road, a better businessman, too.

I got along pretty good in prison. Only one time did someone crack on me. I wasn't at Highpoint long, maybe a couple of days. This big black fucker put the bum on me, you know. We was playing baseball and he says: "I like your ass." I says, "The hell you do." And I cracked him with the fucking baseball bat, across the back. That fucked him up pretty good. Some of the guards seen it and nothing happened to me for doing it. See, the lieutenant was a white guy and the guards hated the blacks there. The other cons saw this too, and then they knew: stay away from that motherfucker, he's crazy. See, I learned that young in life. Do it now, and get in the first shot. If you're gonna play games, you gotta beat me to it. I don't argue much.

After Highpoint, I was transferred to Oldgate on account of the warden there wanted me to work in the furniture factory, to show the other prisoners how to upholster. It was the same thing—I hung with the burglars and con men, the good thieves. I was into a little bit of the merchant stuff but not that much. It was mostly just doing time. I didn't get cracked on, nothing like that, 'cause there were guys in the penitentiary I knew. And the name carries, like from Highpoint. What kind of a con is he? Is he solid or not? The name carries. There's a helluva grapevine.

Sam Moves To American City

After I got out of jail, I went to American City. This is about nineteen fifty-eight. I was right at thirty years old at the time. Right away I was working at two different jobs. I was working at the Night Owl Restaurant as a cook, a short order cook on the latenight shift. And I was working at Bailey's Furniture. Then I quit the Night Owl after about six months and went to driving a tractor trailer, like part-time. I don't remember much about the Night Owl job, except maybe four years later, I met Connie Witzig there. See, I would stop for a sandwich, and she worked there. I took her out, and boom, she told me she was knocked up. I should marry her. So we got married and she was far along, had the kid right away, a little girl. Then the marriage went right on the rocks. I come home one night and everything was out of the house. Not anything was there but a paper plate, plastic spoon and knife and fork, potato chips and pretzels and a couple of pickles. Everything else was out of the house. Even the rugs off the floor was gone. This is the only time I was married. Enough of that shit.

This is funny. One time I get this call from this reformed alcoholic, supposed to be reformed, and he's living with my wife. He says, "Oh, Sam, I love your wife and want to be with her." All that shit. See, he thought I might be upset. So I said, "Why'n the fuck don't you do something for me—marry her. Do me a favor, take her, goddam it. Get her off my neck." So, I didn't hear nothing for awhile. Then I find out he was going to marry her. But fuck, would you believe what happens. He up and has a heart attack and dies. My luck with her was something else, I mean to tell you.

I worked for Bailey's Furniture for about a year, I guess. They make furniture and sell it different places, Sears and Roebuck, Montgomery Wards. They just put different labels on it, that's all. I was a repairman and that's how I really learned to fix furniture. Learned a lot about wood. I had worked in the furniture factory in the penitentiary but nothing like this. Like a load of furniture goes out and maybe some pieces get damaged. They would bring it back and I would repair it. Inside arm, or cushion, or whatever. Learned how to refinish, doctor it up, patch over. Make it look passable.

Secondhand/Antiques Shop: Legitimate Business (Almost)

In the meantime, now, I had opened up a little upholstery and secondhand furniture shop. What happened is, the apartment I was renting didn't have any furniture to speak of. So I bought a couple of chairs at the rescue mission for like fifty cents apiece, a piece of curtain for another fifty cents, and a hammer, tacks, and scissors for a couple of bucks. I recovered the chairs and they looked pretty good, and the lady I was renting the room from wanted to buy them. Paid me thirty-five dollars apiece.

Fuck, this pays off. Decided this was a good racket. So I opens up a little shop. Painted a sign on the window—Goodman Upholstery and Furniture. I starts buying more chairs, like from the rescue mission, and running to the auctions, too, both to buy and to sell. I got business right away. I used to work until 1, 2 o'clock at night doing upholstery work. Find these old chairs, recover them, and put them in the window. Everybody was buying. They really went quick.

I was only in this shop about nine months, opened up a little bigger one down the street. Then I took on lamps and end tables, sofas and other kinds of furniture. I was still working at Bailey's Furniture at this time. I got a bunch of recliners, 99 of them, that I paid Bailey's $15 a piece. They were selling for $89.95. The mechanism for the reclining part was defective. Me being a repairman, I knew where they were sending for their units. So I wrote a letter asking for information on the reclining unit. They told me what to do to eliminate it. All I had to do was get an electric grinder and grind off the little notch by the foot part and then it would work properly without sticking. So, I got 99 recliners and here it come Christmas. I sold every one. Was even delivering on Christmas Day.

I was selling other things from Bailey's, too. If a sofa was brought back, I'd say, "Hey, that can't be repaired, put it in damage." See, I was in with the shipping clerk who was the foreman for all the shipping. He and me used to go out drinking and he would take care of me like that. This was Earl Sweets. He was good people.

Even after I quit at Bailey's, Earl would call me and say, "Sam, I got so and so—maybe eight sofas, nine chairs, whatever." I'd give Earl, say, $85 a set. He'd say, "OK, I'll turn it in." Paid him the $85 and gave him like $20 for his own pocket. Now, supposedly he was turning the money in to Bailey's but I think he made out with the $85, too. See, before I got there, all the damaged stuff was being burned. This went on for about 2 1/2 years. Then a new manager took over and said everything gets burned. I went out but couldn't get no play. The new guy wouldn't sell me nothing.

Into Burglary With Jesse

In the meantime, I'm also getting into sofas. See, before I came to American City, you might say my name hit first. There were a couple of guys who I done time with, ran into almost right away. Pulled a couple of jobs with them.

Then Jesse, Jesse Tate, came in my shop; he became my partner. I had heard of him, that he was good people, a good safeman. We got to rapping and done our first job. After that, Jesse and I was teamed up for a long time.[3]

The way this went down is, Jesse was shopping for a new partner and his brother or somebody recommended me to Jesse, that he ought to check me out. See, Jesse's partner at the time, Dean Howard, was a pretty decent burglar but was losing his heart, getting shaky. He would

---

3. Jesse comments:

"I was looking for a man, for a guy I could trust. Sam was recommended to me. What happened is the guy I was working with was pretty decent but was getting shaky. Losing his nerve. I wanted to get rid of him. And there's only one ·fucking thing to do, is you gotta go shop. There's no other way.

Looking back, this is fucking funny 'cause the first time I met him was in that damn little shop, on Ninth Street. My brother knew Sam cause he had nutsed around with him a little. Said Sam was solid, which was the main thing for me. Then we talked about the jump we were going to do. I says to the other guy I was working with, "Hoyt, we might as well try him out, see what the fuck he's like." We did, and seen he wasn't scared at all when we went into a place, and to me, that meant an awful lot. From then on I felt very comfortable, very safe with him.

'Cause it ain't one thing you're looking for [in a partner] but a number of things. First thing, how tight is his mouth. Next is how good he can handle himself— can't have someone who goes in a place, hears a noise, and runs the fuck out the place. He should know how to find a place, too, and how to go into a place. Being good at planning a job, scouting it out, is more important, really, than knowing how to break into a safe. Sam was good all these ways, but I did have to guide in some ways 'cause he can get careless. Don't ever forget that.

Once me and him got together, why, you could really lay your faith in him. If I was busy doing something, opening one, and if something unforeseen happens, I didn't have to worry about it. I knew he would automatically do what had to be done. Do you follow me? 'Cause, holy fuck, there's very few people you can trust that way. I had some . . . ppsschew, and the motherfuckers took off and there I'm sitting and that's a funny feeling when you're in a situation like that. I felt very relaxed with Sam. It's a feeling within yourself. I don't know how to explain it. Him and me pulled a lot of shit together."

drink sometimes to build up his courage, but it was a false courage. Then, too, Jesse was fucking Dean's wife which Dean suspected. So, there was tension there, too. Really, now, Jesse was a very good thief, but that was dumb on his part 'cause you don't want to have that kind of trouble between partners. There is so much pussy around anyway.

First on, Jesse and me was hitting safes and clipping for metals. Then, later on, we went for antiques, too. We're mixing all three. Hit the safes for awhile, then lay low and go for metals—like copper, bronze, and nickel. Jesse was known for metals. Off and on too, we hit houses, cabins, vacation homes, mainly for antiques—porcelain figurines, good silver, glassware—but some jewelry, too. These jobs were coming more from me 'cause I was dealing legit in antiques by this time, and I had the knowledge and the outlets to go with it.

The safe jobs we did mostly in the fall and winter. Because of noise—people are inside, the windows are shut, they're not hearing. And the worse the weather, the better. That way, if it's a business place or a home, you are less likely to be seen 'cause there's less daylight and people don't want to be out. When it's very foggy, drizzling rain, that is the best. Think about it, when the weather is cold or when it's rainy, really pissy out—even the fucking cops don't wanna be out.

In the summer we were hitting metals, like with the electric companies. They'd be putting in a sub-station, and we'd rob the copper. Load up all we could on a truck, take it to a quarry pit, dump gas on the copper, put sheet metal on top, lit it and burn off the coating. Once the insulation was burned off, we had No. 1 copper which was worth a good dollar. We were also hitting foundries and the trains, too, for nickel. There was a place down in Pilot Grove where they made a nickel. And this car used to come out every Sunday night with nickel. We knew the man that switched the trains and we got him on our side and started paying him to get a nickel car on the one side long enough for us to fill our little load. See, nickel is very, very heavy and it comes in either BB form, powder form, or in 4 X 4 bricks. We used to throw off hunks, all we could while they backed the train in. When they pulled the car away, we would pull in our truck and load it. We got rid of it at a foundry in Frankinburg, one of Jesse's connections. Evidently the train people knew they were getting clipped 'cause they put a cover over the car. You couldn't budge it. There was a lot of money in nickel. I would say our biggest hauls came from that.

We always got a lot of tips on places to clip—like from a bartender, an insurance man, a salesman, maybe a guy that drives a delivery truck. But more from lawyers than anybody. See, your lawyers handle a lot of wills. And many times they know the house and the people exceptionally well. It's too bad, really, that people trust a lawyer that way. Your older people especially talk to their lawyers, open up an awful lot to them. Which they shouldn't, but they do.

It would be like eating cake for us, it was so easy. You can't imagine how nice it is, unless you went through it the other way. When someone can tell you, so and so is going on vacation for two weeks. Even knows that someone two doors down the street checks the place twice a day. And when you get in, the money or whatever is always there where it's supposed to be. Now that makes you feel wonderful in itself.

And opening a safe is an excitement. As soon as you see the money, you feel wonderful. It's just like coming. Not that type of feeling, but a good feeling.

We did a lot of scouting, too. Say, we'd read in the paper about a fire station that is sponsoring a carnival to raise money—we'd check it out, scout the place, maybe hit it early Sunday morning, the morning after the carnival. The money would usually be in a safe that was really a tin can, it was so easy to get in. We watched, like the Moose Hall, the Elks Club, and the Legion—they'd leave the money in the safe until Monday when they'd deposit it.

I don't know if you'd call Jesse a pro or not. In your eye and in the cops' eye, he'd be a professional. But not in my eye. No, 'cause that is not our way of talking but is a law enforcement word. Maybe hear that so and so is in "old pro." That's about it. Now, some of these kids, mostly asshole thieves, really, might be talking and say so and so is a professional, or that they are professional. 'Cause they read that in the papers, see it on TV. But they wouldn't call theirselves that around the better thief or the old timers. That's a cop word, mostly to build theirselves up. Like, catch this guy and claim he's a professional thief and that. Shit, the guy's probably an asshole thief. Maybe way back, "professional" burglar and that was used. I can't say. Not now anyways.[4]

---

4. Jesse has these comments about the term "professional thief:" "That's a cop term. And in the fucking papers, you see it. I never called myself that, never called Sam that. It would be hard to ever remember hearing a real thief use that word. Maybe say, so-and-so is an old pro, or 'he's a pro burglar'—but can't even say I've heard that. If I was to call Sam or somebody a 'professional thief,' this should [Jesse's emphasis] mean he does it for a living, and is making good living at it. Not just fucking around committing crimes. And means he is solid. Really, if the guy ain't solid, he won't do that well cause who in the fuck will work with him. Take the guy in the ghetto that is stealing, hustling his ass off every day. In my book he ain't a pro, and he ain't a good thief either. Holy fuck, no! He is too nickel-and-dime. Now the motherfucker may call himself a professional 'cause I can't say I know how the colored talk. But the thieves I know, even the colored ones, don't talk that way among theirselves. That is not thieves' slang but police slang."

Steelbeams notes: "There is a helluva slang out there, especially from guys coming out of jail. But that [professional] is not used. Maybe call Jesse or Sam an old pro or an "old head," but no more than that. It is the cops and the DA that throw that word around."

Rocky adds: "Say we're talking to some females or to some people we know that is straight at a party or something. They knows we're burglars but don't know what kind of burglars me and my buddies are. So we say 'professional'—means we got skills, know our shit—'cause they understand the word. Don't have to talk no further whereas if we'd say 'good burglar,' that they wouldn't understand.

All I can say about Jesse is that he knew his safes. That he was solid and had the connections, like with a good lawyer and that. A very good safe-man. Actually anybody with any kind of knowledge can crack an old type safe, the old square boxes. They're easy to punch out or can peel it. The round ones, the niggarhead safes, that are set in concrete you can pretty much forget about. Unless you know the combination or can work the dial, you're dead. What I didn't know from prison about safes, I learned from Jesse and from doing it.

You can burn a safe, too. But Jesse and me never did that. No need to. I think all this time there was only three, four safes didn't open. Some of your burglars today are burning quite a bit. Like Bowie and Steelbeams both has their acetylene torch. What they will do, many times, is carry the safe out and then put a torch to it. This is why some of your burglars have a hernia, from carrying out the fucking safes. Some of the better safes you have today, you pretty much have to put a torch to them, or maybe can peel them. But there are still quite a few of the old square boxes around that are really tin cans, they open so easy. And many of new square boxes you buy even today, are tin cans. They're fire protection, not protection from the good safeman. Now, you do see on TV about blowing a safe, use nitro and that. This is bullshit. All the guys I've known that were into safes, this goes way back and from being in different peni-tentiaries, never heard of anyone blowing a safe. This is TV bullshit.

Jesse and me never got popped for safes. Never got popped for metals. Close, got shot at and everything else, but never busted. This one time we're supposed to hit a place, got a tip from a bartender about a safe. Went out and checked the place out. We come back, and me and Jesse went to the house and we're going in the backdoor, Jesse dropped the front off his flashlight. He went down to pick his flashlight up and came up. I said, "look out!" 'cause the door pulled open, right, and Jesse's bent down. Boom! A shot came out. I seen a flash right over Jesse's head, and I took off this way and he took off that way. We headed for the back, which was a gulley. Here the place is full of cops. Bang, bang, shooting like

---

Used that way, professional means crime is our way of making a living, and means the person is no slouch at it. Is fairly skilled and gets the job done. Something he prefers to do rather than work at an ordinary job. But in my own circle, you never talk that way. Will say he is solid or that he's a good 'ace in the hole' which means he is fairly skilled and will hold up his end. More than anything you hear 'good people'—means the guy is trustworthy but can mean he's into crime for a living. Just depends on how it is used. Burglars mainly say a guy is good or decent or is half-assed. The only time I heard professional used, was Duckie Miller would say, 'I'm a professional burglar'—more or less I feel, looking back, to blow himself up, to myself and my buddies 'cause we were fucking greenies then, Don't get me wrong, Duckie ain't a bad thief, is really pretty decent. But he ain't no Jesse or Sam or Steelbeams. No way. My ass is grass, if thieves talk that way [use 'profes-sional' among themselves]. The only one that did was Duckie. So you figure it out."

crazy. They come in with jeeps, made a big circle with the lights on and everything. But they couldn't get the jeeps down the terrain, too steep, you know. I lay under a tree and Jesse is not far away from me covered with leaves. In fact, a man just missed stepping on him. It was getting daylight now, and they went most of the day, looking for us. Just laid there, not moving. And then nightfall, we got out of there. We knew we was set up. See, the way it went down was that this bartender that gave us the tip got nailed for selling drugs, and the state police were leaning pretty hard on him. 'Cause they wanted Jesse and me pretty bad. That's when the setup came in.

It would be hard to find a better partner than Jesse. He is good people, very good people. See, it's usually safer to have a partner. 'Cause four eyes is better than two. But then the other guy can fuck up, too, and it's one extra mouth. But a good partner is a very big boost.[5]

Most of the time, too, we had a dropoff driver. But some jobs Jesse and me pulled ourselves. Ninety-nine out of a hundred burglaries you pull, though, you should always be dropped off, not let no cars around, 'cause that ties you in right away. Even a stolen car is bad to have around 'cause if a cop sees something, calls it in, it's all computerized now. Boom! Boom! Find out it's a stolen car, and your ass is nailed.

This is funny. For a time there, the burglaries I did with Jesse, his brother dropped us off. But we didn't like the way he handled himself—too nervous and afterwards he would throw his money around, show off that he had money. Then, I don't know how it all happened, but he got shot at. Went chicken. Scared him into his fucking retirement. So Jesse and me was rid of him. So what does his brother do? Becomes a cop in a small town, few miles from American City. Then he starts giving us tips on places. Some cop he was.

After Jesse's brother packed it in, we gets a tip on a MacDonald safe. Jesse says, "Bernice will drop us off." I'm thinking, "What the motherfuck you talking about?" But then I seen she knew what she was doing, that she had done this before. See, Bernice is Jesse's wife, and she is good people. She was very dependable, you could put your faith in her, to drop you off and be back at the right time. If we're not there, then go to a spot and wait for us. That's what you want in a drop off, is dependability—that they don't fucking run away, leave you sitting there.

But normally you wouldn't trust a woman that way. 'Cause there's few

---

5. Jesse comments: "Very few guys can work alone, when it comes down to it. Take Sam, he had a lot of heart but he had to be working with someone. How can I put it? A lot of men need that extra person for them to have courage, if you can understand that. Have heart only when someone else is there—Sam's heart was more that way. I don't think he would clip a place himself, say, park the car, walk two miles, hit a place, walk back, and all that shit. And it's not Sam's nature to do things alone, but to have people around. Myself, once I tried working alone, I got to where I liked that better. Some things you have to do different, take your time more. But less worriment. It's just you, yourself to worry about."

women in the world people trust. Women ain't known to be trusted. Another thing, a woman can handle the drop off part but you wouldn't want to take her inside. Bernice was good people, but she would get shook up at that point. Inside a house, inside a building—that's a different world when you go in there than the outside. Say, too, when you're opening a safe, you don't want to worry about anything else, that someone might sneak up on you. You want someone who won't panic, but that he can take care of whatever needs to get done. A woman would be too emotional there. And I don't think she could swing a 2 × 4 or whatever, hit somebody on the head. You don't have to be all muscle, now, but strong enough to swing something hard, and have the heart to do it, too. That, and I would not want to have to worry about her. It would just never dawn on me or Jesse, or other burglars really, to take a woman inside.

Bernice dropped us off quite a few times, quite a few. Then, we runs into trouble one night, couldn't meet her at the pick-up. So she waits in this field, all night she waits. Next morning she comes back, cusses me and Jesse 'cause she is still shook up. That was it with Bernice 'cause Jesse says: "I'm not going to put her through this anymore. We'll have to go shopping, find someone to do the dropoff."[6]

That's when we got Dwayne, a so-so burglar but solid. Dwayne was with us maybe three, four years. Not a full partner, now—well, from his mind, yes, but in our eyes, no.[7] He was mainly the dropoff. Jesse and me usually went inside, so we'd fill our pockets first before we came out. We'd shortchange Dwayne that way but you had to be careful 'cause it sometimes comes out in the papers how much was taken. Many times it's even blown up in the papers 'cause the people are raising the amount to collect the insurance. This is another thing about Bernice which you couldn't beat—she didn't get a cut. Her share was with Jesse. Whatever he wanted to give her from his cut—that was his problem—except we might throw her some loose bills or some coins.

---

6. Bernice (Jesse's wife who preferred that I not quote her in this document, nonetheless requested that I include this comment about her burglary involvement) notes: "I did it for Jesse 'cause he felt safer if I was doing the driving. In some ways it was exciting but nerve-wracking in other ways. The money was good but not like you'd think—'cause a lot was coming in but a lot was going out. Easy come, easy go. Know what I mean. It's not like when you work and bring home a paycheck every week."

7. Dwayne comments: "I was into burglary but nothing big. Knew Sam and Jesse both, a little anyways. Then Jesse asks me about dropping them off. Once in awhile they'd say, 'hey, let Dwayne go inside tonight.' Then Sam or Jesse would be the drop-off. Otherwise, no. I dropped them off, and picked them up. They picked the spots, scouted them, all that. Jesse was the main one on safes, Sam more on the antiques. Why they asked me to pull jobs with them, I can't say. 'Cause, really, I was half-assed, that is for sure, not in their league. I never figured I was a partner in the same way that Sam and Jesse was [to one another] 'cause they was very tight."

Drift Into Fencing

In the meantime, I just fell into fencing. See, I was never just into burglaries. I was always working or running my shop. The thing is, most burglars don't work, and I didn't believe in that. First on, the shop was a
front for the burglary, you might say, but still my legitimate business was
doing okay. See I always hired somebody, say, a woman looking for work,
to mind the store and wait on customers. That way I was free to come and
go. But I still spent a lot of time at the store—mostly working in the back
'cause that's where you'd find me if I wasn't scouting or clipping with
Jesse, or if I wasn't running to the auctions.

That's how the fencing started, 'cause guys I knew—other burglars—
came into my shop at first just to kill time. Then this or that one started
bringing guns and antiques to me, to see if I could get rid of them. These
were all pretty decent burglars who knew me, from being in prison and
from being hooked up with Jesse. Now, in the meantime, I am running to
antique shows and to the auctions fairly regular, maybe two to three times
a week. I would sell chairs, furniture, and that which I had upholstered.
And different people saw my work, including a guy by the name of Brubaker who was a very big man in antiques. He asked if I would do his antiques for him. And this led to other dealers seeing my work, that I was
good at repairing, at doctoring antiques. All the time, now, I'm starting to
buy and sell antiques with these dealers, and I'd mix in some of the warm
stuff from my burglar buddies.

It started very small and before I knew it, it was out of hand. One thing
was Brubaker recommending my work to Scottie—Eugene Scott—a
very big secondhand dealer who at one time lived in American City but
now lives in Oceantown, which is about three hours away. It turns out
Scottie is a pretty big fence, and he's bringing antiques to me that are
warm—like antique furniture, sofas, chairs, rolltop desks—to upholster
and to doctor up so they'd sell better, but also to cover his back. Really, it
was birds of a feather flock together 'cause Scottie knew my background
and I knew about his. He told me, "Hey Sam, if you run into anything,
pick it up and ship it on up to me." So I said, "Solid." Now I could buy
more and different things. I could buy local stuff that was warm and sell it
out of the area.

Scottie was my first main spoke for getting the fencing rolling, but I'm
also getting hooked up with the local clique in American City, too. Not all
the way, but my foot was in the door. A very important contact was Louie
Zarelli who I knew through an uncle of his I met in prison at Highpoint.
Louie ran a used car lot, and was a bondsman. A big man, very powerful,
a toughie. Louie had connections all over. He was tied up with the Mafia,
but he wasn't in the Mafia. Now his old man at one time was tied up, was
in pretty good. Louie had friends in the families. At one time Louie was
in the Park Owls which was mostly young guys who were all Italian.
Angelo, Phil, and different ones were in that too. But they all like grew up
and got out of it. Louie really had American City tied up at one time.

Really good. He had his own connections in town which were Mafia backed. Louie wasn't paying off or anything. He didn't need that. It was more like various ones had different parts. Like Louie might handle bail bonds and was big in the fencing. Nicky Moretti would have the gambling, Angelo would be buying hot stuff and was getting into the gambling. Phil was also pretty big—a bondsman and had a big junkyard in Tinsdale close to American City. They more or less worked together.

Louie and I did a lot of business together, and palled around a lot. Enjoyed each other's company 'cause Louie is an interesting guy and likes to have a good time. Until I got rollin' good, Louie was a main spoke for contacts, especially for unloading stuff. Then I didn't need him that much anymore. Really, later on he needed me more than I needed him. We'd go out to eat, run around together, all the way to the end but we was using each other and trying to out do the other, too. It was like a cat and mouse game. Tom and Jerry, really.

Me and Louie wasn't always tight now. Louie has a name for trying to screw people. He was trustworthy, but he was dirty. He tried to screw me and Jesse one time. Not long after I met Louie, Jesse and me had a small load of nickel and didn't want to bother with running it to the foundry guy. So Louie tells me he could handle it, pay us the same price as we got from the other guy but give him a day to sell it. Jesse was leery 'cause he didn't like Louie, but he went along with it. The next day I went to get our money, and Louie is hedging, fucking around, complaining the price was set too high. Turns out Louie had to unload for a lower price, so he wants us to take less. Jesse says, "Hell, with that motherfucker. A deal's a deal." He starts complaining again. That's when I put a .38 to his head, that we wanted our fucking money. I wasn't going to shoot him or nothing, just scare him. The next day Louie dropped the money by my shop. But he wouldn't talk to me for a long time. I'd see him at auctions and we wouldn't have nothing to say. It was about nine, ten months and then one night at a car auction, he comes up and starts rapping. That's how we got back talking again.

I'd say at this time, Louie was probably the biggest fence in American City, the most wide open anyway. The other two main ones were Ray Weinstein, a Jew guy tied up with the Jew mob and with the Italians, too. At that time, the Jews and Italians worked together. Still do, in many ways. Weinstein dealt mostly with the better thieves. The other main fence was Angelo whose old man, Mario, was very big, very high-up, in the Mafia. Now, there were other people that would buy, especially from the better thief, but these were the main ones.

Joey Page was another one who was pretty wide open at that time. A secondhand dealer. Then he started snitching, and the fucking word spread that he was a snitch—even the bottom-barrel thieves didn't wanna do business with him. I always knew Joey was an asshole, thought he was more than he was. See, he was a cousin of Angelo, and he played on being connected with the family. He was a fucking asshole. Came into my shop one time, says, "Sam, I can use you and you can use me. We should get together." Words to that effect, 'cause he's thinking I will send the better thieves his way. I says, "You can get fucked, and get your fucking ass out of my shop." He was no damn good, really an asshole.

I was just getting in good with the local crowd—with Louie, with Angelo, with Phil and them—and the fencing is starting to roll pretty good when me and Jesse gets popped on the antique burglary. I was doing good on the legit side, and I was getting bigger in the hot stuff. I didn't plan it that way. It just happened.

Antique Burglary

All this time, now, the burglary is changing for me and Jesse. We would still clip for copper or brass once in awhile, but we had quit safes altogether. One time Jesse said to me, "Fella, I'm gonna pack it in, no more safes." And that was it, didn't discuss it no more. No need to, Jesse's mind was made up. See, there was a lot of heat from the state police 'cause they knew we was hitting something fierce.

So, in the meantime, Jesse and me was hitting houses, cabins, antique shops, and that—for antiques, glassware, silver, you name it. This came from me, 'cause of my knowledge of antiques and from my contacts. See, I was getting heavier into antiques, legit now. Was a dealer, you might say, and rapping with other dealers and from going to the auctions and that, I would find out about places to clip.

Then we gets nailed for cleaning out a houseful of antiques. What happened is, we knew about this private collector who had good antiques in his house, that he and his wife would go south for the winter. So, we took my big truck, the twenty-two footer, and parked it back in the hills. Took my little truck and made it look like we was carpenters or plumbers, drove right up to the place, in the broad daylight, now, broke in, opened up the garage door, and backed the little truck in. Load up the little truck, Jesse would drive to where the big truck is parked. He and Dwayne would unload. And Dwayne is staying with the big truck and watching it. I'm at the house, packing and getting the stuff ready for the next loading. Figurines, glassware, and that stuff had to be wrapped and packed carefully. Took down the chandeliers and everything. Jesse comes back, we load up and he goes again. This took most of the day.

My plans were to run the load into Oceantown, to Scottie and some dealers I knew there. What happens is, a guy is fucking around, hunting in those hills and spots the big truck, gets suspicious. Calls the police. It's night now and we're coming out with the big truck. We hits the main road, half-dozen cop cars sirened us in. It was the state police, and they really made a big deal out of it. Handcuffed us and everything. They were walking me with a gun in my back. Pictures in the paper—like we were gangsters and all that shit. Big bullshit, you know, lotta show.

We was wanted in two counties—did the burglary in one county, transported the stolen antiques and was caught in another county. With what the antiques were worth and the damage to the place, and with the owners and insurance company blowing it up, it was listed as $250,000 job. Wally Gleason and Stanley Cohen handled the case, and they also worked with two good lawyers in the other county. It cost me alone $24,000 'cause we had to pay off. And during this time while we're out on bail waiting for the trial, we was pulling safe jobs to pay the lawyers. The lawyers done their job, I'll hand them that. It was arranged to have us tried in only one county, our home county where our lawyers knew the judge and the DA. The other county wanted to bury us. We were looking at a 10 to 20 there. It ended up, Dwayne and Jesse each got six months to a year, and I got one and a half to three on account of my record. With good time and that, I actually done about fifteen months.

It was flukey we got caught. But we coulda been more careful. We was getting sloppy, that I admit. After you do so much of it, and we had it so good in American City with the lawyers and with the cops. As long as we had the bread, there wasn't much we couldn't of done. But you couldn't say I'll pay you later. When you went to Cohen, you hadda take a loaf of bread with you.[8]

Closing Out Of Burglary Career

This part of my life I was a thief, but I was always working or running my shops, had my businesses. And I was getting to be a half-assed fence, too. Now, the first few years after I hit American City I was a thief all the way, and a pretty good thief. Before that, I would say I was a half-ass thief. That's my looking back. But when I was 22, 23 I didn't say I was half-assed. I probably thought I was pretty good, 'cause I was pretty cocky and the guys I was pulling jobs with were even bigger assholes. In those days, knocking around with those guys after work, I didn't know nothing about good thieves. I was green. Terms like good thief, good people didn't mean a damn thing to me. We were more like rough house. More like raising hell. As thieves we weren't nothing but assholes. This I learned in

---

8. Jesse notes: "I'd say me and Sam was getting careless before we got nailed on the antiques, was getting sloppy. After you do so much of it, you think you can't get caught. Whew, you can't believe how many burglaries and that were on the entire list. We were worse than you can hardly imagine. Jesus Christ, we'd drive around some days for hours on end looking for copper or whatever. See, Sam always kept somebody else in the store, usually a broad, to free himself up. We'd go to copper or nickel and then do a safe and then antiques, then maybe back to copper. If you can keep your head together, not get careless, even today your chances are good. But you always have to have the bread, to pay the lawyers and that. That's why I said to Sam one time: 'Holy fuck, we should put so much outta each job aside.' Have a kitty 'cause we knew we could pay off in town. But we never did, just talked about it. Which hurt me in the end 'cause Dwayne never had no money. Sam wasn't much for saving his money either. So you end up putting up the goddamned money; you have to do it to save your own neck, make sure nobody ends up talking and you end up in the hole [doing time in prison]."

prison, from hanging with the better thieves, and from watching all the
assholes. I found out what an asshole thief is, and what a good thief is.

In my eye, a good thief is trustworthy, has heart, awareness, and luck. I
think being brazen has a lot to do with it, too. Myself, I have no fear at all.
No fear of the cops whatsoever. And I'm very brazen, say, about going
into a place or just doing whatever needs to be done. This partly came
from my being in prison, and from when I escaped from jail and was on
the run, and just from doing the burglaries, too. I don't scare easy. In
fact, I don't scare at all.

The good burglar has more contacts than the ordinary thief, too. Like
Jesse and me usually had tips on house burglaries. Something else, a good
thief always has the best lawyer. Like in American City, the good thieves
had the top lawyers in town—Stanley Cohen, Walter Gleason, and Lenny
Savelas—the top lawyers in town.[9]

Some kinds of hustling fall in the same category as burglary. You have
the beginners and the good hustlers, and you have the assholes who think
they're good. You have good card hustlers who can stack a deck, a guy
who palms dice, that's when they're good. And you also have guys that are
assholes who think they are good who will blow themselves up around
other assholes but wouldn't bullshit that way around your better thieves
and hustlers.

A good thief has a lot of class in him. Can see this in jail. Like I might
get into a program or whatever in jail, sort of slide through and get out of
jail. A good thief, I think, is like a notch above. Not in education now. You
can learn from a book, but to really learn, you should experience it. Experience is better than any book in the world. I could have read in a book all
night on how to steal something, but until I done it, and done it with a decent thief, it's a different thing.

The older thieves, the good thieves, know how to do easier time. How
to slide by, get by without being put over. You take me, if you look at my
penitentiary records this last time, I never had a write-up. But before,
like the time I beat up the queer and then escaped, I was a general
fuckup. Somewhere I found out I can bust them. I didn't want to join
them, so I stayed right on the borderline and skated. Same with other
good thieves—check their records, you'll see very few misconducts, yet
they will have their share of privileges. See, we go by the rules. Just on
the outside we go by the rules. Get along with the other inmates and are

---

9. Jesse notes: "To make it, really make it, now, as a burglar—not this penny-
ante shit—whew. You need someone on the inside to give you information, say, a
lawyer or have a contact with somebody that works in a security agency or a place
that sells burglar alarms, 'cause that is fucking nice to have. Need a good partner
unless you can hack working alone, which freaking few can do. [Need] a lawyer to
get you off and help line you up with the right people. [Need] the right kind of
fence unless you're going strictly after cash which is getting harder and harder to
do. And [need] a good woman, to stand by you but not get in your way."

liked by the hacks and the counselors, too. But don't kiss anybody's ass. There's a borderline there.

At penitentiaries, it's funny. You got cliques, what they call cliques. Like a child molester, they were scum. Rapists, they were scum. Your safecrackers and good thieves would hang together. Your stickup men would hang together. And you'd be rapping about what you were into and that stuff. It's still that way but not as many older people in jail, now. See, in the olden days (in the forties and fifties), you got more time than today, have guys in the penitentiary doing ten, twenty years, and up. These older cons more or less ran the penitentiary. And there was a helluva code in prison. Is less of that today, and your older con is fewer in numbers but is still looked up to, left alone if he wants to be. The code is still there but weaker, know what I mean. You have a lot of kids today, a lot of dopers and penny-ante thieves. A lot of assholes, really, and kids who shouldn't even be in prison. You hang with your own kind in prison. I wouldn't be messing around with the baby rapist and the dopers. A different society, know what I mean?

Here's the thing, if you talk to some thieves, they take pride more or less in being a thief, just like an honest man in his work does. Many thieves define themselves as thieves, as good thieves—at least, they wanna think that way and have others see them that way. Say, there are five thieves in a bar. I walk in and they say, "There's a helluva safecracker." It would be like Reggie Jackson walking into a place, and they say, "Boy, can he hit a home run." It makes you feel good, you know. But I didn't want to be known that much, and Jesse even less than me. We didn't hang that much with other thieves.

It takes a lot of heart to be a burglar, especially a good one. Takes a lot of balls. Heart is here. (Sam taps his heart with his fist.) If you have heart, you're not shaky and not too aggressive, and if there's a little bit of risk involved, you won't hang yourself. The chips come down, you can take care of yourself.

What I'm talking about is on a close job, crawling in and cracking a safe and that. Especially today with the communications the cops have. Years ago they couldn't call around like now. Now, of course, thieves have walkie-talkies, scanners and that too. A good thief has to have heart. Myself, I ain't got the heart I had. 'Cause I used to be a nervy sonofabitch, I mean to tell you. Has to have guts, and common sense is important, too. Has to be trustworthy, that's a must. Good people means he keeps his mouth shut. He certainly has to have the trust, and confidence too, of the other guys he's working with. And having skills, that falls into what it means to be a good thief.[10]

---

10. Jesse comments: "When it's used right, if someone was known as a good burglar or good stick-up man—this meant a whole lot of things at once: that he was solid; that he knew how to handle himself; that he knew how to find a good place, how to get in, and what to do when he got in. Meant heart, too, that he

Thieves have to have confidence in each other. That's where heart comes in, too. Suppose we're in a place, right. There's three of us, one other guy is driving the car and me and you are in there. Say something would happen, someone got against me. You just can't run and leave me there. You're going to help me get out, get this guy and get the hell out of there. That's when you're going to have to be able to depend on a person. Not have a guy that's going to get all shitty and run out, and he gets away and you get popped.

That's part of being trustworthy, too. Being dependable. You got to know the man's on your back all the time. I was never worried with Jesse. Knew he would cover my back. With Jesse in a place we knew just what was going on. Knew we'd cover each other's back.

I'll tell you this. A good burglar is very hard to catch. And very hard to convict. The only way you can convict a good burglar is if he was caught in the place. You see guys in prison, 15, 30 burglaries on them, when they tell me "I'm in for 32 burglaries," I don't even want to talk to them. Because I know they either ratted on their self or somebody ratted on them. They're not good people. A man comes up and says, "I'm in for one burglary, I got caught in the place." I would have faith in him. Guy that says he pled guilty to 32 jobs, pled guilty to jobs he didn't even do. Because the police offer him a deal, what he thinks is a deal, and they want to clean their books up. But to catch a burglar, a good one, is very hard to do. I was never caught crawling in a window. Yet, I've crawled through many, many windows. And I was never caught cracking a safe, never. Some close calls, though.

Another thing, if the good thief is caught and has to do time, you will not hear a peep out of him. As long as the cops didn't set him up, fuck him over, you'd hear no peep out of him. To me, if you get me, you got me. That's it. No bitching on my part. These days there are a lot of crybabies in the penitentiary, always whining about they're not guilty or how some

---

didn't scare easy. Good stick-up man, good safeman—this is slang thieves use among themselves. But you have to watch who is using it 'cause most guys can be fucking starving but will blow themselves up. And in jail, holy fuck, you wouldn't believe the ones that will call theirselves good this, good that. It don't mean fuck if a guy says he's a good burglar. It is how he is known to others that means a fuck."

Rocky adds: "Guys use 'good thief' and that more loosely in jail than on the outside. Whole lot more loosely. Someone who is half-decent, say, is just an okay burglar on the outside, might be called a 'good burglar' in jail. That's why you got to watch where the ones using that word is coming from. This you will many times hear—guys will say so-and-so is a good burglar but will tack on whether he's just decent or he is really good. Say guys are talking about Jesse. They would say, 'He's a good burglar, really good.' Whereas, say, they're talking about Steelbeams, they'd say, 'He's a good burglar, is pretty good, pretty decent.' And somebody not as good as Steelbeams, they might say: 'He's a pretty good burglar, not too bad.' But you got to watch who is using that word and where it's used."

other guy got a lighter sentence than they did, or about how they miss their kids or girlfriend on the outside. Hey, man, go fuck yourself, I don't wanna hear it. All that whining just makes doing time that much harder.

Another thing. In my eye there aren't as many good burglars today as there once was. Not that many good safemen left today. Private homes is still pretty good—not so much for safes but for jewelry and maybe antiques. And truck hijackings is good, is good money in that.

The money's in dope now. Some of your better thieves and good burglars are into dealing dope, are wanted by the importers and high-level people to put a layer in between. See, the good thief is solid and knows his way around, with the cops and that. So the big drug people can use them as middlemen, you might say.

Sam Slides Back Into Fencing

After I got out of jail on the antique burglary, I just fell back into the fencing. It is really hard to keep straight what happened. So fucking much takes place. I opened up a little secondhand shop but pretty quick I moved to a much bigger place. I'm running to the auctions and picking up secondhand stuff and furniture. It didn't take me no time to get started again 'cause my old customers were coming back. Saw the sign, Goodman Furniture and Antiques, and they were coming in 'cause I had the best prices in town and treated them fair. The only burglaries I did was a couple of safe jobs—not with Jesse, now 'cause he had packed it in—but with a couple of pretty decent burglars who wanted me to open the safe. Otherwise I was pretty clean 'cause I didn't want to join up with them. If Jesse hadn't quit, it might have been different. I can't say, but maybe I would not have gotten into the dealing so big.

Then some burglars, old buddies mostly, were dropping by. Shoot the shit. Maybe see if I could unload something for them or they'd ask if they picked up such and such, could I handle it? From there, I started dealing more and more with the run-of-mill burglars. Not the street trade so much but your regular thieves, and some truck drivers and that, too. The word spreads fast. Go see Goodman, He'll buy. It just took off like you wouldn't believe.

There's like two periods with the fencing. The first period, say, was before the antique burglary, which towards the end, right before we got popped, I was rolling pretty good in the fencing, but nothing like later on. The first period I was pretty careful who I bought from. Mostly I was buying from the better thieves and I pretty much stayed with antiques. I was leery, you might say, and I was learning. It's a helluva education.

The fencing is much bigger in the second period, after I did the bit for the antique job. Then it becomes a main thing for me. I'm in all the way, you might say. Guys pushing on me, but I'm pulling, too. And Jesse and me is not clipping together anymore cause Jesse has a good legit job and is packing in the burglary altogether.[11]

I didn't plan it to happen this way but, still, I did have an inkling in jail that I'd fall back into the fencing at a bigger level. But I'm also telling myself—I'm gonna quit this fucking shit altogether. Get the fuck outta here, open up my business but be strictly legit. Then, too, I was always in the library in the penitentiary, reading up on antiques, on furniture, and that. It was like I was telling myself to go strictly legit, but if I was ever to fall back into the fencing, this is how I'd do it. See, guys in the prison are always thinking, "Hey, I'm gonna pack it in. This is it." But, in the back of your mind, you're shaky on this 'cause you don't know what you'll do on the outside, when the opportunity is there.

I can say this, though, I did feel I was gonna quit the burglary shit. Maybe not all the way 'cause if you get a good tip where there's really no risk, it would be hard to walk away. Say, too, if you know there's a safe in a place that is easy to get. Maybe you are working on this roof, you look down and see this safe. All the time you're thinking: what's in it, can you open the motherfucker. This keeps itching at you, 'cause you know you will get a kick out of it and the challenge is still there. I don't know how to say this—but jail does not rehabilitate. I'm firm believer that when a person gets to where he says—fuck it, I'm tired of coming to this place, tired of crawling in windows, then and only then will he change. This was the case with me. I left the penitentiary. "Damn, I'm tired. I'm going to quit crawling in these fucking windows." So I quit crawling in windows but, you might say, I had someone else crawling in windows for me.

---

11. Jesse offers this version of why he ended his burglary partnership with Sam: "I forget when we stopped hitting together, but Sam leaves out that me and him did some clipping after we got out of jail on the antique charge. Mainly I quit 'cause we was too hot. Holy fuck, the state police was watching him and me like you wouldn't believe. And Sam is more and more moving into the fencing, and the young burglars and that are hanging at his shop. Sure as shit, I thought, that will lead to trouble. I'm thinking to myself, the hell with it. If I'm going to do something, I'll do it myself. Then I only have one worriment—myself. Then I only gotta pay myself out if I gets popped. 'Cause with Dwayne that time, I had to cover him. See, the lawyers wanted so much money just to take the case and we had to come up with it. Even with Sam, the way that fucker can spend money, I was freaking leery of my having to put up the money if we got nailed—'cause, holy fuck, there would be a helluva price on our heads. I had the feeling it was time to pack it in or go my separate way, work alone if it came down to that. This way I only have me to worry about."

And Jesse adds: "I just told Sam, 'Hey, fella, I'm quitting. I'm packing it in.' In Sam's mind, I'm quitting [burglary] all the way 'cause I had a good legitimate job at this time. To this day, I believe he thinks that."

Chapter 4

Setting of Sam's Business

When Sam arrived in American City in the late fifties, the city looked mostly like an old, rather decayed factory town.[1] Its physical appearance had not changed much since the early twentieth century when, due to a spurt of industrialization, it was transformed from a rural marketplace and trading point into a manufacturing center with a population which over the decades has held fairly stable at 130,000. For many years textile mills and leather-working industries dominated the local economy. Then after World War II, most went out of business or moved to the South. The major industries today include steel processing, heavy machinery, textiles, food products, and energy production. The other major changes since World War II have been the growth of several upper-middle class suburbs and, in recent years, federally funded urban renewal projects which have given the downtown area a more modern look. When the bedroom communities are included in the figures, the total population of American City and its environs is about 200,000.

American City is also the major nightlife spot and trade center for residents of the small towns and farm communities of the rolling countryside around American City. Its immediate rural surroundings notwithstanding, the city is within an hour's drive from several other mid-sized cities in the state (hereafter Midstate) and is within a two or three hour's drive from several of the major metropolitan areas of the eastern seacoast. In addition, the city is within reasonable driving distance to the boundaries of more than half a dozen states.

▶ Two hours south and I'd be in Southstate where I did a lot of business with Tex and Woody who ran big auctions. Really, Woody was probably my biggest outlet. He and his old man ran an auction house

---

1. The writings that were especially helpful in preparing this chapter include: Albini, 1971; Cressey, 1972; Ianni, 1972; Chambliss, 1978; Abadinsky, 1983; Smith, 1975; Reuter, 1983; Block, 1980; Knapp Commission, 1973; Rubenstein, 1973.

in Southfield like you wouldn't believe—Woody could handle almost anything.

Two, three hours east or north, I was into several other states. It would be hard to mention all the places, but for several years I had a very good contact with an auction in Northstate, with a guy named Corky Carter. I did a lot of business with Corky—especially on stuff I could keep in storage for a few days 'cause Corky liked to have a couple of days notice on what I was bringing so he could advertise or contact his buyers.

In Eaststate I had contacts in different places but my main ones were in Oceantown, like with Scottie who was a secondhand dealer like me. I sold stuff to Scottie way back when I was into burglary. He was always a main spoke in the wheel, especially in the beginning when I first fell into the fencing. I also knew some guys from jail that worked on the docks in Oceantown, so oftentimes I would make a trip to Scottie, unload with him, and then pick up a fresh load from the docks.

Don't forget, now, I had good contacts in Midstate, too. There were lots of auctions, half-a-dozen or more, in the area. And some nice size cities within driving distance. Capetown, a good sized city, is only an hour away. Same with Frankinburg [population of more than a million], only an hour away. I had different contacts there but One-Eye Moe was my main one—a fat black guy with a patch over his eye. He was something else, a wholesale distributor and also ran a secondhand shop. I think he supplied half of the city. And on the way to Frankinburg, I might swing over to Glendale, a few miles off the path, and see Grasso, Frankie Grasso, a dirty little Italian that you wouldn't think could even buy a cup of coffee. But he was very shrewd, handled appliances, tools, TVs, shit like that. Had a huge place, maybe three, four times bigger than mine. But Frankinburg was usually my main stop 'cause I had different places to unload, and it is a very corrupt city, even more so than American City. ◄

Recent census data show that the city population of American City is somewhat older, and has a higher proportion of lower-middle class residents, than other middle sized cities. While there is little extreme poverty, there is also little great wealth. Since the early 1960s there has been a fair amount of black and, especially, Puerto Rican migration into the city. At present, these two groups each comprise about fifteen percent of the city population. With the exception of some movement to the suburbs in recent years, however, most of the residents of American City have lived there all their lives. This stability has encouraged the continuation of separate identities for the various nationality groups: the Germans, Poles, Italians, Greeks, and Blacks still have their own neighborhoods, stores, restaurants, social clubs, and political leaders.

Perhaps the most distinctive feature of American City is its reputation as a "loose" town, where menfolk raise hell on Saturday night and where corruption is pervasive in city hall. The control of city officials—police, judges, prosecutors, councilmen—by a limited number of people, has been a dominant characteristic of the politics of American City over the last sixty years. It is a city in which the syndicates work with anyone who happens to be in office and also attempt to have corruptible men elected or appointed to critical positions.[2]

The Italian Mafia has been the most enduring and significant form of organized crime in American City. The Italians have been closely aligned with the Jewish clique both in the past and currently, although the Jews have remained more in the background, their criminal involvement considerably less visible to the press and to the public. The relationships between the Jews and the Italians are amicable but businesslike partnerships, tied together by money and concerns for personal safety, and by the reciprocal resources each group possesses. The resources of the Jews are financial backing, legal expertise, and connections in business and politics; the resources of the Italians are "muscle," reputation, and connections within the criminal community (both locally and intercity), and with the local police, and both the organization and street savvy needed to operate illegal businesses. From about the mid-fifties on, and particularly after the arrest and exit from the city of the boss of the Jewish group, the Italians have solidified their position as the most powerful crime group in the city, with the Greek mob becoming more active and visible in recent years.[3]

Two Mafia families are represented in American City. There is some degree of specialization, with respect to both territory and crime activity, and family members may do business with members of the other family. Both short-term ventures and enduring enterprises exist involving partnerships between members of the two different families. Disputes between families (and between members of the same family) do occur, but the relationships between families are essentially amiable, and the enduring relationship is one of complicated interdependence. Also, the families have relations with other Mafia groups in different cities, linked by a combination of business, personal and family connections.

▶ There were half-dozen, maybe ten, main ones in American City that were connected one way or another. They weren't all connected

---

2. One veteran observer of American City put it this way: "This is the easiest goddamn town to pull shit in. I don't know if all towns are like this but you can pull a lotta shit in this town."

3. Jesse comments: "Your big Italians and Jews could always take care of things. As you come down the ladder, the guy might be protected on some things but not on others, maybe this time but not next time. You don't hear much about the Jews but a couple of them, holy fuck, are very well protected and have their fingers into different things. Still the Italians are the main ones. No doubt. But you got some Greeks moving up. This should tell you freaking something—these days who's the main criminal lawyer in town? Savelas, right? A fucking Greek all the way."

in the same way, now. I mostly did business with Angelo [Cassella],
Phil [DiNato], Nicky Moretti, and Louie [Zarelli]. Angelo's old man,
Mario, and Gus Fiore were the oldtimers—they were both "in" all
the way. They all have their fingers into different things, legit and
illegit.

I did a lot of business with Angelo, Mario's son. Angelo was big in
the fencing, back in the sixties, but now he's mostly in the gambling.
Him and Nick, Little Nicky, pretty well have the numbers and the
big gambling games tied up in American City. Another one I did a lot
of business with was Phil DiNato, a cousin of Angelo's, runs a salvage
yard and is a bondsman. The other one was Louie Zarelli—a bondsman and had a used car lot. Louie is a relative of Nicky. Nicky is tied
up with the family in Frankinburg while Angelo, Mario, Gus, Phil,
and them are with one of the families from Oceantown.

On the surface it would look like Angelo, Phil, and Louie, especially Louie, ran American City. 'Cause they were out front while
Mario and Nicky stayed in the background. They all more or less
worked together, didn't get in each other's way, but if push came to
shove, Mario and Nicky had the backing to do things their way. ◄

As is true in other cities, it is hard to document the Mafia influence or
control of criminal activities in American City. In some ways, the Mafia's
reputation may outstrip actual achievements and power. Though contempt may sometimes be expressed for the competence and toughness of
individual Mafia members, every one—both the police and the criminal
population—shares the view that the group possesses unique resources,
in particular, the capacity to corrupt public authority and the command of
overwhelming violence. Nonetheless, it is probably the case, as Sam believes, that illegal markets in American City are less centrally controlled
by the Mafia than is commonly judged and perhaps less so now than a decade ago.

▶ It ain't like you read in the papers. It ain't one big family. And there
ain't one boss telling the others what to do. They more work together, do each other favors, and have understandings about who is
doing what. And many times the cops are fingering the Mafia when
really they're not involved or are not the main ones. There are lots of
Italians, too, who are into crime but who are not connected.

The other thing is, the Mafia has changed over the years. In the
old days, the Mafia did have pretty good control over some things,
like the gambling. And the Mafia old-timers were more tied to each
other and to the Mafia boss, say, in Oceantown or in Frankinburg,
who would be giving the orders or at least taking his cut from the
Mafia people in places like American City. Now, they're still connected to one another, and the one hand will help out the other, but
it's not so tightly run. The Mafia people in one place are doing their
own thing the same as the ones in the other place are doing theirs.

That, and they are getting into more legit things—restaurants, shop-ping malls—and are more in the background than they used to be.

This doesn't mean they're going away, now. My opinion is they are still very big 'cause they have the connections with city hall, with the police and them. And they have the money and the reputation, too, to back up what they're into, to get rough. And they have the reputa-tion for being into crime and for being "solid," so that if someone is shady he will be more likely to deal with the Mafia than with some-one else. That, and if the Mafia people are pushing for you, that is a very big asset. Put it this way, Angelo and them, made my path a whole lot smoother. ◄

The American City newspapers regularly attack organized crime, and a recurring theme in local elections is the issue of official corruption. In nearly every election, candidates charge incumbent opponents with tolerating or participating in corrupt activities, or both. The issue of cor-ruption, more than anything else, has led to the election of reform candi-dates who, as likely as not, eventually cave in or are overwhelmed in their reform efforts. Nonetheless, as part of the election process, or after the election of a reform mayor and administration, crackdowns on organized crime and on corruption in city hall and the police may take place, along with the arrest and conviction of several local underworld figures. The re-form sentiment usually dies out after a year or two, or in some instances (as when charges of corruption lead to the defeat of city officials) the victo-rious candidates prove to be as corrupt as their predecessors.[4]

For the most part, however, American City voters have not been swayed by charges and countercharges. The interests of voters have been primar-ily on issues such as taxes and services. When they become interested in crime matters, it has been mostly in terms of protection against violence and theft of personal property. The exceptions are when charges of fla-grant corruption are manifest and there exists a heightened sense of citi-zen awareness. This awareness typically does not come from within the city government, or through internal investigations by the local police or prosecutor. Rather, the exposure and publicity is external in origin—

---

4. One American City police officer commented: "You don't see Mafia people doing time, same as some of your businessmen who are into big things. They are all pretty well taken care of in this city."

Along these same lines, a state police officer assigned to a special narcotics squad investigating drug trafficking in the area complained about the difficulty of getting high-level drug cases processed forward once the investigation had been completed: "It's very frustrating, to work four, six months putting a goddamn case together against a top person, say, a main dealer or an importer, only to have the case sat on. Nothing happens and nothing happens, then the word is passed down. Some prick of a D.A. or a judge has kicked the case out. This happens not just here but across the state. It doesn't take a genius to figure out what the fuck is going on."

from local newspapers, national or state crime commissions, or the state police.

Of particular significance has been the more active role of outside police agencies in local law enforcement matters of American City. This stems partly from a statewide policy change toward more involvement of the state police in crime matters of small to mid-sized cities, and also involves the creation of the state crime commission in the late sixties as a spin-off of broader national concerns about organized crime. Thus, from the late sixties through the seventies, both the state police and the state crime commission have mounted major investigative and enforcement efforts aimed at corruption, organized crime activity, and large-scale theft, in American City. The role of these outside police forces will be detailed later, and contributed greatly to Sam's eventual arrest and imprisonment. Says Sam,

▶ I really didn't fear the American City police. It was the state police and the crime commission that were my worry. If it hadn't been for them, I'd still be operating in American City. ◀

This does not mean that all members of the police department, the prosecutor's office, or other officials of city hall are "on the take." Clearly, many are not and some object actively but are unwilling to jeopardize their positions by publicly exposing what is going on.[5] When a reform administration comes into office, or when state or federal investigations reveal the extent of official corruption and seek to undo major underworld figures, these become zealous cops and city officials. Moreover, while some illegal entrepreneurs have virtual immunity in American City, other criminals are not protected but are actively pursued by the city police who are responsive to many community concerns about public safety and street crime.

The lack of police or prosecutorial action against major underworld figures is partly a matter of limited law enforcement resources, combined with the belief that the community wants the police to apprehend more offensive criminals. Many instances of inaction or nonfeasance in American City, however, are clearly based on bribery of extortion. When high-

---

5. An American City police officer offered this assessment of why he immediately retired from the force when he had served twenty years and was thus eligible for pension benefits: "It was getting to me like you wouldn't believe. Not just the payoffs and the other shit that went on, but the state police getting all the credit and our being made to look bad. Different times we investigated a case, are closing in you might say, but the chief or somebody held us up. [Meanwhile] state police come in, make the arrest. They are made to look like Kojaks. Us—we look like fools, real flunkies. I stayed longer than I should of—had an ulcer and other problems. When my twenty years were up, bang, bang, I hit the bricks. Go for a beer with Davey Bumpers sometime, a buddy of mine that is still on the force. This will get you an earful, 'cause Davey got switched from vice to juvenile for pushing too hard on a couple of gambling cases."

ranking police officials are on the take, low-level policemen are likely to feel free to enter into freelance shakedowns, demanding or accepting bribes from motorists, merchants, and others, secure in the knowledge that their superiors are in no position to complain. When rewards given for noncorrupt behavior are low, the relative value of corrupt inducements increases.[6]

Sam's Place Of Business

Sam's secondhand store is located about a block and a half from the downtown and main shopping area of American City. A visitor in the seventies would observe lettering painted on the show windows of the store describing the nature of Sam's general merchandise business. From left to right on the one window the lettering reads: NEW AND USED FURNITURE; on the other window: ANTIQUES—BOUGHT, SOLD, REPAIRED. Then, under the main lettering, Sam simply tallied whatever other kinds of merchandise he was handling at the time. Sam describes the strategic location of his store, the trading-post nature of his business, and the fire that destroyed his store in the early seventies.

▶ I had a neon sign made for the first shop I had. Hung it in the window: FURNITURE, ANTIQUES. Then that broke, so I started lettering the windows, and my trucks too. As my business grew I just added more lettering, beneath the big lettering: TVs, radios, stereos, stoves, refrigerators, kitchen sets, tires, tools, you name it.

I had different shops over the years. The first couple of shops were small. I kept getting bigger, moving to a better spot. The two biggest places were after I got out of jail in '69. They were both on Elm Street, the main drag in American City. I was right in with your better businesses in town. On one side was the Stagecoach Bar and Restaurant. Across the street was Peyton's Candy Store and Luden's Toy Store. Then that store burned down. I opened another one almost catty-corner across the street. The stores were located just where I wanted them to be. I wasn't right downtown, in the main shopping part, but a block to block and a half away. There were eating places,

---

6. Jesse claims: "What the hell, the American City police came to my house one time. Sam wasn't with me then. Took two and half ton of nickel out. Had it in my cellar. They lugged it all out. All that nickel comes out, load it up and take it down to city hall, right, for evidence. About seven months went by and the fucking case was dismissed. Shit, they found the stuff in my house, ha, ha, and one of the city cops comes up to me, younger guy, and says, Jesse, 'listen, I know you paid off.' I says, 'Tell you what. Instead of you playing games, why don't you join them.' I says, 'Take what you get and let live.' And he says, 'Ya know, I'm giving that some thought.' Can you imagine that? Honest to God, he said that. Now, you're talking about nickel they found in my place. Honest to God!"

little shops, and some nice stores all around me. There was always a lot of traffic going by my store.

The fire cost me a lot of money. It was right before Christmas and the place was full. I only had like $10,000 insurance. This was in the early seventies, and I had been in this place about four years. The fire really hurt. I was knocked flat on my back. But I opened up again right away, catty-corner across the street. This was a big furniture place that went out of business like a year before. The chief [of police] helped to get it by inspection, helped it pass. See, the wiring and that was bad. The chief knew the fire inspector and he okayed it as long as I'd take care of the wiring. I was back in business in less than a month.

Both stores were pretty good sized, but the one after the fire was a little bigger. It has two big show windows, with a door in the middle. When you come into the store, there's stairs off to the right which will take you to the showroom upstairs. The main floor had four aisles with stuff spread all over, appliances, TVs, whatever. If you were looking for a piece you heard I had, it would drive you crazy to find it. Stuff in boxes and everything. Then on the sidewalls I had racks of new furniture. Like three sofas and three chairs on the racks, up to the ceiling, pushed against the wall. The new furniture I would always keep on racks. The rest of the stuff was spread out. In the back of the store was my workshop where I worked on furniture, antiques, and whatever else needed to be done. I always had a good business in upholstery, in doctoring antiques, and that. If I wasn't on the road or running to the auctions, you could usually find me in the workshop.

I had a helluva lot of furniture, both new and used. I sold the cheaper, poorer quality new furniture. It wasn't as good quality as what you'd find at Bachmann's or the regular furniture stores. In fact, I bought damaged furniture and that from Bachmann's. By comparison, now, to the secondhand shops in town, mine was a whole lot bigger. Three, four times bigger. It was fixed up better. I sold a lotta junk, too, but I had better stuff and lot more new stuff.[7] ◀

Customers

Sam's customers find him in a number of ways: word of mouth, passing by his store as they shop or go to work, seeing his trucks as they deliver or

---

7. Jesse comments: "There was a hell of a lot of stuff in Sam's store. He kept it nice. Was particular with that store. Some fucking junk but had quite a bit of new stuff, too. Not the best line but pretty good, the type your Puerto Ricans and colored will buy. And the farmers that come from out of town. Did Sam tell you, the colored and the Puerto Ricans come up with the money quicker than a lot of whites? They did, no shit. Sam did turn over a lot of stuff, that I can say."

pick up merchandise, observing Sam buy and sell at the local auctions. On some occasions, Sam pays newsboys a few dollars to distribute a flyer with the local newspapers announcing an upcoming sale.

Sam's major walk-in customers are the lower income and blue collar workers who live in American City and the surrounding small towns, including many Blacks and Puerto Ricans. A small group of more affluent customers intermittently stop at Sam's, for the most part to buy, sell, or trade in antiques. The other major groups of retail customers are farmers from the countryside, policemen, and a variety of local thieves and hustlers who sometimes get a good deal or a favor and also can expect to buy in a friendly, accepting atmosphere.

Sam is proud that his customers keep coming back and that they followed him when he changed stores or when he reopened after doing time on the antique burglary (see chapter 3). Their loyalty stems in part from Sam's low prices, from the special deals he sometimes offers, from his ability to combine a "hard sell" with a good deal of joking and kidding, and from his willingness to extend short-term credit. The fact that he had stolen goods for sale at bargain prices is also an attraction to some customers.

▶ My store was always busy. A lot of my customers kept coming back, followed me from one store to the other. I had the best prices in town. I treated them fair, gave them a fair shake. I never really sold junk in my store, like a chair that would fall apart if you sat in it. I'd ship that off to the auctions.

The other thing is I gave credit. Pay me one-third or one-half now. Then so much per week or month. I never worried about getting paid, especially from the blacks and Puerto Ricans. They were better than the whites, see, 'cause they wanted to do business with me again. With a lot of my regular customers, I might throw in something extra, or I wouldn't charge sales tax. Tell 'em if I don't have to write it up, I'll drop the sales tax. I did little things like that which kept 'em coming back.

I wouldn't say most of my customers knew I was into fencing, but many could surmise it. I don't know if it helped or hurt my business that some of the public suspected I was handling warm stuff, but who do you know who's gonna walk away if he thinks he's gonna get a bargain?

Except for the antiques which brought in the higher class crowd, I catered more to the working man, to the ordinary person, that was my main trade. I sold the cheaper stuff, like in furniture, and lotta used stuff. And I didn't give no warranties and that. No service, either. Once it was in your hands, it was yours. Say it was a refrigerator or TV, my rule was, I deliver it to your place, plug it in, and you're happy, it's yours. My hands are clean of it. With your people that have money, your higher class person, they ain't gonna do business that way, or they will wanna buy a better line of merchandise than I carried. ◀

Store as Hangout and Drop-In Place

Over the years Sam's store has become a sort of hangout both for a half
dozen or so older men who almost daily spend an hour or two in Sam's
shop, and for an assortment of young thieves, "lackeys," and "hanger-ons"
[Sam's spelling]. Sam's store is also a drop-in spot for a number of local
citizens and businessmen in the area who stop by to say "hello" or to see
what Sam has in stock that day.[8]

▶ I'd be working in the back and somebody's always stopping by to
see what's happening, to shoot the shit. Kill time, you know, 'cause
there was always something going on at my store. Take like Charlie
Ciletti, he was a food importer and big distributor in the area, supplied all the restaurants in town. A very big operation. He would
stop by a couple times a week, just to take a break. I did a lot of business with Charlie, sold him a lotta stuff. Same with Winnie, Winston
Burdette, that ran the big TV & appliance place in town. He'd have
coffee across the street at Regina's Diner and stop over and check
what I had on hand that day. Different ones would do that, stop by to
see what I had on the floor that day, or to be part of the bullshitting
and horsing around that might be going on. 'Cause my shop was like
no other shop in town.

The other thing, a lot of your burglars and thieves don't work, and
my store was a place for them to kill time. These I could tolerate
'cause I was doing business with them and I more or less got a kick
out of their antics and bullshitting. Now, some of the other hanger-
ons and lackeys, I could have done without. See, your hanger-ons are
more or less asshole thieves and hustlers. Too lazy to work, too dumb
to be good at stealing. They just hang around different places in
town, like at the secondhand places, looking for something to do.
The ones that hung at my shop were bad enough, but the other secondhand places had even worse assholes hanging around.

Lackeys are lackeys! They don't know how to work and they don't
wanna steal. More or less, they're bums. Hanging around to pick up
a penny, free meal, or just to be part of something. Take
Chubby—he's a lackey. I'd have him run errands for me, wash windows, and that. They are more a nuisance than anything. I don't
know how many years Chubby hung in my store—shit, this goes way

---

8. Tommy, a truck driver who off and on sold pilfered merchandise to Sam and
who also killed time in his store, notes: "There was always a lot of activity in Sam's
store. Not just customers but friends and people that knew Sam, that were looking to pass the time or hear the gossip. A couple of hangers-on, like Chubbie,
were always around, were there every day. And young guys, like Rocky would be
there a lot in the afternoon. Myself, when these types came in, I'd make an excuse, say, I'll see you later. I was there to see Sam, not to mess with the other
hangers-on."

back to the early sixties. A fucking lamp fixture, but in many ways I got a kick out of him. ◀

Finally, Sam's store is a kind of information bureau for finding out about underworld activities, about the police, etc., particularly on behalf of the more professional criminals in the city. These include a mix of active burglars and underworld figures as well as a number of inactive or semi-retired thieves who are interested in keeping up with what is going on.

▶ Some of your better thieves and your higher-ups might stop by just to get the gossip, to find out what was going on. 'Cause there wasn't much that happened that I didn't know about. Many times they would stop by and check if the hangers-on and them were around. If the place was empty, they'd stay. Otherwise it was "hello" and leave right away, come back later. Now, some of these were no longer clipping, weren't active anymore. But they was still curious to hear the gossip, and to reminisce about the old days. ◀

Work Routine

It's not easy to describe what a typical day or week is like for Sam because of the assortment of happenings and activities that take place. The unpredictability of the traffic in stolen goods—fencing may be busy one week, dead the next—precludes a tight schedule or a set routine. Periods of inactivity are rare for Sam, however. A slowdown in theft activity and fewer opportunities to buy stolen property means more time for his legitimate business or for tending to other matters associated with his illegal trade. There is always something to do, so that putting in long days and short nights is the rule rather than the exception.

▶ I couldn't tell you what I did from day to day, what all happened, or all the people I saw. It depended on different things. It seemed like every day would have something different. Never knew what was gonna happen. I was always on the go. I didn't sleep very much. ◀

Most days have a pattern to them, however; there is more predictability to Sam's life and to the way he runs his business (or, the way it ran him) than Sam himself recognizes. Also, while Sam interacts with and makes contact with a rather large number of individuals during the course of a week, there is a fairly stable group of individuals with whom he regularly has social and business dealings.

Some mornings, very early, Sam might make a trip to one of his out-of-town outlets for purposes of unloading recently purchased stolen merchandise. Otherwise, by 7:30 he is at his store, entering it by way of the rear entrance, checking on the way in to see what, if any, stolen merchandise has been left out back by one of his regular thieves or truck drivers. Once inside the store, Sam greets Clyde, a long time employee who for

several years running has lived at the store. Clyde, an avid horserace
player, is kidded by Sam about how he fared at the races the previous
evening. Then if Clyde has not done so, Sam takes down the closed sign
from the front door and the store is officially open.

The two then discuss and make plans for the day, while at the same
time either unloading furniture that Sam may have purchased the evening before at one of the nearby auctions, or moving existing furniture
around the store. On the principle that people are more likely to buy if
they think others are buying, Sam believes strongly in the rapid turnover
of merchandise. Sometimes the appearance of doing a good business is
achieved simply by shifting merchandise around.

Sam relies on Clyde for much of the everyday running of the store—
moving and stacking the stock, making deliveries and pickups, and waiting on most customers. Oftentimes Clyde is assisted by part-time help or
by one of the regulars or hangers-on who offer a helping hand. While Sam
does most of the buying and setting of prices, Clyde does much of the actual selling and has leeway in negotiating with customers over prices.
Clyde may also do some of the buying from the walk-in trade, but Sam
does the buying on the larger deals, many customers specifically asking to
deal with him.

▶ Clyde was with me a long time. I picked him up off the street, you
might say. I found him sleeping in an old van in the parking lot in
back of my store. It was winter, colder than hell. I said, Clyde, come
in here or you'll freeze to death. So he came and more or less started
working for me. I just let him flop.

Told him, look, no use fucking around, if you're going to work for
me, you're going to work for me. So I paid him like $75 a week. No
expenses. I put a room in for him, bed, shower and all that. He runs
the store. That's actually what he done. Selling, making deliveries,
going to the auction and picking up furniture I bought the night before, that was all up to him. That way, I could come and go, or be in
back upholstering or working on furniture, 'cause he'd take care of
things. I always operated that way: have someone in the store to handle things so I could be free to come and go.[9]

Before Clyde, it was Lester. They're both good workers. Clyde
could fix anything, like TVs, refrigerators, and that. Lester was really
good with furniture. See, they both worked in secondhand places in
town before they came to me.

They were really something. Clyde's a horse player. Has a helluva
head on his shoulder. Brilliant man, really, had a football scholarship
and graduated from college. Then went to the army, sent all his
money home to his girl. When he comes home he finds out she's

---

9. Jesse comments: "Sam usually had some broad in there to run the store, too.
That way he could just take off, go to the auctions or whatever, and have a little
nooky on the side, too."

spent all his money and married someone else. He just gave up on life. Betting on the races—that's his life now. Lester's an alkie. He had a bad experience with a wife, and he never got tied up with another woman, except once in awhile he goes for a fat woman. He'll go for a real fat woman. Otherwise he drinks, will go on a four or five day drunk. Then, he might not drink another thing for four or five months. Lester's drinking got so bad, I had to let him go. But he still worked off and on for me after that—depending on the drinking thing.

They're both pretty sharp. I always let them have store money. I kept money in the desk at the back of the store. Just a little cash box 'cause I didn't have a cash register and that. Just bills, sales slips, and that in the desk drawer or on top of the desk. It was a mess, really. Clyde was a horse gambler, but he could be trusted to handle the money. He would blow what I paid him, just like that, but he was safe with the store money. I was a little leery of Lester when I'd see him getting edgy, wanting a drink; otherwise he was safe. ◄

More often than not when Sam arrives at his store, a customer or a thief is waiting for him with something to sell. This is especially true on Monday mornings, when Sam may come in earlier than usual to accommodate the extra trade.

► Lot of your burglars are hitting places on weekends, so they come in early Monday morning to unload. Same with thieves hitting trucks. They're gonna hit them late at night or very early morning when they're full. Or take your truckers or delivery people, they're hauling early in the morning, so if they put something extra on for me, I'm gonna get it early.

Like Tommy Bosco, he worked for a trucking and storage outfit which hauled local and interstate. For awhile there, I could expect Tommy almost every Monday morning. He'd drop off a couple of pieces, like a box of tools or a couple of chain saws, typewriters, or whatever. ◄

By 9:00 A.M. Sam has organized Clyde's day, may have handled a transaction or two with a burglar or driver, and has probably chatted with a local businessman or sold something to a customer who has stopped by on the way to work at one of the nearby office buildings or stores in the downtown area. Sam then goes to his workshop in the back of his store to upholster or to repair furniture until someone stops by to go out for breakfast or morning coffee. Frequently, Louie, Phil, or one of Sam's business friends will stop by. If no one does, Sam will wait until noon to eat. As with sleeping, Sam eats when it is convenient and can be fitted into the rest of his schedule.

The trickle of customers into Sam's store picks up abruptly from around noon to 1:30 when customers on their lunch hours come in to check on bargains or just to see what Sam has in the store today. The other busy times in terms of customer trade are late afternoons from 4:00–5:30, Friday evenings, and most of the day on Saturdays.

▶ "Mammy Whammy Day" was about my busiest time. This was every other Friday—your black and Puerto Rican mammas and some whites, too, would come in 'cause they had picked up the welfare check, and had the cash to buy things. Some Saturdays were very busy, too, especially if I'd have a sidewalk sale. Say I'd been to the auctions and had bought a lot of stuff, or maybe had bought a couple houses full of furniture—like an estate deal where a relative dies. Just put up signs around town the night before or have the paperboys include a little announcement with the evening paper. Pay them a couple of bucks, you know. You wouldn't believe the crowd you would get for one of those sales.

There's a funny story here, 'cause I had a hookup with the Salvation Army in Frankinburg, with Cletus, a reformed alcoholic, who was like, foreman of the docks, ran the warehouse. This is a huge place, 'cause it brings in stuff from a three state area. Cletus would set aside good pieces for me. I would pay for maybe one-third of a load, then the rest would be free. I'd give Cletus a kickback of like two hundred dollars.

It was beautiful. I got a lot of good stuff, lot of junk, too, for little bit of nothing. I've already gone up very early Saturday morning, with my 18-footer, come back around 10, 11 o'clock and the people are buying right off the truck. I would sell most of the load right there. Cletus made me a good dollar. He was really "reformed," I mean to tell you. ◀

The customer trade slows down considerably after the lunch hour break. Sam will usually send Clyde out to bring back sandwiches, or may go out for a late lunch with somebody with whom he is presently doing business.

▶ Many times I ate at Regina's, was a restaurant. A lot of your working class people and truck drivers ate there. The woman that ran it, Regina, was very attractive, maybe forty-five years old. Lotta guys tried to put the make on her, but I don't think she'd played around. She and I were friends, no hanky-panky between us.

Say Gordie Rupp or Bowie Williams that were both good thieves gave me a call: "Meet me at Regina's for lunch, okay?" We'd meet and go over what they had, make arrangements for picking the stuff up, close out the deal, you might say. ◀

By mid-afternoon, there is a steady in and out trickle of hangers-on, lackeys, and young burglars who drop by to see Sam or just to kill time. Sam keeps busy upholstering furniture or arranging merchandise in the store while he visits with them or observes their antics. Frequently, one or more of the hangers-on will lend Sam a helping hand or perhaps accompany Clyde to pick up merchandise that has recently been purchased at an auction, at a real estate sale, etc. Among the young burglars who almost daily kill time at Sam's store are Rocky Lozier and Reggie Rhoads, two burglars who eventually become a core part of the scenario leading to Sam's arrest and conviction on receiving charges.

▶ The hanger-ons and the in-between burglars would come in late in the day, like from two, three o'clock on. Just killing time, looking for something to do, wanting to be part of something. There was a lotta horsing around, bullshitting about women, the cops, who was pulling what. It was more talk than anything 'cause some of them couldn't hustle their way through a paper bag.

A lot of them thought they was closer to me than they were. I would let them think that. The only one I was really pretty tight with was Rocky. He'd show up 3:30, 4:00 o'clock just about every afternoon. He brought me a lot of stuff. He was pretty young, like 22, 23, but was getting decent. The guy Rocky clipped with, Reggie Rhoads, is the one that fingered me, was part of my getting popped by the state police. Not Rocky now, 'cause he stood up, but Reggie snitched on me. Louie got popped the same time 'cause he was buying guns from them, and Reggie snitched on Louie, too. ◀

Around 5:30 Sam may go across the street to The Stagecoach for dinner. This or that burglar, and maybe one of the hangers-on may tag along, knowing that Sam usually foots the bill. The Stagecoach is one of Sam's favorite places. He kids and jokes with the management and the help, and finds the location convenient should he be needed at the store. The evening hours from roughly five to seven are prime times for warehouse, platform, and other employee thieves to bring in their stolen merchandise.

Sam keeps his store open until about 8:00, or as long as there are customers in the store. Some evenings he will work late in his workshop, upholstering or refinishing furniture. Other evenings he will attend one of the auctions in the area. The auctions are a major part of Sam's business and have been the setting for some of his more important contacts. Sam knows, and is known by most of the auction regulars, including Dorothy Ford, a local antique dealer, with whom he has, over the years, done a fair amount of business, mostly legit but some illegitimate. More important, it is Dorothy Ford who eventually betrays Sam by providing information to the state police which leads to his arrest for criminal receiving.

▶ I went to the auction on the average of 2–3 times a week. There were different auctions in the area. I might take a load of junk to sell. Or I might buy. I'd take Clyde along, go with Louie, or go by myself. Other times I went with Dorothy Ford. She was probably the biggest antique dealer in the area, legit now. Dealt in more expensive antiques than me.

She was a funny woman. Her and Albert, her husband, kept foster children who helped out with the business. Ran their business out of a big red barn on their place. Albert is a helluva nice guy. Hardworking but a little slow mentally. Every other word is a cuss word. I don't think he ever knew Dorothy was doing a little fencing. See, she did a little buying, like from a couple of her cousins who were into burglary. Many times she was then selling the warm stuff to me. That's how she set me up, tipped off the state cops, when she got jammed up herself from buying from her cousins. I should have never trusted her the way I did.

You run into all types at the auctions. More than anything, that's where many of my main contacts came from. That's where I met Woody who had the big auction house in Southstate, about a three hour drive from American City. The Chief, Melvin Pulaski, was another one. Was chief of police in American City at this time, lasted longer in that job than any of the chiefs before. Met Melvie at the auction cause he was into antiques and guns, and we became friends.

A big boost at the auctions was Cooper, Dale Cooper. A real spoke in the wheel. Was the auctioneer at several different auctions in the area. He and I would rap a lot, maybe have coffee after the auction. It came out he would chisel. The way we worked it was, I would mix in some warm items with the legit, and he would auction off the warm at good times. Afterwards, I would throw him a couple of bills.

He also sold me some hot antiques and gave me tips on places to be clipped. See, Cooper was an appraiser, too. He was like me that way. Say, somebody died, the relatives wanna settle the estate. So, they have someone appraise the household goods and that. If the place had good antiques, Cooper would let me know and then I'd have a good burglar or maybe Rocky clip the place. Other times, if it was small antiques, Cooper might box some of them up, and sell it to me. It's the way the police do it when they investigate a burglary. They may take more than the burglars. ◄

After attending the auction or after working late in his store, Sam frequently stops at Casey's Pub for a sandwich and drink before heading home. Casey's is somewhat of a thieves' hangout, although many of its patrons are blue collar workers from the neighborhood. Sam is a good customer: he greets and jokes with many of the people in the bar; before he leaves, he will have bought a round or two of drinks for the house. Sam does not drink much himself, but he is generous, known as a big spender among his friends.

▶ I stopped at Casey's Pub fairly regular, either after an auction or maybe late in the afternoon, whenever. It was a place to relax. Lot of your thieves hung out there and your ordinary working man that lived in the neighborhood. Everybody knew everybody. On Friday nights after the races it would really be hopping; otherwise it was pretty tame.

I was good friends with Casey and Lois that ran the place. I would always check with them if there were any messages 'cause a lot of people knew I stopped there so they would leave a message for me with Casey and Lois. ◄

Sam seldom makes it home before midnight. Home in the mid-seventies is a house in a middle income suburb on the edge of American City where Sam lives with his girlfriend, Becky, and her three children. Sam has been separated from his legal wife for more than ten years and pays alimony and child support to their daughter who regularly visits him at his store. Sam is not a family man, but he enjoys his daughter and is generous to her.

► Becky was married to a real asshole. Left her with three kids, wasn't paying support or nothing. They was going hungry when I met them. I more or less took 'em in, helped pay the bills and that. See, my real wife, Connie, and I split way back in the sixties, but she wouldn't give me a divorce. All these years I kept hoping some guy would take her off my hands. I could be so lucky, no way. But I did see a lot of my daughter cause she stopped regular at the store to pick up the support money or whatever. We'd go across the street for ice cream or maybe I'd take her along in the truck when I was picking up furniture.

I was good to Becky but it was tough for her in some ways. I was always on the go, spent very little time at home. Saturday nights and maybe Sunday afternoons were our main times together. Saturdays, I'd usually take Becky out for dinner. Maybe take the kids along, then go roller skating. The kids got a bang out of that. I enjoyed it too, see, 'cause I used to skate when I was a kid.

Becky knew, but didn't wanna know that I was dealing in warm stuff. She more or less went along with it, pretended it was all legit. See, some of the regular thieves would stop by my house, all hours of the night. Or call me, "Can you handle this or that?" "Where should we drop it?" If I wasn't home and Becky knew where I was, she'd call and leave a message for me. ◄

Come Sunday, Sam's pace slows down a bit. Usually he opens the store for a few hours, from about 10:00 to 2:00, to catchup on the upholstering and antique work. A few customers may drop in, but the main traffic is cronies of Sam's, such as Louie or Ciletti. One who shows up frequently is Sam's onetime burglary partner, Jesse. The group may go across the street for breakfast or, more likely, Clyde will make coffee and someone will go out and pick up doughnuts. The talk includes some reminiscing about past exploits and former associates, but is mainly about what is "going down" presently in American City. There is a good deal of kidding and self-mocking humor, and the language is rough and repetitious with a ribald sexual tone.

Probably the big event of the week for Sam takes place on Sunday evenings, when the local gambling club meets to play poker or roll dice. The club's membership includes many of the major underworld figures in the city as well as a number of local businessmen and free-lance entrepreneurs. Participation is more or less by invitation from someone connected with the Mafia, such as from Louie or from Nicky Moretti, who act as "sponsors" for the game. As Sam describes it, the gambling club is a loosely linked "clique of guys who each has his fingers into something." For Sam the club is both work and play, good for relaxing but also good for business, particularly since it brings him into the inner circle of men who have a great deal to do with criminal and quasi-legitimate activities in American City.[10]

▶ Nicky Moretti was the main organizer. Always came with a bodyguard. Ciletti came, Angelo, Phil and that whole crew. Different businessmen would be there. The two main pimps in town—Stokes and Cain—were usually there. They were the big losers. Would blow their money and run out, round up their girls, come back in, and blow their money again. The dumbest gamblers I ever saw.

Another strange one was Jerry Gucci—ran the vending machine business in town, big drug dealer, too. Jerry wasn't in the Mafia really, but he was connected with them. He'd show up, say, at 9 o'clock. Then it was bang, bang, a couple hundred bucks a roll. Go around the table once, maybe twice, then he'd leave. If he won, he won. If he lost, fuck it. He did it quick. We all got a kick out of that.

For a crap game there may be as many as 25–30 guys, but sometimes they'd bring in fresh money from the outside, say, a salesman or a businessman that was visiting in town. We'd start around 7:00 and there were times some of us played until morning. It was a friendly game but we wanted to beat each other. It was a way of relaxing for me and finding out what was going on. Just by listening and watching you could get a good notion of what was going down. It more or less put me in touch with a lotta people and helped me get hooked up with the police, too. ◀

On balance, there is some pattern to the way Sam runs his business, to the way he works and plays, but his week is far from routine or scheduled. Not only is the the trade in stolen goods unpredictable and highly variable, but Sam possesses a spontaenous nature and an inclination towards action. He may have dealings with a particular thief or dealer almost daily for a certain period of time, but then the trading may abruptly drop off. In other cases, Sam may deal regularly with someone for a sustained period of time but at an infrequent pace.

Whatever is Sam's schedule, he is in "business" to make a profit. The

---

10. Jesse notes: "The card playing group has been going on a long time, a fucking long time. Myself, I never cared for the gambling, 'cause that is a way to make yourself more known. I didn't need that worriment. Sam is different—likes to gamble, and be seen with that crowd. That's his nature. They all had their fingers into something—Sam is right there. Not all the way now, but they sorta controlled things in American City, without a doubt.

advantage of trading in stolen goods is that he can buy merchandise at less than it would cost in the legitimate market, and hence can make a greater profit. How Sam manages to "buy cheaply" is examined in the next chapter.

Chapter 5

Buying Stolen Goods

Probably the most important middleman function of the fence is getting the stolen goods off the hands of the thief, a term used broadly here to refer not only to burglars, shoplifters, and drug-addict thieves but also to truck drivers, dockworkers, shipping clerks, and others who steal or pilfer property and then sell it to criminal receivers in order to convert it into a more negotiable medium — cash.[1]

Fence-thief dealings are similar in some ways to exchanges in the legitimate market in that both transactions involve willing participants motivated by self-interest, and working together for mutual benefit. Whether buyer or seller, both expect that the rewards will be greater than the costs incurred from participation. When profits are unsatisfactory, the participants may negotiate to change the rate at which the goods are traded or withdraw from the operation altogether.

But trading in stolen goods has special problems. For one thing, locating a market is difficult. In legitimate exchanges, advertisements and telephone directories list buyers or sellers, as well as the times and places they can be contacted. In contrast, the market in stolen goods is relatively concealed. Participants find out about each other by word of mouth within social networks (friends, kin, work) or at locations frequented by thieves. Furthermore, in legitimate exchanges, prices are often conventionally established and nonnegotiable, and the mechanical elements of the transaction are usually minimized and routinized, making the actual transaction as convenient as possible. But for every deal involving stolen goods, the thief and the fence must come to terms on price. Even agreeing on a time and place for the exchange may be a problem. Consequently, the fence and the thief have a good deal of flexibility in selecting a marketing strategy because of such factors as the low cost of the goods

---

1. The authors and writings that were most helpful in preparing this and the next chapter include: Hall, 1935; Klockars, 1974; Roselius, et al., 1975; Stanton, 1964; Wilken, 1979; Caplovitz, 1973; and Clinard, 1952.

sold and freedom from some legal constraints (e.g., regulatory practices). But factors like the risk of detection may render them considerably less flexible in their marketing behavior.

Risks for Thief and Fence

The risks faced by the thief and the fence may overlap, but there are some differences. The thief faces one major type of risk—that of detection during and after the theft. Unlike the legitimate marketer, the thief usually can't store the goods while waiting for better market conditions. So he puts distance between himself and the stolen goods to minimize the risk of detection. Also, the thief may be under real or imagined pressure to get cash as soon as possible after the theft.

In addition to the risk of detection while performing any one of a number of middleman functions, the fence faces a significant economic risk. He has committed resources for goods which he may not be able to sell at a profit, perhaps because of the deterioration of the merchandise during transportation, or because of his falsely appraising the quality of the goods or his ability to market them. While the fence is better able to protect himself against the risk of detection by means of alibis, covers, and fronts, he is less able to protect himself against economic risk.

More so than in legitimate exchanges, either the fence or the thief can exploit each other during their illicit transaction. The thief, for example, can "burn" the fence by obtaining some or all of the cash payment and failing to deliver the goods, just as the fence can cheat the thief by not paying him in full for the goods received. Or the fence can deceive the thief about the quality of the goods, or may conspire with another fence against a thief who makes the rounds trying to get the highest price for goods. More importantly, either may betray the other to the police or to other control agents.

To reduce the potential for exploitation, both the fence and the thief attempt to control each other's actions. The thief typically will not release the goods until he has been paid in cash, just as the fence typically refuses to advance money before taking possession of the stolen goods. Similar to consumers in legitimate markets, should the fence try to deceive the thief, the thief may refuse to sell and may avoid the fence in the future. Stated another way, to minimize their risks, thieves often return to fences who have dealt fairly with them in the past, so that established trade relationships are developed. Consequently, thief-fence situations are not equally vulnerable to exploitation; a fence and a thief are unlikely to exploit one another if they have developed a stable, long-term partnership.

The potential for exploitation, the absence of the strong arm of the law to enforce "contracts," the need for secrecy, and (perhaps) the thief's need for money, all contribute to a general rule in fence-thief dealings: the fence pays on the spot. Consequently, much more so than in legitimate commerce, running a fencing business requires substantial up-front cash, or at least the capacity to get cash very quickly. Furthermore, how much upfront cash is needed at any time can be quite variable, since the fence controls neither *when* the thief steals, nor *what* is stolen. (Granted, the fence's preferences, the information he may provide, etc., may influence the thief's stealing behavior.) Though paying in cash is the standard practice, a thief may give short-term credit to a fence with whom he has a stable relationship. In rarer instances, a thief may agree to wait for the fence to resell the goods before negotiating a price and collecting the money. Sam comments as follows:

▶ In fencing, it is strictly cash upfront. The rule is "no pay, no get." The bread has to be there, 'cause the thief wants his money, not tomorrow, not next week, but now. That's very different from the legitimate business. Even in the secondhand trade, like buying from the auctions, I could charge it to my account number and wait a week to pick up the merchandise, and this would give you a chance to raise the money if you're running low. Except for some of the regulars who might be willing to wait a day or two, I always paid the thief right away; it was "cash on the spot."[2] ◀

---

2. Chubbie notes: "Sam mostly paid right on the spot. Very few times I've seen otherwise. He always had cash in his pocket. I'm talking about the walk-in people, now. With Steelbeams, Rocky, and them, there wasn't that big a rush. This would happen. Say Steelbeams was supposed to stop by to pick up his money but Sam had to be gone somewhere. He'd say, 'Chubbie, if Steelbeams stops by, tell him I'll be back at such and such a time, or tell him to meet me at Regina's for lunch.'"

Rocky agrees: "Sam always paid on the spot. A few times, he'd say, okay, I'm low on cash—give you so much now, come back tomorrow for the rest. We'd go along with that. Once in awhile even, say, Sam wasn't sure what we had [what the merchandise was worth], we'd let him have a couple of days to unload the stuff, then settle up. It was no big deal."

And Steelbeams adds: "Most times if it was something big or even half-big, say, more than a couple thousand, and if Sam wasn't expecting us, he would need a little time to raise the money. He didn't have, say, $5,000 in his pocket, unless if we called ahead. He'd go to somebody for the money or he'd sell it right away. You'd get paid, usually a day later. Now on smaller stuff, Sam would pay right out of his pocket."

Also, Jesse comments: "This did happen to me, eight, ten times with the foundry guy, especially on a Saturday. I'd go down, deliver the nickel or whatever, he didn't have enough bread on him. Now, holy fuck, this guy is full of money but I just caught him at a bad time. He'd say, come back Monday. I'd go back Monday, the bread was always there. No worriment on my part whatsoever. Ninety percent of the time, though, I'd say the thief gets paid right then and there. But you may hit them at an awkward time. That's why you want to notify them that you're coming, so they can be figuring what the fuck they will need. This depends, too, how much bread the guy has to get together. If it's a fence I have faith in, I'd wait. No big deal. But with a stranger or a guy I don't feel comfortable with, no way."

Fence as Dominant Trade Partner

More so than in many buyer-seller exchanges in the legitimate market, the fence tends to dominate pricemaking in negotiations with thieves. First, the fence enjoys an advantage because of his experience and greater knowledge about the quality and value of stolen goods and about the intricacies of the fencing business. Secondly, the fence's capacity to reward the thief is greater than the thief's capacity to reward the fence: (a) because the thief needs to transform stolen goods into the negotiable medium of cash which the fence controls; (b) because the thief may have limited options, of knowing only one or two fences while the fence may know a large number of thieves who provide a steady stream of stolen goods; and (c) because the thief is under pressure to get rid of the stolen goods while the fence is better able to protect himself against detection by means of covers and fronts.

The fence's dominant role in pricemaking is somewhat akin to that of any merchant, businessman, or wholesaler who is in the business of buying products from producers or clients, particularly when the products are perishable, and the seller is under pressure to market them. In this context, the fence is viewed not so much as a customer of the thief who is selling stolen goods to him, but rather as a wholesale *buyer* of the thief's product. As such, the fence enjoys the advantages of market knowledge and resources that accrue to a legitimate buyer. The thief is like the farmer peddling produce to food wholesalers, a trade situation strongly dominated by the wholesale buyer on account of the farmer's need both for an outlet and for transforming goods into cash. In a similar vein, the fence provides a service to his "client," the thief, by paying him cash for a "perishable" product.

Though the fence tends to dominate pricemaking, this does not mean that he pays the thief the lowest possible price; nor does it mean that the thief is simply the puppet of the fence who pulls the strings. Thieves steal property and sell it to fences voluntarily and out of self-interest. Both the thief and the fence behave autonomously but within a framework of *legal* and *economic* constraints which shape and color their transactions, dampening the freedom and desire of either party to exploit the other. What exists is a mutually beneficial relationship in which both parties, typically, desire safe as well as profitable ventures.

Legal and Economic Constraints In Fence-Thief Dealings

On the legal side, the fence's trading with thieves is influenced by how safe it is to buy since some kinds of goods, some situations, and some kinds of thieves increase the possibility of legal hassles. In general, the greater the risk, the cheaper are the prices the fence offers and pays. On the *economic side*, the fence faces a dilemma when buying stolen goods: on the one hand, he must buy the goods at bargain prices so that he can resell them at "discount" prices and still make a profit; on the other hand, he must pay a fair price or risk losing the thief's patronage.

The buying and selling of stolen goods takes place within a range of market values. Sam is constrained to buy stolen goods cheaply by the wholesale-retail pricing formula of the legitimate trade in mass-produced goods and by the discount pricing of goods sold in his general merchandise store. What Sam pays for stolen goods must be less than what he would pay if he could have purchased the same or comparable goods through legitimate channels such as wholesale outlets, factory closeouts and seconds, auctions, or estate settlements. This means, for example, that his prices must take into account the wholesale-retail markup of about 25–50 percent on many items such as TVs and appliances, or the 100 to 200 percent markup on items such as furniture and jewelry. Or for those stolen goods Sam plans to merge with his legitimate stock, the prices he pays must anticipate the 15–20 percent discount on most items sold in his store compared to prices at regular retail outlets. Also, as with any business ledger, but perhaps more so for an illegal trade, the prices Sam pays for stolen goods must take into account a variety of "overhead" and operating costs. (These costs are discussed in the next chapter.)

These considerations must be balanced against still other forces which restrict Sam from buying too cheaply but encourage him to pay at least a reasonably fair price for stolen goods. If the thief *thinks* Sam buys too cheaply, the thief may take the stolen goods to another fence, may peddle the goods himself to friends or neighbors, or may discontinue theft because it is no longer profitable. What's more, the thief may spread the word that Sam is "cheap," thereby discouraging others from trading with him.

Thus, although at first Sam may profess that "the fence buys as cheap as he can," in the next breath he spells out how the fence's buying practices are more complicated and less a matter of quick-and-easy profits than is traditionally believed.

▶ The fence is gonna get it as cheap as he can, same as any business-man, so he can make more money . . . But you can't beat the thief too bad. You can't pay him nothing, know what I mean. Your ordinary thief is not hard to satisfy. He's got nothing but his time invested. He don't wanna be caught peddling the stuff. But he isn't gonna steal for nothing. You can be cheap but you got to be fair too. I would never cut off the hand that was feeding me.

The risk factor has to be figured in there, too. What good does it do to buy something dirt cheap and then have the cops come walking in your shop. And what if you can't get rid of the stuff 'cause it's too warm.

Now, sometimes you can buy dirt cheap, 'cause the thief doesn't know what he has, and you don't give a shit if he peddles elsewhere. Usually, though, what you want is that the thief is happy, that you got a place to unload, that there be no hassles from the police, and that you make a good dollar for yourself. ◀

In other words, to "buy right" is to buy and sell stolen goods profitably and safely while maintaining the patronage of thieves. This means, among other things, that the thief's norms about a fair price and his perception of whether he has been treated equitably will influence the prices the fence offers and pays for stolen goods.

Pricing Norms of Thieves

For centuries thieves have been guided by the norm that the fence ought to pay "one-third" of the retail value of the goods, although for more experienced thieves the asking price is more likely to be a percentage of wholesale or is based on the fence's selling prices.[3]

▶ For thieves, their rule of thumb is like one-third. That's the thief's opinion. Whereas my rule of thumb is to get it as cheap as I can but not beat the thief too bad. Now, on some deals I might pay the one-third or even better cause there was still a good dollar for me. This will depend on the thief, too. 'Cause your penny-ante thief is thinking about one-third of retail but your good thief is thinking about wholesale, like he will shoot for half the wholesale price.

Or the better thief is figuring he wants half of what the fence can sell the stuff for. Say, I buy jewelry from Rocky. I can't pay him half

---

3. Jesse's comment is typical of the seasoned thief's viewpoint on pricing: "I would want a little less than half of what the guy has to pay for it in the legit market. Take the foundry guy, he was paying seventy, eighty cents a pound for nickel. So, he's making about one hundred percent which is fair to him, fair to me. See, I made it my business to find out the going rate on nickel, which was $1.50 a pound. This is even more than fair to him [to the fence] 'cause he fucking pockets what he'd have to pay in taxes."

Rocky adds: "You hear the one-third of store price quite a bit which we more or less was going by for awhile. How this came about, I don't know, but we dropped that. Never used the one-third anymore but the pricing was figured on our surmising how much the fence could resell it for. That was our thinking."

Mickey—a general thief who sold to Sam also states: "We wanted thirty to forty percent of retail, the price the stuff would sell for in your regular stores. Sometimes we got it, sometimes we didn't."

Steelbeams notes: "I shot for one-third to one-half of wholesale, or I'd shoot for one-half of what I thought the fence could get for it. Didn't pay retail no mind, 'cause the fence ain't going by that anyway. Say you have a carat and a half diamond that's in its setting—no flaws, no bubbles, no carbon, no nothing on it. With the right dealer, you're gonna get one-half of wholesale, maybe even a little better. 'Cause there's no risk at all for him. As soon as you pull that diamond out of the setting, forget it, it's cold. He doesn't have to worry, can sell that to the same guy it was stolen from. Now, if you have to sell that diamond to a fence like Sam, you're gonna get a lot less. 'Cause he will have to unload to a regular jeweler. [But note that Sam can sell cheap jewelry in his store.] The more ways it's cut, the less there's in it for the fence, so you got to take that into account."

of wholesale 'cause I can't get full price for it 'cause I got to unload to a jeweler. So Rocky has to take that into account, that the profit has to be cut another layer. Now, say, Rocky sells direct to the same jeweler, he can shoot for half of wholesale 'cause this guy ain't having to cut the profit again. Most of your thieves can be reasoned with on this. ◄

When examined closely, the economics of fencing simply do not fit the one-third norm in many buying situations, if at all. The norm will apply only to those items which have a low wholesale to retail markup, say, 25% rather than 100%, or to those items which the fence will himself sell at retail. Suppose Sam pays one-third or $33 for an item which in the legitimate market retails for $100 and wholesales for $50. To be competitive he must sell below wholesale. Thus, if Sam sells at 30 percent below wholesale ($35 for a wholesale cost of $50), he will make only $2 on each item. At that rate Sam is quite likely to go broke or at least find it as profitable to remain in the legitimate market.

In other instances, however, the fence can still make a good profit when paying one-third or even one-half of retail. Say Sam buys ten TVs which retail in the legitimate market for $500 and wholesale for $400. If Sam pays $200, and resells them to a business-buyer outlet at 25 percent below wholesale for $300, he pockets a thousand dollars. ($100 each for ten TVs equals $1000.) Or if Sam places the TV's on the shelves of his store and sells them to upfront customers at or near legitimate market prices, say, at $400, he makes even a larger profit. ($200 each for ten TVs equals $2000.)

▶ I had thieves say to me: "I know a dealer that will give me a third." That's bullshit. Say you brought me a gun that sold for $79. The thief would be figuring a third on that. But it don't come out like that. It would be more like $20.

Now, if a thief came in with, say, cameras or TVs, I might pay one-third. 'Cause the markup is very small on TVs and there's still room for a good dollar. But not if it's jewelry 'cause the markup is so big, I'm better off buying that legit than paying the one-third.

It's funny the thief's opinion on this. This one thief was bringing me grandfather clocks, good ones. The guys says I seen that advertised for $600. I said, yeh, sure, try selling it at the store you priced it at. What do you want for it? He says, he wants $200. So, I said, okay, I'll chance taking a beating on it. Now, this time I paid one-third. But the place I'm taking them is paying me $1400. See, the price he sees in the store is way off, it ain't for the same clock. The thief may think he's getting one-third but he's not, no way. ◄

The implications for Sam are that he may sometimes pay one-third of retail, that he may begin bargaining with the thief at one-third, or that he may attempt to dupe the thief into believing that he is being paid one-third of retail. On the whole, Sam pays little, if any, attention to the one-third norm, except possibly to placate the thief. Rather, his pricing policy is mainly governed, on the one hand, by a desire to buy the goods at one-half of what he can sell them for, and, on the other hand, by a desire to make a hefty sum of money irrespective of whether he sells the goods at a low or at a high price markup.

Shoot To Make 100 Percent

▶ What I shot for was to make a hundred percent. Say someone brought me five Smith-Corona typewriters. If they're new, I know I can sell them for like $140. I'd pay maybe $60 or $70 for them. If they're used, I could get like $80 for 'em, so I pay $40.

From going to auctions and just buying and selling, I pretty much always knew what I could get on something. I'd always try to deal where I could make 100 percent, but many times I would settle for making fifty percent. Other times I made 200 percent profit, even more than that.[4] ◀

Aim To Make A "Good Dollar"

▶ What it came down to, really, I wanted to make a good dollar—not a percent of this or that. Say, oriental rugs came my way and the thief knew what he had. I could pay 8, 9 grand and sell them for 11, 12 grand. That's 3, 4 Gs for me. Same with liquor and cigarettes, I could unload them easy, say, to Angelo. Even if my cut was only 25% I was making several grand with no hassles and very little work on my part.

I didn't care shit about a percentage if a big dollar was involved. This would depend on who I'm doing business with, too. Does he know what he's got, can he peddle it elsewhere, how much risk is there for me, how sure am I of my outlets. ◀

In sum, Sam has neither a consistent nor unified pricing policy. His goal is both to "make a good dollar" and to "stay in business," with the two juxtaposed norms—buy cheaply and pay a fair price—acting as boundaries or guidelines within which Sam negotiates in actual trade situations.[5] ◀

---

4. Thieves generally believe, perhaps falsely, that fences at least double and sometimes triple their money in fence-thief dealings. This doubling (but not necessarily the tripling) of the fence's investment is accepted by most thieves as being "fair." Rocky notes: "To our thinking Sam was trying to double his money —which, when you think about it, is fair. Fair to the thief and fair to Sam."

And Tommy states: "Sam was fair—he would pay me like $20, $25 for a portable typewriter that would retail for $80. He'd double his money—put a tag on it and sell it in his store for $50."

5. In recent "anti-fencing sting operations," where police pose as fences and buy stolen goods from thieves, it is claimed that the phony fences pay as little as *two* percent (see Weiner et al., 1983) to *seven* percent of retail value for the stolen goods purchased (Shaffer, et al., 1978; U.S. Dept of Justice, 1978, 1979). Consider

Future Transactions With Thieves

▶ I would always try to keep the thief in my pocket, especially the ones that were bringing pretty good stuff. I was known as a "nice guy," you might say. You want to keep them happy so they come back and give you a shot at what they're peddling. ◀

Sam's desire to keep a particular thief coming back with merchandise cuts across a great many buying situations, directly influencing the prices Sam pays for stolen goods, especially if the thief has other outlets and can peddle the goods elsewhere. Less directly, because Sam's reputation among thieves in general is at stake, he tends to pay fair prices even to thieves he is inclined to beat badly-suspecting that he might want to do business with that thief at some time in the future, or fearing that the thief might spread the word that Sam is "cheap."[6]

▶ You always got in back of your mind about next time, about whether you're going to be doing business again. I might pay the man more than I'd have to, this time, hoping to chop him on the next bid. Wait for an antique or something he don't know much about.

The only ones I beat bad were the real assholes. I would pay them

---

what two cents (or the higher seven cents) on the dollar means on the purchase price of some commonly stolen property. It means that one can buy a $20 watch for 40¢ (or for $1.40 at seven percent), a hundred dollar stolen suit for $2 ($7 at seven percent), a new $200 ten speed bike for $4 (or $14 at seven percent), and a new $400 TV for $8 (or $28 at seven percent). In a report evaluating the anti-fencing stings (there are other kinds of "stings"), Klockars (1980) has expressed his disbelief at these pricing claims with the statement: "Any two-bit thief in any city in the United States on any day of the week can do better than that."

How much anti-fencing stings must pay for stolen goods will depend on the kind of product and the kind of thief, so that paying only seven cents or even two cents on the dollar may be possible in some circumstances. For example, a large legitimate market exists for cars and vans but few people are willing to buy a stolen car because they have no idea how to go about dealing with title and registration problems, altering serial numbers and the like. Thus, while the streets are filled with such vehicles, few in fact are stolen and the majority of those stolen are found abandoned. But should a young car thief find an outlet who will pay seven percent or even two percent of the dollar for a stolen car or van, he can make out quite well. One $15,000 car will bring $1050 at seven percent and $300 at two percent. It is not surprising then that fencing stings frequently report the buying or "recovering" of high-priced stolen cars (Weiner, 1984). At issue, obviously, is whether the initial theft of the vehicle would have occurred without the available outlet provided by the sting project. In a study evaluating the "success claims" of fencing stings, Klockars (1980) concludes that the claims have virtually no validity in fact but are puffed up police versions aimed at defending and manufacturing the image of exemplary policework efficient in use of monies and careful not to entrap.

6. One thief commented that, "Old Man Goodman was pretty fair with everybody. If some nutball came in and had something good but didn't know what he had, Sam would take advantage of that. Fuck yes, who wouldn't."

shit cause no one will bother with them anyway. And you don't want to associate with them either, 'cause that can drive off the better thieves, the ones you really want to do business with.

Even with the penny ante thieves and the dopers, I would seldom beat them too bad. Many times I would have Clyde do the buying, treat them as if they were the walk-in traffic selling strictly legit. I would just tell them, I'm too busy, deal with Clyde. They were better off peddling elsewhere 'cause Clyde was so tight he would "take a nickel out of your eye." ◀

Thief's Experience and Skill Level

Some thieves are more informed about the quality, the price and the market for the goods they have to sell than are others, and thus fare much better in their price negotiations with Sam. Experienced burglars may know very little about the market value of a particular antique piece or the value of certain unusual kinds of goods, but they usually have a working knowledge of a wide assortment of both new and used items of merchandise. By comparison, the marketing knowledge of the younger or less skilled thief is more limited to checking prices at retail outlets and to what he learns by "word of mouth" from thief-associates or at thief hangouts.

▶ If a man knew what he had, I didn't mind paying a fair price. I respected that. Quite a few of your thieves are pretty sharp, know the prices and what they got. Sometimes your warehouse thief and truck driver will even have the bills of lading, so they'll know wholesale, retail, shipping cost, and everything. But your dopers and walk-in thieves only know what they can see by checking the store prices or what they hear from street talk. On the secondhand stuff and your antiques, it's hard for the thief to know the prices. Your average burglar will have a ballpark idea on most items, but on some antiques, even your good thief won't know, and you can chop the price way down. Now, most of the time, I had to pay the good thief a decent price cause, even on antiques, they know what they have. ◀

Character and Integrity

Sam strongly prefers dealing with, and treats especially well, thieves and drivers who are unlikely to bring trouble either because they are solid or because their theft activities are not known to the police. In contrast, Sam deals especially hard with those thieves he considers to be "snitches," "crybabies," or both. Snitches bring hassles with the police while crybabies are "pains in the ass." Sam holds both in contempt: to be an informant or a whiner violates the code Sam lives by and also strikes him as unmasculine, the mark of a weak person.

▶ In some ways I preferred dealing with your truck drivers, dock-workers, and your warehouse thief 'cause they don't bring no heat. If they're just a little bit cautious, there's no risk at all. I really had no hassles with them. When they first come in, they might haggle on prices 'cause they don't know anything about the way fencing works. So you got to explain how you have to ship it out, how there has to be a cut for the next guy, and all that. Once they get that through their heads, then they are easy to deal with. No hassles, really. Maybe just have to slow him down, if he's clipping too much, to keep the people he's working for from getting suspicious.

Your ordinary thief can bring more hassle 'cause he's known to the police, especially if he's into burglary. But as long as he's solid, I could handle that. Your doper thieves are even more known. And as soon as they get popped, they'll start talking. After a while, if the cops hear your name often enough, they'll haul you in, and you got to take care of that hassle one way or another. See, you can buy dirt cheap from the dopers, but they can be more trouble than they're worth. Same with kids, you can get jammed up very easy if you buy from kids.

Some of your hustler types are the biggest pains 'cause they're try-ing to "get over" on you all the time. Many of your black thieves are that way, always hustling. Set a price and they keep finagling. Or they'll come back later, badmouth or cry about what you paid them. Real pains in the ass. More times than once, I've put a shoe in some-one's ass and told him to never show his fucking face again. ◀

Sharply contrasted to the hard bargaining he does with doper and hus-tler-type thieves is Sam's favorable treatment of the active burglar who is trustworthy and "plays by the rules," even though this type of thief will be well-known to the police and may bring Sam a hassle or two.

▶ If a man was solid and didn't whine about it afterwards, I was willing to treat him right, not be too greedy even if the police were after him something fierce, and he had to unload quickly. I didn't mind the kind of hassles he might bring. But your "crybaby" and your "snitch" I would chop them bad. ◀

Consistency of Thief's Stealing Behavior

It is an exaggeration to say that the thief is to the fence what the depend-able employee is to the legitimate businessman, but a thief who works regularly at his trade and steals quality merchandise is a valuable asset to Sam. Sam "caters," for example, to the in-between burglar who steals reg-ularly, who at least occasionally steals merchandise of high value, and is fairly solid.

▶ A man who is bringing me pretty good stuff and is clipping pretty regular, I would cater more to him. Maybe even go overboard on some things he knows the prices on. But if he mostly is bringing me junk, just mediocre stuff, then I'd have to deal with him strictly on a business basis, have set prices.

The other thing I would do, like with the in-between burglars, is when they come back next time, I'd throw 'em a couple of extra bills, tell them what I bought last time was worth more than I had thought. To them I'm coming across as a pretty decent guy. To me, I'm keeping them in my pocket. ◀

The last anecdote reveals what in a broader sense is a standard operating procedure for Sam in his dealings with thieves: the use of "bonus" practices to sustain the opinion that it is better to do business with Sam than with one of his less receptive and less generous counterparts. As is described in chapter 8, the use of perks of one kind or another (free meals, short-term loans, advice) represent attempts on Sam's part to maintain a positive reputation among those who sell to him.

Risk and Market Demand

Sam pays less for stolen goods whose resale entails greater financial risk on account of low market demand, uncertain outlets, or uninformed pricing situations.

Low Market Demand

▶ Say, a thief has something—like guns or video recorders—that are easy to peddle. You got to pay a fair price to get it. But what if he's peddling something unusual, say, it's a load of batteries or a load of canned mushrooms or musical instruments, that are hard to get rid of. You can buy these things cheaper 'cause you know the guy is gonna have a hard time peddling them.

And the fence may not be sure about his outlets, either. I bought stuff already which I didn't know where I would unload and didn't know what I might get. I figured if I made enough calls I could peddle it. So I'd buy, but buy cheap 'cause I'm taking a big risk.

Too "Warm" To Peddle

▶ Some merchandise is so warm you know the thief can't be peddling it; he has to unload it quickly. You ain't gonna touch it either, unless you can make a good dollar. If it's really warm, hotter than hell, say, the state police will get involved, and you may even get heat from the local police. There can be a lotta hassles on some pieces, especially antiques. And what if you can't unload: The stuff is so hot nobody will touch it. ◀

Inadequate Marketing Knowledge

▶ I was probably the cheapest on what I didn't know much about. I wouldn't buy jewelry unless I could get it dirt cheap 'cause I didn't know enough. Same with clothes, fur coats, and that, I didn't buy 'cause I didn't have the knowledge of the quality and the prices.[7]

Now, if I could buy it cheap enough, I would take a shot at almost anything. I would bid low and take a chance on it. Like, I had drawers full of rings, watches, and jewelry that was really junk. After awhile I would take it to the auction, rent a booth, and unload it. Take whatever I could get. See, I was buying this stuff from the walk-in trade, paying nothing, hoping this or that piece would be worth a good dollar, that it would turn out to be a pot of gold for me. ◀

Time and Convenience

Some goods are easier to store or to transport, or they involve less in the way of overhead, than do other kinds of stolen goods. Marketing the stolen goods through the fence's legitimate store or selling them to local merchants is generally less costly and more convenient than shipping the goods out of town. This, however, does not necessarily mean that the fence will prefer to sell to local buyers—convenience may not outweigh the advantage of reduced legal risks that tend to inhere in out of town and more distant outlets. Indeed, on balance, Sam is more inclined towards safety than convenience, generally preferring outlets away from the city and nurturing, in particular, out-of-state outlets.

▶ You have to figure your time and gas, too. If I could run it through my store or sell it to one of the local boys, that was easier, and I would make more 'cause there was less overhead. Like, the two biggest TV places in town would buy from me. I would call one or the other and just drop the TVs off. I never worried about hassles with them.

But many times you got to figure the chances of hassles are greater if you sell local. So I would look for places out of town that were still pretty close by. That way, there's a little extra gas and time but a lot

---

7. Rocky contradicts Sam's claim that he didn't buy much jewelry: "I don't know how Sam can say that. All the jewelry we stole was going to him. The same was true for some other guys—the jewelry was going to Sam or to Louie. Sam pretty much knew what different pieces were worth. If not, we'd give him time to check it out and come up with a price."

Steelbeams adds: "I had an outlet in Frankinburg but I still sold some jewelry and coins to Sam, just to avoid the hassle of making that trip. Sam would pay a fair price but he was cautious, didn't have the confidence in his knowledge of jewelry, not like he did when it came to antiques."

less risk. The chance that the cops would hassle the guy you sold to or trace the goods back to you would be very, very small.

But shipping it to another state is probably the best. I could go 70, 100 miles in either direction and be in another state. I generally preferred that, 'cause you cut down on the risk and it's still pretty convenient. ◀

In sum, along with the type of thief and the desire to maintain a positive image among thieves, what Sam pays for stolen goods is influenced by ordinary market considerations of financial risk and convenience. A final factor influencing Sam's purchasing prices is competition from other fences or criminal receivers.

Competition

▶ In the back of your mind, you're thinking whether the thief can unload elsewhere, and how much the other dealer will pay. Does the thief have other places to go? Can he peddle to somebody he knows? Or can he pass the stuff off as legit and sell it, say, to a regular merchant or maybe unload it at an auction? ◀

When a number of dealers handle the same products, competitive pricing may occur on a temporary basis under one or two conditions. In the one situation, a fence may raise prices to purchase stolen goods if he is attempting to develop the patronage of a promising thief or if he is seeking to lure an established thief from another fence. The other situation occurs when a fence's business drops off because other fences are expanding. He may then outbid his competitors in order to regain a portion of the local business.

▶ I didn't worry much about what the other dealers were paying, especially the little ones. Now, if a decent burglar came to me who had been selling regular to another dealer, I'd be thinking he's shopping around, and then I'd pay a better price than usual. I'm trying to get him to come my way, give me a shot at what he's peddling. Same thing if it was a young thief that was pretty good, had promise, I guess you could say. I'd pay him a better price when he first came to me. But once he was coming regular, I wasn't worried about what he might get elsewhere. I know if I treat him fair, he ain't gonna take the extra risk and peddle elsewhere.

My prices were decent, always in the ballpark of what others were paying. I would never beat the thief too bad, but I wouldn't go overboard just because another dealer was paying more. Now, Louie was different that way. In fact, it was kind of a joke among the thieves and them: how Louie was very greedy but that he would jack up his prices if myself or another dealer was cutting into Louie's business.

Normal Economic Dealing Does Not Fit Fence-Thief Situation

Normal economic dealing simply does not fit the fence-thief situation, for several reasons. First, in order for economic competition to occur, those who sell to Sam must have the alternative of selling to others. But many thieves and drivers are ignorant of the markets for stolen goods and simply may not be able to judge the relative monetary advantages of doing business with one fence rather than another. The underworld grapevine and the channels of information about fences are informal and rather unreliable. Thus, were another fence paying substantially higher prices than Sam, many of Sam's thieves and drivers would have no information network through which to learn about it.[8]

Second, while those who sell goods in the legitimate market tend to sell to whomever pays the best price, those selling stolen goods are more choosey—selecting buyers on the basis of trust and loyalty rather than simply for economic payoff. As long as the thief does okay financially (i.e., isn't "beat too bad"), he will opt for a smaller profit for the sake of selling safely, particularly if the fence in the past has been a reliable market for the thief and has in no way jeopardized his freedom.[9]

---

8. Rocky comments: "Reggie and me stayed pretty much to ourselves. For a long time the only fence we knew was Louie. Then Louie couldn't handle some antiques we were peddling, that's how we met Sam. 'Cause Louie sent us to Sam. He said, 'Go see this guy, Goodman. Has a shop on Elm Street. Tell him I sent you.' Turns out Sam will pay a better price on most things, but we had no idea on that until we was hooked up."

Tommy notes: "I was satisfied with what Sam was paying me. I couldn't tell you what other dealers were paying. It never came up in conversations I was around. Out on the street, with your regular thief, maybe, but with my buddies [other truck drivers], no. I knew some were taking stuff to Sam, too, but we never talked about what Sam paid."

Jesse notes: "A lot of what you hear is fucking bullshit. A guy will say, 'I got so much for this, so much for that.' He's blowing himself up. Holy fuck, I've heard guys talk like they are doing so wonderful, when they are fucking starving. Unless I knew the guy very well, that his word was good that way, I would pay it no fucking mind. No fucking mind at all."

9. Seasoned thieves (e.g. Jesse, Steelbeams, Bowie) strongly assert the priority of safety over price in selecting a fence. Jesse describes what the established thief looks for in a fence: "It's very important to have the right fence, not a fence but the *right* fence. That once he has it you never have to worry about it. There would have to be a relaxation in myself, that I felt trust in him and that we hit it off. Trust is *the* thing, nothing is close to that. Then I'd have to like the guy—his personality has to be okay with mine. Then does he pay top dollar and how good can he handle what you're bringing. Myself, I would not go down the road to another guy just 'cause he's paying more. If I felt relaxed, felt good about the guy, that there was no worriment involved, he could still be paying me less. Now it will usually work out the other way: if they like you they will even treat you better. Understand? The foundry fence—we got along exceptionally well. Was never no bullshit. And he was paying top dollar, too."

▶ A thief isn't gonna go across the street to a dealer he doesn't know or is leery of, just for a few extra bucks. The thief has to trust the fence, especially your better thief. That's the most important thing.

If you're treating the thief right all along and this time your price ain't what he thinks he should get, especially if the price ain't too far off, the thief ain't gonna take the extra risk and peddle it elsewhere. ◀

Third, the processes by which someone becomes an established dealer in stolen goods are sufficiently treacherous to virtually ensure that, within a particular locale, only a handful of criminal receivers will dominate the market in stolen goods. Ready money and reputation, as well as the ability and willingness to buy stolen merchandise on a regular basis, account far more in the thief's choice of receiver than the prices he will be paid for the merchandise.[10] Generalist fences like Sam are especially attractive to the nonspecialized burglar, the shoplifter, the warehouse worker, or the truck driver who tends to steal whatever is available.

▶ The big thing in fencing is to be known and to have the outlets. Say a thief is stealing regular or is stealing real good stuff, or, say, he has a truckload of something. Where's he gonna go? The little dealers can't handle that, so he has to come to someone like me or Louie. ◀

A final reason for the lack of competitive selling among thieves is that relationships among fences are sometimes cooperative rather than competitive in character. Thus, even when the thief knows about other fences, access to them may be restricted on the one hand by collusion, as in the occasional practice of price fixing, or on the other hand by the rise of short-term monopolies.

And, to the extent that they have choices, common burglars and general thieves tend also to emphasize the importance of the fence's trustworthiness. As Mickey notes: "A thief wants to get his value out of the merchandise, and know that it's gonna be kept quiet. I would take a cut on price if I knew the fence wasn't a fucking snitch."

Agent Bogart agrees: "I'd say that's right—whether one fence pays more than another is not the main factor. I found this, if thieves like a guy and get along and joke with him, and if they feel there's more trust than with the other guy, they will go to this fence even though he might be paying a little less. If there's a clash of personality or the thief has to wait for the money, he won't sell to someone just because he can get more money."

10. Agent Bogart notes with respect to Vincent Swaggi: "The big thing for Vincent was, he always had the cash. And he would buy almost anything. Especially with the black thieves and the thieves on narcotics—the thief that needed cash quickly, like the thieves on dope who had no other place to go. See, many fences are leery of dealing with the narcotic thief, afraid he'll open up. Another thing, was Vincent's location—he was right in the main retail district. The ordinary thief—the shoplifter, the guy on dope, the black thief—usually can't transport what he steals. He is looking for a place close by to where he does his stealing."

Price Fixing

One fence may occasionally conspire with another fence against a thief
who makes the rounds trying to get the highest price for goods. According
to Sam, these fixed-price arrangements typically involve an inexperi-
enced local thief or a thief from outside the area who is peddling merchandise which is worth a "good dollar." Also, since dealers lack strong in-
group loyalty and tend to be quite greedy, when collusion in pricing
does take place, it is seldom, if ever, very far-reaching.

▶ Say, it's merchandise I want but we can't agree on price. If he's a local thief and he walks out, I know pretty well where he has to go. I'll
call the guy up and tell him to buy it for me at such and such a price.
Or maybe it's something I can't handle, like fur coats. I'd send the
guy to another dealer. Call the dealer up and tell him he can get it for
a good price. I would do it as a favor, that way he would owe me
something.

I mostly done it when the thief thought he was more than he was, a
smart-ass and hassled and hassled over price. Then I would bid low
and call the other dealer and have him chop the price even more. It
was more to put the thief in his place than anything. But this isn't a
main thing at all. Very seldom happens. It isn't like the public thinks.

Here's the thing, you can't pull this with just any thief and it has to
be something that's worth a good dollar, otherwise it ain't worth the
time and hassle. With the better thief, you ain't gonna pull this
'cause you don't want to lose his business—you're gonna offer him a
fair price to begin with. Or, say, another dealer sent a thief to me. I
ain't gonna beat him too bad just 'cause the other dealer sent him.
No. I want that thief's business, and I'm not gonna pass up a good
dollar on account of another dealer.

Another thing, one dealer might be able to get another dealer to
work against a thief, but if the thief has several dealers he can go to,
that dealer will not be able to get all of them to go along. No way,
'cause they're too greedy and there ain't that kind of honor among
fences—there's more honor that way among thieves.[11] ◀

---

11. Sam's conclusions conflict with this oft-quoted illustration of collusion that
is reported in Walsh (1977:74): "An interview with Greg, a professional thief, produced this chilling tale of collusion and its enforcement in the fencing industry:
'Finding himself in possession of a truckload of stolen furs, Greg, unused to handling property in such volume sought to make a quick deal. He approached a fence
with whom he had had satisfactory dealings previously only to find that this individual, appreciating his predicament, was bent on taking some advantage of it.
Unwilling to let his efforts go so cheaply, Greg began to survey other fences to see
if he couldn't negotiate a more equitable bargain. It was then that he discovered
that, as he put it, 'the word had gone out,' that is, other fences had been alerted to
the prior claim placed upon the merchandise by the original fence, and, knowing
the exigencies of Greg's situation, had agreed to uphold the territorial rights of

Monopolies

The thief's alternatives for selling stolen goods may be further constricted by "monopolies" which occasionally arise within the larger fencing industry. That these monoplies tend to be relatively fragile and unstable reflects not only the very loosely organized nature of the traffic in stolen goods, but also the reciprocal linkages that often exist among fences, as well as the shifting power alliances within the underworld more generally.

Fencing monopolies tend to be one of two kinds. In the one, there is an understanding among criminal receivers that a particular fence or crime organization has "property rights" to certain *kinds of stolen goods,* as for example in American City where Mafia-connected fences held the rights to purchase stolen cigarettes and liquor.

▶ I don't know if you'd call it a monoply now. It's more just an understanding: you handle this and I'll handle that. You're doing it as a courtesy to each other, really, and to avoid hassles. Take guns. For a long time I never bucked Louie on guns. If guns came my way, I sent the business to Louie. Same with liquor and cigarettes—they came my way, they went to Angelo, to the Mafia you might say. It worked the other way too. Louie and Angelo were sending a lotta antiques my way. Now, this doesn't mean that Louie got all the guns that were stolen, no more than I got all the antiques. But we got our share, and more.[12] ◀

---

their fellow fence. Knowing he could not expect a fair price nor even the original price at the data site (since there would undoubtedly be a 'penalty' fee assessed him by the first fence), he took the furs to another large metropolitan area and sold them. On his return, the local industry's displeasure with having been scorned met him, in the person of two 'enforcers.' He was beaten and the money he had acquired for the furs was taken from him."

I have shown this incident not only to many thieves but to police as well. They report never having heard of an incident like this happening, and express strong disbelief at the notion of several fences conspiring together and of their employing muscle against established thieves (or any thieves for that matter) in the fashion described by Greg. The incident provided for burglars, in particular, an opportunity for derision at academic naivete, with Jesse asking: "Holy fuck, is this what you university professors believe? The guy's got a good imagination, I'll hand him that. Wonder what he says about his sex life—that oughta be good." Agent Bogart notes: "Not in my twenty-six years in Mid-City, that never happened. Fences aren't that reliable with one another."

Rocky states: "Really, can you imagine that happening [getting roughed up] to someone like Jesse or Steelbeams? If that happened, the fences would be answering to them."

12. Sam's frequent claim about "not bucking Louie on guns" is disputed by several thieves I talked to. Steelbeams notes: "As long as I knew Sam he would buy guns. Now, at times he'd sell them to Louie but for a fact at other times Sam was running them down South or to Oceantown."

The other kind of monopoly involves the fence controlling the patronage of a *thief* by threatening to inform on him or, perhaps, by intimidating him in some other way. Also, some receivers may be effectively discouraged from buying from a particular thief who is associated with a more powerful fence. Nonetheless, using the threat of force or police set-up as a "stick" to maintain the patronage of a thief—usually the young thief—is likely short-lived, since with experience and contacts he becomes less easily managed.[13]

▶ Louie would sometimes keep a younger thief in his pocket by threatening to snitch on him if he peddled elsewhere. Louie knew who he could push around, an he would play dirty sometimes, especially with the run-of-the-mill thief. Say, Louie had put up bail for him; he'd threaten to take the bail away or have it raised. See, Louie was in thick with the magistrates. That, and Louie had a reputation for getting rough, and some thieves—mostly your younger ones— feared that.

Same thing with some of the little dealers. They were afraid of Louie, that he might get rough with them or set them up, if they cut in and bought from one of Louie's regulars. They would still buy now and then, but they were leery to buck Louie, 'cause of his reputation, that he had ties in the Mafia, and because of Louie's connections with some of the cops, and the D.A., too. If Louie found out a particular thief was selling to another dealer, he might finger the guy to the cops. Or say the thief came back to Louie with something to peddle, Louie doesn't buy this time—so then the thief goes to the other dealer. In the meantime, Louie contacts the cops, and they bust the thief and nail the other dealer red-handed.

I never had trouble with Louie that way, not to my face at least. But I do believe that when my fencing really got going, that Louie had the fire set to my store to slow me down. Louie was losing a lot of business to me, 'cause the better thieves and even the walk-in trade was coming my way.

I believe this now, not when it happened. It was rumored that Louie had the fire set, but I didn't suspect Louie 'cause we were pretty thick. And Louie and I kept on doing business, even more so,

---

Rocky comments: "After Louie hooked us up with Sam on the antiques, we started taking everything to Sam. The first couple of times we had guns, Sam told us to drop 'em off at Louie's or, if we wanted, he'd hold them for Louie. Then Sam didn't bother with Louie no more. This pissed Louie off 'cause he had always been the main one for guns."

13. Rocky reports that he was threatened by Louie, after he switched to Sam as his outlet for stolen wares: "I ran into Louie a month or so after he hooked us up with Sam. Louie says: 'Hey, where you been? I guess I put you on to a good thing, with Goodman. I can do you damage, you know.' So, I told this to Sam. He says, 'Don't let him bluff you, the man's mouth and reputation is bigger than the man. Tell the mother-fucker, to get fucked'."

after the fire. 'Cause once I got on my feet again, it was as if Louie accepted my being the main fence. He never really bucked me, at least not that I know of.[14] ◄

Paying a Fair Price and Competition Reconsidered

There is competition among fences—sometimes fiercely so—to develop and to sustain suppliers of stolen goods but competition over price *per se* is probably greater in the legitimate than in the stolen property market. Certain assumptions made in normal economic dealing simply do not fit the fence-thief situation where trust and camaraderie typically play as important a role as the prices offered and paid.

► There are a lot of similarities between fencing and running a legit business but competition isn't one of them, not really. In legit business you're gonna buy from whoever you get the best price and you're gonna sell to whomever pays you the best price. That's where the competition comes from. But it don't work that way in fencing, not really. I worked harder trying to outdo the other secondhand dealers on the legit side than I did on the fencing.

I don't know how to explain it but it works very differently. The trust and how you carry yourself, what kind of a guy you are, is there with the fencing. Is the guy "good people" or is he an asshole. The thieves knew I was good people, that I would treat them fair and that the cops could never come to me to help them out. Once the goods were in my hands, it was my problem, not the thief's, and he would never have to worry about it. As long as I wasn't too greedy, I knew the thief would come back, and I bothered very little about what he might get peddling elsewhere. ◄

These comments help to further clarify Sam's pricing policy and what he means by *paying the thief a fair price*: (1) that even if the thief has no other outlet, it still holds that "you can't pay the thief nothing"—the thief must receive reasonable compensation to justify the risks of stealing; (2) that the prices Sam pays are in the ballpark of prevailing fence-thief market standards—the thief can't do much better by peddling the goods else-

---

14. Whether Louie had the fire set to Sam's store is debatable. One view is expressed by Rocky: "I think Louie did it 'cause Sam was getting most of the fencing business. Louie couldn't take that, always wanted to be the kingpin." Chubbie comments: "Sam and Louie had a falling out about this time but it wasn't that serious. They were still friends. I'd say the fire was from bad wiring 'cause this was a pretty old building." Jesse notes: "The talk was Louie did it, but I don't figure Louie would have the balls to do it, even to have someone do it for him. Louie was mostly mouth—he wouldn't fuck with Sam that way. Could of been a piece of equipment was left on in the work area 'cause Sam was pretty sloppy that way. I wouldn't rule out, now, that Sam set it himself—the cocksucker claims otherwise, even to me—but I wouldn't put nothing past him."

where; (3) that should another dealer be willing to pay more, Sam's lower price may still be fair *all things considered*—when taking into account the bonus practices, the safety, the convenience, and the other attractions that come from doing business with Sam.

Sam's assertion that the fence pays the thief a fair price is at odds with the conventional view that the fence pays low-level or rock bottom prices, a view in large part based on the image of the hapless thief being exploited by a cunning and heartless fence. To be sure, there are significant pressures within the fencing industry to restrict competitive pricing among thieves, as described earlier. But equally important, there are also pressures (e.g., that the thief keep stealing in the face of high risks) to maintain more middle-of-the-road rather than strictly low-level prices. Thus, while the trade in stolen goods is relatively insensitive to differences in price, even a "greedy" fence like Louie ends up paying fair prices, at least to many of the thieves with whom he does business.[15]

▶ Altogether my prices were probably a little better than Louie's 'cause I was dealing with a better thief, and I wasn't as greedy as Louie. But across the board our prices were pretty even 'cause Louie many times paid a fair price. With Louie, it was more that if he had something over a thief, he would take advantage of that. Say, Louie put up bail for a thief, then he might cut his prices. And Louie would buy from kids, even 15, 16 years old, and he would pay them nothing. See, Louie was big 'cause he had the connections to operate and he would buy anything. That, and he always had the cash so the thief knew the money would be there. My advantage over Louie was the thieves trusted me more. ◀

In sum, Sam's reputation as solid and as a ready market for almost any kind of merchandise, more so than the prices he pays, influences the thief to come to him in the first place, giving Sam the chance to apply some of the bargaining tactics described next. In running a fencing business it is important that one gets the first opportunity to buy stolen merchandise. Sam paraphrases an old proverb to make the same point.

---

15. Agent Bogart comments on Vincent: "If it was a decent thief and he knew what he had—like some of the good hijackers—Vincent would pay an okay price. He would think about what someone else down the road was paying. Vincent was locked into the addict trade, mostly blacks. This was tailgating, shoplifting, and small burglaries: He didn't worry about their going elsewhere, and that was a lot of his business.

Another thing, Vincent wanted to give the impression that he always bought cheaply, that was important to him. That he was a good conman, could outhustle these guys. Your man, Sam, comes across as wanting to be seen as solid, as a good guy who paid decent prices. My guess is they fall somewhere in-between: that Vincent paid more than he'd admit—paid a decent price to the decent thief; and that Sam beat thieves more than he says."

▶ Once the thief comes to you, you got to figure he's gonna sell unless you beat him too bad. He don't want to chance peddling elsewhere. To his thinking, why chase two birds in the bush when you got one in the hand. ◀

Price Negotiation

In actual trade situations the fence may employ any one of a number of tactics in price-bargaining with thieves and drivers, tactics that are shaped by the fence's greater knowledge and experience, and by the thief's urgency to sell. A standard feature of Sam's bargaining strategies is to begin the negotiation by "making the thief set his price."

▶ The first thing the thief or driver wants to know is "what will you give me?" I'd say to that, "what do you want, tell me what you have to have." I want them to set their price. That way I can find out if they know what they got, what they think is a fair price, how cheap I might get it. Then I go from there. If I don't like their price, I tell 'em: "I don't like them apples." After that, if we can deal, fine. If not, he has to peddle elsehwere. ◀

Once the thief sets a price or Sam has made a price offer, Sam may claim the merchandise is damaged or incomplete, or is junk, to convince the thief that his asking price is too high, or that the price Sam is offering is fair.

▶ Many times on antiques and secondhand items I would tell the thief: it's missing this or that piece. Maybe it's a leg that's broken on a rolltop desk, or the chimes don't work on an old clock. I would play this up to the thief, that it will be much harder to peddle because of this defect. Now, I know it ain't gonna make no difference when I sell it, or that I can doctor it up and will get a good price.

One time I bought a load of 3 × 5 rugs which were stolen off a truck. The thieves were "greenies," and I could tell from our conversation they didn't know what they had. I told them the rugs were rejects because they were the wrong size, that they were made for a bathroom but were too small. I got them dirt cheap and turned right around and sold them to Abram's, the big carpet place in town, for top dollar.

Especially with your antiques, even your good thieves often don't know what they have. But even more so, your ordinary burglar that's hitting houses, he will come in with a bunch of stuff—anything from glassware, silver, pewter, figurines, jewelry, rolltop desks, different furniture pieces. What I would do is ignore the good stuff like I wasn't even interested. I'd offer a price on the rest, tell him the other pieces are junk. Sometimes I'd even pay for the other stuff and walk away. Now, nine times out of ten I know he don't wanna go elsewhere. Besides, if it was a piece I really wanted, I could always say, "Let me take another look at it." ◀

On other occasions, Sam may play tricks with wholesale-retail markup, he may display for the thief low prices in his store on comparable items, or he may show the thief a phony sales receipt of stolen merchandise recently marketed.

▶ If I was getting a run of certain things, I would keep my prices low in my store on those items. Like, cameras or tape decks would come in streaks, it seemed. Then, I would mark down my prices, legit now, on that stuff. Tell the thief to check the prices in my shop. Or I might show him something that I had priced very low, which was close to what he was peddling. That way, in his eye, I'm paying a fair price.

Another thing, say, I'm paying $80 for stolen wicker furniture that I'm unloading at an auction for like $300, $400. The thieves have no idea what wicker is worth, what I'm getting, but they is jacking me up for a better price. So the next time they come in, I says: "No, I'm not interested. Maybe Louie will take a shot at it." I might do this the next couple of times they come in. So they want to know why I'm not buying. "Hey," I says, "I can't make any money. Look at what the fuck that stuff is bringing me." So I pulls out a sales receipt from the auction on the wicker they brought me last time, which is a phony: the price is marked way low. I would do this, too, to slow down guys who are clipping too regular; that way, I'm keeping the heat off them and me, and I'm keeping my prices down, too. Some guys you can string along this way, especially the ones that are stealing just to get a few extra bucks, say, for dope [marijuana] or extra pocket money.

The other thing, even your general public doesn't know about wholesale pricing. The markup in your stores is a lot less than people think. This depends on the item. There's a big markup on furniture, maybe 100% or higher. Same with jewelry. But for most items like TVs, appliances, and that, it's closer to 25 to 50 percent, maybe even less. But your thieves don't know that. They think its a lot higher. So, if a thief says this or that is selling at such a price, you can tell him what you want about wholesale. I say, "Yeh, that's marked up two to one and maybe three to one if they are bought in quantity. I can get it cheaper legit than paying your price, without any of the hassles."

That's why the one-third don't mean shit. Many times I can pay one-third and still make a good dollar, 'cause the retail markup is small. Other times, like on good furniture, I can buy it legit at wholesale as cheap as if I would pay the thief one-third of retail. Now, your good thief may know about wholesale and your driver and warehouse thief will, too. But your average thief don't know nothing about wholesale to retail markup. ◀

Finally, Sam seeks to sustain the impression that he does not need the thief to make a living so much as the thief needs him to convert the goods into cash and make ends meet. As a fence, Sam buys from many thieves and also has a steady income from his legitimate business.

▶ With your average thief that doesn't know his way around, I would let them know that I could make a living without all the headaches of dealing with them, but what the hell could they do. Now, when you come right down to it, I needed the thief, too. But I would never let on that way.

I may even explain to the thief, hey, look, how am I gonna make anything if I pay you what you're asking. Look around this store. I got stuff that's been sitting here for months. I'm gonna take all the risk, and go broke? I got to eat too. I might explain to him what it costs to run a business, the risks I'm taking, how if I have to ship it out of town, the guy on the other end has to have his cut, too. ◀

In every deal the fence and thief must come to terms on the price to be paid for the stolen goods, nonetheless, in many transactions there may be very little, if any, real negotiation. Sam may simply pay the thief's asking price, sometimes with the intent of "paying well this time but chopping him down next time around," or Sam may offer a "take-it-or-leave-it" price.

▶ Really, your ordinary thief has been around and knows the score. From talking to other thieves, peddling to different dealers, and just checking prices at regular retail places, he understands what kind of price he can get. There wasn't that much hassle over prices, it was pretty cut and dried. With your walk-in trade, I'd say "I'll give you a couple of bucks for it," and that was it.

I think the word spread on that, too, about my not going for the hassles. Couple of times a thief has kept hassling me, and I've had to put a shoe in his ass, right out the door. Like, Jeremiah Walker was a half-assed hustler and thief, brought in some coins one time, kept crying about he oughta get more for them. It really got to me. I chased his ass out the store and told him never to show his face again. I wouldn't do business with him no more. See, I didn't go for hassles. That doesn't mean you couldn't jew with me. But there was a limit there. ◀

Standard Prices

In many buying situations, Sam has worklike agreements or understandings in which he more or less pays standard prices for certain items. Usually these situations involve either a regular thief who knows from prior transactions what Sam will pay, or one who steals on order: "If you run across such and such, I'd be interested." Moreover, agreements over price may be worked out, or at least are roughly understood, in those situations in which Sam provides tips to thieves on places ripe for burglary or states his preferences for certain kinds of merchandise.

▶ A lot of the thieves I bought from were regulars, you might say. There were three or four burglary crews that might come in two, three times a week. They might be out every night of the week, hitting houses, trucks, or whatever. They knew what I would pay. Like, a colored TV, two-years old, with 19-inch screen, last year's model, I would pay eighty dollars. A good camera, I'd pay sixty-five dollars if it was new, maybe thirty-five for a used one in good condition. These are ballpark prices: you could give or take a little either way. Even on antiques it was pretty well understood what I'd pay. There wasn't that much haggling over prices.

Lotta times with the regulars they would just drop the stuff at the back of my store, say, like three or four in the morning. Next day they'd stop by to get paid. They knew the money would be there and about what they had coming.

It happens, too, that we sometimes talked prices before a place was even clipped. Say, guys are bringing in antiques, but not good antiques because they don't know the difference. Well, you let them know what you're looking for, what will bring a good dollar. It's natural they would ask, okay, what will you pay for that. You give a ballpark price which still gives you some leeway. ◀

Settle Up Later Deals

While Sam appreciates the trust signified in these standard price arrangements, he is even more proud of "settle up later" deals—situations in which, although regular price arrangements have not been worked out beforehand, the thieves deliver the stolen goods, trusting Sam will pay them a fair price after the goods have been more thoroughly appraised or even marketed. These situations usually involve regulars who have in their possession unusual antiques or a shipment of out of the ordinary merchandise. And, in comparison with Louie and some other fences, who are notorious for promising to pay a certain price prior to the theft of merchandise and then either dropping the price after it is stolen or claiming they can't unload it themselves—Sam maintains that he lives up to prior price agreements.

▶ Sometimes a thief would call me, maybe late at night, and describe what he has and wants to know if I'm interested and what I will pay. Say its antiques, but I can't tell what he has from what he's telling me. So I'd have him drop the stuff at the back of my store. Then in the morning I'd look it over, and I'd pay him what he had coming whenever he came by. Or say, its a load of something, and you don't know what the hell it's worth. Take the time I got the load of batteries. I told Steelbeams and them, I think it's worth about so much. I'd give them a range, but I got to unload it first before we settle up. Then, after it was sold, I'd pay them so much but maybe chisel them a little, and make sure they were happy with that. [16] ◄

On the whole, although some negotiation is taken for granted, Sam downplays the use of deception, gimmickry, and other ruses in his trade with thieves, maintaining that he bargains as hard or harder with the general public wanting to sell merchandise to him, the legitimate secondhand dealer. Thieves "know the score," and their expectations on prices are more in line with actual market values than the ordinary "Joe Blow." Then, too, some thieves fare better in their price negotiations or price arrangements with Sam than do others. He deals hardest with thieves who are more likely to bring trouble or hassles and with one-time or occasional thieves who, because of their isolation from the criminal community and underworld grapevine, are unlikely to jeopardize his reputation as a generous fence.

▶ I would rather deal with a thief than with the general public. Any day. Your ordinary Joe Blow thinks whatever they own, what they bought at one time, is worth more than it is. And they will whine and

---

16. Rocky states: "This would happen sometimes—say, it was fifty guns. Sam would give us a rough price, an estimate, maybe give us a few hundred bucks to hold us over. He'd say, 'I have to sell them first, 'cause I'm not sure what they're worth. I'll treat you fair.' We'd come back, maybe two days later, he'd settle up with us. I can't say if he chiseled us or not, but at the time, no. We were happy with what he paid us." But another thief states: "I found this out later, that Sam screwed me more than a few times on stuff we sold to him. Then on, we always had to be paid on the spot. Anybody will fuck anybody if they get the chance, really. There's not that much honor. Sam would fuck you, maybe not as much as Louie, but he'd still fuck you."

Steelbeams comments: "Whether you let a fence check out what the stuff is worth or have him sell the stuff first, depends on what you're peddling. Some things you want to get rid of right away, other things there's no hurry. For small things like jewelry, silver, coins, little porcelain pieces, you can hide that easy. You give the fence or the buyer a couple of days to come up with a price offer—just fucking warn the guy to come back with the stuff and the *same* stuff. We did this with Sam, and a couple of other dealers, too, and never had any problems. But, say, you got a couple of garden tractors or a load of meat [a perishable item], you need an off for that right away. Can't fuck around and hold it, waiting to get a better price. So, we'd take it to Sam; say, okay, give us a ballpark price. Once he sold the stuff, then we'd settle up."

In related fashion, another burglar in the area observes that the thief may give the fence *temporary* possession of merchandise for purposes of appraising and making a price offer, a practice that apparently is fairly commonplace with respect to unloading expensive stolen jewelry: "Our thing was hitting houses for jewelry, good jewelry. We took our time selling it 'cause we had a couple of good outlets. Let each one have a couple of days to check out what they could pay, then we'd sell to the one that paid the best price."

hassle, check prices here and there, to see if you're paying a fair price.

The actual buying from the thief is more straight business than anything. I didn't pull many tricks with them. Like, you asked me about flashing a roll of bills in front of the thief, to soften him, to make him more eager. You got to be dealing with the bottom barrel for that to work. Most of your thieves are smart that way, more streetwise than the average person. They don't fool that way.[17]

Altogether, I was cheapest with the Joe Citizen thief, the ordinary guy who is trying to to sell something quick. 'Cause I know I ain't gonna see his face again. Not your truck driver or warehouse thief, now, I wouldn't bid that low with them. They come back, and spread the word, too. Another thing, they're not regular like your ordinary thief, but they're safe. Never had no hassles with any of them. See, the police don't know them, don't expect it. Just have to make sure they don't grab too much or clip too often. ◄

Buying From Other Fences

There is one final buying situation left to describe—Sam regularly purchased stolen goods from other fences and part-time dealers. (Perhaps, strictly speaking, these do not constitute fencing on Sam's part, since he is not dealing directly with the thief.) These fence-fence transactions are affected by many of the same factors which govern Sam's dealings with thieves—skill level, experience, consistency, and the desire for future transactions—but there are some important differences as well.

The purchasing of stolen goods by one fence from another fence is less random and less complicated, and bears considerably more resemblance to normal economic dealing than is true of fence-thief dealings. First, the fence's advantages in thief-fence exchanges—his greater marketing knowledge and the thief's urgency to sell—are much less variable in fence-fence dealings where the partners are on fairly equal footing. Both will usually be businessmen who know the quality and value of the merchandise and understand the intricacies of running a fencing business.

▶ The first thing is, your fence is a businessman. He knows what he's got invested, what the going prices are, and all that. The thief don't have the same knowledge. You can't get over on another dealer that easily.

There are exceptions now, say, if a fence is handling stuff outside his line of business. Take antiques. A fence may get antiques once in awhile but doesn't know what he has. When we had the flood in American City, there was ransacking and looting of houses, people

---

17. Klockars (1974:116), however, reports that the ploy of "flashing money" in the thieves' face was used by Vincent (apparently successfully) in price negotiations with some thieves.

bringing in good antiques to the secondhand places in town. These places were buying and I was buying from them, and dirt cheap 'cause they didn't know what they had. But your dealers will usually have pretty good knowlege of what prices are in different areas, and if they don't know they can find out. ◄

Second, matters of risk and trust are less at issue in fence-fence transactions, not because fences are more trustworthy than thieves, but because fences are better able to protect themselves from detection and because they seldom receive the intense police attention that is oftentimes directed at the active thief. Indeed, a major attraction of fence-fence exchanges is their extra safety: when the fence is on the buying side it provides a layer between himself and the thief; when the fence is on the selling side it reduces risks by allowing for quick disposal of stolen goods. Thus, when buying from another dealer, Sam is satisfied if he can purchase stolen goods at "cheaper than legit" prices.

► The fence is not under the gun in the same way as the thief, 'cause the fence ain't gonna be short of money and you have to figure, if he bought it from the thief in the first place, he has different places to unload. That, and the fence can cover his back better.

More or less, I was trying to get it cheaper than legit. If I could make a 100 percent or fifty percent, I'd grab it, but even if it was only a small edge over what I'd have to pay legit, I'd buy. 'Cause there's very little risk when you deal with another fence. Many times you couldn't say for sure what was legit and what wasn't 'cause the legit and warm were mixed together. You could surmise what was warm but unless it was something really warm, we didn't discuss it. That's part of covering, too, 'cause what you don't know won't hurt you. Know what I mean? ◄

Of course, Sam's trade relations with other fences involve more than the purchasing of stolen goods. Sam also sells to them; they are a major outlet for disposing of stolen goods. This dimension of fence-to-fence linkages is described in the next chapter which examines the economic aspects of selling stolen goods and the would-be profits that derive from a fencing business.

Chapter 6

Sales and Profits

Here's the thing: any damned fool can buy stolen goods. It's being able to get rid of the stuff and have your back covered and still make a good dollar that counts.

There are two major problems with the conventional view that the fence buys stolen goods at very cheap prices, resells them at a considerable price markup, and pockets a handsome profit. First, this view ignores the market forces that constrain the prices at which stolen goods are both bought and sold. On the buying side, as was reviewed in the last chapter, the fence's price markup on stolen goods is constrained by having to pay the thief a fair price. This means that the fence buys stolen goods at less than wholesale but not at rock-bottom value. On the selling side, the fence's markup is restricted by his having to sell the goods at a comparatively low price. That is, the potential buyer of stolen property is unwilling to buy unless he believes that he will be obtaining the merchandise sufficiently below legitimate prices to warrant the additional risks and disadvantages. One may complain to the Better Business Bureau or even take civil action against a seller of defective goods if one is dealing in the legitimate market, but the courts will not enforce a similar claim in an illegal transaction.

Second, this view of the fence's handsome profits obscures the extra operating costs inherent in the precarious market environment in which the buying and selling of stolen goods take place. Not only are fences like Sam saddled with ordinary overhead costs that accrue to any business ledger (e.g., transporting and storing goods), but they are also faced with idiosyncratic costs. In fact, the operating costs involved in running a fencing business may easily exceed those of a legitimate business.

Fence-Buyer Dealings

Lower selling prices as well as high operating costs limit Sam's fencing profits in a general sense, while specific aspects of fence-buyer dealings influence actual selling prices and whether, in the long run, Sam is able to buy and sell profitably. That is, considerations of risk and trust, and the consistency with which he does business with a particular buyer, influence not only what Sam pays thieves for stolen goods but also Sam's selling prices. Just as Sam wishes to maintain the patronage of some thieves, so also does he desire to keep the patronage of buyers who are safe and reliable outlets.

► I let go the cheapest on stuff I didn't have my back covered. Like food products or the load of batteries, I unloaded cheaply 'cause you can get jammed up on that easier. I would make a profit and be satisfied with that. Now many times you come out better than otherwise, 'cause you're gonna pay less to get it, and what you're handling is worth a good dollar.

The other thing is, an item can be very warm, an antique gun or a namesake piece that's been in the family. You know the police are going to come looking and these can be traced easier, too. Those times, I'd unload real quick and wouldn't even think about making top dollar. I'd make a quick dollar and be content.

It depends on how much faith I have in the buyer, too. Can he be trusted, is he good people? Will there be any hassles for me? If it is somebody I've been dealing with for some time, I'm not going to be too greedy, 'cause I'm thinking of down the road, of wanting to do business again. ◄

But more so than in his dealings with thieves, the trade Sam enjoys with those he sells to bears considerable resemblance to conventional market descriptions. Sam's thieves and drivers may know little about their products and may be under strong pressure to sell what they have. In contrast, those who buy from Sam, upfront store customers, auction patrons, antique dealers, wholesalers, retail merchants, and other fences, are likely to know the market for the goods they wish to buy, are able to buy the goods elsewhere, and are able to shop around for the best price. Consequently, Sam's selling prices will be strongly influenced by market demand and by the threat of competitive buying among his customers and buyers.

Distribution Paths

The prices Sam asks and receives for stolen goods are tailored to the various paths by which stolen property passes from thieves to Sam and then is resold to eventual consumers. One path is relatively uncomplicated and may involve only the thief selling the stolen goods to Sam who resells the goods to upfront customers of his store. Other paths lead less directly from Sam to eventual consumers and may involve his distributing the stolen merchandise to business merchants who then sell the merchandise to consumers under the cover of their legitimate business; or the path may involve Sam distributing the stolen goods to wholesale buyers who sell the goods to business proprietors who, in turn, sell the goods to customers of their legitimate business establishments. Still other paths lead from thieves to Sam and then to other fences who may resell the stolen goods to customers of their legitimate retail outlets, or to business merchants who then sell the goods to eventual consumers. The different patterns of the sale and distribution of stolen property from thieves to Sam and from Sam to eventual consumers are diagrammed below.

Selling to Upfront Store Customers

The prices Sam sets for goods sold in his store are generally the same, regardless of what he paid for the goods and of whether they are illicit or not. That is, the prices are consistent with the overall image of a discount business and are determined by what the selling prices are for the same goods purchased legitimately. Sam, however, is more inclined to negotiate and lower the price on items he has purchased illegally. Also, even though "getting a bargain" is a strong buying motive for most of Sam's customers, those who suspect that what they are buying is stolen expect even better bargains:

▶ I might drop my prices more on the warm merchandise 'cause I would rather get rid of it. See, you could bargain on the prices in my shop. But a lotta people didn't bargain at all—paid the price on the tag. Other ones would bargain hard, 'cause they more or less suspected I was handling warm stuff. As long as they didn't hassle me too much, I would drop the price down. ◀

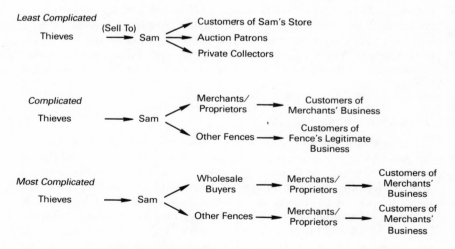

Figure 6.1 Distribution Paths For Stolen Property

Selling to Auction Patrons

The prices Sam receives for stolen property are probably more unpredictable when he is "peddling at an auction" than in other buying situations. Sometimes he barely breaks even, while at other times, say if he hits "auction fever," Sam makes good money.

▶ The prices I got peddling at the auctions was very variable; I could never be sure what I'd get. If you take into account the time and gas, the auctions overall paid less then my store. But then I was always running to the auctions anyway to buy for my store and to help me cover. Most of the time I'd do okay 'cause I was hooked up with the auctioneer who would help keep the prices up and also mix in the warm with the legit.

Now if you hit "auction fever," then you can really clip. Can make a bundle by mixing in junk with this or that good piece. People can be very funny that way and get taken very easily. If the auctioneer works the crowd, gets them going, they will pay top dollar for junk, and all the more so if you can make them think the stuff is a little shady. ◀

Selling to Antique Dealers

When selling stolen antiques to local or out-of-town dealers, Sam pretty much retains the 100 to 200 percent markup, a norm in the antique trade, regardless of the prices he has paid for the goods. The situations in which Sam offers stolen antiques at comparatively low rates involve antiques that are very warm or trading with a preferred dealer who is a reliable and consistent outlet.

▶ If I sold out of the area, like to Scottie in Oceantown or to the dealers down South, I cut my prices a little on the warm antiques but not that much. Otherwise, no, I tried to get top dollar. Like the grandfather clocks I was getting from the docks, I knew what they would bring. I didn't say to Tex, "these are warm—how much you gonna give me?" No, I knew what they were worth and we did business like they weren't warm. He could surmise they were hot but he didn't ask questions. We didn't talk about it. ◀

Selling to Business Buyers

The primary advantage in dealing with Sam is, of course, his price. The upfront store customer may be able to buy merchandise at discount prices anywhere from twenty to fifty percent less than at conventional retail outlets, and the business buyer anywhere from twenty to eighty percent off normal wholesale prices. An added advantage for the wholesaler or the retail merchant is that there need be no record of the sale and, therefore, the profits on the subsequent sale of the merchandise need not be declared for business taxation. With the business profit tax anywhere from thirty to fifty percent, this can represent a substantial savings. At the same time, because Sam is a licensed merchant, the business buyer, in order to legitimize the transaction, may obtain a bill for the stolen goods he buys.

Even when there is not a bill of sale, buying through Sam puts a layer between the purchaser and the thief, thus making the buyer relatively safe from detection should the thief be caught. Many of the customers and buyers who do not hesitate to deal with Sam would have absolutely nothing to do with a thief selling the same merchandise (and vice versa the thief may want nothing to with the merchant).

▶ With your store people, there's a range there that you both have to operate within. I would sell for a little less than wholesale, just so there was a good dollar in it for him and a good dollar for me. If I'm selling to a local businessman who has never given me any hassles, then my prices will be cheaper than if I sold to someone else or if I had to ship it out. Not always, now. Sometimes I'd sell cheaper what I shipped out cause then there's less chance of any hassles. Then I'd try to come back with a load for myself, make up for the time and gas. ◀

Selling to Other Fences

Sam probably sells stolen goods at the cheapest prices to other fences, in what oftentimes are stable trading arrangements in which both parties appreciate how each contributes to the safety and economic well-being of the other. The roles of buyer and seller tend not to be fixed in fence-fence dealings but are reciprocal and overlapping where the parties may buy, sell, and swap stolen goods. The comparatively equal stature of fences as trade partners, the fact that they are frequently compatible in personality and in attitude, and that their dealings are not only a means of legitimizing stolen goods but may also be effective business practice, all contribute to a process of price negotiation in fence-fence exchanges that Sam calls "friendly business." This does not mean there is no haggling over prices: Sam and his fence-associates are businessmen who expect some degree of haggling; if they don't get it, they think something is wrong.

▶ I did a lot of buying and swapping with other dealers. If I sold to them I'd ask, "Now, what you got for me?" Especially with Woody, Grasso, and One-Eye Moe, they'd get a load from me and I'd get a load from them. It would be, "I'll give you these pieces for that;" or, it'd be so much for this and so much for that, and then we'd total it all up at the end. We would both know what we had in it, what we could get at our end. Now, if it was a fence I hadn't dealt with, say, someone recommended to me by someone else, I covered my back more, and I would offer a take-it-or-leave-it price. It was more similar to the way I dealt with thieves or with your regular store people.

Dealing with another fence is covering your back, too. It's another layer, and if they're from out of the area, there's really no risk. This is good business, too, 'cause maybe we each had things we couldn't get rid of in our store. Some items I could move better than Woody, say, like furniture and antiques, while he could move tools, lawnmowers, bicycles, and that better. We could help each other out that way even with the legit stuff.

I would say price-wise I could make more if I peddled it elsewhere than to another dealer. The more ways it has to be cut, then the less there is for each one. There has to be room for the other guy to make a dollar, too. It's that simple. What if he can't run it through his store, and has to ship it out? You can't be too greedy when you deal with another fence. But, in the long run, I'm coming out ahead because I can turn it over fast and because many times I'm buying from him, too.

Now, we would try to beat each other, try to outdo the other. But it was friendly business. We would try to get over on each other and then laugh about it later. Maybe buy the other one dinner. But we wouldn't beat each other too bad. We more or less helped each other, we were content as long as we could both make a good dollar. ◀

Standing Orders

Because the flow of merchandise from thieves and drivers is irregular, those who buy from Sam may alert him to the kind of merchandise they are interested in.[1] These standing orders and Sam's promise to "keep my eyes open" influence his decision to buy when the opportunities become available and also nurture stable arrangements with a particular thief to fill such requests.[2] The advantage to Sam of these regular arrangements is that it is possible to agree on a relatively fixed price with the buyer (and perhaps with the thief, too), thus lessening the time and work involved in setting up deals.

---

1. Chubbie notes: "A lot of stuff Sam bought was planned ahead—he knew right where he was going to get rid of it, had different places where the stuff was spoken for. Take Burdette who ran the TV place, was very brazen. He'd say to Sam: 'I can't keep enough of those little colored TVs in my shop. If more come your way, you know where to find me.' Sam had different ones like that—so, bang, bang, the stuff was gone quick."

2. Mickey notes: "It's only natural the thief will want to know what the fence will handle, what he will pay a decent price for. We knew Sam wanted colored TVs, so we was hitting a lot of motels." Tommy notes: "When I worked at Hilary's [Freight Storage & Shipping Co.], Sam would ask me: 'Hey, Tommy, what can you get your hands on?' Same way, me with him: 'What can you handle? What do you need?' It was a two-way street."

▶ Lotta times I would know what somebody needed. Maybe this or that businessman or store owner would stop by my shop, or we'd just bump into each other over coffee. They might say, "Hey Sam, if you run across such and such, give me a call." Sometimes I might ask them, "What do you need? What you in the market for?" The prices could be worked out or would be roughly understood. Then when the thief is peddling this stuff, you got the outlet all set up and know what price you're gonna get. It would be fewer hassles all the way around. Just easier for everybody. ◀

Selling Piecemeal

The frequency with which a buyer may trade with Sam fluctuates according to the type of goods and thief involved, and the number of buyers in different businesses willing to take what he has to sell. Having two or several outlets for a given product gives Sam the option of choosing the buyer and of keeping the price level up, for with stolen, as well as legitimate merchandise, the dealer can make higher profits on smaller amounts. Spreading the merchandise around also helps to maintain a steady supply of would-be outlets for stolen goods.

▶ You can make more money if you sell piecemeal. On some things I had several places that would buy. I would try to spread it around, drop off some at each place. Sometimes I would call ahead and shop around first, check prices. Say, it was typewriters, "What are you paying?" Then, I would sell more of them to the one that was paying the best price.

But I would never cut a guy off completely 'cause I didn't want to lose him. I always sold him a few, gave him a chance to make a buck. I'd take that few cents loss. Never cut my nose off, 'cause you may need that contact in the future. You can never tell when you might get a big run of something or if this or that outlet will dry up.

But you got to figure the risks of shopping around, and your time. Say, I bought 75 tape recorders. If I want to piecemeal them, I can get $75 each. But this time I would rather sell them all at one shot to one man for like $60, $65. Because everytime I'm selling to a different one I'm taking a chance on getting busted. So I'd take a little drop, make a little less, unload it all on one person. I never liked to peddle. ◀

There is considerable paradox in Sam's comments: the two policies of "spreading the merchandise around" and "not peddling" juxtapose. How Sam resolves them reveals much about the interplay and tension between the opposing considerations of profit and safety that inhere in the running of a fencing business. The advantages of piecemealing are the greater profits and, perhaps, the maintenance of contacts with would-be buyers. But piecemealing also involves the risks that come from peddling: to trade with more partners lessens secrecy and raises the prospect of something going awry. There are no hard and fast rules to guide Sam in deciding whether to piecemeal or not, so his strategy is to rely on "how he feels at the time" and on his sense of the need for extra caution in some situations.

Operating Costs

The emphasis so far has been on how the price markup and the profits Sam enjoys on stolen goods are constrained by his having to pay a fair price for the goods, as well as having to resell the goods at comparatively low prices. As a consequence, the fence's price markup and, ultimately, his profit margin is probably less than is commonly believed, and, in fact, may be less than that of the merchant who buys fenced stolen goods and then resells them to unaware customers at regular retail prices.

Equally important, the fence's profit margin is more than just a matter of price markup: as is the case with any business ledger, operating and overhead costs must be considered. Not only are fences like Sam saddled with the ordinary operating costs that accrue to almost any business (e.g., transporting and storing of goods), they also face idiosyncratic costs triggered by the precarious market environment in which the fence buys and sells.

Goodwill Expenses

The first set of costs is "goodwill" expenses, of which there are basically two kinds: promotional and protectionist. The former is aimed at establishing a fencing business: recruiting thieves, developing contacts with business buyers, or currying the favor of the local crime elite. The second is aimed at staying in business: attorney's fees and perks of one kind or another to police or judicial officials.

▶ In a fencing business you got to scratch a lot of backs. There are lots of little expenses that crop up. You got to be a nice guy in different ways, help this one out, do this one a favor. Not be a tight-ass with your thieves and other dealers, but be a good sport. Same with the cops, you got to keep them happy.[3]

---

3. Chubbie notes: "This is funny. But as much as anybody, cops and thieves were Sam's main customers. The thieves, especially the burglars, bought from Sam 'cause they liked him, not so much 'cause he gave them good deals. The cops are the ones that got the good deals. Different cops would pop in: "Hey, Sam, what's for nothing today?" Sam would laugh about it afterwards: 'what does a burglar and a cop's house both have—the stuff in it come from my shop.'"

Jesse comments: "Without a doubt, when Sam got in with the card playing group, he was giving them guys stuff very cheap. I know some of those people very well. For a fact, Sam got a half load of paint one time, from a hijacked truck, and damn near gave it away. In some respects, there, he's not a very good businessman. He always like to impress some people, and, holy fuck, you find out he's too generous with people."

These are more day-to-day, but there can be big expenses, too. Say, you get jammed up, you're gonna have to pay your lawyers and they can really bleed you. ◀

Bad Deals

The second idiosyncratic expense that affects Sam's profit margin is the "bad deal." While the promotional and protection costs described so far are both expected and accepted parts of running a fencing business, not so expected, much less accepted, are those occasions when Sam gets burned and loses a substantial sum of money because he wrongly appraises the value of stolen goods or because he overestimates his capacity to market them.

The traffic in stolen goods takes place in a hustling setting that lacks the strong arm of the law to protect property rights and to prevent partners from exploiting each other. While attention is usually directed at how the fence exploits the thief, the thief can also exploit the fence: by obtaining some or all of the cash payment and failing to deliver the goods to the fence; by deceiving the fence about the quality or quantity of the stolen goods; and by making the fence a target of theft because he can't complain to the police.

Being a victim of theft is much more likely to be a misfortune of the smaller dealer or the part-time receiver than of large-scale fences, although even fences like Sam and Louie face some risk. The smaller dealer is more vulnerable because thieves may view him as an unimportant or trifling outlet, unable to effect reprisals.

▶ You wouldn't think that a thief would steal from his fence, that he would be cutting off the hand that was feeding him, but it don't always work that way, especially if you're dealing with the assholes and the dopers 'cause they will do anything for a fix. And what about the thieves you're not dealing with? They can rip you off.

I never carried a gun when I was a burglar, but I did sometimes with the fencing. See, the thief knows the fence is carrying a lot of cash and that he can't go running to the police. It's not your regular thieves I worried about but the ones I wasn't buying from. But even one of your regulars might clip you if he thought he could get away with it. Take Bill Toscano. I don't know how many times he got clipped by the same ones that he was buying from. Really, it's the smaller dealers get hit that way. The thieves know who they can pull that shit with. ◀

Sam insists he has never lost money by advancing cash before taking possession of the stolen goods, nor that he has ever been the victim of theft, but he has been duped or burned by thieves more times than he would like to admit.

▶ You can get taken over the coals real easy. One time I bought two rings, thought they were diamonds. Paid $750 a piece for 'em. Turned out the diamonds were windowglass pane. I got rid of one in a card game, and the guy who got it didn't say anything 'cause he didn't want it known he got taken. The other ring I got stuck with. I took a chance and lost.

This is a funny story that didn't happen to me. I'm having coffee at Regina's and I overhear Bill Toscano and two other secondhand dealers, Honest Jake and Eddie Torsell, talking about this thief who had burned them. They didn't wanna tell me, but they finally let it out. This thief was from out of town, and he had sold a few things before to Bill. This time he comes with a U-Haul load of appliances and refrigerators. But Bill can't handle them all. So he goes to Honest Jake and Eddie, and they go in on the deal with Bill. They pay the thief and he tells them, "Look, I don't wanna unload in town, meet me at a certain spot on the edge of town. Be there in 50 minutes." Turns out, when Bill, Jake, and Eddie go to pick up the stuff, the U-Haul truck is there, but it's empty inside. The thief had their money and the merchandise, too. This was the dumbest thing I ever heard of, trusting a thief that way. I laughed like hell. No wonder they didn't want me to know.

Another thing, the temptation is strong to take a shot at what you can buy cheap—but what if you can't rid of it. Maybe it's stuff that is so warm, you can't unload it. I had to dump a whole set of porcelain dishware one time, the pieces were catalogued, photographed, and everything. Nobody would touch it.

Take the fence we talked about, the one who was written up in the paper recently who got popped with $300,000 worth of antiques in his place. Now, the cops have blown up the figure to blow themselves up. The way that went down was, the antiques were so warm that he couldn't peddle them. He was buying what he didn't have the outlets for.

There ain't no warranties and returns either. Say there's a fire. You got to pocket the loss cause there's no insurance on what's warm. I lost my shirt that time in the fire. Or say something gets damaged or gets stolen. Take the time Louie and me buys the razor blades. We didn't know it but they weren't wrapped. Just a whole damn load of razor blades lying loose in cartons. We held them for more than a year before Louie found a place that would wrap them, so we finally got rid of them. What we made wasn't worth the hassle. If that had been legit, we could've just shipped it back to the company. ◀

All things considered, the economic realities of running a fencing business pressure many prospective fences into giving up criminal receiving altogether or force them to dabble as part-time dealers. That is, there appears to be a high *dropout rate* among dealers in stolen goods, not only because of the legal risks that come from trading in stolen goods but also from the intermittent character of the trade and the smaller-than-expected profits.

▶ If you're talking about big money and a good dollar that is steady, not a one-shot thing, it would just be a handful in American City that qualify. Going back twenty-five, thirty years it would be Angelo, Louie, and myself. You also could count Weinstein, the Jewish guy, who for years was a big, big fence. This was when the Jew-Italian Mafia was big, way back when I first hit American City. If you're talking about now, I would say Phil is the main one. See, Phil always did some fencing, off and on, but he more or less took over when Louie and I got popped.

A lot of your dealers are nickel and dime. The fencing they do more or less helps keep them afloat, get over the hump in their legitimate business or gives them a little extra pocket money. It's not big bucks at all. I would say that many of your dealers pack it in 'cause they ain't making the money, not the big bucks anyway. Maybe they ain't got the heart and can't get the contacts, too, but you have to be able to hack the business side of it. Fencing ain't all its cracked up to be. There's a very fine line for making good money. Any fool can buy, but can he sell for a profit? ◀

How The Fence Makes Money

Obviously, in spite of the market pressures and the idiosyncratic operating costs described above, for at least some dealers, the profits from fencing stolen goods are quite substantial. These profits derive not only from the advantages of paying less for merchandise than one would have to pay in the legitimate market but also from the tax-free nature of illicit transactions. Less directly, one's fencing involvement may spill over into other illicit enterprises, making one's criminal career even more lucrative.

Rapid Turnover, High Volume of Trade

The fence's price markup may or may not be greater than that of the legitimate businessman; it depends upon what kind of fence he is. If he is a "secret" dealer selling to customers who do not know the goods are stolen, the markup is usually higher than in the legitimate market, because he buys the goods below wholesale price and sells them as if they were legitimate. If he is a "public" fence like Sam, however, the price markup is generally similar to that of the legitimate market. Although goods are purchased at lower than wholesale prices, they are also sold at lower than regular retail. Thus, the advantage that fences like Sam have on the legitimate businessman is not higher price markup, but rather the greater volume of their trade and the rapidity with which they can sell merchandise because it is being offered at lower prices than in the legitimate market.

▶ My thing was to turn it over fast. Not make a big buck, but a quick buck. I had the best prices in town and that brought people to my shop. Even better prices than the other secondhand places. See, on most of the warm stuff, you ain't making that much. Not more than what you're making on the legit. The advantage is not the markup but that you can turn it over faster 'cause you're selling it cheaper.[4] ◀

"Good Dollar" Transactions

The ability to turn merchandise over rapidly is especially attractive when goods of high quality or in large quantity are involved. Sam refers to these as "good dollar" deals—transactions in which the fence stands to pocket a handsome sum of money, not because his price markup or profit margin is unusually large but because he is handling merchandise of high value.

▶ The way Louie and I made a lot of money was from turning over fast a lotta small stuff and from handling this or that which was worth a good dollar. Like maybe a load of something or some good antiques or good guns would come my way. It wasn't that I was beating the thief 'cause I would pay him a fair percent. But see the percent don't mean shit. It's how many dollars are in it for me. Same as your car dealer, he'd rather sell a Cadillac and pocket $3000 than sell a Chevy and make only a $1000.[5] ◀

"Pot of Gold" Deals

While rapid turnover and large dollar transactions are the principal grist of Sam's fencing operation, he does sometimes pull off a deal in which the price markup and profit margin is exceptionally large. Sam refers to these as "pot of gold" deals—when the fence purchases high-value merchandise

---

4. Chubbie comments: "Sam had a big turnover. Many times, if he got something at 8 o'clock, 9 o'clock he was rid of it."

Jesse notes: "On the penny-ante stuff, what Sam couldn't sell quick in his store he would run to the auction or run in down South to Woody. The price he was getting wasn't that wonderful, but, holy fuck, if you turn enough over this adds up."

5. Jesse states: "A fence can handle a lot of penny ante stuff but still not be making big money. The big money comes from handling a good product or getting a truckload. In my mind, Louie and Sam fucked too much with the run-of-the-mill thief, the guy selling off the street. The lawyer and foundry guy did it right—were making a helluva lot without all the hassles—'cause they only fucked with a good product. One deal worth some real freaking bread is more wonderful than a shit-pile of the penny ante ones. I don't think Sam had that many deals where you're talking really big money, nothing like the foundry guy anyways."

very cheaply and resells it at a high price markup because of the thief's urgency to sell or his ignorance about the market for the goods.

Whereas "good dollar" deals tend to involve established burglars or drivers with whom Sam regularly trades, "pot of gold" deals involve penny ante and walk-in thieves with whom Sam is somewhat reluctant to deal. Indeed, the major incentive for Sam's on-and-off-again decision to buy from the walk-in trade is the gamble that a doper or a Joe-Citizen thief would, once in awhile, be peddling high-value merchandise that Sam could buy very cheaply.

▶ I was closing the place up one night when this guy comes in that's been drinking heavy and he's peddling two rings and has a back seat full of junk: TV, cassette tape recorder, and that. Apparently, he ran out of money and took this stuff from a woman he was shacking up with. I offered him some ridiculous price just to get rid of him—and he took it. It was like $55 for the whole shebang. Turned out the rings were ruby rings, a man and a woman's set. I sold the one for $1,400 and gave the other one to this woman I was seeing.

Another time, a woman comes in the shop, wants to sell an apartment full of furniture. Is in a big hurry on account of she's dumping her boyfriend, wants to skip town. So I scoots over with the 22-footer, loads up everything—table, chairs, bedroom set, all very nice furniture. Cleaned the place out. Paid her like $800 and shot down to Woody's. Tripled my money twice. A beautiful deal.

Profit-wise, whew, deals like these are a pot of gold 'cause I was getting 4, 5 times what I paid, even more, and on stuff worth a pretty good dollar. ◀

These pot of gold deals best conform to what conventional wisdom presents as the typical fence-thief situation—the hapless thief who sells the goods he has stolen for virtually nothing to a cunning, Fagin-type fence. Sam maintains, however, that high-value merchandise is seldom stolen by hapless thieves but by established ones who are apt to know the market for the goods in their possession. Consequently, pot of gold deals are an infrequent and relatively minor part of a fence's overall profits. What the fence can expect from trading with walk-in thieves, Sam claims, is not so much easy money, as headaches.

▶ After the ring deal, I started buying more from the walk-in trade and even dealing with the dopers, hoping to run across a deal like that. I would buy from guys like Lemont Dozier and them, to keep the flow coming, so when he gets the good stuff he brings it to me. Now, once in awhile I did catch a good piece that way, but not very often. See, the walk-in trade don't bring in the good stuff very often, and when they do they still might know what they got. With them, you got to rely on the turnover to make a dollar.

In the long run, unless you can really turn it over, it don't pay to deal with the walk-in trade. It's too penny ante, and they can be a lot of hassle and bring you a lot of junk that you got no use for. The thing is, you're inclined not to turn the thief away 'cause you're hoping maybe next time he'll come with something really good which you can buy dirt cheap. The temptation is very strong to do that. You can get too greedy and buy from anyone that walks in the door. ◄

Bypassing Restricted Legitimate Opportunities

Finally, a major attraction of dealing in stolen goods for some fences is being able to generate income by trading merchandise which they have limited opportunities for buying and selling in the legitimate market. Sam, for example, fenced a variety of products—guns, cigarettes, liquor, food products—which he lacked the resources, the contacts, and the business apparatus for buying and selling in the legitimate market. While trading in one may facilitate trading in the other, the legitimate and illegitimate markets are stratified in such a way that an individual may be able to trade in one or the other *but not in both.*

▶ Say, I was interested in being a food importer and wholesaler, like Ciletti, selling food, meats, and that to the restaurants in town—that would be very difficult 'cause you have to be in business for that, to have the contacts and to have the operation in place. I might be able to handle food products that are warm but I can't handle them strictly legitimate. Just because you can deal in merchandise that's warm doesn't mean that you can deal legit on the same merchandise. And it goes the other way, too: because you're a legit businessman doesn't mean you can deal in hot stuff. Know what I mean? A lot of things I handled, even if I wanted to, the legit side wouldn't be there.

That's why a lotta times you find your blacks and Puerto Ricans in the small-time fencing, say, operating out of their home or out of an eating joint. Won't even have a legit business as a front, 'cause what the hell kind of legitimate business can they run? The legit side ain't open. It is a fact, your whites won't trade with a black that easily, and many times the blacks won't either. So, if a black opens a legit business, he's gonna go broke whereas he might be able to make it if he peddles the warm stuff on account of the good prices he can offer.

Myself, whether I could make as much handling the same stuff legit, don't mean shit. Fuck the price markup, I just wanted to make a dollar. 'Cause if I don't handle it warm, I ain't gonna handle it at all. ◄

In sum, there are three main sources of direct profit in a fencing business like Sam's. First, because a fence can buy stolen goods cheaper than legitimate goods, his price markup may be greater, and he stands to make a greater profit—especially if he can sell the stolen goods at regular retail prices or, perhaps, if he has been able to purchase the stolen goods from thieves at very cheap prices (e.g., what Sam calls "pot of gold" deals). Second, probably the major advantage of being able to buy stolen goods more cheaply than legitimate goods is that the fence generates more income by being able to sell stolen merchandise rapidly because it is being offered at lower prices than in the legitimate market. Third, largely because he can sell stolen goods so cheaply, the fence may profit from being able to trade merchandise in the illegitimate market which he lacks the opportunity of trading in the legitimate market. For a highly public and a generalist fence like Sam, overall profits are probably derived mainly from the high volume of trade and from the capacity to trade in merchandise at the strictly illegitimate level rather than from the high price markup on stolen goods.

The discussion so far on the sources of the fence's profits are suggestive of how the economics of fencing can hinder the dealer from buying both profitably and regularly, depending on the kind of fence that he is. The trading of the specialist dealer, say, in antiques or jewelry, for example, may be so intermittent that he is able to buy and sell profitably but not regularly. On the other hand, the generalist fence may be able to deal regularly but not always profitably.

▶ Say, you wanted to deal only in really expensive antiques. That would be very hard 'cause you have to know the good thieves, first of all. And they got other places to go, so you're gonna have to pay them a good price. The other thing is, they're not clipping that often, so you can make a good dollar, maybe, but you can't depend on it.

Even with your jeweler fence, there are just a few that turn enough over to make a good dollar *and* a steady one. There is a lotta jewelry stolen but there are different places to peddle it 'cause it's so hard to trace jewelry. I was buying jewelry from the walk-in trade. Your regular Joe Blow citizen might buy, or maybe the thief can peddle it at an auction, or his lawyer may buy once in awhile. Even your legit dealers will buy sometimes, if the guy's not known as a thief, or, say, he has his girlfriend do the peddling. It would be the same as you going to a jewelry store in your town, say, with a diamond ring or necklace. The guy is gonna buy without asking questions if he can buy cheap. Now, he won't if the police have posted him on what's been stolen or told him to watch out for this or that thief. Then he's taking some risk, and he can get burned if he has to return the jewelry that's been stolen. ◀

In comparison to the intermittent character of the specialist's trade, a generalist fence may be able to deal regularly, but not always profitably. Thus dealers like Sam, who tend to buy those things which are commonly stolen, may become oversupplied with particular items. On the other hand, if he buys from non-specialist thieves who steal whatever is conveniently available, the generalist fence may end up with unusual items which are difficult to sell.

▶ Now, for dealers like myself, that are more wide open, the turnover is not a problem. Many times you get more of some things than you know what to do with. Watches? I had drawers of watches 'cause whatever the walk-in thief can steal easily, you're gonna get a lot of. Remember the fire—the watches all melted into a couple of big globs.

You can get stockpiled on some items very easy, especially if you deal with the shoplifters or the thief that steals whatever he can grab easy. To get rid of the stuff, I'd haul it to the auctions. Sell it for a penny if I had to, just to get rid of it. ◄

The risks and the market forces surrounding a dealership in stolen goods are such, moreover, that a thriving legitimate business, besides helping to mask an illegal trade, can serve as a financial boost or buffer for a fencing business.

► My legit business always did good and that was a big help 'cause you can't always depend on the fencing. If there was a slack in the fencing, the legit side could pick me up. Or, say, I needed cash quickly, I could always take on more upholstery work or run a sale on the legit stuff and raise some extra bucks. And what if you get popped and have to put up bail or pay the lawyers? Your legit business can be collateral and can keep you afloat, help you ride it out if you have to shut down for a while. ◄

No Taxes

Whether he makes money by rapid turnover or by large money transactions, there are other features of a successful trade in stolen goods that may enhance the fence's overall profits. To begin with, he does not pay taxes on the stolen merchandise he handles. Also, because of the way Sam runs his secondhand business, he manages to avoid taxes on much of the legitimate merchandise he buys and sells.

► I paid very little in taxes. What I had, really, is two sets of books, one for myself (which is in my head) and the other for the taxman. Now, this comes not just from fencing but from the secondhand trade itself. I would say that most of your secondhand dealers pay very little in taxes, if they pay anything. Because you deal in cash much of the time. Many times there is no record. Couple of times I did show my book to the state taxman but it was pretty hard to figure out. And I have to eat, too, you know. ◄

Ruse of Selling "As If" Stolen

Whether stolen or not, most of the merchandise that Sam buys and sells does not cost his customers the same as it would in a department store or at conventional retail outlets. Rather, Sam purchases secondhand merchandise at cheap prices from estate settlements, auctions, the Salvation Army, and from the walk-in trade in general; he also buys dead stock, damaged merchandise, factory close outs, overruns, and the like at especially low prices. Thus, Sam is able to sell at lower prices even on legitimate merchandise, an important factor in attracting customers. Furthermore, the fact that Sam's business buyers and many of his walk-in customers know he has stolen merchandise to sell at "discount" prices also figures importantly in his trade in legitimate goods.

▶ Some people will grab up junk if they think it's stolen. They figure if it's warm they can buy it cheap. But many times they don't know what they're buying 'cause they're all hepped up about it being warm. They're so eager, you can get over on them very easy. Even some of your businessmen and other dealers can be taken in by that, easier than you'd think.

I would pull this on Woody: call him up very early in the morning and, say, "Hey, I got a load of such and such, are you interested? I'll give it to you for so much." He'd jump at it. Shit, he coulda bought the stuff cheaper legit.

One time I bought a whole pile of rugs from a factory that had a defect in them that was hardly noticeable. So, I called Abram's that ran the big carpet place in town, and told him what I had but let him think they were a little shaky. He grabbed them right away 'cause he thinks he's getting a bargain. I got a helluva laugh out of it.

I especially pulled a lot of shit with antiques. I'm talking about selling what people believed was an antique, but wasn't. Many times I would buy a reproduction and doctor it, maybe upholster or even scratch in an old date. I fooled antique dealers already. It's funny. If it had been legit, they would check the piece out very carefully. But when it's hot, people are too eager. This protected me, too, their thinking it's warm. 'Cause if they do find out it's a fake, they would figure I had been duped and got burned, too. ◀

Sideline Illicit Enterprises

Because of the skills and the connections that coincide with being a dealer in stolen goods, the fence's business portfolio may spill over into other illegal and quasi-legitimate activities. It is hardly surprising, for example, that racketeers oftentimes either "moonlight" in fencing as a sideline to other criminal enterprises, or they drift into fencing as a more or less full-time criminal occupation. The contacts and reputation they enjoy, not only within the criminal community, but also among local businessmen and law enforcers, are important advantages. The effects here are probably reciprocal: established criminals or underworld figures are likely to have the reputation and connections that strongly contribute to running a fencing business; and successful fences, by virtue of those same qualifications, are well suited to assorted kinds of illicit enterprise.

My being a fence made it easier to fall into different schemes. One time

Arnie Binder comes to me. Arnie had a big place that sold mostly women's dresses. "Sam," he says, "I can use all the dresses you can get me, don't matter what kind of shape they're in." This is the only time I ever handled clothes, but whenever I went to the Salvation Army, I would have Cletus give me all the dresses he had. I'd drop them off at Arnie's and he was selling off the good stuff and replacing it with junk. Then, when he had nothing but junk left, he had somebody put a torch to his store and he collected the insurance. It wasn't as if Arnie came to me and said, "Here, help me fill up my store with junk merchandise, so I can burn the place down and collect the insurance." But you could read between the lines, so I knew what was going down.

A couple of times I handled counterfeit money. The one time it really helped me a lot, 'cause it was right after the fire and I was very short of cash, very short. Danny Walker came to me trying to unload $15,000 in counterfeit bills. Danny was a real bullshitter but a pretty good all-around thief, and solid. So, I checked the bills out and whoever done it, did a good job. I paid like $3500 for them. Meanwhile I hear from Scottie about this old hotel in Oceantown which is going out of business and is having this big furniture auction. So, I painted my big truck, changed the plates, and went to the sale. I mixed in the counterfeit with like $5,000 of my own money and bought like $20,000 worth of good antique furniture. I would bid and then pay cash right away, 'cause I told them I couldn't stay for the end of the sale on account of having to make some more stops. They didn't ask any questions, just took my money. It was beautiful. ◀

Sam has burgled while a fence, but explains that this was not an offshoot of fencing skills or connections:

▶ I still pulled some burglaries when I was into fencing. But this came more from my having been a burglar, although the fencing helped with getting the tips. See, if I had a good tip, I might hook up with a good burglar and clip the place. That, and I did a couple of truck jobs that Louie had information on. See, Louie had the contacts to find out things, but he didn't have the heart for burglary or for hitting a truck; and your good burglars wouldn't work with Louie. So, Louie would come to me and I would take care of it. ◀

In general, however, for reasons of time, connections, and personal taste, the burglaries and other scams are episodic sidelines to Sam's main business of dealing in stolen goods. In comparison, Louie was as involved in gambling and the rackets as he was a full-time fence.

▶ I pretty much stuck to fencing. I didn't screw around with different things the way Louie did. Louie was into every damn thing. Louie even messed in drugs, and I could have gotten into the dealing end of drugs very easily. But I was always leery of drugs. That, and I didn't have the connections the way Louie did. Louie would go whichever way he could make the most money. I was more content just to stay with the fencing. That, and you only have so much time. I didn't want to spread myself that thin. ◀

As Go-Between or Contact For Another Dealer

A final financial arrangement that fences like Sam may enjoy is kickbacks or rake-offs for working with or helping another fence in actual trade situations, for example, as a go-between or as a contact man.

▶ On some kinds of merchandise I was more or less a layer in-between for Angelo or for one of the other dealers that had ties [in the Mafia]. It got to where Angelo didn't want to deal direct with the thieves anymore, unless it was a real good thief. So, maybe once or twice a month, I would get a call: "Sam, will you handle such and such." Mostly, it was sugar, liquor, and cigarettes. What I'd do is meet the thieves and deal with them, pick up the stuff, and drop it with Angelo's boys. Later in the week I'd go to Angelo's place and settle up. Depending on how much the load was worth, I'd get anywhere from $500 to a couple of grand. It was a kickback arrangement, but not a set percentage. I got whatever Angelo gave me and never cried about it.

The other arrangement was like a rake-off of 10 or 15 percent when I'd hook up a thief, or maybe a fence, with an outlet. Say, a fence calls me looking for a place to unload some stolen merchandise he's bought, or say it's a thief who comes to me with something I don't want, maybe like furs. Now, I don't know nothing about furs, so I send him down the road to somebody else. I would say, "Okay, but I want a cut off the top or I want a couple of bills [$200] for making the contact." Then, too, next time I see the fence, I'd get my rake-off from him which would usually be about ten percent.

Actually, now, I very seldom ever took the rake-off. I would do it more as a favor to the thief or to the fence; that way he would owe me a favor. In many ways there's more talk about getting a kickback or rake-off than there is. Most of the fences I dealt with never pushed for their rake-off, same as me. Louie might 'cause he was very greedy that way, and for one-upmanship. ◀

Sam's Profits Reconsidered

Sam dislikes talking about how much he made from trading in stolen goods, although on occasion he will comment on a particular transaction. It is impossible, therefore, to apprise in exact terms how profitable fencing was for Sam. That he fared at least moderately well can be gauged from what has already been said, as well as from his statements comparing his profits as a full-time fence with his profits as a legitimate general merchandise dealer, or as a full-time burglar prior to becoming a fence, or as a dabbling dealer in the early stages of his fencing career.

Fence vs. Dabbling Dealer

▶ When I first got into fencing it was nickel and dime. It wasn't until I got into it with both feet, when I got the contacts, that I made the big money. Take the small dealers in town; they ain't making that much from the fencing. Maybe a couple of thousand a year; maybe ten or fifteen thousand, if they're lucky. They're making more on the legit side, with the fencing bringing in a little extra cash. ◀

Fence vs. Good Burglar

▶ When Jessie and myself were clipping, we was making a lotta, lotta money, and some very big hauls. Same way with Rocky and them today, they're rolling in the bread 'cause they're making some good hits and they have different places to unload, so they're getting a good price. You'd be surprised at how much a good burglar can make. It would be for a fact that some of your burglars, the really good ones, are taking in more than some of your fences. And they don't have the overhead and the investment that the fence has. Once I got rolling, really rolling, then I made more, whole lot more, on the fencing. But otherwise, no. I made more from the burglary. ◀

Fence vs. Legitimate Merchant

▶ It depends on what kind of business a fence is in, how big a business does he have. I always made a good living from the legit business. Now, when the fencing went "swoosh," there was no comparison 'cause the fencing was bringing in a whole, whole lot more. Not only that, but the fencing can open up other doors for making a buck, 'cause one thing leads to another and with the fencing you've got the contacts, and you're running with a different crowd that plays for a big dollar. ◀

Then, Sam muses as follows:

▶ I enjoyed the excitement of fencing, but the money was the main thing. I made a lot of money and spent a lot, too, and on crazy things. But I spent it the way I wanted to. It was beautiful.[6] ◀

---

6. There is some disagreement among Sam's associates as to how much he profited from his trade in stolen goods. Rocky comments: "From the talk I heard, Sam was a good burglar but I can't say what he made from that. When I knew him I would say the fencing was bigger than anything, by a long ways. His legit store turned over a good business but the big money came from the fencing." Chubbie states: "Sam made more with the hot stuff. No doubt about it. But it came and went faster 'cause Sam was a big spender and was too generous with the little people. He would give the hot stuff away a lot easier." However, Jesse states: "I believe he made more from the fencing than from the legit side. But, you put it alto-

If buying and selling stolen goods for a profit is at the economic core of running a fencing business, then doing so safely by, in one way or another, "covering one's back" is at the legal core. This side of running a fencing business is examined in the next chapter.

---

gether what he had left at the end, he made more from the burglary. Holy fuck, it is hard to realize how much we was hitting—hit safes for awhile, then go after metals like nickel or copper, then knock a place off for antiques, back to safes. And with the burglary, you don't have all the other expenses—just need to keep some bread on the side to pay the lawyer if you get busted."

Chapter 7

Covering and Corrupting

In the wording of criminal law, a person is guilty of the crime of receiving or fencing stolen goods if he "knowingly buys, sells, possesses, receives, or conceals any goods or property that has been stolen."[1] To convict a dealer in stolen goods under the receiving law, the prosecution must establish: (1) the receipt or control of the goods by the fence; (2) that the merchandise was stolen at the time of receipt; and (3) that the fence knew the property was stolen. These three legal constrictions pose obstacles to successful prosecution and provide the context of the fence's modus operandi.

The crime itself (of receiving stolen goods) usually does not offer any easily observed evidence of its occurrence, and the evidence needed to move forward the charging and prosecuting of an individual for fencing is stringent. Successful prosecution requires not only proof that an individual engaged in an illegal transaction but also that he did so knowing that the goods involved were stolen. Since the parties to such a transaction are usually only the thief and the fence, it is hard to get testimony against the fence which would convict him; merely receiving the property without guilty knowledge is not sufficient. Even with the thief's testimony it is difficult to prove the fence's participation if the latter cannot be apprehended with the goods in his possession to corroborate the thief's testimony.

▶ By the law it's hard to get a conviction. 'Cause you got to prove that he had the stolen goods, in his hands now, and that he knew they were stolen. If you're careful, it's hard to prove that.

In my eyesight, now, it isn't important to know much about the law. Not me anyway. Just don't get caught. My policy was to avoid trouble before it came. I'm a firm believer in looking ahead, covering

---

1. The writings that were most helpful in preparing this chapter include: Blakey and Goldsmith, 1976; Hall, 1952; Adler and Adler, 1980; Klockars, 1974; U.S. Congress, 1973, 1974.

my ass from behind. The less anybody knows about your business,
actually knows now, not just surmising, the better. ◄

Methods Available to the Police

There are a number of methods available to the police for gathering sufficient proof to gain a conviction for fencing stolen property. One method
involves a buy-bust program in which the fence is arrested immediately
after having purchased bait property purportedly stolen from an informant or undercover officer.[2] In this approach, the fence can only be
charged with conspiracy or with "attempt" to receive stolen property
since in fact the property is not stolen. A second method involves buying
property from the fence and then determining if, in fact, the property is
stolen; if it is, a search warrant is obtained for additional property stolen
under the same label but not recovered. Methods one and two are often
combined in practice—that is, begin by selling merchandise and then
buy other goods as well.

A third method involves surveillance—staking out a fence's place of
business, taking photographs, or phone-tapping. But this method is time-
consuming, expensive, and beyond the manpower, equipment, and resources of most police departments.[3] Also, as with methods one and two,
surveillance may require an element that is usually lacking both within local departments and between law enforcement agencies and jurisdictions:
effective police cooperation and communication. Methods one and two,
furthermore, may lead to charges of police violation of the fence's lawful
rights or of entrapment; and the methods not only are beyond the "buy
money" of most police departments but entail risks of substantial sums of
departmental money being passed into the hands of a fence who may not
be convicted later.

---

2. Chubbie points out: "The state cops did this a few times, came in wearing
plain clothes so Sam wouldn't figure it was them. The cop would say, 'Hey, I got a
couple of things here.' Sam would say, 'How much you want?' Sam was right out
in the open. He wasn't too leery. This got Sam arrested one time, I remember
'cause I went to the hearing [preliminary hearing]. The magistrate throws the
charges out, so the one state trooper tells Sam afterwards: 'Hey, we're gonna get
you. Just wait.' This was Cecil Martin. Him and another state cop, Larry Kuhn,
were really hot on Sam. I will never forget their names. They would give their left
nut to get Sam. They would more or less kid Sam about nailing his ass which they
really meant to do. And Sam would clown back with them."

3. Jesse comments: "Put yourself in the freaking cop's place. They are human,
too. How many 24-hour days can you put in, around the clock, watching. Then
nothing the fuck happens or you can't do nothing about what does happen. The
cop's the same as you and me, don't want to fuck with something as boring as that,
that can have very little in the way of a payoff."

A state trooper who did surveillance of Sam and Louie notes: "I hate to think of
all the time I spent watching those two. I could tell you how many times a day
Sam went to the bathroom."

A fourth method involves police inventory of businesses for purposes of discovering fences. Indeed, there usually are state or local statutes that require the records of certain types of businesses, such as pawnshops and secondhand stores, to be open to police inspection. One approach is to check serial numbers at repair shops, auctions, and secondhand places, but this is not very effective because of the property owner's failure to record the serial number, or to, in other ways, tag identifying marks on his property.[4] As with the other methods, moreover, the inventory method is time-consuming and is also tedious and not very glamorous police work, so that little use is made of these laws. Sam explains how he dealt with the local ordinance requiring that secondhand merchants, on a daily basis, report to the police all purchases of merchandise.

▶ To be a secondhand dealer, you have to get a merchant's license from city hall. The secondhand dealer is supposed to turn into the police within twenty-four hours what he buys from off the street. It's not the same as a pawnbroker, but it's close.

Now, it turns out the police don't wanna be bothered. See, for a while I was taking sales slips up to city hall pretty regular. Then, one time I went up with a whole fistfull and the cop says: "Goodman, what the hell you doing bringing this crap up here? What the hell we gonna do with all those damn slips?" Then I knew I had clear sailing, didn't have to worry about having the slips. Too much trouble for the police, didn't want to take the time to keep track of 'em. Once in a while I'd still go up, take a shoebox full, more as an excuse to chat and to find out what was going on.[5] ◀

Thief as Informant

The principal method by which the police discover and prosecute fences is to *use thieves as informants* who, in exchange for immunity from prose-

---

4. Agent Bogart notes: "We tried this on Vincent and other big fences in Mid-City. But it doesn't work that well. Lot of time and work for nothing. One problem is an inventory one—it can take the manufacturer or the shipper a long time to discover that something's missing. For example, this one pier reported losing 500 bicycles which, looking back, we thought Vincent was involved in because he had a friend that had a big bicycle shop. But the inventory on the piers didn't turn up they're short on the bicycles until a year later. Where are you going to find the bicycles now? The tires are worn out by that time."

5. According to Chubbie, it was Police Chief Pulaski who initially suggested to Sam that he keep sales slips, but that the officer in charge of keeping such records didn't want to be bothered: "Sam was friends with the chief of police. So, the chief tells Sam to protect himself he should use cards. Pick them up at the police station. Anytime somebody sells you something, have them fill it out. So Sam started doing that but the cop at city hall didn't wanna be bothered. Sam got a kick out of that: 'The chief gives me cards to fill out, but the motherfuckers at city hall won't take 'em.'"

cution or reduced charges, agree to testify against the fence. Were it not for thief-informants, the detective's task in apprehending (and building a case against) a fence would be next to impossible. Typically, it is the thief as informer who provides the police with initial identification of the fence and is the major state witness in court against him. The thief may also furnish the information on which a search warrant is issued (e.g., of the fence's place of business), with the warrant specifying the property to be seized and identifying it as stolen. While the detective usually has some leeway, it is often impossible to identify and specify property not in police custody.

Any fence who regularly deals in stolen goods can expect that, at one time or another, a thief will give information or "tips" to the police that the fence is going to buy or has bought particular merchandise; or, even worse, the thief may work with the police to "set up" the fence by agreeing to sell alleged stolen goods to him.[6] For fences like Sam, an occasional informant is not worrisome; but too many thieves willing to cooperate with the police can spell trouble even for a well-connected and resourceful fence.

▶ You got to expect this or that thief is going to snitch once in awhile. I could manage that. But if too many are snitching, and to both the local cops and the state police, that's a different story. If your name comes up too often, the police will feel the pressure to do something. It's much better to avoid trouble before it starts. ◀

Against the threat of the informant's tip, Sam is less likely to deal with some thieves than with others, but mainly he relies on a mix of incentives to encourage integrity. On the positive side, these incentives include paying the thief a fair price and using bonus practices, and the like, as means for cultivating camaraderie and loyalty. On the negative side, there is the threat of ostracism within the criminal community if Sam spreads the word that a particular thief is a snitch. And Sam's reputation as someone who would resort to violence deters some prospective informants.

▶ That's why, say, it's a burglary crew of three guys, the fence may deal with only one of them—the guy he trusts the most. The less contact you have with different thieves, the better off you are. Angelo

---

6. A run-of-the-mill burglar who sold to Sam notes: "I got pulled in several times by the state police, wanting me to finger Sam. This last burglary I got sent to the hole for, I could have walked if I gave Sam up. The one trooper [Kuhn] kept pumping me: "Tell us where you're taking this stuff and we'll get you a pass.""

Another burglar reports, that he admitted selling stolen merchandise to Sam, but balked when the state police offered him "a break" if he'd help set-up Sam: "They worked it out of me that I did sell the stuff to Sam. Kept telling me, 'you can do a lot of time for a lotta little shit, for nothing really.' Bullshit like that. 'Help us get a handle on Sam, and we'll let it ride this time.' They had me by the balls but that was going too far. No way would I do that."

used to operate this way, and I have done that already, too. Louie, too, but Louie was doing it more to screw the other thieves—he would connive with the one thief he was dealing with to chisel his partners.

You can't keep all the thieves from snitching, no way. But you can limit it. If the thief thinks you treat him fair and if he knows that once he unloads the stuff with you, his worries are over, the police will have a harder time getting him to snitch. But a few times I did have to get rough. Really, I had very little trouble from most of the thieves I dealt with. Very little. ◀

There are other defenses the fence can use against the thief-informant system (and the other police methods as well), but these are better examined after a more complete portrait is drawn of Sam's operating procedures and the artifices he employs to cover a trade in stolen goods. These procedures are inseparable from the character of Sam's legitimate business and the tailoring of his illegal trade to fit it.

The Front

In the vocabulary of the underworld, the "front" is any ruse behind which illicit activities can be undertaken. In terms of a fencing operation, it refers to the multiple advantages that a legitimate business identity gives to a trade in stolen goods. The buying and selling goods or the transportation of property are not inherently illegal. They are common business activities engaged in daily in the commercial sphere. Thus, in most cases the fence trades both legitimately and illegitimately. In his illegitimate trade, he molds his operations after the normal procedures and practices of the business world. In his legitimate trade, he buys and sells with an eye toward covering his illegitimate activities. This managed similarity of one trade with the other is designed to lessen suspicion and to make difficult the detection of the illicit transaction amidst many legal ones.

▶ Your legit business is your best cover. Even on goods that don't match your legit line, it helps. 'Cause who would know, who would suspect the warm dealings from the legit ones, the hot goods from what's clean. ◀

Some Businesses Mask ("Front") Better Than Others

Simply by owning a secondhand and general merchandise business, Sam is entitled to hold various kinds of merchandise, some of which is new, some old, and some damaged or altered, the market value of which is not easily established; to buy merchandise at the best possible price, taking advantage of bankruptcies, liquidations, production overruns, and private sales (thus, for example, Sam is not especially suspect if he has in his possession goods taken from private residences); to buy, sell, and trade with the public, with other merchants and secondhand dealers, and at auc-

tions; to possess bills of purchase which may only vaguely cover possession of it; and to conduct many transactions as cash deals in which there
may or may not be a record of the transaction. Also, Sam is a dealer in antiques, a designation somewhat amorphous in meaning which does not
preclude carrying items whose "antique" claim may be many years away
and whose market value is not easily established.

Sam's drift into fencing may have been happenstance, but he soon appreciated the predatory possibilities of this business environment, including the ease with which its trading post atmosphere could accommodate
an expanding trade in stolen goods. Sam's legitimate business and his
fencing business both changed over time as each shaped and was shaped
by the other.

> ▶ Let's say you wanted to become a fence. It would be hard to find a
> better cover than the kind of legit business I had. I could handle al-
> most any damn thing. And I was an antique dealer, too. Now, who
> can say what an antique is?
>
> First on, the fencing I did was separate from my legit business.
> But once I got rolling, the one was helping the other but mainly the
> fencing was pushing the secondhand business. My legit business
> kept getting bigger 'cause the fencing was getting bigger. Take an-
> tiques. I got into antiques 'cause I wanted to cover for the fencing.
> Now, once the legit side of antiques got going, it was making me
> good money and carried on by itself.
>
> I never sat down and figured out what I was going to handle. If I
> was handling this or that warm stuff, this encouraged the legit side. If
> I was handling something legit already, like furniture, then naturally
> I would be more likely to deal in furniture. ◄

No Questions Asked

An integral part of the front is the protection offered in many situations by
claiming that one does not know the goods in question are stolen; that is,
the fence can claim he believed the thief's story or, if no story is offered,
invent a convincing one of his own. Equally important, if accused of failing to inquire about the origins of merchandise, the dealer can feign oversight on his part or can convincingly claim that conducting an inquiry
would offend prospective legitimate sellers, thereby losing their trade.

Indeed, at any given moment, it is difficult to gauge both what percent
of the retail stock on Sam's shelves is warm and what percent of his total
trade (e.g., not on store shelves) is illegitimate. First, there is the rapid
turnover of merchandise and Sam's continuous buying and selling of
goods, both legitimate and illegitimate. Second, the "no questions asked"
environment of the traffic in stolen goods may mean that Sam, in fact,
sometimes does not know for sure (nor care to find out) what is stolen and
what isn't. Third, Sam's interpretation of what is warm is not cut and

dried but takes into account whether the merchandise, in fact, was stolen as well as whether the merchandise has in any way been "legitimized." Merchandise that Sam purchases from other dealers or buys from certain employee-thieves (e.g. Cletus at the Salvation Army), even when he knows or strongly suspects it is stolen, is not "hot" or at least not "hot" in the same sense as goods purchased directly from known thieves. Neither is stolen property which Sam has purchased from another fence and which has crossed state lines "really warm," especially in comparison with merchandise purchased from burglars stealing from local residences or commercial establishments.

▶ In my eye, what I bought from Woody, say, is warm down there but not up here. Know what I mean? The chances of getting caught are so small on account of there's a layer between me and the thief, and you're going across state lines. Strictly speaking, you can say it's hot, same as what I bought from Cletus at the Salvation Army. But in another way, no. It would be hard to blame me for what they're doing. Now, if you call "warm" everything I bought that I knew or surmised was stolen, then a pretty high percentage of my business was illegit. This varied, but I would say overall about thirty percent or more of the stuff in my store was warm in one way or another. Altogether, fifty to sixty percent of all the merchandise I handled would be warm.

But it was a lot less if you consider only what I bought direct from the thieves, and what I also had in my store. Anything that was local hot, like from the local residences or a bigger business burglary, I shipped out. Except now for the little stuff—toasters, coffee pots, cameras—the shoplifters and them were bringing in, little stuff you ain't gonna get jammed up on. I would run this to the auction or put it right on the shelves. If you traced everything I had in my store, maybe twenty-five percent would be stolen but no more than five percent would be what I called really warm. ◀

Moreover, the "no questions asked" norm is reciprocal. Not only is it attractive to the dealer in stolen goods, but also to many of his business buyers, store customers, and others glad to be in on a bargain. That is, while some of the fence's customers are honest consumers or business-men, other customers simply do not want to know how the distributor is able to undersell the competition, and why he wants to be paid in cash. Rather, under the precaution of not asking questions or looking further, "they turn a blind eye." The norm, then, serves as a kind of collective ruse for disguising the trafficking in stolen goods.

▶ Many times you can read between the lines or surmise that some-thing is warm, but really you prefer not to know. It works the other way, too. Many of the ones I sold to don't wanna find out if its stolen or not, 'cause they don't want to have that facing their conscience and 'cause this way the prosecution can't prove there was knowledge, that they knew the stuff was stolen. What they're doing is turning a blind eye—figuring what you don't know can't hurt you. ◀

By skillful employment of the front, and by ingenuity and industry in other ways, the fence can make it difficult for the detective or the prosecution to build a successful case against him which requires substantiation of three separate elements of the receiving law: receipt, identification, and knowledge.[7]

Proving Receipt and Knowledge

The law on receiving stolen goods requires that the stolen property must have been received by the suspect. For the police this means first finding the stolen property and then establishing the fence's possession or control of it. For fences like Sam it means developing devices and procedures aimed at averting the discovery of stolen property in his possession. Principal among Sam's practices is the extra precaution he exercises when he purchases merchandise stolen from local residences or businesses.

Were The Goods Stolen Locally?

The thieves and drivers who sell stolen goods to Sam are subject to one hard and fast rule: if Sam inquires about the origins of specific goods, the thief must forthrightly state whether they were stolen "locally" (within American City or its vicinity) or outside the area. The rule is most strongly in force when residential burglaries or commercial thefts of merchandise of substantial value are involved—that is, when the owners of the property are more likely to be able to identify their property and are more likely to pressure the police toward intensive investigation. On the other hand, when low-priced consumer goods stolen from regular retail outlets are involved, Sam seldom bothers to inquire about their origins because the owner's identification of these goods is highly unlikely.

▶ That's how Lemont Dozier got in trouble. Lemont was bringing me a lotta stuff, most of it from house burglaries. This one Monday morning, about 10:00 o'clock, he brings me a couple of stereos and three TVs. He tells me they are all from Capetown, which is about sixty miles from American City, but it turns out the stuff was local. In fact, he had stolen it that very morning. The next thing happens, this same day now, the lady he stole it from is window shopping during lunchbreak and sees this TV in my window that looks like hers. Sure

---

7. The organization of this section around the three elements of the receiving law follows that of U.S. Congress *Hearings on Criminal Redistribution Systems* (1973) and Klockars (1974:80ff). The organization also reflects Sam's sensibility to the receiving law and how he oriented his "covering" strategies towards it.

enough it is and she calls the cops, and I had to give her the TV back and the hassle that went with it.

See, Lemont had been a pretty good thief at one time. Then he got on dope and I should of dropped him but I didn't. Lemont had it figured out that I would pay a little more if it was from outside the area 'cause then I didn't have to ship it out, could put a price on it and put it right in the store window. After Lemont fucked me that time, he and I couldn't do business anymore.

The major thing I wanted to know from the thief was whether it was local or from outside the area. Was it locally hot, 'cause if it's local I ain't gonna put it in my store. I got to put it in storage or get rid of it fast. Not on the small stuff now that comes out of department stores, say, like a transitor radio or Kodak camera; put that right in the window of my shop. But something bigger, like a TV or appliances, then I wanted to know, especially when the house burglars came in. ◀

Don't Clip Too Often

▶ Another thing is, you sometimes got to slow the thief down. That, or at least he should clip a different product, to keep the heat off. Especially with the truck driver or the guy that works on the dock, if they're clipping too much, this can lead to an inventory check. Like the grandfather clocks that were coming in at the docks, I'd tell Danny, the guy that ran the tow fork, "Hey, don't break into the fucking crates too often, [let's] keep the fucking eyebrows from being raised." No need to get somebody's suspicions up, you know. ◀

Drops and Storage Places

Another form of protection sometimes used by Sam is the "drop" (Sam simply calls them "meeting places."),[8] usually impromptu, agreed-upon

---

8. The term "drop," along with the expression "swag," are sometimes presented in the crime literature as underworld slang of fences and thieves, as "The fence told me to leave my swag at a drop." Swag supposedly refers to stolen property while drop refers to a secret location for stolen property or a location for transferring stolen merchandise from the thief to the fence or his agent. Sam and the thieves I interviewed do sometimes use it in verb form, as: "Drop the stuff at such-and-such a place" or "where do you want me to drop it." "Drop" was seldom used in noun form, however, and then only as reference to a temporary storage or transfer location, for example: "I left it at a drop" or "where's the drop site." The word "drop" was not used to designate a more permanent location, as when a fence or a thief supposedly says: "I kept the merchandise in a drop."

Regarding "swag," Sam (and others I interviewed) insist that it is strictly a jailhouse term for contraband of one kind or another, and that swag is not used in

locations selected for the purpose of the fence-thief transaction: (a) where
the thief leaves or "drops" the merchandise to be picked up later by the
fence, or (b) where the thief transfers possession of merchandise directly
to the fence. In some instances the fence's agent or the ultimate consumer
may take possession of the goods after it has been determined that the
goods are not being kept under surveillance. The drop may be a loading
platform, a parking lot, a country road, or some other kind of temporary
meeting place.

▶ Say, I get a call and the guy tells me, he's got a load of this or that. I
might have him bring it right to my shop. But other times, if I'm
leery of him or think maybe the police have a tail on him, then I'd
meet him somewhere or maybe have him drop the stuff off at a certain spot. Then, I could check to see if the coast was clear. It would
all depend on how I felt, 'cause you always had to worry about a set
up. That, and there can be a lot of police heat on some of your burglars, and so with them you got to take the extra precaution.

The other thing is, some of the good thieves would rather not
come to my shop when they were peddling. So, I'd meet them somewhere. This would depend on what they had. Say, it was a van filled
with antiques that I was gonna unload in Southstate. I would meet
them on a country road on the way and run the antiques straight to
my contacts in Southfield. ◀

After Sam has purchased the goods and their possession has been
transferred, he may store them until they are eventually resold. In the
case of bulk merchandise, a warehouse, a garage, a parked trailer, an un-

the criminal world by thieves and fences as an expression for stolen property.
"Yeh, that [swag] is used in jail. *Not* on the outside. I don't know how'n the hell to
say it, but a lot of these words you ask about are not used by thieves and them, not
really. That is more something you see on TV, whatever in the hell for I can't say.
To make the story more interesting, I guess.

Really, there is slang among thieves but not like what you're asking. You don't
hear Jesse, Angelo, Steelbeams, Bowie and them talking like that—swag this or
drop that. Maybe an asshole thief that just got out of jail 'cause that is where the
slang really is. But otherwise, no."

Agent Bogart generally agrees with Sam's assessment, and adds an interesting
anecdote about Vincent Swaggi (but see Klockars, chapter 8): "'Drop' I would say
is used, like 'leave the goods in a drop.' But swag, no. The only one I ever heard
use that word was Vincent. He picked it up somewhere. He might stand in front
of his store, people pass by, he'd call out: 'Anybody wanna buy some swag? Folks,
come on in. All the swag's inside.' Whether this was ploy on his part or Vincent's
being a ham, playing the part you might say, I don't know. But this is why, I
would guess, that your man Klockars gave him the alias, *Swaggi*." (emphasis
mine)

Note, however, that both "swag" and "drop" appear in the major collections of
criminal argot, and supposedly both expressions have been in use, at least among
English thieves, for more than two centuries (see Eric Partridge, *A Dictionary of
the Underworld*, 1968).

used railroad car, or any other location which is stable and secure for storage, may be used as a sort of permanent hiding place for stolen goods.[9]

▶ You warehouse it until you can move it out. Maybe I need the time to find a buyer, or I want to build up a load to make it worth a trip to Oceantown or to Southfield. Yoy keep one step ahead. You ain't gonna get popped if they [the police] can't find it.

One time I had a garage where I just kept antiques. For a long time I had an old railroad car that was out in the country. I've used parked trailers already. With the last store, there was a big warehouse on the side and to the rear of my shop. It was beautiful. You could drive a big truck right into it. It's funny, you may think it's risky to have a warehouse and use it this way. But the cops never had any suspicion. My store was searched a number of times, but the police never checked the warehouse.

How long I'd keep it in storage all depends. Usually I would move it out in a day or two, at most a couple of weeks. I never liked to sit on it. Now, Louie was different. He had things stored for more than a year already before he unloaded it. I was more willing to take a lower price to get rid of it. ◀

In the case of merchandise which is not bulky but is of high value and very warm, Sam may employ what he calls "special hiding places" to conceal stolen property until he is able to resell. Items such as personal jewelry, a coin collection, or a set of antique silverware are likely to be easily identifiable by victims of the theft, and the victims are usually higher status members of the community who are more effective in prodding the police to investigate and zealously seek recovery of the stolen property.

▶ In the one store, I put a fake ceiling in the john. In the last store, I used a trap door that opened up into a stairway to the basement. I covered this with a rug and with my desk. One time the police had a

---

9. Burglars, too, may have "storage places" (the designation they use rather than "drop") for keeping stolen merchandise until they sell or transfer possession of it to a fence or another buyer. A number of burglars I talked to joked about the garage Bowie, a good burglar in the area, used for storing stolen antiques. Steelbeams notes: "This was a brick garage, and Bowie had bars on the windows, big lock on the door. It was like a fucking fortress. See, Bowie was mostly after cash and jewelry but if he saw a good antique he would pick it up. He'd keep the stuff in this garage, then he'd contact Sam or maybe a private person he knows to come to the garage and look over what he had." Rocky notes: "Reggie and me had a trailer. We'd hold stuff there until Sam could come to check it out. The way it worked was, say, we had some guns, some antiques or whatever—we'd call Sam or stop by his store, tell him what we had. Sam says, "Okay, I'll stop by this evening." He'd do that, give us a price, and settle up more or less. Then we'd just keep the stuff in the trailer until Sam was ready to move it. Usually the next day or that same evening, Sam would pick the stuff up and run it to wherever was his outlet."

tail on me when I picked up a couple of very rare guns, real antiques.
I went in the store, into the john, and shoved the guns into the fake
ceiling. Another time, the police were after some coins that were stolen. Came in my store with a search warrant and everyting. Tore the
store apart but never found a thing. All the time, the bag of coins is
right under their nose, under the trap door. ◄

Sell The Merchandise Quickly

Although drops and hiding places are an important part of Sam's illegitimate business, by far the most important way Sam protects himself
against a charge of possession of stolen property is the speed with which
he can sell the merchandise he receives. This requires a number of reliable outlets for various kinds of merchandise.

▶ The most important thing is to be able to get rid of the stuff quickly,
not have it sitting around. If you get it warehoused, it ain't necessary
to get rid of it right away. 'Cause the police don't act that fast. What
I'd do, say, it was appliances, is store them for a few days, until I got
enough for a load. Then I'd make a trip to Frankinburg or Southfield.

It depends on the item. On stuff that was worth a real good dollar
and if there was much risk, I would ship it out right away. See, on
some things the police know where it's coming, that I'm gonna get a
shot at it. I'd move this out real fast. In a couple of hours, it would be
gone. In the front door of my shop, and out the other.

It depends, too, on how much heat there is and on whether I could
make more if I held it. Like sugar, liquor, and cigarettes, I wasn't
covered on them, and it don't make no difference price-wise whether
you hold them or not. I knew what I was getting. So, I would move
that out quickly. Altogether, I didn't like to sit on the merchandise. I
would rather take a price cut than take the extra risk. ◄

Sam's thriving trade with upfront store customers and the fact that he
has merchandise for sale at bargain prices also helps ensure a quick turnover on the stolen goods he places on his store shelves. That Sam frequently offers an extra incentive of "no sales tax," provided the customer
will forfeit a receipt, further helps to turn over the merchandise quickly.
And it also means that there is no record of the transaction.

▶ Tell 'em, pay in cash and I don't bother to write it up, no tax. This
was a break for them and then there would be no record either. I
could always say, hey, they didn't buy that from me. ◄

Finally, Sam uses the watchful eye of a Doberman or a German Shepherd
as a sort of last resort protection against unexpected police searches.

▶ This is funny—but Muffin, this one Doberman I had, hated cops. If
you were in a cop uniform, she would take you on unless I called her
off. If a cop comes barging in, sudden like, they would have to an-

swer to her. This one time the state police were trying to set me up—had an undercover cop peddle some jewelry. Soon as he left, I had that feeling, felt something was fishy. Out of my eye I see two state troopers coming for the door, and I'm telling Muffin to let them have it. Now, I'm heading for the john, to flush the jewelry down the toilet, cause they're afraid to come in. When they finally got in, they couldn't find shit. I always have a Doberman or a Shepherd for that reason, to give you that few minutes, which has saved my ass more than once. And to guard the place at night, too.[10] ◄

Proving The Goods Are Stolen

The property must be positively identified as being stolen—often a difficult task even when the goods are found in a fence's possession because of the relative impersonality of property items and the lack of adequate identifying marks on most categories of goods. In many cases, for example, the police may find persons in possession of property which they believe is stolen but which cannot be traced with any certainty to a legitimate owner, either because of lack of serial numbers on the property or the failure of the owner to maintain adequate records. Indeed, many manufacturers of small appliances and similar items maintain that serialization is too costly in terms of labor and recordkeeping. In most cases, therefore, identification of specific items depends on certain markings (name of consignee and shipping number) that are stenciled on the cartons or shipping crates in which the products are packed. Obviously, one of the first things done by the fence or the thief is to dispose of or "strip" the cartons.

Similarly, the police may "know" a theft has occurred and the goods fenced, but there is inadequate inventory control by large companies to prove that they were actually victims of theft. Because a company may not be able to document its own legal ownership of property that has been stolen, the prosecution lacks sufficient elements of proof to make a formal charge.

Identification of stolen property is difficult with respect to mass-produced name-brand products, (e.g., appliances, liquor, wearing apparel), but is especially difficult with so-called fungible goods (e.g., metals, foodstuffs, grain, livestock) that are virtually indistinguishable as stolen once they are merged with quantities of similar products. The lack of any specific identifying marks makes it difficult, if not impossible, for the man-

---

10. Chubbie reports that: "Sam spoiled the hell out of Muffin. She couldn't do no wrong. She liked riding in trucks, would whine and bark. Sam would say: 'Chubbie, give that motherfucker a ride.' I'd take the little pickup truck and give Muffin a ride. Other ones that hung around the shop, like Rocky or Mickey, if they were going somewhere, maybe running an errand for Sam, it was the same thing. I think Sam called her motherfucker more than he called her Muffin."

ufacturer or owner of, say, a set of tools to state positively that a particular item is his own property.

Besides the beforehand shielding that is part and parcel of these patterns of merchandising and product labeling, Sam can merge stolen merchandise with legitimate stock, he can thwart identification of goods by altering them, and he can use false or vague receipts to legitimize his possession of particular goods.

Merge With Legitimate Stock

Sam's diverse buying practices in his legitimate trade make identification of stolen property exceptionally difficult by assuring that an especially precise identification of alleged stolen goods will be necessary.

▶ Who is gonna be able to tell (what's warm, what isn't)? I'm buying and selling all the time, legit now. Somebody dies, I buy out the house. I'm running back and forth to the auctions. I'm getting stuff regular from the Salvation Army. People are coming in off the streets, selling and buying. This place goes out of business, I'm buying from them. I've got new stuff and used stuff, this brand and that brand; some of it's junk, some isn't. You could find almost anything (in my shop). And full. You could hardly walk through it. ◀

Altering Merchandise

Another way to thwart identification of goods as stolen is by removing identifiable characteristics and by changing or destroying identification numbers. Gold, silver, and other metals can be melted down, jewels can be removed from their settings, consumer goods can be removed from their identifying cartons, and secondhand merchandise can be further refashioned or "doctored." Because Sam's legitimate trade is often with distressed merchandise and also because he is a legitimate craftsman who repairs furniture and antiques, his possession of goods that are altered to avoid identification is not especially suspect.

The frequency with which a fence removes serial numbers or in other ways alters merchandise to cover an illegal trade can be easily exaggerated, however. While alteration is a part of the mechanics of covering, Sam relies much more on rapid turnover of merchandise and on the lack of traceability of most consumer goods as protection against possible proof that he possesses particular stolen goods. The sheer magnitude of goods produced and shipped, as well as the many changes in possession, ownership, and location of goods between production and consumption, practically assures that many goods can't be traced.

▶ Who keeps track of serial numbers anyway? I never bothered to change a serial number. Never had a hassle on it, either. Even your business places may not know. All they can identify is the make and model number. And that ain't enough for the cops to go on.

If you have to, you can tear off a label or exchange backs on a TV or refrigerator. But I didn't bother even doing that very much. I've never had any hassles on that, either. What you have to watch for, is merchandise that comes from private homes, like your antiques. If I was leery, than I'd break off a leg, or upholster part of a chair. Or, say, it was a clock, I might take the stain off, and then refinish it. I was most careful on the antiques; even the ones I bought from outside the area, I would many times "doctor" them just enough so there would be a doubt in the person's mind that this piece was theirs, and it had been stolen from them. ◄

False or Vague Receipts

Falsely claiming that particular receipts cover stolen property or maintaining receipts with vague descriptions of merchandise also help lessen the risk of possessing identifiable stolen property. And keeping a supply of purchase receipts of legitimate goods that cover purchase of similar stolen goods at a later date, protects both against proof of possession of stolen goods and against proof that they are stolen.

► More than anyting I tried to have receipts that covered different items I was handling at the time. Say, I was at an auction. I might buy TVs, lawn mowers, furniture, and that which was selling cheap. Maybe it was even junk. Just to get the receipts. Then if I would get jammed up on TVs or whatever, I had this piece of paper and my back was covered.

This is where Cletus at the Salvation Army was a big help. He would give me a fistfull of blank slips, with the "Salvation Army" inscribed right on it. I could fill them out whatever way I wanted. The Salvation Army is a charity and who would ever suspect them. ◄

Proving The Fence "Knows" The Goods Are Stolen

The most difficult problems of proof in the crime of receiving relate to the *mens rea*, or mental element, of the crime. That is, even if it can be established that a fence possesses, or has possessed, stolen property and that the property was indeed stolen, it is still necessary to prove that, at the time of the purchase, the fence knew, or had good reason to believe, the property was stolen. In the absence of direct information about an individual's thoughts, circumstantial evidence is needed to prove foreknowledge.

This is normally determined in court by the unexplained possession of recently stolen goods, or by demonstrating that something about the character of the goods, their price, or the person selling them should alert a reasonable person to the probability that they are stolen—for example, receiving stolen goods from a known thief or buying goods at some fraction of their real value (such as a new ten-speed bicycle for twenty dollars). The fence's protection against possible proof of this element of receiving rests, therefore, on devices aimed at casting doubt on the question of whether a reasonable businessman would have suspected that the goods he purchased were stolen.

Probably the strongest defense Sam relies on is the use of phony or false bills to display an unaware "state of mind," as well as to establish a record of reasonable price. This procedure—an extension of the vague receipt tactic described above—involves securing a fictitious signature either from the seller or from somebody else and frequently involves "jacking up" the purchase price paid in cash for the merchandise.[11]

▶ Say, someone comes in my store and sees his TV, has the serial number written down, all that. What you need is a piece of paper which says you bought it from so and so. If you got the sales slip, you're usually home free, especially if the cop who investigates wants to give you a break. See, the sales slip protects him, too, and allows him to go to bat for you. You will lose the merchandise, but that will be it.

Most of the time I would have the thief sign a slip, saying he sold such and such to me, or I'd write up a bill of sale and have Clyde or one of the hangers-on sign it. I didn't care what name is put down, as long as I have a signature. I might jack up the price, too, so that if they checked, it would cut down on the suspicion that comes from buying too cheap.[12]

Having the sales slip saved me more than a couple of times. This was a very close call, but one time twelve rolls of cemetery vault wire came my way. I put eight rolls in the warehouse and took four rolls to the auction. Now, it turns out the guy the wire was stolen from is at the same auction and he spots the wire, and calls the cops. When the cops come, they had me dead 'cause I hadn't bothered to make a sales slip or anything.

So, I made a call to Tommy, a very regular truck thief I was buying from, and told him to go to my shop, make out a bill for four rolls of

---

11. Another strategy, one not employed by Sam, is the false bill-cancelled-check procedure which, according to Klockars (1974:90), was used frequently by Vincent Swaggi. This involves the fence making out a check to the seller at a plausible purchase price, have the seller endorse it, and bank deposit the endorsed check in the business account. If questioned, the fence will then explain that he paid the seller the (reasonable) price shown on the check, but after doing so, the seller asked him to cash the check. The fence then claims that he agreed to do so and requested the seller to endorse the check; the fence then deposited the check. The story is, of course, untrue but it gives the fence a receipt and a cancelled check as evidence that the goods were purchased from an apparently legitimate seller and that a fair market price was paid for the goods.

12. Chubbie notes: "Sam might have me, or anybody else that was around, sign a piece of paper. He'd say, 'Chubbie, knock out a name, scratch it on this.' I got pretty good at knocking out some helluva good names."

vault wire, purchased from so and so, on such and such a date. Then, crush up the bill and throw it in the wastebasket. Well, when we all got back to my shop, I headed for my desk to show the cops and this guy my sales slip. Now, my desk is piled with everything, from paper to thumb tacks, you name it. And the cops and me are looking but we can't find the bill. Finally, the one cop says, "Maybe you threw it in the wastebasket." I says, "I don't think so, but let's check." So he checks, and sure enough he finds it. Then he tells the guy he don't have anything on me but that I would have to return the four rolls of wire.

Now, later on, the guy calls me back and asks me to keep a watch for the other rolls. So, a couple of weeks later, I call him and tell him somebody just brought the wire in and I'm holding it for him. He can just pay me what I had to pay the other guy. I won't take my cut. See, I had the other eight rolls in storage, so I'm selling him back his own wire. ◄

This last anecdote not only reveals Sam's ingenuity but suggests how careless or casual bookkeeping can be used, even inadvertently, to circumvent the law. Sam's sloppiness, as he well appreciates, makes it difficult to prove where poor bookkeeping ends and illicitness begins. From the point of view of the investigating detective, moreover, poor bookkeeping may be an acceptable alibi, particularly since Sam was typically contrite while conveying the impression that he was not smart enough to set up elaborate recordkeeping or that it was an oversight from being too busy.[13]

► I would always let the police think that I knew I needed to keep better records, that I should take the time to carefully write everything down and work out a system of keeping on file what I bought, from whom, and all that.

This was all bullshit on my part 'cause in this business you're better off not to keep good records. You don't want to make it easier for them but make them dig for whatever they get. ◄

The false bill procedure has its limitations, moreover. First, it is not applicable to all varieties and quantities of goods. For example, false bills cannot be used when Sam buys stolen goods which do not match his general merchandise front (e.g., food products) or other commodities that require a special license to trade in (e.g., guns, liquor, cigarettes). Second, writing up a phony bill in an amount adequate to establish a reasonable purchase price on a very large quantity of merchandise would appear to be exceedingly suspect if the goods are not a major part of the fence's le-

---

13. Jesse notes: "I never knew that sonofabitch to keep books. That way who in the fuck's going to connect one to another. Say he goes to Frankinburg, pays cash for a load—this is legit now—comes back and sells it. Another time it might be hot stuff. How in the fuck can it be checked out?"

gitimate trade. For example, it would be difficult for Sam to convincingly use the false bill procedure to explain his possession of a truckload of car batteries since he seldom sells them in his store. Third, this same suspicion surfaces when the seller of the property could not possibly have been the legitimate owner—for instance, if Sam purchases fifteen television sets from someone having no legitimate connection to the industry. Fourth, in situations in which the police have apprehended a "known" thief and he confesses to selling stolen property to Sam, the availability of a phony bill (e.g., even with a fictitious signature) may provide evidence of possession and the presumption that Sam had reasonable cause to believe the merchandise is stolen. Nevertheless, for many general merchandise goods in the medium quantities in which a store like Sam's would normally trade, the false bill procedure creates a believable image of normal business practice.

▶ If I bought a load of furniture, that would be okay 'cause I handled a lot of furniture. But say, I bought a load of snow tires or tools. The sales slip may help but I will still have a lot of explaining to do. The other thing is, anytime you buy from a thief that is well known to the cops, the cops got to figure you know he's a thief and that what he's peddling is warm. Same with the jury, they ain't gonna believe that piece of paper.

That's why, if it was something worth a good dollar or a truckload, especially if it involved a known thief, I didn't bother with the sales slip—my best cover was to ship it out quick. But, on a lot of things, the day-to-day stuff, the sales slip was a good cover. If I had the time and thought about it, I would get a bill of sales. ◀

Moreover, under some of the circumstances described above—where the law reasons that a normal person would have cause to believe the goods were stolen—it is the fence's task to create a plausible alternative explanation. In the case, for example, of someone with no connection to the TV industry selling fifteen TVs, the fence may argue that the thief represented himself as a friend or a relative of someone who had had a legitimate business and that the business had failed, and its merchandise was being sold at a discount to other dealers. In this regard—and no matter how much Sam or any fence relies on the phony bill procedure—he must be able to claim convincingly, both under interrogation and in court, that he believed the thief's story or, in other ways, did not have reasonable cause to believe the merchandise was stolen.

▶ The fence has to think quickly on his feet and have some heart too. Come up with a story, and stick to it. You can't let the cops scare you 'cause if they want to, they can pull a lotta shit, can crack on you pretty hard. I would never let them think they could get the upper hand. ◀

To this point, the descriptions of Sam's operating procedures suggest that legal proof of the crime of receiving is difficult to attain, and how the

difficulty of convicting a resourceful fence is inseparable from the character of the business he conducts. But Sam's employment of a front, and his
tailoring of his illegal trade to fit it, can be easily overstated. Depending
on time, convenience, or whim, Sam may or may not alter merchandise,
use a drop for stolen merchandise, or take advantage of the false-bill procedure. A surprising finding is how casually Sam treats secrecy and how
free and easy he sometimes is about the way he runs a fencing business.
That he is such, perhaps, is because the skillful use of various artifices and
manipulations to cover a trade in stolen goods is only a part of the business of being a fence. For if fencing is an illegal business, then law enforcers and the fence's relationship to them are at the core of it.

Complicity of Law Enforcers

Particular dealerships will require particular solutions to the problem of
protection from "the law"—the term broadly used here to designate the
police, the prosecutor, and the courts. As a general principle, as the fence
becomes more public—usually because of dealing more regularly or because of dealing with a wider mix of thieves—he will be under increasing
pressure to gain the complicity of police or other legal officials. The private collector or buyer who deals with a small number of established
thieves, as well as with the small merchant who occasionally buys stolen
merchandise, places it on the shelves next to his legitimate stock, and
resells it, may have little need to conciliate the police. Their chances of
being discovered are small, and, if discovered, the evidence is likely to be
too slender to lead to arrest or to prosecution. Even the specialist fence
who regularly buys from seasoned thieves and has quick disposal outlets
outside the area, may need little in the way of slack from the police. As
Sam notes:

▶ The police can surmise, but do they really know? If a jeweler fence
is careful about who he deals with and has good outlets, the police
will know but will not know in the sense of doing much about it. But
if he does the fencing for a long time or if he gets more wide-open,
the chances are the police are giving him some slack, for one reason
or another. ◀

In comparison, the generalist fence who deals with generalist thieves
will be both highly known and exceptionally vulnerable to law enforcement efforts aimed at larceny-theft and burglary activities. Therefore,
fences like Sam have a distinct need for police protection.

▶ You can't be a dealer like me or Louie, or like Angelo was at one
time, without the police knowing and being taken care of. You can't
operate without their cooperation. One way or another they have to
give you some slack, really a license to steal.
    Mainly what you need is a break now and then. Take the time this

woman called, wanted to sell all the furniture in her apartment. Is running out on the guy she's living with. Remember? So I quick buys the stuff. Then this guy gets wind of this 'cause someone saw my trucks loading up the stuff. Goes to the cops, and they come to my shop. "Yeh, I bought the stuff," I says, "Here's the paper with the lady's name." They tell the guy, "Sorry, it's a bad mistake but we can't do nothing." Now, they coulda made a hassle for me but they was two cops that shopped regular in my shop, so they was turning their heads.

Then, too, I've already been called down to city hall, to the police station, 'cause this or that thief was fingering me, that I was buying hot stuff. Different times Lorenzo—who was Captain of the detectives—was on the sidelines you might say. He'd tell the other cop: "Hey, we can't go to the D.A. with this. This ain't for shit. Let the man go." ◀

The dealer in stolen goods can opt for one or a number of strategies for gaining this "license to operate." These strategies may be directed mainly towards the police, they may be aimed at other legal officials, or both.

The Fence As Informant

Informants are persons who for favors, money, or revenge give information to the police. As observed earlier, were it not for thief-informants, the detective's task in apprehending and building a case against a fence would be next to impossible. The thief-informant system can be turned upside down, however: just as thieves can inform on a fence, so also can a fence inform on thieves.

The fence is likely to be an especially valuable informant either because he typically deals with many thieves (versus the thief who knows only one or two fences) or because he has information, or access to it, about criminals and their activities more generally. Consequently, the police may cultivate fences as suppliers of criminal intelligence in exchange for what may be virtual freedom to buy and sell stolen goods.

The fence's value as an informant intertwines with two related elements: (1) with public concern about personal safety and the security of residences and thus with more offensive criminals such as robbers, burglars, and drug-addict thieves; and (2) with the police's vested interest in "clearing" many arrests since the latter is the principal standard for judging police performance. Fences acting as informants can help the police make many arrests and thereby increase the detective's and the department's efficiency. And because a resourceful and well-connected fence may often be able to thwart police investigative efforts directed at him, the detective may be further inclined to focus on that portion of the criminal landscape—robbers, burglars, and drug-addict thieves who will more expeditiously enhance his chances of doing well (e.g., promotion, favorable assignments, good publicity). Consequently, cooperation between the police and a particular fence may be mutually beneficial: the detective is assisted in making many arrests and in ably enforcing the law; the fence is able to practice his trade, knowing that he, too, has fulfilled his obligations to the state.[14]

▶ A fence can give himself some slack if he's willing to be a snitch. What the police get out of it, is to keep their arrests up, clean their books. Makes the detective look good and the chief, too, 'cause in the public's mind they're solving all those crimes. It's all bullshit. What they do is get the fence to snitch on a few burglars or a couple of dopers. And the ones the fence is turning in are usually your real lackeys, the penny ante thieves and the blacks who are into dirt. They will end up admitting crimes they didn't even do.

Now, it doesn't mean the fence has to set the thief up or testify against him. Usually it won't involve that. Maybe all the fence has to do is identify that a particular thief stole such and such, or pulled a particular burglary, so the police know they have the right man and they can turn the heat on. Or maybe the fence knows who is dealing drugs or who is mugging the old ladies, 'cause that's a crime the police very much want to solve. See, the fence hears what's going on in different areas, and he can help the police out in little ways.

It's a fact that Louie was a snitch, and he would use that to save his ass, and as a club, too. Say, a thief was busted and fingered Louie. The police would call Louie and then Louie would say, "Okay, next time he comes peddling I'll let you know." So the thief comes and Louie doesn't buy but tips off the cops. The cops tail the guy, and he gets popped with the goods in his hands. And Louie could be very

---

14. Evidence that the fence may achieve immunity by acting as an informer can be traced at least as far back as Moll Cutpurse and Jonathan Wild. As noted earlier (see chapter 1, and also see the appendix), thief-taking was the cruder eighteenth-century equivalent of giving information to the police and currying the favor of the judiciary. This was not a new system: Luke Hutton complains of it in 1596, and the historian Gerald Howson says: "It is clear that when Wild embarked on thief-taking—that is blackmail, bribery, informing, grassing . . . he was entering an already well-developed, 'sophisticated,' profession with a long and important history behind it." (Howson, 1970:42)

Indeed, students of the fence have consistently pointed out the complicity of authorities in fencing operations. Crapsey, a newspaperman with extensive contacts with the New York underworld, observed in 1892 (p. 501) that there are "many flagrant cases of collusion between the police and plunderers . . . it is to the interest of everybody that the case shall not go to court; the owner wants his property, the policeman his reward, and the fence impunity . . . (as a result) dealing in stolen goods has become and threatens to permanently remain, one of the leading industries of the metropolis." (Crapsey, 1872: 502) And the 1928 Association of Grand Juror's study concluded "one of the problems of supressing the fence is caused by the tendency of the police in some localities to wink at the receiver because he can frequently tip them off to criminals whose misdeeds have aroused special resentment." (Association of Grand Jurors, 1928:11)

dirty with the other dealers, has already set them up, tipped off the police that they were going to buy. Lot of the little dealers feared Louie that way, 'cause they didn't have the connections with the police. See, the police can give one fence a license to steal and be fucking over another dealer so he can't operate.[15] ◀

While the advantages of the informer relationship may be considerable for the fence, so are the risks—particularly since the police may keep pushing for more information and may come to expect it on a regular basis. The fence-informant risks the violent reaction of those whose criminal confidence he has betrayed, as well as of their friends and associates.[16] And the fact that a particular fence is a "snitch" may become widely known through the underworld grapevine, causing at least some thieves to avoid doing business with him. This partly explains Sam's refusal to be a police informant but also reflects his strong allegiance to the underworld code against snitching.

▶ Some fences will throw the police a bone now and then to keep the heat off themselves. But the fence has to be careful 'cause if he snitches on the better thief, that can hurt his business. What Louie would do is turn in a bottom-barrel thief or a doper, and the police would be happy with that.

Several times, now, the police did try to open me up. "Just tell us if so-and-so is the one, so we can check it out." "Let us know if we are on the right track." But there was very little pressure 'cause they knew where I was coming from.

For me to snitch, I could never look at myself in the mirror. It

15. One retired American City detective comments, "It did come up in the department that if somebody was buying hot stuff, and was getting too big, Louie would have the DA or somebody in the [police] department hound the guy, so he'd slow down. Whether this in fact happened, I can't say, but that was the talk." When I asked why Louie didn't do this to Sam, the detective replied, "I can't answer that. Don't forget now, they were doing things together, helping each other out, you might say. Then Sam got tight with the chief and with Duggan, too, who was really the chief's right hand man, so Sam was pretty well set himself. Sam wasn't somebody you wanted to mess with, either. And Louie was having his troubles at this time, with Angelo and some of the higher Mafia boys. Keep in mind, Sam was in with that crowd, too." Agent Bogart notes: "Vincent was an informant for the city cops. The way he figured it, if he worked for the cops, they worked for him, too. That he could go to one of the captains or one of the higher-ups, 'Hey, I want this guy [another fence] knocked off.' I'd say a lot of your big fences operate this way."

16. Steelbeams recounts this episode: "I was hooked up with Bowie and Danny Spence at the time. We was selling jewelry and that to Jules Blerkom over in Ironwood. Blerkom gets popped and fingers us to save his ass. We got off but Bowie was pissed, fucking pissed. "I'll get that motherfucker," he says. So we goes to Blerkom's house, roughs him up a bit, but mostly messes up his house. Broke furniture and that. Afterwards we laughed how scared shitless he was. Ask Bowie about that some time."

would be hard to shave in the morning, to look at myself, knowing I did that. The other thing is, you will pay for it in the long run 'cause your better thieves will be less likely to deal with you. You can end up dealing with nothing but the bottom-barrel. I wasn't worried about the city cops anyway. There wasn't that much need to throw them a bone, and once you start the snitching, it can be very hard to stop, 'cause then they got their foot in the door, and the police can play very dirty, too, if they want to. ◄

That Sam will not act as a snitch does not mean that he will never assist the police in crime-fighting matters.

► Different times, I did help the police get back stolen property. This has nothing to do with snitching, now, 'cause many times you're really protecting a thief. One time some cousins of Dorothy Ford robbed a very wealthy, old established family in American City. Broke into their house and carried off a gold bed frame which had been in the family for years, which they peddled to Dorothy. Couple of detectives came to me, to help them out, 'cause the family was raising quite a stir. So I worked it out with Dorothy and the family got back the gold bed frame.

Another time, the district attorney came to me, asked me to watch out for a coin collection that had been stolen from his daughter-in-law. Now the coins already came my way. I had unloaded them to the lawyer who was my main outlet for coins. I told the D.A., I'd keep my eyes open. So, I get the coins back, wait a couple of days, and calls the D.A. — I has run down the coins, he can pick them up.

It has happened, too, that someone from the public has come in and asked me to watch for such and such. Say it was a namesake piece, and it came my way, I might contact them and have it returned. See, I never liked to take something that meant a lot to the person, like a piece that's been in the family for years. It would depend on what the piece was worth, too. You ain't gonna return something that is worth a really good dollar.

I think a lot of your fences help out the police this way, to give themselves some slack. I could have made a very good dollar on the coins, but by helping out the D.A., he owes me a favor which will pay off in the long run.[17] ◄

---

17. Agent Bogart notes that fences do strategically cooperate with law enforcement in the recovery of stolen property, and that Vincent occasionally did so. Bogart maintains, however, that one incident reported in Klockars (1974:159) alleging that Vincent contacted and turned in two black thieves for stealing Army rifles simply didn't happen. "If Vincent contacted the FBI, like he claims, this would have come to me. Absolutely would have to come to me. It didn't come to me, so it didn't happen. Vincent is giving your man, Klockars, a line of bull there." [Bogart frequently made reference both to Sam and to Klockars as 'your man, Sam,' or 'your man, Klockars.']

"Perks": Fence As Generous Merchant

As legitimate merchants and also because of their overall reputation and
contacts, fences are able to offer various "perks" or payoffs to the police
and other legal officials. The fence need not, however, ingratiate himself
with all members of the police department but mainly needs to gain the
complicity of some members of the burglary-theft detective division. In
return for these perks, the police may be less zealous in responding to
complaints against the fence or may sabotage an ongoing investigation.
From the point of view of the individual officer, moreover, the compensation offered by a fence is especially attractive if corruption exists at other
levels of the department or legal system.[18]

▶ It is hard to convict a fence, to make an arrest stick. That in itself
will turn a few cops your way 'cause they're figuring they can't nail
him anyway, might as well get what they can. Then, once you get
your foot in the door, other ones will give you even more slack. The
one is feeding into the other.

Another thing, it is mostly the detectives you have to worry about.
The ordinary cop don't have nothing to do with you anyway. You
want to get your foot in the door with a couple of the detectives.
'Cause, if one cop knows another cop is dealing with you, he is leery
to interfere. Say, I get reported to the cops by a thief for buying stolen goods; chances are the case will go to the cop I'm paying off. The
police have a helluva code that way, of standing up for one another
and not interfering in the other's business.

My way of paying off the cops was selling them merchandise in my
store at cheap prices, very cheap. There was maybe ten, twelve,
fourteen city cops that were coming to my store very regular. Whatever they were in the market for, "Hey, Sam, I need snow tires on
my Chevy, can you help me out?" It don't have to be good deals on
merchandise, now. Louie ran a used car lot and he would give the
police old cars for their driver training.

I felt very safe with the local police. Same with Louie. We knew
they would give us slack if they could, wouldn't push an investigation
as hard as they could. This is very funny to me. The way I see it, I'm
buying the cops off. But to them, I'm not 'cause it isn't cash straight
up. It's more like a favor or gift they would get from any businessman
for looking the other way at this or that violation. See, you don't need
to have the cops in your pocket all the way. If you can cover yourself
in other ways, and they're giving you a break now and then, this will

---

18. Herbert Ashbury (*Gangs of New York*, 1928:215) reports that Marm Mandelbaum, who survived as New York's largest fence from 1860 to 1884, did so with
the help of "police officials and politicians." Marm, he writes "entertained lavishly
with dances and dinners which were attended by some of the most celebrated
criminals in America, and frequently by police and politicians who had come under the Mandelbaum influence."

do. And someone like Angelo is so tied up, the police will give him slack anyway. ◄

Most of the detectives who shop at Sam's store are more or less passive recipients of Sam's generosity. A few are actively on the take, however.

► Duggan and Lorenzo, two detectives, were fucking corrupt cops. When I first got into the fencing, they're both biding their time, waiting to see how I handled myself. Once I got rolling and was in with the local clique, like with Angelo and them, Duggan comes around. "Hey, Sam, what you got for nothing? What price will you give me on this?"

This even happened. One Saturday afternoon, Duggan and a couple of cops are watching a football game at the police station and the TV breaks down. Duggan calls me up, "Sam, the TV went on the blink, can you help us out?" I sent Clyde right over with a TV.

With Duggan and Lorenzo, it was more than just the deals on merchandise. They might grab something at the burglaries they investigated. So now, they're coming to me with good antiques, say, wanting me to fence them. They were both fucking corrupt cops.

Until I was hooked up with Duggan and Lorenzo, I had to cover my back more and not get too careless 'cause the slack I had wasn't that great. This or that cop might help me out a little. Then when Melvie became the Chief, I had no worries at all with the American City police, cause the chief and I were good friends on account of his interest in guns and antiques which I could help him out with. And the chief made Lorenzo a captain, put him in charge of the detectives. Then, he made Duggan in charge of internal affairs and that shit. Duggan was really the chief's right-hand man. It all fell into place like you wouldn't believe. I had more protection from the local cops than I really needed.[19] ◄

All things considered, the police may have little to gain and much to lose by devoting time and manpower to arresting dealers in stolen goods. The difficulty of proving the crime of receiving, limited resources, public definitions of "serious" crime, the rewards for doing "good" police work, the corruption of justice at all levels of the legal system, the gains that come from working with a fence—all combine to encourage police and prosecution to apprehend thieves and discourage law enforcement efforts aimed at fences.

In effect, both the fence and the police (especially the detective) have access to resources desired by the other. The fence is able to give infor-

---

19. Agent Bogart notes: "Vincent was an informant but he was also paying off the city cops. He was connected all the way to the top. A hell of a lot of them shopped at Vincent's store—they got a lot of stuff, top of the line clothes and that, from Vincent. And once a cop is on the take, the fence is in to him, too. What's to keep Vincent from going, say, to a U.S. Attorney: 'Hey, I'm paying this guy off.'"

mation about thieves and is often able to assist in the recovery of stolen goods as a result of his knowledge and contacts; and he is able to offer the police bargains on legitimate merchandise. In some instances the payoff may be more blatant, as when the fence pays cash to the police in exchange for non-enforcement, or when a fence with links to the rackets provides, say, sex or drugs, to an official, or when the fence buys property pilfered by detectives in the course of burglary investigations. In return for some or all of these favors, the police can overlook complaints against the fence or not pursue their enquiries should their investigations lead to him, or they can warn the fence of impending investigations or of the danger of purchasing certain goods.

Payoffs To Court Officials

Infrequent police investigation is the fence's first line of defense against legal interruption of his business. If strategies of avoiding arrest and police investigation fail, however, the fence must turn his efforts toward exploitation of the criminal justice system. For one thing, he may enjoy, as a result of personal contact, favors owed, or payoffs, the complicity of one or more of the main actors of the justice system: the prosecutor (or one of his assistants), the district magistrates or lower court judges, and the trial court judges. Less directly, the fence may rely on the services of a skilled or well-connected attorney to manage his dealings with the prosecutor or the judiciary.

Sam has no special connections with any of the local trial court judges (except possibly through his lawyer), but he can expect some slack from the local prosecutor's office as well as protection from several of the local magistrates. The actions of these lower court judges seldom receive any scrutiny from the press or the citizenry, and they are responsible for the initial processing of all criminal charges.[20]

▶ Of the seven magistrates in American City, there were always a couple that could be paid off. I got hooked up with them through Louie and that was a big help, especially with the state police. See, after you get popped, before it can even go to trial, there's a hearing in the magistrate's court. The magistrate can throw it out for lack of evidence or because of some screw up by the police, a technicality.

This is funny, but when I was into burglary, I would always let my lawyer handle it. I knew he was paying somebody off, but didn't know who. It turns out, once or twice, he paid off the magistrate. So

---

20. District magistrates in East State have broad powers. In criminal cases, the first stop during an arrest is before a magistrate who officially records the charges and sets bail. The first court appearance of any suspect—from shoplifter to burglar to murderer—also comes before a district magistrate who, during a preliminary hearing, weighs the evidence to decide if a trial should occur. He then may pass the case on to a judge in Trial Court. As such, the lower-court judge or magistrate serves as a crucial gatekeeper for criminal cases.

now a couple of times I was able to do this, too, and this saved me a lot of money. Helluva lot cheaper than paying the lawyer.

It helped, too, that the D.A.'s office wasn't pushing hard. See, all this time the district attorney is someone that Angelo or maybe Louie helped put in office. It wasn't that I was paying them off, nothing like that, but like Mike Cummings and Sylvester Abbott hung with the same crowd I did, and they would never push too hard. ◄

Access To Good Lawyer

Being able to avail oneself of a good lawyer is a final safeguard for the fence, and one which frequently dovetails with one or more of the defenses already described. It is usually the case in places like American City: (a) that among the many lawyers who at least occasionally practice criminal law, only a handful qualify as "good lawyers"—skillful, well-connected, or both; (b) that these good lawyers tend to be selective in the clients they serve, so that they are more likely to vigorously defend that small and more professional segment of the criminal population.

▶ For many years, the main lawyers were Walter Gleason, Lenny Savelas, and Stanley Cohen. Gleason and Savelas worked it both ways; they had the connections to pay off but they were good lawyers in the courtroom, too. Cohen was mainly paying off. He was connected something fierce, and he would take very few people as his clients.[21]

---

21. Jesse comments: "To get Cohen you had to have some kind of connection, some personal link-up 'cause he wouldn't take on just anybody. Mine came from Harvey, a safeman who pulled a lot of jobs on tips from some of your very big people, like the main Italians and Jews. Sam's connection with Cohen came from me." An up and coming criminal lawyer in American City adds: "Someone like Cohen can do that [defend a few select clients] but a lawyer like myself has to take on clients as they come, to keep the cash flow going. But you pull out all the stops only certain cases. Say Steelbeams gets busted, I have a few favors that are owed me. I would use whatever weight I have at that time."

This same lawyer has this to say about the ethics of "fixing" cases: "Sure, it's illegal for a lawyer to offer a cop, a DA or a judge a kickback or a payoff. A bribe is illegal. But if it's the right client and you think he'll take your offer, you do what you have to, to get your client off. Any lawyer who says different is lying through his fucking teeth. But most lawyers can't work the system this way. And there's very few that really know what's happening. That information is kept in a pretty tight circle. Lenny [Savelas] and I go drinking once in awhile, Friday afternoons usually. Few too many beers, Lenny's tongue loosens up because he trusts me now. Remember the old saying, "the facts are better than the fiction?" Come have a beer sometime with me and Lenny, you'll find out how true that is." But another lawyer in American City disagrees: "You sometimes hear about this or that case being tossed out, so-and-so getting off. I'm sure it does happen but not like you suspect. A lawyer has to look beyond the case before him, that when this case is over, he still wants to practice law. So the risk is too great [to offer or make a payoff]."

The way a lawyer gets his connections is through someone like Angelo or Louie or maybe by helping a judge or a prosecutor get elected. There are a lot of little ways a judge and a lawyer can scratch each other's back. And usually the connections stay in the same law firm—like Gleason and Savelas got their connections from Cohen, when he took them in as junior partners.

I pretty much always dealt with Stanley Cohen. This came from my burglary days. He would tell me, "It will cost you so much." He wasn't cheap but it would be taken care of. There wasn't much that Cohen couldn't get you out of. He could pay off all the way to the top.

Don't forget, now. I would never leave it entirely up to the lawyer. Say the state cops have a thief that is going to testify against me, are making him promises, I am going to be working on that: lean on the guy or have someone else lean on him. Do whatever needs to be done. ◄

In sum, Sam has, or at least feels he has, a "license to operate," a license that is linked into the larger network of mutual favors, corruption, and exploitation that prevails in American City. This network has managed to perpetuate itself through relationships of interdependence and support, as well as through a sort of collective eagerness to cover up improper or illegal operations. Moreover, Sam's immunity and that of other network members is enhanced by the inclusion of prominent local representatives of the police, the judiciary, and other law enforcement agencies. Therefore, any real attempt at vigorous law enforcement against specific individuals or specific kinds of criminal enterprise (e.g., gambling) would have multiple negative effects for the authorities as well.

► American City is a fucking corrupt town, probably more than most. But every city will have its share. Different ones will have a license to operate—say, in gambling, in the fencing, or in the higher-up drug dealing. It would be very hard to get rid of the corruption. 'Cause too many people are involved and it's hard to pull back once someone is involved. He will like the extra bread, and now he has skeletons in his closet, too. It's like a spiderweb really, the way it is joined together. There's something in it for everybody. ◄

So far, the focus has been on the legal and economic obstacles that confront the world-be dealer in stolen goods. The *tour de force* of how well he copes with the social and economic realities of running a fencing business is examined in the next chapter.

Chapter 8

Making Contacts

"The hardest thing is getting the connections, 'cause you have to have the contacts with all different kinds of people."

The Network

The network map in figure 8.1 depicts the varied individuals that are linked to Sam's trade in stolen goods.[1] The map reveals not only the organizational side of a fencing business but also suggests something about the importance of the fence's reputation and the need for contacts in maintaining his career. As characterizes the underworld more generally, Sam's contacts derive from mutually beneficial exchanges with persons who trust each other and whose skills and resources are mutually supportive. Especially when these exchanges develop into relatively stable arrangements or partnerships, they also depend on the compatibility of the individuals involved. Typically, the trust and the connection is based on a pre-existing tie or develops through the mediation of a third party who introduces the participants and vouches for their reliability.

Sam's network is a comparatively fluid and negotiable set of relations or working associations that are subject to considerable vacillation, even termination, as the varying parties attempt to come to terms with their lives and the relative payoffs they associate with one another. Thus the process of making contacts is never complete but is ongoing. Sam makes contacts by "word of mouth," by existing contacts introducing him to others, and by his own active recruiting.

---

1. The writings that were especially helpful in preparing this chapter include: Granovetter,1974; Adler and Adler,1983; White,1970; Albini,1971; Blau,1960; Hall,1972; Ianni,1974; Kanter,1977; McIntosh,1975; Moore,1977; Prus and Sharper,1977; Prus and Irini,1980; Katz,1962; Dubin,1976; Shover,1972; Steffensmeier,1983; Sutherland,1937; Weick,1976; Zuckerman,1977; Whyte,1955; Fisher, et al.,1977.

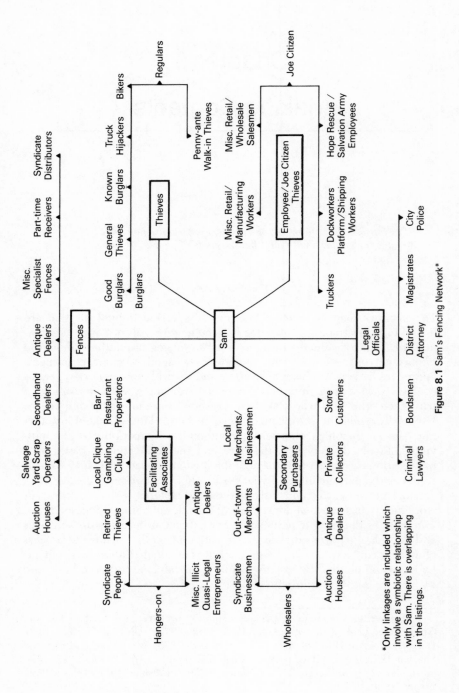

Figure 8.1 Sam's Fencing Network*

*Only linkages are included which involve a symbiotic relationship with Sam. There is overlapping in the listings.

Word of Mouth

▶ Word of mouth, from one trucker to another, one guy to his buddies, was a bigger source than anything. Word of mouth is your best advertisement. ◀

In contrast to the legitimate businessman, the dealer in stolen goods cannot advertise publicly but must rely on informal channels of communication to locate prospective partners with whom to buy, sell, or trade illicit goods. "Word of mouth" is far from being a monolithic process, however. There is not one but several grapevines by which particular thieves, drivers, and businessmen find out about fences like Sam. The information carried in these grapevines is a mixture of rumor and fact, of knowing and surmising, with some grapevines providing more reliable information than others. Access to these grapevines also varies—the "street grapevine" is accessible to almost anyone acquainted with the criminal community, whereas other grapevines may interface with it but are more narrowly confined to individuals in specialized locations. The latter grapevines tend to be almost personalized gossip channels that are linked both to specific cliques of offenders and to particular kinds of criminal enterprise.

▶ There's a helluva grapevine out there—well, really, what you have is different grapevines. Say, you are a greenie in town and want to find a fence—so you hit on a doper or an alkie and pay him twenty bucks to tell you who the fences are. You may find a fence but more likely you will be throwing away twenty dollars 'cause most of your good fences will not be known, not really known anyway, by the dopers. Now the dopers will hear about this or that fence but chances are they don't know what the fuck he buys or how he operates. Must you be recommended by someone before he will deal with you? Is he buying now or has he closed up shop until the heat dies down?[2]

See the doper and the penny ante thief has the street grapevine and it ain't for shit—and what if the doper fingers you to the police. The good thief would never rely on it. Even many of your in-between burglars won't pay it no mind. They will have their own grapevine, say, that's just between burglars. Myself, I knew shit about the street talk when I was into burglary. My grapevine was with other burglars and with the higher-ups, like with Louie and Angelo. It's the same with your businessman, he ain't gonna use the street talk to find a fence—unless he's desperate as hell. The "word of mouth" that brings him to me will be very different from the one the dopers and the walk-in thieves use.

---

2. Mickey points out: "Yeh, you sometimes hear on the street of people buying —but you have to be part of a pretty tight circle to really know. Who the good fences are and if they will buy, you ain't gonna get that information off the street. You will have to know somebody to get connected with them."

With the fencing, now, I did tune into the street grapevine 'cause it has an all-around bullshit that can be helpful or that I would want to check out. The big thing is to sort out the bullshit from the real shit, cause half of the street talk is bullshit, even more. ◄

Third Party Referral: "Being Recommended"

Another path bringing Sam and prospective buyers and sellers together occurs when a thief, a truck driver, a businessman, or another dealer refers or recommends someone to Sam. Unlike "word of mouth" through the underworld grapevine, third party referral is less diffuse and the information more reliable. More established offenders and those not associated with the underworld, such as many businessmen and employee thieves, usually link up with Sam on this basis. Sometimes the grapevine and third party referral work in tandem: for example, when an established burglar hears through the gravevine that Sam is buying stolen goods, checks it out with a trusted associate, and then contacts Sam. Or the burglar may have a fellow thief recommend him to Sam before initiating contact. Establishing contacts by way of referral or recommendation tends to be more an outgrowth of friendship networks and business or work associations than is true of the street grapevine which derives more from peer relations or involvement in specific criminal subcultures.

► One thief can recommend you to another, one dealer to somebody else. This will especially happen with your businessman, and your truck driver or dockworker, 'cause chances are they ain't gonna have a grapevine. Not the ones the thieves have anyway. It can come out different ways. Maybe two, three businessmen are having coffee and the one tells the others, "I hear Goodman can get hold of TVs and will unload them cheap." See, then, the other ones will perk up, their minds will click and they can check it out theirselves. The other way is, say, it's a businessman I'm already doing business with or I know—he tells his buddy, "Hey, go see Goodman, he'll give you a good deal on TVs. Tell him I sent you." Or, he tells the other one, "I'll give Goodman a call and tell him you're gonna stop by."

It's best when somebody is recommended. The way both sides is not so leery, will have more confidence in each other because they know the other person. ◄

Third party referral, moreover, is more than a one-way process of thieves and buyers being sent to Sam by an intermediary. Over the years Sam has come to know a variety of individuals or "contact-men" from different walks of life whose assistance he solicits, usually on an impromptu basis and usually for the purpose of finding an outlet for stolen merchandise he has recently purchased or is considering purchasing.

► This happened one time. Couple of bikers, motorcycle guys came to me, if I'd buy motorcycles. They were going to steal them from a rival gang. So I checks this guy I know who works on motorcycles. He said, "Yeh, I know this guy [in another state] who'd be interested. I used to work for him." So, that's where I unloaded the bikes. Another time, this same guy put me in touch with a place that would buy riding lawn mowers. See, there are different people you can go to that is your contact for making the contact. Can be almost anybody, just have to treat them right, throw a few dollars their way or whatever. They is more or less a "contact-man," but I can't say if they is called that or not.[3] ◄

Sponsorship

Closely allied with being recommended, and overlapping with it, is sponsorship. Sam has been "blessed" over the years with a number of sponsors who vouched for him and made connections on his behalf. In return, Sam may give the sponsor a kickback or share of the profits; more likely, however, Sam is expected to reciprocate in kind, to return the favor. The significance of sponsorship is especially strong in Sam's case, since he was an outsider both to the local underworld and to the local business community when he first arrived in American City. By comparison to the established criminal entrepreneurs in the city, he could not rely on childhood friendships nor on kinship nor on ties with the local syndicate as a source of contacts.

► One person can go to bat for you, pave the way—recommend you and put you in touch with someone else. Especially when it's something big, like needing a place to unload. I was blessed that way 'cause a lot of my contacts with different dealers and even some of your businessmen came that way. Like Louie put me in touch with the magistrates and with a couple of dealers, and with some thieves, too. Woody paved the way for me in Southstate—showed me around, introduced me to others. Took me by the hand, you might say. Same with Charlie 'cause he would line me up with different restaurant people in town.

When I came to American City I was a "greenie" you might say. I knew a couple of names but that was it. I had to start from scratch. That's a whole lot different than say Phil or Louie, see, 'cause they got connections going back to when they was even kids. And both of 'em is tied up, too. That's a very big help on account it's natural a lotta connections will come your way. Take Louie, his old man was pretty big in the Mafia. Right away, Louie is gonna have a lot of con-

---

3. Agent Bogart comments: "Almost anybody can be a contact-man, but we found some lawyers to be, maybe more than anybody. The lawyer will know an auction man or a jeweler or a dealer or a wholesaler in some other state. He will make the contact for the fence; sometimes even for the thief, if it's a decent thief and there's enough money in it."

nections. The other thing is, Louie knew everybody. Some guys in
the police were old buddies from schooldays. Him and Cummings,
the one D.A. were thick from way back. Same with some of the businessmen; they would go way back to when Louie or, say, his old man
were kids.[4]

Just being Italian helps in this town, too. Like Ciletti, he doesn't
have ties but he's Italian and there will be a lot of openings for him
because of that. Your Italians stick together 'cause there's a certain
trust there.[5] ◄

Differences between word of mouth, third party referral, and sponsorship are a matter of degree and in practice may shade one into another.
The emphasis in word of mouth is on the process whereby a would-be
thief or buyer hears that Sam is dealing in stolen goods and seeks him out.
In referral, someone already linked to Sam sends him an associate, perhaps as a favor to Sam but more likely as a favor to the associate. Sponsorship involves third party recommendation, too, but usually the sponsoring individual has a stronger tie to Sam and acts in his behalf on a sustained and more diversified basis.

► Charlie, Woody, Louie, and them were doing this for me 'cause we
were pals—that was part of it—but, see, I'm lining their pockets in
other ways. The favors go both ways. They ain't gonna do nothing for
nothing, same as me. ◄

What each of these paths to Sam has in common is that his role in making contacts is relatively passive; he is more acted upon than acting. In
point of fact, of course, the process of developing and sustaining connections is a two-way street: if Sam is "worked on" by his environment, he
also "works" his environment—by encouraging and soliciting referrals
and sponsorships, and by personally hustling and recruiting thieves, buyers, and others.

---

4. Jesse comments: "I believe a lot of Sam's contacts came from Louie, like for
getting rid of a truckload. I never fucked with the cocksucker but Louie did have a
lotta connections, I will give him that. The man did have a reputation which to
this day I will never understand why. In jail that time on the antique job, you'd
hear guys talk: 'Louie's *the* Mafia. Don't fuck with Louie, he'll break some bones.'
He was a help to Sam, but, holy fuck, you would not have to go through him
'cause there are ones around here that were fucking bigger than Louie. Sam
knows this, too. He fucked with Louie a lot less when he got in with Angelo and
them."

5. When asked whether it helps to have "Mafia ties," Jesse responds: "Holy
fuck, yes. 'Cause then you know the right people, right away! Have the cops, the
lawyers, right down the line 'cause you're trusted and people know you got the
bread. And that you can get rough, don't forget that. Can break up a few heads.
But if you got to work your way up, it's fucking hard."

Recruitment

▶ Word of mouth and being recommended are your main advertisement. But you have to help it along, put out the word yourself. ◀

Sam's recruiting of prospective buyers or sellers sometimes begins as a
spinoff of what are largely accidental or fortuitous encounters. At other
times, he explicitly seeks prospective trade partners, for example, by
checking out someone he knows or suspects is a little shady, or by going
to the "right" places where thieves, drivers, or businessmen are likely to
be found. Sam not only initiates contacts and builds camaraderie with
truckers and businessmen at these places, but is also solicitous and congenial with the proprietor and employees in order to encourage them to
send him their customers.

▶ I would go to places where your truckers hang out, the diners and
truck stops, see their trucks parked and stop myself for breakfast or
lunch. Then I'd rap with them, get in a conversation, let them know
about my shop, that if they ever needed anything or come across
something, they should give me a shot at it. They can read between
the lines. Same with your businessman. I would go to the coffee
shops where they hung out, just to meet them and build a friendly
relation.

Another thing, I always tried to get along with people that ran the
business or worked there, say, at your diners and bars, 'cause they
can send people your way. Now, I would treat them right too—I was
more or less known as a nice guy that way. Maybe I'd buy the house
drinks or if they came to my shop I'd give them a good price on whatever they wanted.

Many times, now, it's unexpected. You can't predict it. You're at
this place and you run into somebody, maybe an old buddy, or somebody you knew somewhere. Or maybe it's somebody you never met
before, but it comes out he's after the easy dollar. I was always on the
lookout for that, say, especially at the auctions 'cause you know the
people there have some larceny in them. One thing leads to another,
especially if they've seen you around before and they can check you
out. ◀

Providing An Opening

Many of Sam's contacts, especially with persons not linked to the theft
subculture, derive from Sam's standard practice of "opening someone
up." This strategy entails knowing when to provide an opening, knowing
when to use hard or soft sell tactics, and being able to instill in the other
person a sense that he can safely trade with Sam.

▶ You have to "open people up," feel them out. Let them read between the lines—what the fuck, you ain't gonna come right out and

say, "Hey, I buy hot stuff." They got to surmise it, pick up on it. Most people will take the extra dollar if they can get away with it. But you got to make it easy for them, set it up so there ain't no hassles. And you got to create a trust, so they will have confidence in you that it's safe or that they got a way out should something go wrong.

With some of your people you got to start them small 'cause they're leery at first. It can be they're scared or they're thinking if they chisel small, it ain't really stealing. So you start them small and once they see the good dollar coming it's hard to turn away. You got to know when to come on strong and when to back off.

Almost anybody I dealt with, legit now, I would hit on one way or another. Say, I bought furniture from a place, legit now. I'd hit on the salesman or the guys doing the loading in the warehouse— maybe bitch about the prices, kid them about how little they get paid, about how the people that run the place make all the money and the little people can't make a living. Joke to them about throwing on an extra piece so they can have a little extra bread and this would help me out, too. What I'm doing is feeling them out, giving them an opening. Same way if a businessman or one of your local store people come into my shop, I am ready to give him an opening if I think a play is there. ◄

Spokes in the Wheel

However they have come about, say, by third party referral or by his own active recruiting, certain of Sam's contacts have played an especially important role in fostering his fencing involvement. A favorite expression of Sam's is "spokes in the wheel"—designating someone who, in a major way, helped him overcome either the economic or the legal obstacles associated with the running of a fencing business. Probably more so than in legitimate occupations, one or a few powerful "spokes" can strongly shape a criminal career.

► It would be hard to name all the spokes but the main ones in the beginning were Jesse, Scottie, and Louie. And Angelo and Phil were right up there. Later on, it was Woody and Tex, and Grasso and One-Eye Moe. A couple of the cops, like the Chief and Lt. Duggan, and Stanley Cohen, my lawyer, were also main spokes 'cause they gave me the slack to operate. I'd have to put Charlie right up there, too. Gave me a lotta contacts with the business people in town. And Charlie was the main one I would go to if I needed quick cash, say, if I was buying heavy and I was short of bread. Cooper was a big boost, too, helped me out with the antique dealers and with the auction people. Another one would be Norman Hirsh, 'cause he could put me in touch with dealers who would handle antiques that were very warm, so warm my regular outlets wouldn't touch them.

Those would be the main ones, but there were lots of little spokes, too. Couple of the local businessmen—Ziggie, Elliot Abrams, and

Winnie Burdette—were good outlets. Same with Vinnie Zabella that ran the big pizza place in town. It would be hard to name them all. The Salvation Army hookup, with Cletus, was a good spoke while it lasted. And some of the thieves were good spokes, too, not so much on account of their bringing me stuff, but 'cause they spread the word or recommended people to me. Like Tommy Bosco and Davey Reilly were truck drivers that sent other drivers to me. Same with Steelbeams and Bowie—they brought me a lotta good stuff and recommended some good burglars my way.

A good contact or two can be very important—what you need is a few spokes in the wheel, to get you rolling. Once the wheel is spinning, if you lose a spoke here or there, there will always be another spoke to replace the one lost. Louie was important first on, and Scottie, too, but later on I didn't need them 'cause I had other ones to fill in the gap. Same with One-Eye or Woody, I would want to keep them on the string 'cause there's no point in losing them, but I could replace them. Take what happened to Frankie Grasso—he has a heart attack and packs it in, so that contact dries up. It didn't hurt me a bit 'cause I had others to pick up the slack. ◄

So far, the description has been on the general processes by which Sam develops the contacts necessary for running a fencing business. Obviously, which of these processes comes into play, and in what ways, will depend on whether Sam is connecting with thieves, with truck drivers, with local merchants or with out-of-town dealers.

Connecting With Thieves

Some thieves discover Sam through word of mouth and the underworld grapevine. Others find him through a third party referral—perhaps from a thief-associate; a dealer the thief is selling to; or, perhaps, the referral comes from a criminal lawyer, a bondsman, a drug dealer, or another illicit entrepreneur. Still other thieves learn about Sam as a result of checking out "suspect" businesses to see if the proprietor will buy suspect goods. And at least a few thieves chance upon Sam—at an auction or at a thieves' bar, where Sam is solicitous and friendly towards them.

How difficult it is for a fence to make contacts with thieves, and which of these paths is typically taken, varies considerably with the type of thief. It is comparatively easy for a fence like Sam to connect with drug addict and walk-in thieves who are strongly tuned into the "street talk" side of the underworld grapevine and who also are frequently in search of a market for their stolen wares. They routinely check out secondhand places and the like as prospective outlets, particularly, if they have heard "on the street" that a generalist fence like Sam is operating. They may do so neither knowing whether he can handle the kinds of merchandise they are peddling nor whether he, in fact, deals with their brand of thief. But should Sam or a dealer like him buy regularly from only a handful of these walk-in thieves, this would be rapidly communicated to similarly-situated thieves.

▶ Danny Turner was a main one for spreading the word to your general thief. He knew a lot of boosters and your half-assed burglars. See, for a long time, I wouldn't buy from the walk in trade. Unless it was something I couldn't pass by. And this was known on the street, the way I operated. But the doper thief and the shoplifters would still keep checking me out 'cause I had a big secondhand place and they would hear I was doing some buying. Same with Danny, I was choosey on what I'd buy. He was going to Louie, to the other secondhand shops, and peddling to his friends. Then, when I started buying more, and different things, Danny put the word out. He's a real bullshitter, knows a lot of people, a real bullshitter. Thinks he's a lady's man but the women he gets are like has beens. He likes to brag. A real talker. Now he was a good shoplifter—he can go out and get the stuff—I will give him that. Different ones would ask Danny, "Where you getting rid of your stuff?" Danny would say, "Goodman's." With someone like Danny and his crowd, it spreads.[6] ◀

In contrast to the kind of street talk and contacts that envelop many drug addict and less established thieves, good thieves, as well as many in-between burglars, view the street grapevine as unreliable and also prefer not to associate, much less be seen with, the dopers and the penny ante thieves.

▶ Your good thieves, and even many of your ordinary burglars, pretty much stay to themselves. Won't hang with the shitass thieves. And your good thief won't advertise where he's selling, except maybe will tell another decent thief or a buddy. So, the word spreads slowly.

The better thief will come to you on the recommendation of another good thief or somebody else they know, maybe like their lawyer. If they hear somebody's buying—say, from the street talk or

---

6. That it is not difficult to build up a clientele of thieves—if one is willing to buy anything and from any type of thief—is borne out by the numerous "sting" operations in which police pose as fences in order to trap thieves (see, also, the discussion of "anti-fencing stings" in appendix). The "success" of the police in these undercover operations is interpreted by Sam as evidence of just how bottom-barrel is the criminal clientele developed in "stings." They nab small-time thieves and hustlers who almost randomly seek a fence who buy their stolen wares. "This is very funny to me, how the police can blow themselves up. 'Cause I've followed this on TV and bullshitted with different ones about this—where the cops will open up a little shop or a business, pretend they're fences to catch thieves. In my eye, the ones they're popping are the dopers, the blacks, the bottom-barrel. The real losers, you might say, who got no place to unload. And listen to this. The cops doing this will buy any damn thing the thief brings in—so what they're doing is sending the assholes back out to steal. The police are using these set ups to make themselves look good, to blow themselves up in the public's eye. What they are doing is blowing the public's money. That is my belief."

maybe from an in-between burglar they know—they'll ask another decent thief: "Hey, what's he paying," "Is he solid?" That, and they'll check it out for theirselves. Like, I knew all the good thieves in the area and they would usually come to me, give me a shot, 'cause they knew me, knew I was solid.

Here's another thing. A lotta times one thief knows another thief from being in prison. He comes in my shop, or calls me at home, and says: "Joe so-and-so told me to give you a call. I've got some good antiques, are you interested?" Your better thief will usually have a number of places he can go, to get rid of his stuff. But sometimes he has to go shopping, too. That's when he's gonna check with his buddies or look for himself.[7] ◀

Some in-between and younger burglars find out about Sam through the street grapevine or through checking out the local secondhand shops, even though the prospective dealer may have problems handling the variety and bulk of the merchandise being peddled. Others may find out about Sam from an established thief they are somewhat friendly with, from another dealer who can't handle the merchandise the burglar is bringing, or perhaps from a bondsman or drug dealer. That Sam himself had been a burglar means that many active burglars have at least heard of him and that they are more likely both to seek him out and to refer other burglars to him.[8]

▶ With the doper and the walk-in thief, once you start buying it goes swoosh. And the better thief, he'll come your way if you're good peo-

---

7. Steelbeams notes: "Someone on the street might say so-and-so is buying hot stuff but most of your thieves don't give two shits for this kind of talk. Bowie's the one that told me to check out Sam. Once Sam knew I was okay with Bowie, he felt comfortable with me and we was set."

Jesse notes that while it is best to be recommended, there are times when even the good thief may have to "shop around": "This one time Sam and me had antiques, were taking them to Scottie in Oceantown. Holy fuck, he's not there. Now this is a three hour trip so we decides to check out a couple of secondhand places. Feel them out. Which we did, and unloaded the stuff and for a decent price. But, holy fuck, this was dumb on our part. Nine times out of ten you are safe doing that. But that is still too much risk. You should always know the man you are selling to."

Another burglar comments: "Unless it's somebody you're pretty tight with, you don't bother with talk about other fences. I was content with the price I was getting from Sam. Why risk going to someone else?"

8. One burglar (nicknamed "Bulldog" because "it looked like a truck ran over his face") explains the involved sequence of how he hooked up with Sam: "I was selling stuff—mostly tools and guns—to a guy in the Warlocks, the motorcycle group. They have the contacts to unload different things. Once in awhile I'd grab like pewter or a porcelain piece 'cause I knew this stuff was worth something. Turns out, this guy couldn't handle it. But he checks with another biker who knows another burglar who knows Sam, from when Sam was into burglary. That's how far back they went."

ple. But your ordinary burglar, especially your younger one, usually don't know much. He may run with just a few other guys or a clique. Unless he's done time, been in jail, he ain't gonna know many people. I more or less kept up with who the burglars were, so that if we came across each other—maybe at an auction 'cause burglars often hang there—I'd come across as a nice guy and let him know what kind of store I had. For a while there, I was stopping at this one tavern where a lot of your burglars hung out. You might say I was putting the word out.

Really, you would be surprised at how little some burglars know about what is going on 'cause they stay to theirselves. Take Rocky—when I first met him, he didn't know nothing about nothing. The only burglars he knew were the ones he was working with and Louie was the only fence they knew. Then Louie sent Rocky to me 'cause he couldn't handle the antiques that Rocky had picked up. Different ones would do that: "Check out Goodman, maybe he'll buy." Unless you got a hook-up, somebody who will bring you together, a burglar like Rocky is a whole lot less likely to come your way.[9] ◄

Employee Thieves

There is overlap in the paths leading criminal and employee thieves to dealers in stolen goods but there are some differences as well. First, employee thieves typically are neither integrated into, nor very aware of, the underworld grapevine; nor are they very familiar with the mechanisms of theft, such as in locating a fence. Second, their stealing is usually an individual rather than a group activity, so they are less likely to spread the word to fellow employees than is the case with full-time thieves. And whatever spreading of the word does take place, is likely to be confined to a small group of peers or fellow workers. As a result, the self-generating effects of word of mouth and third party referral are not as operative among employee as among criminal thieves. Third, the theft activities of employee thieves tend to be sporadic and their theft careers short-lived so that there is rapid turnover among them. Consequently, more so than with full-time thieves, a more sustained recruiting stance is required of the fence if he intends to maintain a steady supply of driver and employee thieves as suppliers of stolen goods.

▶ One guy can tell his buddy or can recommend him if I'm buying off the other one already. Especially with your truck driver, there's a trust that's there between them. Maybe they rap at a truck stop, "Hey, I got a couple of extra refrigerators, know any place I can unload them." "Go see Goodman, I hear he buys."

---

9. Rocky comments: "Louie sent us to Sam 'cause he couldn't handle the antiques we were peddling. Never heard of Sam or any other dealer before that. We stayed to ourselves. Now, as time passed I found out Sam was handling a lot of stuff, that he was the offman for a lot of the burglars."

Another thing, some of your truck drivers and warehouse people are gonna know thieves 'cause these are the kinds of jobs your ex-con and burglar is gonna get. Maybe they know each other from old school days and maybe they hang around in the same taverns because they are both your ordinary working man. If this thief is unloading stuff with me and if he thinks the driver is solid, then the word will spread that way. Maybe the guy isn't even chiseling yet, but his mind is gonna click. "Hey, this guy I'm working with is crawling in windows, and is selling to Goodman." So, next time when the chance is there, he's gonna be more interested 'cause he thinks he can get rid of it.

You got to put the word out yourself, and keep working at it or that trade can dry up. That's why I'd stop at the truck stops, rap with the truckers and let them know what kind of a shop I had. And keep the help and people that worked there on my side, too, so they could send people my way. Like Regina that ran Regina's restaurant, she was pretty hep—if she heard the truckers talking, she'd put a word in for me. Same with this one tavern where a lot of your working men hung out. The owner and the bartender knew me 'cause I would stop by and buy drinks for the house, and the owner's boy did odd jobs for me. You have to make a lot of little things add up, 'cause your hookups with drivers and the warehouse and shipping people come and go.[10]

It's funny all the ways it can happen. One time I'm seeing this woman who worked at a large department store. I picked her up from work a couple of times and through her I got to know a main guy that worked in the shipping department. I started buying used refrigerators, and that—trade-ins, you know. He was giving the stuff to me for a few bucks, rather than throw it away and pocketing the

---

10. Tommy describes how he met Sam: "I was working at the time at Hilary's, the big truck terminal and freight storage place in town. There's this guy that comes in, picks up this or that, bullshits all the time with the help. So I'm helping him load one time. Tells me about his store, I should stop down sometime. So I did on account he was fun to talk to, and to see what he had in his shop. I can't say the exact words but he says to me, if something gets damaged at work or it's unclaimed merchandise, I should give him a shot at it. Hey'd pay me a fair price, be just between him and me. That the motherfuckers don't pay me enough anyway. Always talked about how the motherfuckers fuck the little guy. I remember he was pretty straightup about it. So I started bringing him stuff, like Smith-Corona typewriters, the electric ones and the portable non-electric ones. Maybe twice, three times a month I'd bring him stuff. See, I got to know the guards good, too. I was bringing home a lot of "empty" boxes on account they was turning their heads." Another of Sam's regular drivers comments: "Right after Sam got out of jail [for the antique burglary], he and me was working for this trucking outfit. Boss introduced us, told me to show Sam around. We started hanging together some, 'cause when you work together, you play together. Then Sam quits after a couple of months. Said he was gonna open up a shop again. So I says, 'Then I got a place to drop things off.' He says, 'Solid.' That's all there was to it."

money for himself. Then I moved to better stuff, even new stuff. Once I got my foot in the door and he saw the dollars coming, it got to where he was approaching me. Not just appliances, now, but lamps, chairs, mattresses. Would pull my truck right in 'cause he was covered, could say it was used or damaged. ◀

Maintaining the Patronage of Thieves

While initially attracting thieves and drivers is a somewhat fortuitous process and is partly beyond the control of the would-be fence, maintaining their patronage, once attracted, is a matter the fence can influence considerably. The two processes obviously intertwine in that satisfied thieves are a major advertisement for attracting other thieves. And factors like trust, money, and camaraderie which contribute greatly to recruiting thieves in the first instance are at the core of sustaining their patronage.

As was touched on earlier, there are a number of attractions which encourage thieves to keep doing business with Sam, especially in comparison with some of his competitors. First, Sam pays a reasonably decent price for stolen merchandise, at least in the thief's eye. Second, Sam usually has the upfront cash to pay immediately for what is offered to him, or is able to raise the money quickly if he does not have it.[11] Third, Sam is a reliable outlet and is able to handle just above whatever the thief has to sell. Being a ready market for the thief's stolen wares not only inclines the thief to avoid the risk of "shopping around" but also fosters in him feelings of loyalty and reciprocity.[12] Fourth, Sam's store is conveniently located and is also a kind of social sanctuary for a number of thieves, providing a familiar and relatively secure setting for killing time. Sam is an amusing fellow and interesting things happen at his store.

▶ A lot of your burglars don't work. If they do work, they want a job that won't tie them down, or a part-time job. I'd be in back working, they'd come back, bullshit, horse around. Say, somebody got a new

---

11. A small secondhand dealer tells this story about the importance of upfront cash: "I had this driver coming by, from out of town, that was selling me stuff, very cheap. Mess of stuff, brings it in a van. Lotta, lotta radios. Sam's in my shop, says "Where you getting all these fucking radios?" I made up a story, was afraid I'd get hooked out of the deal if Sam found out. Maybe he'd show up when the guy's in my shop, get the guy to check his store out, cut me out. One time the guy comes, wants to sell a whole van packed full of stuff for like $1500. Mostly radios but half-dozen portable TVs too. But I didn't have the money. I couldn't do it, could only buy a couple of pieces. Never heard from him again, except this happens: I'm at Sam's and the guy comes in. He's selling to Sam, would you believe. I guess he got discouraged I didn't have the money to buy that much, so he goes down the road."

12. Mickey notes: "Once I was hooked up with Sam, 99% of the time I sold to him. Only if it was shitass stuff, I would try to peddle at the other secondhand places 'cause I knew Sam wouldn't wanna be bothered. Otherwise, no need to go elsewhere. I was satisfied with the way old man Goodman treated me."

motorcycle, they would want to show it off. Couple a times, even, somebody would bring a girl in from off the street, and the guys would use the back room and all take turns with her. There was always something going on at my store. I don't know how to say it, I guess you want to be where something is happening.[13] ◄

Finally, Sam maintains the patronage of some thieves by offering advice and by perks other than simply buying their stolen goods.

► I didn't finance thieves. Nothing like that. But I'd help them out, say, if they're running a period of bad luck. Here's the thing, even your good thief spends money something fierce—easy come, easy go. Even more so, your ordinary burglar. In case they needed money to case a place, I'd give them three, four hundred dollars. Or, say, a guy has the hots for some broad, needs the money quick. Not just any thief, now, but for some of them—if they were short of cash, I would lay it right out. Then, the next time around I would many times just take off what he owed me. Same way if they needed bail, I would contact Louie or Phil, "Hey, this guy's okay, put up the bail." I was more or less a job sponsor, too, for some of the guys in the county jail. Sign the papers to get them out. Hire them for three days, then I'd tell the parole officer the guy no longer works for me. I can't use the man no more.

Here's another thing: Say, you sold me an antique and I give you $200 for it. Next time you come in, I say, "Hey, that piece you sold me was worth more than I thought. Here's another fifty bucks." You're gonna think I'm a pretty great guy 'cause I don't have to do that. This was something I frequently did, to make the thief think that I was really doing him right. The thief is like anybody else, he more or less thinks he owes it to me to give me a shot at what he has on account of my treating him fair, and just from being his outlet in the past.

With the in-between burglars, I had them almost always in my debt. If not on a money basis, then more or less a feeling of guilt 'cause I would buy their meals and that kind of stuff. I was a helluva nice guy to them. I would always keep them where I was one step on their toes. Nothing big, just little debts.[14] ◄

---

13. Rocky comments: "Sam's store was a stopping off place. Guys stopping by to see what Sam is doing and to bump into other guys. Way to kill some time. Sam liked to talk to people, to have people around. How can I say it—Sam is comical, fucking comical. If you're down in the dumps, he brings you right out of it." Chubbie notes: "This wasn't a regular thing, nothing like that. But already a broad comes in and one thing leads to another. Maybe Sam would say, "Hey, how about an orgy. Put smiles on our faces." She'd end up screwing all the guys. And never one come in that wanted money. I guess they just wanted it."

14. Mickey comments: "Sam would help guys out, if they were down on their luck or had to lay low for awhile. He gave me a "plate" [fifty to a couple hundred dollars in cash] more than once."

That Sam's "bonus practices" are aimed at in-between thieves and younger burglars is because they are more easily swayed by extra services and a friendly atmosphere than at good thieves who are more influenced by profit and safety. And good thieves are harder to monopolize because they have less need for many of the services and other devices that Sam effectively uses to keep particular thieves coming back with merchandise.

That good thieves are strongly concerned about safety also spills over and affects Sam's opportunities to deal with other types of thieves: dealing with one type of thief may lessen, if not eliminate, the chances of doing business with more preferred thieves. Good thieves are apt to be leery or "gun-shy" of fences who deal mainly with "kids, dopers, and asshole thieves."

▶ I preferred dealing with the good burglar. But, see, they have other outlets. And with them, it's more strictly business. "What can you pay?" "Have you got the money?" "Can you be trusted?" You can't get them in your pocket. With the younger guy, say, I could help him out with bail or give the bondsmen a call. But with your good thief, he ain't gonna mess with the bondsmen anyway. His lawyer will handle all that.

You can drive away your better thief if you deal with the kids and the assholes. That hurt Louie 'cause the better thief is leery of that. I think I lost some business, too, with a couple of good burglars when I started buying from the walk-in trade. I could feel they were more gun-shy. Even your ordinary burglar can be funny that way, that you don't just buy from anybody. Your burglar more or less looks down on the shoplifter, the hustler, and the general thief. He don't want to be hanging around with them.[15] ◀

Connecting With Buyers

As with thieves, word of mouth and recommendations by a third party are important paths by which businessmen (e.g., store merchants, wholesalers) find Sam, or he finds them. But more so than with thieves, Sam seeks out and recruits business buyers, although there are occasions when merchants seek out Sam and let him know what they are in the market for. However they develop, the recruitment and the contacts are usually an outgrowth of Sam's legitimate business activities, particularly when the stolen merchandise matches his legitimate product line and when his identity as a general merchandise dealer provides both him and the

---

15. Jesse states: "First on, Sam's store was a social place for the better thieves. They'd stop, just to shoot the shit. Sam was handling some of their stuff—guns, antiques, shit like that. Then more and more Sam is buying from the fucking kids and your lower class thief—cause you fucking better believe there are classes of thieves—so the better thief shied away. Wrong crowd. Know what I mean."

would-be buyer with an "opening," as well as the cover for illicit trade relations.

▶ On the things I was covered on, I would go to different places in town like the furniture and carpet places. See if they had seconds or damaged items. But I'm really feeling them out, too. Letting them know that I handle what they have and can get it for them at a good price. If they bite, then first on I deal with them as if it's strictly legit, but we're both reading between the lines. If it becomes bigger and gets to be regular, then it will be more out in the open, on the table, that it's warm.

It goes the other way, too. Once it got around that I was buying, then some of your store people came in theirselves. See, the businessmen talk among themselves, one guy tells his buddy. And the fact that I was known as a pretty decent guy brought business my way. The two biggest TV and appliance places in town was buying from me. They both came to my store first. Looking around, seeing what I had, small talk and then one thing leads to another. Like Winnie Burdette started buying my TVs that were two, maybe three years old. Eventually I asked, "What do you do with all those fucking TVs?" He said he hustles them to the Puerto Ricans, sells them as new but as demonstrators. Now, it's in the open with Winnie, and he and I did a lot of business together.

My shop was in a good spot, little coffee shops and eating places mixed in with the stores. So your store people go for coffee, maybe stop by just to see what I had in my shop, what was on the shelves today 'cause you would never know what I would have. It was a way of breaking up the day, breaking up the monotony for them.

I got to be buddies with some of them, too, especially once I got in with the gambling clique. Then, I could ask one of them about so-and-so, or if I needed an outlet for something special, they could maybe recommend somebody. Ciletti was a big help here 'cause he knew about everybody. I would ask him, if so-and-so is "up and up." Take like Ziegfeld that handled the truckload of lobsters. Ziggy had a big seafood place in town. I ate there a lot and met him. From what he said I surmised he was out for the extra dollar. So, when I got the call on the lobsters, I checked with Charlie, "What about Ziggy. Will he take 'em, is he okay?" Charlie said he thought it was worth a try. So, I called Ziggy, and he grabbed them just like that. ◀

In the initial stages of a fencing career, it is probably far more difficult to develop contacts with business buyers than with full-time thieves (but not necessarily more difficult than making contacts with drivers and employee thieves). There is less of a grapevine among businessmen and store merchants, and they also tend to be strongly cautious and fearful of discovery. This means that there will be a more intensive "feeling out" process on their part and a more deliberated "opening up" on the part of the fence. However, once a fence like Sam does become widely known and accepted, then, with a little prodding, contacts with business buyers tend to be self-generating. And fewer contacts with business buyers are needed to sustain a fencing trade because a handful of buyers has the potential of disposing of the bulk of property stolen by a large number of thieves. ("A really good contact, a Winnie or a Charlie, can handle a shitfull of what different thieves are bringing.")[16] Lastly, once made, these contacts frequently turn out to be fairly stable, long-lasting arrangements. There is comparatively little turnover as there is in the case of thieves so that, with time, Sam finds it easier to sustain adequate outlets than to maintain a steady supply of thieves.

▶ Until you're known and different ones have confidence in you, it's hard to get your contacts with your businessman and with your store people. This is about the hardest thing there is in being a fence. But once you get it going and get in with the right crowd, once they know they can deal with you without worrying about hassles, then it can go swoosh. You can't get the hot stuff fast enough. ◀

Contacts with Antique Dealers and Auction Houses

Because Sam's fencing trade revolves heavily around antiques and secondhand goods, how he establishes contacts with antique dealers, private collectors, other secondhand dealers and auction houses is especially significant. While almost any thief or part-time criminal receiver can, as some certainly do, sell stolen merchandise at auctions, flea markets, and similar "open trade" settings, to do so regularly and in volume requires contacts with the key individuals associated with these operations. Even more so than with store merchants, these contacts emerge from Sam's legitimate dealership in secondhand goods and are frequently linked to legitimate business exchanges already in existence. There is also a strong snowballing side to developing contacts with antique dealers. Not only is there a grapevine among dealers that is somewhat akin to the grapevine among a subset of thieves, but dealers frequently bump into one another at common meeting places, so that dealers covering a wide geography may know of one another.

▶ Your secondhand people, your antique dealers, and them hang at the same places, run in the same circle. If you stop at one secondhand place, you might bump into other dealers. When I would take stuff to Scottie, many times there were other dealers at his place, just

---

16. Klockars (1974:109) points out: "a dozen different businesses, if chosen properly, can cover almost the full range of merchandise that is ordinarily brought to him [Vincent]. Indeed, five willing contacts—a small retail store (clothing), a drug store (cosmetics), a medium-size contractor (tools, building supplies), a market or restaurant (food, groceries, dishes, liquor, cigarettes), and an auction (almost anything)—in addition to his own store could satisfy the need for markets for the merchandise that ordinarily becomes available to Vincent."

killing time and talking about business. Same thing with the auctions, you will bump into regular antique dealers and their pickers [people who shop around or "scout" for regular dealers], and your secondhand people like myself. You get to know them that way first, then it might develop into something more later on.

That's how I met Woody. He came up one time and said, 'You must have a helluva big shop to be handling all that stuff.' 'Cause sometimes I would damn near buy out the auction myself if it was furniture and antiques. I told him to stop by my shop and he did. Then he told me he could get furniture at a good price and what did I have for him. We was both reading between the lines but we still dealt legit the first couple of times. Then it just came out in the open that we was both handling stuff that was a little shaky.

Another thing, I met a lot of people from working on antiques, doctoring them up. That's how I met Norman Hirsh. He came into my shop to ask me to work on his antiques. We was on friendly terms. Then one time I got my hands on a shitpile of good antique pieces which I couldn't unload; the dealers I had were too leery to buy 'cause the stuff was so hot. That same day I got 'em, in fact, the state police checked my store. So I called Norm, said: 'Hey, I bought some good antique pieces but it turns out they're hotter than hell.' I didn't know if he'd take a shot at them or not. But he did, and that was a main connection cause on the really hot stuff he was a big help. Then, another time I got what turned out to be a Louie XVI cabinet and china set, only a few of its kind in existence. Came my way and I grabbed it. Norm wouldn't touch it this time, but put me in touch with a dealer down south who would. I ran it down to the guy that same day. Now I had another contact who could handle the really warm stuff.

I can't say for anyone else, but for me it was easier to make contacts with the auction people and the antique dealers than with your ordinary business people. The auction people are shadier and they're not as afraid of taking a little risk. They don't ask many questions. They figure, what they don't know won't hurt them. If it was very hot, then I would let them know, tell 'em it's 'pretty warm.' Just so they know, to protect them, so they don't sell it to just anybody, and everybody gets jammed up.

Another thing, almost anyone can peddle this or that piece, little shit you know, at your auction or flea market. Who's gonna know it's stolen, and there won't be any questions asked. But if you're gonna do it regular or if its good pieces, worth a good dollar, then you got to know some of your auction people—the auctioneer, the "ticket" people, and maybe even the guy that runs the auction. They can help you in a whole lot of ways 'cause the police, especially the state police, watch your auctions pretty closely. Just getting to know the people that work there, being friendly with them, buying a guy a cup of coffee, maybe throw a few bucks his way if he does me a favor—goes

a long way. You need them to help you in little ways, look the other
way or give you a break. ◀

Contacts with Fences

As with business buyers and antique dealers, Sam's contacts with other
fences and criminal receivers come about partly through word of mouth,
partly by third party referral, and partly as an outgrowth of legitimate
business links which already exist. But more so than with business buyers, Sam's contacts with fences derive from his "criminal" reputation and
from his associations with the criminal subculture.

▶ The fact that I had been a thief, was a good safeman, that I done
time and never took anybody down with me, that I was hooked up
with the local clique, all this helped with the fences but was not a
main thing with the business people. The reputation does help with
the local store people but with them it counts more how comfortable
they feel with you, how well you can open them up and get them
over their leeriness.

It ain't necessary to have this criminal element, now. Take Woody.
How can I say it? Woody wasn't into crime in the same way as Louie
or me. He really wasn't a crook, you might say. Woody more fell into
the fencing because he and his dad had this big auction and, see,
hooking up with me was a big push there 'cause now he had an outlet
for stolen goods and he could buy more from thieves down there.
Even a big auction like he had, you don't want to run that much
through your own place, too much risk. Woody was a "free spirit"
and if he liked you then he would do favors for you. Woody gave me
the Salvation Army connection, hooked me up with Tex and others
—now that hurt Woody in some ways. See, most of the time, you do
a favor for somebody, you expect one in return. Woody wasn't that
way.

My best fence contacts were mostly ones where we was brought
together by someone else we both knew. But I did find a couple of
very good fences just by checking out my suspicions. That's how I
met Grasso from Glendale. I wasn't getting any business from that
area, so when I heard about this guy who had a big secondhand
place, huge place, in Glendale, my mind clicked. So, one time when
I was in that area, I played my hunch and checked it out. It was
Frankie Grasso, little dirty Italian. I just knew he was dealing, I had
that feeling from what he said when I rapped with him. And there
were a couple of guys there that I would say were burglars. I told
Grasso about my shop, what I handled and he showed me around his
place. In fact, I bought about half a load of stuff right there, legit
now. Then when I was leaving, Grasso told me to keep in touch, that
I should bring a load up to him sometime.

I said that was fine but that in a secondhand business like I run, you never know if what you're selling is shaky or not. "Yeh," he said, "You never know in this business." After that, Grasso and me did a lot of business. ◀

Spider Web: Interlocking Fencing Networks

One of Sam's favorite analogies is to link his fencing trade to a *spider web*. The imagery highlights the interwoven and configurational side of contacts and network development—how contacts build and feed on one another, and how the settings, the people, and the paths linking Sam with others frequently converge. In addition, the spider web analogy illustrates how fence-to-fence linkages criss-cross and intertwine and frequently interlock.

Each fencing network—Sam's, Louie's, Scottie's, One-Eye Moe's—is a separate entity of loosely structured relationships made up of thieves, drivers, buyers, and corrupt officials, but each network is also loosely interconnected both with the underworld more generally and with the networks of other fences. Sam and some of the other fences know and associate with some of the same people; they refer patrons and make connections for one another; they socialize during work hours as well as outside the work setting; and, although there is little in the way of planned collusion, they draw upon each other's resources in their business relations.

▶ A lot of the people I did business with also did business with Louie and Angelo. And we made contacts for each other, knew a lot of the same people. Take the cops and the magistrates—they was working with all three of us. Many of the good thieves, especially the older ones, at one time were selling to Angelo; now they're selling to me. It goes back and forth.[17]

Even the fences away from American City, say, Woody—he knew people up here and I was acquainted with many of his people down in Southstate. Grasso, too, we never rapped about it, but I feel for sure that he was doing business with some of the same dealers in Frankinburg, say that I was. It even came out one time he done business with One-Eye Moe.

This doesn't mean that we're dealing with all the same people. No way. But many times you're connected with one another without even knowing it 'cause this isn't something you talk about. You stay out of each other's business. But bumping into so-and-so or hearing someone's name come up—it turns out that many times fences are

---

17. Agent Bogart notes: "I don't think fences *necessarily* help each other out that much. Vincent knew and traded with different fences but he snitched on some of them too."

working with the same people or with people that know of each other. It's funny how small the world is that way.

With some of the fences we was buddies, you might say. And we helped each other out. If I couldn't handle something I would send the guy to Louie or whatever, and he was sending people to me. Louie and I ran around together, went to Vegas together, had lunch, would see each other every day almost. Same with Woody, when he was in town we had dinner or met at the auction.

Just getting in with a couple of main dealers, like Louie or Scottie can be a big, big help, 'cause they can recommend you to others, put you in touch with so and so, and then the next guy can help you out that way, too. This is very important, especially until you get established yourself, that you are tight with a main dealer or two cause each has his own spider web—not just with other dealers but with thieves and businessmen, too. See, a legit businessman can put you in touch, say, with another businessman he is buddies with—but that's about it. In my eye, being tight with a couple of main dealers is very near a must—that is when the contacts can go swoosh. ◄

The existence of interlocking fencing networks, however, does not mean that there exists powerful combinations of criminal receivers or that they are united in a few large associations. The latter are hardly possible in the conditions under which criminals operate. That is, the high degree of uncertainty that characterizes illicit enterprise, the need for constant mobility that makes difficult the accumulation of stolen property, and that the danger of detection increases with size, all contribute to working units being typically small so that they can respond flexibly to changes as they occur. Also, fences (e.g., Sam) tend to be fiercely individualistic and by temperament disinclined to form lasting associations.

Contacts with Law Enforcers

Sam's contacts with the police and with other legal officials in American City have come about in several ways: through prior associations or friendships; through ongoing business relationships; through association with the local crime-elite; and through the active "grassing" of some members of the police department. While long-term relationships that grow out of earlier friendship and work ties are not restricted to crime circles and are found in legitimate social relationships, they seem particularly potent—because of the trust and loyalty they imply—in more organized kinds of criminal enterprise and in crime networks.

► The first two cops that helped me out were ones I knew before I got into fencing. I knew Paul Daggett from the skating rink when we was kids. He moved to American City and became a cop which itself is hard to believe. The other one was Herschel, Herschel Dokes, a black cop. When I first hit American City we worked together at Bailey's Furniture and got to be pretty good buddies. Then later he was a cop, a detective, too.

Paul and Herschel both helped me in little ways. Nothing big, now. Just let me know what was happening or give me a break if they could. I would treat them right, like with good deals on stuff in my shop, but I wasn't really buying them off. They were both pretty straight cops. We were old buddies more or less. That was the main thing. As long as there wasn't too much heat on, they could give me the benefit of the doubt. You don't need more than that most of the time.[18] ◄

Sam's most important contact among the local police—with the chief, Melvin Pulaski—derives partly from a mutual interest in antiques that emerged initially from Sam's acquaintance with the chief's son, Chip. The "breakthrough" came when Sam began helping the chief add to his gun collection.

▶ I met the chief through Chip, his son, 'cause he was at the auctions a lot. And the chief would be there, too, sometimes. I got to know the son, then I got to rapping with both of them, buy 'em coffee, and that. I advised them on antiques, sold them some stuff cheap—just little shit like that. But this was my breakthrough, 'cause later on it came out that Melvie, the chief, was into guns. See, a lot of your cops, especially your police chief, are big on guns, will have a gun collection. And I could help Melvie out that way 'cause I was getting my hands on some good guns.

In fact, one time his son was linked to a shady gun deal, and I more or less took the heat for it on account of I knew the state police couldn't really touch me on it. Melvie and I were pretty good friends. I had no worries from the Chief.[19] ◄

At about the same time that Sam is connecting with the chief of police, his contact network with the department as a whole is expanded by his entry into the gambling club and by his association with the local crime elite. These involvements enhance Sam's reputation with the police as someone with whom it is safe to do business, and reveal how Sam's connections within the city police (and also with other local officials) are symptomatic of the broader political and legal corruption in the city as a

---

18. Chubbie comments: "As long as I knows Sam, this one colored cop came in a lot. They kidded each other a lot. The colored cop would tell Sam, 'Hey, your name came up at the station.' So Sam always pretty much knew what was going on with the local cops. When he'd leave, Sam would say: 'Hey, buddy, thanks for stopping.' Sam didn't like the colored that well but he did like this one colored cop."

19. Jesse notes: "Sam was in with the Police Chief, Pulaski. Holy fuck, yes. But so were other ones. Maybe not as much as Sam was, but far enough. And Duggan, Jesus Christ, he was so fucking corrupt—ask the state police about Duggan. They can tell you. After his ass for years. Sam coulda walked this last time if he'd turned over Duggan. That's how bad the fucking state police wanted Duggan. Jesus Christ, there is a fucking corrupt cop. But very few of the local cops are clean all that way. Very, very few."

whole. Sam, with time, is linked into an ongoing system in which some individuals, but not others, receive special treatment from local police, prosecutor, and judiciary. These officials not only accept but sometimes solicit "favors" from illicit entrepreneurs if they can do so safely. In some ways, it isn't so much that Sam has corrupted local officials as that he has become part of the group able to corrupt them.

▶ Getting in with the gambling crowd was a big kick in the ass as far as the cops were concerned. It wasn't long before a number of them came into my shop with their hands open. In fact, Lt. Duggan's brother was in the club, a building contractor. I figure he put the word to his brother 'cause Larry, the Lieutenant, was in my shop almost like the next day.

After Duggan, there was more of them. Especially the detectives. They would stop by, maybe just to kill time but also to see what they could get for nothing. I guess they figured if Duggan can do it, why in the hell not me. I feel for a fact, too, that Duggan personally put the word to his buddy, Jerry Lorenzo, who was corrupt as hell and later became captain of the detectives. Lorenzo was always hitting on me. "Hey, Sam, I need such and such [maybe a TV]. Can you help me out?" Lorenzo and Duggan didn't pull no punches, they were pretty blunt about it. A couple of the other ones would kid me: "Hey, what you got for nothing today?" "What you selling cheap?" "My snow tires are old, got any coming in?" Shit like that. I don't know if you'd say I was buying them off. But I knew I had my foot in the door, put it that way. ◀

Furthermore, once begun, many of the same mechanisms that helped to establish police contacts in the first place help maintain them. Thus Sam is continuously currying the favor of individual police officers, and he is careful not to damage their confidence in him by gossiping about their "arrangement" or by bringing it up in their presence. Rather, Sam's interactions with the police are aimed at sustaining the impression that they are not corrupt, that they are not being bought off but are just getting good bargains on merchandise. Also, as in the case of thieves and buyers, Sam's connections with the police are based not only on mutual benefit or profit, but also on mutual trust and responsibility. Nonetheless, damaging information about an officer gives Sam leverage with the corrupted officer and helps to sustain the connection.

▶ Say a cop is looking around my store and I see he's interested in something—I would tell him, "Hey, I won't let it go for nothing but I'm tired of looking at it. I'll take half the price that's listed." This way, too, I'm making it easier for him 'cause I'm not coming right out and saying, "Hey, I want to buy you off." Or say, I was at the Stagecoach and a couple of cops were there, 'cause that was a watering hole for them. I might buy them drinks, pick up their tab, but be discreet—just let the bartender know I'd take care of it. The police appreciated that. ◀

Contacts With Other Officials

Besides his police connections, Sam has access to the top criminal lawyers in town, is "in" with several local magistrates, and is on friendly terms with the local district attorney.

▶ My first contacts with the good lawyers in town came through Jesse when he and I were doing burglaries. This just continued. Your lawyers can handle the payoff for you, or maybe somebody owes them a favor cause they contribute, say, to a judge's or the D.A.'s campaign. But later when the fencing got rolling, I myself was hooked up with the magistrates and a little bit with the district attorney.

My connection with the magistrates came mostly through Louie who would sometimes call and ask if I wanted to go up for a bail hearing. Come along. Really, I was just going along to be sociable. But in the end this hooked me up with the magistrates, too. See, all this time in American City, most of your magistrates would take kickbacks on bail. Raise the bail and then Louie would throw a few bucks their way. As long as the case wasn't too big a stir, and they had some leverage, they would take a payoff.

I wasn't really connected with the prosecutors, not directly anyway. But I knew them, and I hung with some of their people. See, for years Abbott was the D.A. and he was a relation of Angelo. Then, it was Cummings who was Louie's man. I got along with both of them. I always tried to stay on the good side of the D.A., not buying him off or nothing like that, so they wouldn't push so hard if a case came down. But it was never a sure thing, not like with the police or the magistrates, 'cause the prosecutor has always got to worry about the public and the papers.

Another thing, I always tried to get along with Louie, with Angelo, with all the local gang 'cause if the D.A. parts ways with one of them, it's harder for me to do business with the D.A. It's very shaky that way. I never banked on the D.A. to help me out. If I could do him a favor, I would. Not snitch, now, but maybe help get back some property that has been stolen, say, a piece that's been in a family for years. This helped to stay friendly with whoever was in office. ◀

Major Factors Building Sam's Contact Network

It is no easy matter, obviously, to describe the complex of relationships and linkages that comprise Sam's dealership in stolen goods, much less to delineate how these linkages came about. But several factors in the process particularly stand out.

One factor is Sam's prison experience—a "testing ground" where Sam's personal qualities (e.g., trust, heart, loyalty) were recognized and observed by peers, made him more accepted as a member of the criminal community. And the prison experience acted like an "old school tie" bringing Sam and prospective partners together with the assurance that they can rely on certain values and standards of conduct from an earlier shared experience.

▶ In a way my name hit American City before I did. The name carries from jail—people can find out if you're an asshole or not. Then, too, it's amazing how many guys I bumped into, got hooked up with, who I knew from the penitentiary. But the main thing is, your name carries from prison. I was known as a good con, did my time without any hassles. That's why when I first came to American City, my name got there before me. This was added to, when Jesse and I got popped for the antiques. 'Cause after I got out of jail on that, the local gang and them were really coming my way and giving me the openings. See, I didn't take anybody down with me. And the fact that we got off so easy, that with my record I only did fourteen months. Our lawyers did one helluva job, and this really made it known that I was good people, and that I had some connections, too.

Looking back, it is hard to believe the different guys from prison I later hooked up with. My main connections on the docks were guys I knew from jail. Other guys I did time with ended up working in warehouses, in the shipping departments of your large stores. One was Squirrel [a burglar so nicknamed because he was "kind of nutty" and because he was good at climbing onto rooftops or into windows, for example]. Worked the night shift at a big place that made furniture, in the warehouse. I wasn't tight with him in jail but we was friendly. I knew he was a good con. So I just came out and asked him, if he wanted to make an extra buck for himself. Mainly he was getting upholstery material for me. See, upholstery roll is like 54 inches long, has maybe 105 yards on it. Fits right into a car trunk. Roll might cost $1000, like $10 a yard. I'd give him $300. Squirrel made me a lot of money. ◀

A second factor is Sam's stint as a burglar, particularly his partnership with Jesse. He not only connected Sam with specific individuals (e.g., criminal lawyers, several fences) but, in a general sense, quickened Sam's acceptance within the local criminal community as a whole as someone who is solid, skillful, and well-connected.

▶ Jesse was well known and this helped get me in with the bigger people in town. Some of the fences, too, came from the burglary—some were my contacts, some were Jesse's. Selling to them just continued when I started dealing. More than anything though, my contacts with thieves, especially your better thieves, came from my burglary 'cause they all knew me and I knew most of them. ◀

A third factor contributing to Sam's contact network is his acceptance by the local gang and induction into the gambling club. In the sense that a reputation is dependent not only on what one does (or does not do) but also on those with whom one is closely affiliated, "being tight with the right people" can be a powerful mechanism in establishing a reputation.

One can achieve "nodding" acknowledgments fairly easily, but to become "well connected" generally takes considerable time and sponsorship, such as what Sam received from powerful insiders like Louie and Angelo.

▶ One time Louie just asked me, "Hey, you wanna come to our card game." Some nights they play cards, other times it'll be rolling dice. Not anybody could come. It was only if one of the main ones—like Louie or Angelo or Nicky—would bring you. There was about twenty guys that were part of the regular gang. It was like a clique and everybody had his fingers into something, were connected with city hall or with the money downtown. I wouldn't say all the main operators in town were part of the club. Some of the Jews weren't. But they were still connected with the Italians and others that were.

The fencing was starting to roll before Louie invited me in, but it really took off after that. I started doing business with some of them and, the ones I was already doing business with, it got heavier. And they could recommend me to others. If something came my way I couldn't get rid of, or if I needed a hook-up with somebody, I could check with one of the gang. It just made me more known. I feel it helped a whole lot with the magistrates and with some of the police.

Really, most of those in the club were getting police protection one way or another, and I benefited a lot from that. Face it, hooking up with Jesse was a big boost but getting in with the local gang was an even bigger step. They threw a lot of openings my way. And just people knowing I was doing business, say, with Angelo, opened up a lot of doors. ◀

A fifth factor is Sam's legitimate identity both as an antique dealer and as a secondhand merchant, as well as his frequent presence at various auctions. Just as some businesses mask an illicit business better than others, so also and partly because they mask so well, do some businesses more readily bring together illicit trade partners.

▶ A business like mine was good for a cover, but it also helped in making contacts. A lot of people surmise that a place like mine is dealing in warm stuff—not just thieves, now, but your truck drivers, your store people, your ordinary Joe Citizen, and different ones all the way down the line. And with my business I could handle damn near anything—old stuff, new stuff, whatever.[20] ◀

A sixth factor adding to Sam's success at making contacts is a lifestyle which includes few, if any, strong interpersonal ties, but many weak ones.

---

20. Employment in certain kinds of occupations, Jesse claims, facilitates the making of contacts: "Bondsmen, I'd say most of those motherfuckers are mixed up in different things. Many times they are fences 'cause it's easy to get the contacts —not just with thieves, now, but with the magistrates and the fucking cops, too. Same with your lawyer or even a judge, you'd be surprised the shit they are into. Jesus Christ, you should check into that sometime."

Rather, as appears to be generally true of successful entrepreneurs, legitimate or illegitimate, Sam knows many people on a first-name basis and is friendly with many persons, but the relationship is largely centered around his dealership in stolen goods. In contrast to primary group relations, these friendship contacts are casual. And yet they have a degree of permanence to them, and can be activated upon occasion.

Not weighted down by family ties or close friendships, Sam is free to move through different social and criminal work settings and to organize his life around the people and activities in these settings. As Sam moves in ever wider circles and becomes acquainted with people in them, his pool of personal contacts and his awareness of opportunities grows. With time, he builds a network or "spider web" whose complexity is even a bit bewildering to him.

▶ Looking back, it's hard for me to believe all the ones that were involved—how big the spider web got to be, how it came about, how this led to that. ◀

A final factor, perhaps the most important one, contributing to Sam's connections is tied to an apparent need in American City for someone to assume the role of dealer in stolen goods: *there was a vacancy in the position of fence in the city*. That is, fencing is like many legitimate occupations in that an individual's preference for one occupation over another does not by itself determine occupational entry. Whether his choice can be realized, or must be modified, or even set aside, will depend in part on factors which are beyond his control and which may even be unknown to him. The first factor is whether there is a demand for new members in an occupation, that is, whether vacancies exist at that time. The second factor, decisions of selectors, refers to all persons whose actions affect the candidate's chances of obtaining a position. The criteria affecting selection will be those experiences, attitudes, and skills that are seen as matching the requirements of the role.

So too, Sam's rapid rise as a generalist fence in the late sixties occurs not only because he has *chosen* a given career line but because he has been *selected for it*.[21] Indeed, in many ways, Sam simply drifts into fenc-

---

21. A fairly common observation, in this context, is the difficulty a black person would have if he aspires to become a fence. Agent Bogart comments: "We never had any black fences that were really big, not to my knowledge anyway. I can't say why this is so but my gut feeling is the better thieves are mostly white and they won't sell as easily to a black fellow, afraid he'd open up on them, that he'd break. Never knew of a good burglary team that had white and black working together. It is this way all the way down the line—there's a problem between the races. The white businessman would not buy as easily from the black fence. And the black fence would find it hard, very hard, to get the protection of the police. Whatever it is, the black guy isn't likely to be associating with the right kind of people." Jesse adds: "It is hard, period, for the colored person, and many whites, too, to make it big in crime. You don't see many colored going out doing big jobs, getting

ing without ever having made an explicit choice among alternative ways of making a living, although there are a number of crossroads (e.g., the breakup of the burglary partnership with Jesse) at which his life took decisive turns narrowing the range of future alternatives and influencing his ultimate choice.

▶ When I first hit American City, say, in '58, '59, there were two, maybe three, main dealers. It was Weinstein, big Jew dealer. Angelo and his old man, Mario, were operating, and Louie was already getting pretty big. Then Angelo's dad pulled back and Weinstein had a heart attack and packed everything in. Just retired, left town and went to Arizona, 'cause the feds were after him something fierce on account of his being hooked up with the Italians, and his being part of the gambling, prostitution, and the different rackets. That left a gap 'cause Weinstein could handle anything and some of the better burglars were peddling to him. Then later on, Angelo pulled back and that really left a gap which opened up even more when Louie was falling down as a dealer 'cause he had made too many enemies and had fucked over too many people.[22]

See, one place only has room for so many fences. This will depend on the size of the place. But the whole time in American City there was never more than two or three, maybe, four main fences. I'm not talking about nickel-and-dime dealers, now, but ones like an Angelo or a Louie who the thief can count on to buy, and who may even handle a truckload. It would be same, say, if we was talking about priests

---

into bigger things. They may have the guts and that, 'cause many do. But not the know-how and the contacts. They don't think big either but stay in their own vicinity of thought—Jesus Christ, four, five hundred dollars would be a lot to them."

While partly a matter of racial prejudice, this exclusion of blacks from lucrative fencing networks reflects, more broadly, the tendency towards homosocial reproduction in dangerous or high risk activities, as characterizes criminal enterprise. Members of crime networks choose others with whom they feel comfortable, who are predictable and can be trusted, and thus reproduce themselves in kind. This principle of homosocial reproduction or the tendency to exclude "outsiders," helps explain why the criminal world tends to be strongly segregated along lines, say, of kinship, ethnicity, race, and sex (see Steffensmeier, 1983).

22. Jesse comments: "Angelo had the money, and knew the right people, too. He never fucked with nickel and dime shit. If it was good stuff he'd buy. Or he'd buy in quantities, big quantities. He got out 'cause he had his fingers in other things, better things, where there was less worriment, less bullshit to put up with. Face it, if you fuck with the hot stuff, there are many cocksuckers you have to put up with. And you can become very well known, too known. Angelo was getting tied into the gambling, other shit, too, from his old man [Mario] who was a top mafia. Think about it, Jesus Christ, that's a lot more bread than the freaking fencing. A freaking lot more. So why fuck with the fencing? Understand what I'm saying."

and bishops—there are only so many slots for getting to be a bishop. The opening has to be there. ◄

It is one thing, of course, to be initially selected as a dealer in stolen goods, quite another thing to carry out that role ably. Obviously, being selected as a fence is a continuous process, involving a networking of contacts and an ongoing appraisal by prospective associates of Sam's skills and qualifications. What these talents are, is examined in the next chapter.

Chapter 9

Qualifications for Success

Unlike many occupations, criminal or otherwise, dealing in stolen goods is not something that can be managed by just anyone.[1] The successful dealer must possess skills and attributes that will enable him to cope with the economic and legal problems endemic to running a fencing business. As a "middleman," he must be able to sustain and manage relationships with different audiences from both legitimate and illegitimate walks of life, and must have a working knowledge of the theft subculture, the business community, and the society at large.

The fence traverses two worlds, the legitimate and illegitimate, that are not necessarily set off from one another but are distinct with respect to knowledge, skills, and practices. The majority of fences are very much a part of the underworld, although few are wholly submerged in it. The significance of their affinity with the underworld and not only with the realm of seemingly honest business is in terms of the skills and contacts necessary for a dealership in stolen goods. That the fence is not your average businessman does not overlook the greed of many legitimate merchants. After all, one of the major outlets for stolen goods handled by fences is that of legitimate merchants who are willing to buy suspect merchandise if it assures them of a higher profit. But running a fencing business is another matter.

▶ Your ordinary businessman couldn't make it as a fence, same as most of your thieves. Your thieves are streetwise, but they don't know the business side. They couldn't deal with the businessman and with the public. And they wouldn't have the connections. An-

---

1. The authors and works that were especially helpful in preparing both this and chapter 11 (on "rewards of fencing") include: Applebaum, 1984; Hughes, 1958; Letkemann, 1973; Miller, 1981; Peterson and Truzzi, 1972; Polsky, 1969; Prus and Irini, 1980; Prus and Sharper, 1977; Shover, 1972; Sutherland, 1937; Inciardi, 1975; Bryant, 1974; Nosow and Form, 1962; Freidman and Havighurst, 1962; Katz, 1962; Dubin, 1976; Vroom, 1964.

other thing, most of your thieves won't work, and fencing is long hours, can be very hard work.

Even more so, your businessman couldn't hack it. Main thing is, they're not known and it would be very hard for them to get the connections, except maybe with the assholes who will deal with anybody. And that will affect their legit business to have the bums and the riffraff around. The businessman would know the business side, know the prices and that, but he ain't world-wise, doesn't have the street knowledge to deal with the thieves and the cops, and maybe he doesn't really have the larceny in his heart, not enough larceny anyway to really clip and to get over on others. He wouldn't have the heart either, would be too shaky and others wouldn't have confidence in him. The big thing is the connections—who would do business with him? ◄

Success as a dealer in stolen goods requires that the practitioner be a good student of social patterns and arrangements. The fence must be sensitive and informed about what is going on in the world around him. He must be familiar with his business environment, the habits of its people, its usual and unusual processes. He must understand the nature of conventional work roles and business routines in order to exploit them. Furthermore, such exploitation will frequently demand that the fence use or follow work habits strikingly similar to those of the ordinary worker or businessman. It is in the fence's ability to reinterpret commonsense knowledge in ways relevant to his illegal trade that his learning becomes unique. Even this statement must be qualified in recognition of the fact that the civilian, too, by knowing the rules of the game, is somewhat equipped to break and exploit them. It is probably more accurate to say that it is the refining and focusing of this knowledge that make the fence's learning different.

Many businessmen or salesmen may acquire some of these same skills in varying degrees, but the extent and intensity of the learning experiences needed to be a fence are greater than one is otherwise likely to encounter except by way of delinquent or prior hustling experiences. Their value for becoming and being a successful fence are for developing thief orientations or composure, for providing some rudimentary skills, and for providing an early testing of one's suitability as a criminal. The learning of dealing skills and a criminal attitude begins long before a person becomes a dealer.

A jail or prison experience can be helpful, too (albeit, it certainly is not a necessary condition for being a successful fence). That prison is a "school for crime" is probably exaggerated, but prison does provide a setting in which some contacts may be made and some skills learned. A prison experience (or a delinquent experience, too) is useful, maybe even essential, for learning how to evaluate and profitably use the considerable information relevant to criminal activity that is passed along informally by and among criminals. Not being able to sort out "good" from "bad" information can expose one to unknown and unnecessary risks. Also, a prison experience (and the inmate code) reinforces norms operative in both the street and thief subcultures: that the "solid guy" will not "squeal" and will take a "bum rap" rather than incriminate others; and that persons stand up for themselves, grabbing what they can, however they can, settling any differences between themselves without recourse to outside authorities.

▶ You don't become a fence out of the blue. That's my opinion. All the fences I knew had a background that was shady; they had their fingers into different things. Were raised with the hustling or the clipping, you might say. I don't mean they were strictly into crime, at least not all the way. But somehow they got the street knowledge and the eye for the easy dollar.[2]

The biggest things are knowing how to deal with thieves and knowing how to sort out the good information from the bullshit. See, there is a lot of talk, lotta gossip, about the cops and about different things—the fence has to be able to tell what is bullshit and what isn't. Different dealers get that in different ways, but being in prison helped me a lot.

It was a helluva education, all the way along. Not from books, now, 'cause that don't mean shit as far as being a fence. Take in your college, you have majors in business, masters degrees and everything. This would give them a little business knowledge but what the hell else would it do? Fencing is knowing about people, and knowing how to clip and how to see an opening. And the business side of fencing would be hard to learn from the books anyway. Now, say you had the hustling in your background or did time in prison, and then got the masters in business, this could be a good combination. Otherwise, the college don't mean shit. ◀

Learning the ropes of how to deal successfully in stolen goods, moreover, is an ongoing experience. The fence learns by trial and error and by

---

2. Agent Bogart concurs: "Not just Vincent now, but the other fences I knew came from that kind of background, mostly from the Italian or Jewish neighborhoods where there was a heavy dose of hustling, gambling, swindling. If not illegal, on the borderline. Maybe hooked up with the rackets in one way or another. This is how they got their contacts with thieves and other fences, and with the cops, too. And how they got to be streetwise, really. If you look at their backgrounds, the guys from the Polish neighborhoods and that become the burglars, the Jews and the Italians, and the Greeks in recent years, get into the shady business stuff. Now there are some lawyers and that which don't fit this pattern but, see, their contacts come from being a lawyer, from associations with the criminal element that way. That's how they got to be streetwise, too, how they learned the ropes, you might say. Works the same with the bondsman. You got to be shady to get into that in the first place, then you get the contacts and that by handling bail and dealing with the thieves."

innovation, and he also may learn from others both through occasional tutelage and through listening or rapping with other dealers about job problems and remedies. This learning is not confided to the handling of actual transactions, but also involves coming to terms with one's business setting, the police, and one's colleagues.

▶ I got my education from doing it, from the dealing itself. And from watching and listening, like at the auctions and from being around Louie and Angelo. Here's the thing: most dealers in an area will know one another, will bump into each other here and there. It's only natural that you will rap about things. You don't say, "Hey, teach me about fencing." Many times you won't even acknowledge that the other one's a dealer. But things will come up in conversation, and you can watch how he handles himself. ◀

The specific talents and qualifications described next are prerequisites for becoming a successful fence, although some dealers may be able to compensate in one area for what they lack in another.

Larceny Sense

Consistent with the general thief orientation, the fence must have, or develop, what criminologists label as "larceny sense"—the ability to perceive and capitalize on less than legitimate activity.[3] Larceny sense is an indefinite body of appreciations favorable to theft and fraud that is partly attitude and partly acquired knowledge. To have larceny sense means, first, that one has "larceny in his heart," which implies an orientation unconstrained by conventional beliefs in what ought to be done or what one is supposed to do. In the hustling or business context in which fencing takes place, the dealer is expected to capitalize on every opportunity to make money.

▶ You have to be a little shady to be a fence 'cause really you are a thief. You're stealing, although you don't call it that. It's a must that the fence have larceny in his heart, 'cause you have to be looking for the angles, be aware of them, cash in on them when they come your way. Be willing to clip or get over on somebody, not worry if it's crooked or not. ◀

A second and more subtle aspect of larceny sense is that one be observant and sensitive to circumstances and opportunities for illicit gain, and know when to take advantage of them or to desist.

---

3. Steelbeams notes: "Thieves don't use that expression [larceny sense] but will say: "A guy has to have a good eye, know what to pick up on, what to pick out, and what not to pick out. A good eye for a score, for information that will help out in pulling a job."

▶ You have to be able to see the openings. And know, too, when to pick your spots. See, my mind would just click that so and so would buy hot stuff or that I needed to do such and such to cover my back. It's the same as the con man, the burglar, or the guy in the Mafia. The fence has to read his environment with an eye towards clipping.

There are lots of little things you need to know, that you pick up here and there. That's where my being a burglar helped, 'cause you have a different outlook, a way of seeing an opening or just a feeling to be leery. I really can't explain it. It's not this or that thing, but where you (or another straight person) are seeing or hearing one thing, I am seeing something else.

Take this one time: I am at this auction, rapping with another antique dealer, and he mentions that old man Frazier, who is a big antique dealer, is having his place remodeled. Just like that, my mind clicks; this would be a good time to knock it off. Then I passed that information on to Steelbeams, and he hit the place. It's knowing little things about the police, too, the way they operate. Like the time I came back from Southfield with the guns, right before I got popped. I just had the feeling I was being tailed, so I skidooed. Found out later, there was a tail.

It becomes like second nature, without even thinking, 'cause you're not really aware of it. It wasn't that I was always looking, but my mind would just click. It's more than just seeing an opening, now. It's knowing when to back away, let the opening pass by, not get too greedy or careless. ◀

Larceny sense has its basis in common sense interpretations of society, so that the average citizen also has the ability, say, to detect when police surveillance is greatest in a neighborhood, or to pose as an "unaware" customer when buying stolen goods. It is the more specific socialization, such as that which occurs in early hustling experiences or in association with other criminals, that forges in the fence a complex series of visual clues not readily observed by the layman or the average businessman. Fences like Sam may be ignorant or unmindful of many social conventions but they are criminally sensitive to subtle social expectations and routines (as has been periodically illustrated in this book).

Street Smarts

Dovetailing with larceny sense, the fence must be "streetwise," meaning he knows the underlife of society: what's going on in it or how to find out; knows when to keep silent about other people; knows who the snitches are; knows what to say or not to say to the police; and it means having the angles and not being easily duped by thieves and others who are both prone to, and skillful at "ripping you off." Furthermore, being streetwise is not static. It is an ever-changing and ongoing process.

▶ The fence has to be streetwise. That is a must. Has to know where the thieves are coming from, and the cops, too. I would always try to stay on top of things, know what is going down, 'cause things can change very quickly and get very hairy. I knew just about everything that happened in American City from my contacts with Louie and the local gang and from knowing the thieves. The thieves are the most important 'cause they're on the front line. They know who's solid, who the cops are after, who's clipping, who's lying low or who just got popped. ◀

Business Skills and Knowledge

The fence must possess at least rudimentary knowledge of business practices and conventions, such as those utilized by the small businessman: knowledge about the product that is traded, its pricing, and its marketing, all of which can generally be acquired by simple trial and error. Some knowledge of technical regulations, practices, and procedures is also required, as well as sufficient capability at money management to keep on hand enough upfront cash to purchase stolen goods in an unpredictable market.

▶ Learning the prices and knowing about the different kinds of merchandise is hard at first, especially with the antiques and because of all the stuff I handled. But once you have a good general knowledge it is pretty easy. This goes way back: even when I was a kid I was following the prices of things. Going to the auctions helped a lot 'cause they handle damn near anything. For antiques and that, I always kept up-to-date books on what different pieces were worth. I always got along with the secondhand dealers and with different businessmen, too, so if I needed to know the price on something I could check it out. A dealer like myself, you need to know at least a little about many things. I know ballpark prices on almost anything. Not an expert, now, but general knowledge.[4]

What the fence needs to know on the strictly business side is not that much. In some ways it is less than in the legit business 'cause the fence doesn't worry about paying business tax and that, doesn't have to figure it in his profit margin. Other things can be simpler, too, like handling and shipping costs are less of a factor in most of the stuff you

---

4. Jesse comments: "Sam has a good business head, I will give him that. Just about anything you ask him about, he can pretty well figure what it's worth. His mind works well that way. Not for keeping books now, 'cause he couldn't be bothered with that. But knowing what a piece is worth, what he could sell it for, fucking sharp that way. Another thing, he kept his store nice, always very particular with that, so the people enjoyed coming in. Is a good salesman, can sell stuff. The cocksucker could sell ice to Eskimos. No shit. To this day, if he wants to go strictly legit, he can make a very good living. Without a doubt. But he's not happy unless he's pulling something, that he's doing somebody in."

fence. This will depend on what the fence is handling. Like antiques can be hairy on account of all the reproductions and 'cause the prices can change so quickly. Otherwise, the business side of fencing is no big thing. It's knowing how to cover your back and deal with the thieves and them, that is hairy.

The business knowledge I feel I had. Where I fell down was not always having the cash in hand. That's where Angelo and Louie, or the foundry guy, had the edge. I never saved my money like I should of, that I will admit.[5] ◀

Particular dealerships will require particular kinds of business knowledge, a fact which helps explain why the dealer in stolen jewelry is likely to be a jeweler or the dealer in stolen cars, an automobile dealer. The fence who deals exclusively in one type of product can be expected to have considerable product intimacy, while the generalist fence like Sam must be broadly informed about many products and their prices, and needs to enlist the aid of specialists from time to time. Additionally, some products require more sophisticated knowledge than others, not only with respect to their quality and marketing but also with respect to their care and handling. In Sam's case, for example, the antique side of his trade was especially "hairy" not only because of the uncertainty surrounding the pricing and marketing of antiques but also because it required some expertise in their handling and upkeep. Consequently, in Sam's line of trade, the fence must not only possess business acumen but be a good craftsman as well.

▶ Here is something you wouldn't think about, but a fence has to know how to take care of what he buys. If I bought an antique, say, I had an advantage. Because I knew how to take care of it. Many times I could doctor up an antique and double my money, which another fence couldn't do 'cause he doesn't know about antiques. It's the same way with other things—appliances, TVs—if they get damaged, you can't send the warm stuff back to the manufacturer. For a

---

5. Chubbie comments: "I seen Sam spend every dime in his pocket. Then he'd turn people away [thieves, truckers, etc.], unless they'd give him time to get the money. He didn't really have the type of money where he could hold onto something until he got a good price. Had to turn it over quickly to keep up his cash flow. Whereas Louis was full of money. Could sit on something for a year, and wait until he got his price."

Rocky disagrees somewhat with Chubbie: "Sam didn't have the cash in the bank like Louie but the better burglars would give Sam time to come up with the money. Because Sam had places to go, like to Ciletti or to Woody. So not having the cash right there wasn't that big a deal."

Jesse states: "To do the fencing right, you need a lotta bread, not just in your pocket but in the bank, too. That way, you don't have to take unnecessary risks to keep the money coming in. And can pay off if it comes down to that. Sam was not saving enough to be big, a really big fence. He never accumulates a lot of money. Makes it and blows it."

fence like me, it was very important to be good at fixing things, to doctor them up, or whatever. ◀

Worldly Wisdom

In Sam's view the knowledge most required of the fence is that he be "world-wise"—meaning that he has been around in a general and far-reaching way. To be world-wise complements and extends the fence's business sensibility and street knowledge described above. A kind of all-around knowledge which blends together the suppositions of the theft subculture, the business community, and the society at large, "world-wiseness" is not something that can be learned from books but must be experienced, must be lived.

▶ More than anything else the fence needs to be world-wise, on account of he's dealing with so many different people. You have to know where different ones are coming from, what they're thinking, what their angle is. Otherwise, you can't get over on them, and you can't get the contacts you need. From having been a thief, from doing time, just being around different people was a good education. See, you can't learn it from books. You have to be there yourself. It's knowing how to handle yourself in different crowds, in different situations, with different kinds of people. ◀

Because the fence trades in a shifting and complex environment and because he interacts with the full range of peoples, from thieves to businessmen and from the police to the public, being world-wise is the bedrock of the fence's capacity to exploit his environment and to effectively gauge the feelings and perspectives of others for purposes of manipulating them.

Ability To Con

The successful dealer in stolen goods must be able to hustle and to gain the confidence of others regardless of whether he is dealing with a thief, a businessman, another dealer, the police, or the public. Akin to any confidence or con game, fencing requires finished acting ability, versatility, keen insights into human behavior, judgment, and sense of timing, all skills which are not easily acquired. The fence must take on the role of the "other" and be capable of fitting in and, thus, take full advantage of the situation, whether his purpose is sharp trading with a thief, playing on the greed of a would-be customer, or making contacts.

Hustling—attempting to realize one's own interests at the expense of others, such as by talking people out of their money—is a very diversified phenomenon, one not limited to the underworld but very pervasive in our society as a whole. Within a criminal context, the fence's hustling resembles that of the con man or the racketeer rather than the "no holds barred" approach of the street hustler. Fencing is far too reciprocal an activity for participants to abandon norms of fair play, largely nonexistent in street hustling. The hustling a fence does also takes place within a business context and involves "sharp business practices," that may be carried out by merchants and salesmen who use various ploys to break down sales resistance, to advertise a product, or to receive favors from the powers-that-be.

▶ To me, hustling is when you try to get over on somebody, to make a buck or to have them help you out in one way or another, like to give you information or make a contact for you. It doesn't mean you're "beating" them 'cause many times there's something in it for them too. See, that's where the street hustler is different 'cause he will beat anybody and will do anything to make a buck, really lower himself if he has to. The fence doesn't hustle like that, but he has to be on his toes not to get outhustled by the street types.[6]

The hustling a fence does is really like that of a businessman. Being shrewd and advertising your business. Play on the greed of the person looking for a bargain, who wants something for nothing. A good conman. Being a shyster, really. The difference is the businessman has the law on his side, the fence don't. So the fence has to watch much more so he don't get ripped off 'cause who is he going to complain to.

When it comes right down to it, a legit business can have more hustling than the fencing. As far as just the buying and the selling, I did more hustling with the legit secondhand side, except that with the fencing you're pulling the strings more to keep up your contacts, and make new ones. It's more like what Angelo or somebody in the rackets does, 'cause they hustle that way, too. ◀

---

6. Jesse comments: "A good hustler is one who really gets out there and makes a buck. I don't mean the street hustling, the ghetto shit. Sam was a hustler but a conman hustler. All the shit he's pulled on people, yet they don't stay mad at him. He's still a friend. Now, holy fuck, how many people do you know can get away with that?

Sam was a good con man. More than anything else, that's what he was. He is a hard man to figure out sometimes. Like, I trust him as far as some things. As good friends as him and me were, as tight as we were—now I'd never have to worry about him ratting on me if he gets pulled in—if he could steal five grand from me, con it off me, you could bet your fucking ass he would. You always hadda be one step ahead of him. He'd rob his mother, just to be doing somebody in. That's the only way he's happy in life. But you can't get mad at him. I know he pulls some shit even on me. I just let it go."

Agent Bogart notes: "Vincent was a con man, a swindler. That's what he was. He would take somebody over the coals, all the time they're thinking he's dealing straight with them. Vincent could be anything to anybody, could come up with a story just like that. And if the guy found out that story was bullshit, Vincent had another one just as good. Even with some of the better burglars and hijackers, what he could convince them of is hard to believe."

Ingenuity

In the lexicon of the fencing literature, the real genius of the fence lies in his *ingenuity*—meaning that he has the ability to actively exploit his environment, to create and control his opportunities.[7] To have bought and sold stolen merchandise when the opportunity presented itself is one thing. To become a successful fence, however, one cannot rely on chance opportunities alone. It is as true of illegal life chances as it is of legal ones, that people not only discover or act upon opportunities, they also *make* them.

The fence's ingenuity builds on his larceny sense and springs from his intimacy with the suppositions of the underworld, the conventions of his business environment, and the discretionary workings of the law. His ingenuity is a combination of cleverness and cunning, and is an ongoing creation of the dishonest possibilities of the fence's environment. If he is to be successful, the would-be fence must make it so. He must make his buying and selling of stolen property appear to be no different from what others in his environment normally and legally do; he must hold his own and not be outhustled by thieves and other trade partners; and he must make the contacts and gain the confidence of lawbreakers, law enforcers, and all others on whom his success as a dealer ultimately depends.

In the language of legitimate society, the fence represents, in its strongest form, what is meant by the term entrepreneur or "capitalist"—someone who, in the pursuit of profit, takes the initiative in order to manipulate other persons and resources. In Sam's vocabulary:

▶ The fence is really a schemer, an operator. There is hustling, but it's more wheelin' and dealin' with the fencing. A lot of scheming. The fence has to take the openings that come his way, but even more so, he has to make his own openings.

I was always trying to be one step ahead. Say, I was at the auction, I might buy some junky TVs, furniture, or whatever, just so I'd have the receipts and have my back covered in case those things came my way. The fence has to make the adjustment if something comes up, but the big thing is to keep one step ahead. Covering your back, setting up a deal, whatever, you're always thinking of down the road. ◀

---

7. In reference to Jonathan Wild, for example, Pike writes: "Genius may display itself in crime as well as in science, or art, or strategy; and there arose, in the first quarter of the eighteenth century, a great leader and a great organizer in the commonwealth of criminals . . . Johathan Wild. Like many a better man who has risen to eminence, he had the discrimination to perceive the great want of his age." [Pike, 1876:225] Later on the historian, Gerald Howson, who has written the definitive history of Wild's life, expands on Pike's sketch: "Wild had no sensitivity, probably little creative imagination and, morally, he was an oaf. But he did have an abundance of what the eighteenth century called 'Genius'—that is, ingenuity, cunning, resource, energy and that mysterious power we sometimes call 'personal magnetism'" [Howson, 1971:286]

Hardworking and Energetic

To be ingenius and, more broadly, to manage both the routine affairs and the happenstance goings-on of his business, the fence must be hardworking and energetic. In a kind of free-floating fashion, dealers like Sam find that something always seems to be happening, that one thing or another needs to be checked out or tended to. The flow of stolen goods, for example, is irregular and unpredictable: shoplifters and the walk-in thieves peddle their stolen wares from noon to late afternoon, truck drivers stop by in the early morning hours, and burglars may call late at night or in the wee morning hours. In many respects, the fence is like the physician—always on call.

> ▶ It can be hard work, very hard. I didn't sleep much. Getting calls two, three o'clock in the morning from this or that thief, "Hey, I got such and such, can you handle it?" Then shipping the stuff out, running to the auctions, having to be at the store. I was always on the go. And you got to be on your toes constantly, to deal with the cops, with your thieves, and different ones.
>
> In my eye, the fence is a go-getter, more so than most people. He has to have a lot of ambition, 'cause you have to put in long hours, and you have to know your limits, too.[8] ◀

Charisma

From the time of Jonathan Wild to the present, the fence has been characterized as having uncommon persuasive skills and even mysterious powers which attract others to him and predispose them to his cunning and resourcefulness. In the more romantic sketches, the fence is described as having the fullest attribution of presence, personal magnetism, and even charisma.[9]

Sam says the fence must have "personality"—an elusive attribute to which he attaches two subtly different meanings. First, by "personality," Sam means social skills and talking ability: the fence must be affable and able to get along with people; he must be able to change roles with ease, to move from one subculture to another; and he must be able to mix with a variety of people, to fit in and role play in appropriate ways in differing situations. More than anything else, perhaps, the fence makes his living by talking.

---

8. Jesse comments: "Sam could work his ass off. Doesn't need much sleep. Even to this day, as old as he is getting, he doesn't sleep much." Rocky notes: "Anytime of day or night, he'd meet us. Which is very nice to have, from the burglar's eye now, that you can unload when you need to and at the right time."

9. "A bold heart, a thundering voice, and a steady countenace," Henry Fielding numbers among Wild's "more transcendental qualities." Dickens describes Fagin as a "crafty jew," with apparently mysterious powers over youth.

▶ In my eye the fence has to have a lot of personality. This is his trademark, you might say, 'cause you have to mix with so many different
people and relate to them at their level. The people have to like you,
find you interesting and have confidence in you, too.

The personality side was a very big thing for me, that I could talk
to anyone, mix in any crowd. And I have a knack for remembering
names and faces, and little tidbit things about someone. I don't know
what you would call it, but I always had the gift of gab, not just in
bullshitting my way around but in getting others to reveal themselves to me, to give me an opening that I could maybe use later
on.[10]

A lot of people stopped in my store just to talk, to see what was
going on. If someone wanted to talk sports, I talked sports. If it's
women, I'd talk women. My shop was like a "Dear Abby" column, a
soap opera. You wouldn't believe the stuff that came up. You'd hear
everything in my shop. ◀

Second, in a broader sense, by "personality" Sam means "how a man
carries himself"—a kind of all-around display of a man's character, wits,
and style. This, in part, is determined by how well he has responded to
certain tests, (e.g., arrest, incarceration). But it also refers to the air that
one manifests of being in control of himself and the situation, of having
the poise and experience to think quickly and to act in a self-assured way,
of having leadership qualities.

▶ A big thing is how you carry yourself. Is the man an asshole or not.
Is the man honest or not? Will he hold up his end of the deal. This is
one part of it. The other part is being on top of things, that you know
what is going down and can take care of it. Even if I wasn't sure of

---

10. Chubbie comments: "Sam would kid people a lot, and build them up, too.
Had a knack for names and faces, and could keep in his mind a little something
about a person." Rocky states: "Sam liked to talk to people, to have people around.
How can I say it—Sam can sense peoples' moods, and he is comical. If you're
down in the dumps, he brings you right out of it." Jesse notes: "Sam is easy to
shoot the shit with. Very easy. You meet him, just like that you feel very comfortable with him. He is fun to nutsy around with, to have a conversation with.
Really, his store was a social place, too much so because of all the fucking kids that
would hang there. They looked up to Sam, thought he was more than he was.
Which Sam ate up. He would try to impress them."

A state trooper adds this evaluation of Sam, and also of Louie: "Crooked as Sam
was, he was likable as hell. We'd joke back and forth. He'd ask about my kids.
Maybe talk about crimes you'd read about in the papers. Shit like that. Same with
Louie—he was cocky sometimes, especially in public, but he was an interesting
guy. You'd stop at their places, either one, end up spending the afternoon. They
were enjoyable to talk to."

Agent Bogart comments: "Vincent was a *friendly* businessman, same as the
other fences I knew. They have likable personalities. It was hard not to like Vincent. He was entertaining, put it that way."

myself, I would always let the thieves and them think I was. I would
not show a weakness that way.[11]

And not letting it go to your head; not become a big shot and come
across as better than you are. I was always very careful that way, not
to badmouth someone or look down on them. Here's the thing. Say
you bad mouth one thief to another thief, behind his back. You do
that, you got to figure the guy is thinking, "Hey, if he talks about this
guy this way, what the hell does he say to others about me." I was always very careful not to run somebody down that way.[12] ◄

In the world in which he operates, Sam possesses an attractive and win-
ning personality, not in the sense of being refined but of being "rough on
the edges." Sam is a man's man, so to speak. His casual manner, the easy
equality, and self-mocking humor combine with a kind of energy and
moxie which thieves, police, and others find appealing. Thieves in particular put great stock in how a man carries himself; in whether or not he is
loyal and manly.

► This is funny, but a lot of different ones, some businessmen and especially your thieves, felt they were friends of mine. I wanted them
to think that, but no way was that true 'cause, when it came down to
it, I wanted nothing to do with them. I was always very sociable to
someone's face, but I really am a loner. I might say so-and-so is my
buddy or my friend, but deep down I have few friends. I enjoy rapping with people, but in my own way I'm a very private person.[13] ◄

---

11. Steelbeams expresses a common viewpoint of thieves: "You watch the way
people carry themselves—do they carry themselves right or not. You watch how
the people walk, or the way they act. Or the way people dress, the way they speak
to you. You can see if they know anything or not, if they think they are something
which they ain't."

12. Rocky notes: "Sam didn't run people down. But he would tell us to watch
out for this or that thief, which was an asshole, no damn good. Louie, too, he
warned us about, that he'd cut your throat to save his own ass. In a way this kept
us coming back to Sam, but it was the truth, too, 'cause Louie could be a dirty bastard." Another burglar commented: "Never heard Sam badmouth anybody, except a doper or a snitch. He hated snitches."

13. Rocky states: "Didn't matter who it was, Sam would make the person feel
welcome. Won't put them down but would be interested in them. So a lotta guys
were thinking they were buddies of Sam. Of the younger ones now—not thinking
here of Jesse or Louie—I was probably the closet to Sam. He and me was pretty
tight. He more or less took me under his wing, you might say." But Mickey notes:
"Once I was 'in' with 'Pops' [a nickname some of the younger thieves and hangers-on attached to Sam], we got to be pretty close. Didn't pal around and that, but
he was different towards me than he was to the other guys [including Rocky] that
hung at his shop." And Tommy adds: "I'd stop by Sam's store, and the young set
were there, I'd make an excuse to go. I came to see Sam, not listen to the other
bullshit. Sam would walk me out, says to me: 'Come back in the morning, come
on Sunday afternoon—the big mouths aren't around then.' I think he musta got
awfully tired of different ones being around."

Fence Must Have "Heart"

Besides the interactional and psychic skills described so far, the fence must demonstrate that he has "solidness" and "heart." "Heart" is a set of traits, a combination of courage and coolness, of tenacity and self-assurance. To have heart is to be a good money player, able to perform at one's best when the action is heavy, the stakes high, and the risks great.

▶ It takes a lot of "heart" to be a fence, a lot of heart. What I mean is you have to be a nervy son-of-a-bitch, not scare easy, not fall apart when there's a search warrant on your shop or when the police pull you in for questioning.

It's the same in dealing with the thieves and the other dealers— you got to be tough in a lot of little ways, or they'll take you to the cleaners. Really, the fence has to put up or shut up, be able to stand up in different situations. He can't be a pussyfoot—you do it or you don't, and if you don't, you can kiss it good-bye.[14] ◀

Heart not only implies a kind of mental toughness but also the ability to "get rough," should the need arise. With often enormous temptation and fragile relationships, "honor among thieves" can disintegrate rapidly; in this context, some "muscle"—the use of force or its threat—is essential for coping with threats from other criminals, for enforcing contracts, and for managing associates. Sam's reputation as someone who could get "very rough," and as a man with important contacts lessens the likelihood of trouble and deters some potential informants and would-be predators.

▶ This one morning I'm at Bill Toscano's and the night before a couple of thieves he'd been buying from broke into his shop. Robbed him. They know who they can pull that shit on. Same with snitching, you can't stop all of it, no way, but you can make them think twice.[15]

---

14. Jesse comments: "Very brazen, is how I'd describe Sam. He don't scare easy—it don't matter a fuck if it's the cops or whoever. And the cocksucker can lie through his fucking teeth. Just in general he can do that but with the cops he can fucking make himself believe what he's saying."

15. Jesse notes: "Sam was known, what the hell, that he could be a son of a bitch. I seen him screw up a couple of guys pretty bad, know what I mean. On the surface you wouldn't know it, but, holy fuck, he could get very violent. Can handle himself, don't kid yourself." Rocky comments: "Sam could get a little crazy, if he was crossed the wrong way. Ask the colored guy, Dozier, about that. To tell the truth, I think Louie was afraid of Sam. Somewhere along the line, Louie knew he couldn't buffalo Sam." Steelbeams notes: "Sam had a reputation as an all-around guy, a good fellow. Easy-going, really. If you treated him right, he'd treat you right. But if you gave him some shit, he wouldn't hesitate to deliver a load of shit for you. Was no doubt about that." Mickey adds: "Myself and other guys would get hauled in by the state cops, 'Hey, give us Sam, give us Louie, we'll let you go.' Shit like that. I wouldn't do it 'cause I'm not cut out to be a snitch. Let's face it: the other thing is, you're looking down the road, that they'd lean pretty hard on you."

I was pretty easygoing, but it was well-known I could be very nasty, if I had to. Couple of times I've handled things myself, right in the store. Another time, with Lemont Dozier, Angelo's two boys gave me a hand. This is the time I got jammed up 'cause Lemont lied to me about where he had stolen the stuff and the woman spots her TV in my store window. Lemont got more than just a kick in the balls, now. Even the cops didn't have to worry about Lemont stealing for awhile. I feel this helped to get the word out, too, 'cause I really had very few hassles with thieves.[16]

I would say it would be very hard to be a fence, say, like me or Louie, and not have that side of you, roughness or whatever. That you can lean on someone if it comes down to that. Not that you use it very much, but that they know where you can come from, that you can do it yourself or you got the backup to do it for you. Take Louie, he was a very big man, very powerful, and he had "ties," which itself scared a lot of people. You'd be surprised—even the police would think twice before messing with someone like Louie.

There were just a few times I had to get rough. I was more known for being a nice guy. But you can't be a pushover either. That little suspicion that you can lean on someone helps with your thief and even with your businessman. All the way down the line, really, 'cause there are quite a few assholes out there.[17] ◄

The criminal subculture, like the larger society, relies first and foremost on relationships of trust and reliability (as well as on money and friendship). But it is also the case that violence or its threat is a critical part of the fence's world (as it is of the underworld more generally), an indispensable resource for inspiring respect among one's associates. The

---

16. Rocky notes: "Sure, a thief will steal from a fence, especially one he's not selling to. Why not? Who in the fuck can the fence complain to? This will depend on who the fence is now—you wouldn't wanna steal from somebody like Angelo, that could lead to a lotta headaches. Most guys ain't gonna steal from the fence they're doing business with, makes no sense. You don't want to upset the thing you have going, and many times there's a trust there between you. But half-assed thieves and dopers would steal from their own offman, they're dumb enough to do that."

Agent Bogart comments: "The narcotic thief, in particular, the fence would have to worry about, same as any other shop owner, because if he needs a fix he is gonna steal from whomever he can. But take the good burglar, if he knows someone like Vincent has money or something of value in his store and he can get at it easily, he isn't going to be stopped by knowing the victim is a fence."

17. Agent Bogart notes: "Vincent played the image of a tough guy, played the gangster type, that he had Mafia ties. With the black thieves and the narcotic thief especially, he'd threaten them, talk tough you know, that if they fucked with him, he'd have them blown away. That's his way of talking, not mine. Physically Vincent was not a powerful man, nothing like that, but if he had to he could have someone worked over or dumped in the river. Either way, he put on a good bluff."

enforcement of economic arrangements between criminals is not, of course, subject to civil law, but rather to informal norms and unofficial "policing." In a sense, the underworld relies on violence to enforce promises as conventional society relies on the courts to enforce its contracts —as a last resort.

That fences need to have "muscle" does not mean they need to be "toughs" or heavies. Indeed, within the criminal community, persons thought too reliant on physical force for doing business or resolving difficulties tend to be distrusted. While it is fairly common in the underworld to hear persons expressing threats to injure or kill others who have violated their notions of fair play, these threats are carried out infrequently. A more likely response is that of slandering or blackballing the offender and encouraging others to avoid dealings with him.

Fence Must Be "Solid"

A "solid" person is capable of taking care of himself and is one upon whom others can place considerable confidence; under pressure, he is reliable, dependable, and trustworthy. "He keeps his word," has personal integrity, and seldom contributes to another's trouble with the law. "Snitching" is the most visible violation of this norm.

For those with whom the fence does business, reliability is highly valued in terms of expediting ongoing transactions; those with whom the fence deals must be confident that he is able to deliver, that appointments will be kept and agreements honored. Even greater value is placed on trust. Some degree of trust is generated by the shared recognition that "we're all doing things we're not supposed to," but concerns over whether the fence is solid are maximized when trouble arises with victims or with the police. These concerns are greatest among established thieves and among experienced buyers and dealers.

In Sam's view, his reputation for being "solid" was a prime reason for his rise and eventual success as a dealer in stolen goods. Thieves, other dealers, businessmen, and even the police were more likely to do business with Sam, because they trusted him. Sam not only takes personal pride in this recognition but cultivates it.

▶ The big thing for me was I was trusted, my word was good. Once the goods were in my hands, the thieves and them didn't have to worry about it. It was my worry, and if something happened, I wouldn't take anybody down with me. If I said I'd pay so much, or set it at this price, they knew my word was good. It was known that I would handle my end of the deal, be there at such a time, do this or do that. They knew they could depend on me. All the way down the line, I was trusted. But the main thing was the thieves trusted me. You have to have that. ◀

That Sam's career as a dealer in stolen goods is strongly anchored in a "solid" reputation, does not mean that fences as a whole are paragons of integrity. Some fences compromise the police and gain immunity from the law by informing on thieves or by assisting the authorities in other ways, and some fences set up other dealers as a way of eliminating or sabotaging competition. Nonetheless, even though it is sometimes violated, the rule of not informing is generally respected, if for no other reason than that general compliance with the code of "honor among thieves" is essential for sustaining an illegal business.

This also means that those fences who do inform, usually do so *selectively*. They may quickly inform on the "riffraff," the garden-variety thieves and hustlers who lack status within the criminal community. But they probably would not inform on a business buyer, nor on a good thief or another established criminal unless they were under very strong pressure to do otherwise. In this regard, the fence evades the rule against informing that is at least partly accepted in the underworld: that "creeps and assholes" are less deserving of protection from the police.[18]

▶ The rule is you should never snitch, cause trouble for someone with the cops. But it makes a difference who the guy is. Say, it's a doper who is snitching on everybody, or say it's a baby rapist—very few eyebrows will be raised if the police are given wind of that.

There are fences who are snitches now, like Louie, but he was careful who he snitched on. Louie never took anybody down that was important, that could hurt him. Louie was very solid that way. See, a thief might overlook it if Louie just turns in shitass thieves, figuring Louie wouldn't snitch on him. But the suspicion is still there.[19] ◀

---

18. Agent Bogart doubts whether any fences are really "very solid":

"The fences I knew I wouldn't trust that far. That's why I object to your definition of fence—as *reliable* market for stolen property. Now I know what you mean by reliable there, but in other ways the fence is anything but reliable. He's a swindler, a conniver, will pull the wool over somebody's eye if he has the chance, and will stab you in the back to protect himself. Would you trust Vincent? Would you say he was *reliable*? He was a snitch, and everybody knew he was a snitch. We'd ask the tailgaters, 'If you know he's a snitch, why do you go to him?' It was always the same answer: 'Cause he's got the cash. You don't have to wait for the money.'

But this is something I hadn't thought about, what you write here: Vincent never snitched on his outlets. To my knowledge, he never did. As far as that he was very trustworthy. I know he has snitched on other fences, to have the cops slow the guy down or knock him out of business. Not another big fence, now. Vincent was smart enough not to mess around with the real big boys. The common thief, in particular, the blacks and the narcotic thief, Vincent was a snitch all the way. With the hijacker or the better burglar, Vincent would snitch if it came down to that but he would cover his tracks a lot more carefully because some of these guys can crack on you pretty hard."

19. Steelbeams states: "Louie wasn't a big snitch, nothing like that. But enough of a snitch that you were leery, so you're more likely to shy away from him. Sam, you could trust all the way. Sam's problem was he didn't have the money like Louie or, say, somebody like Angelo would have. So you might have to wait for Sam to come up with the cash, which was okay for some guys but maybe not okay

Fences probably violate the rule against informing more frequently than do good thieves and some other underworld types, but less frequently than many criminals. Also, fences apparently are more trustworthy and much less likely to squeal than the average citizen or the legitimate businessman who finds himself under pressure from the police. Two factors enter into the fence's reluctance to act as an informant. One is the detrimental consequences that could result: loss of prestige, loss of business, or possible reprisals. Of these, the loss of business due to the reluctance of thieves to deal with a suspect "offman" would be the most severe consequence. The other factor is the loyalty and identification that many fences have with the criminal community, growing out of the common experiences that they typically share with thieves and other underworld members.

▶ Some of the fences I dealt with, if they got jammed up, I would be leery they couldn't stand up. I wouldn't trust them all the way. But, in general, most of them were pretty solid. Like Angelo and Scottie, I would trust all the way.

I would rather trust a good thief than a fence. A lot of your decent thieves are more trustworthy than many of your fences. But not your penny ante and your walk-in thief, no way. The same with your businessman; if they got jammed up I wouldn't trust them, not at all. They would break down or they'd be saying things that would get you and themselves in trouble without even knowing it.

This can happen, too. You can get fucked over pretty good for the snitching shit 'cause some of your thieves can get pretty rough. That's what happened to Duckie Moore, Angelo's cousin, a couple of guys he ratted on busted him up, and good. Ribs, jaw—Duckie got his due. Then, a couple of years later Duckie got jammed up for gambling and he got worked over by guys in jail who he had snitched on.

Myself, for me to snitch, it would be hard to shave in the morning, to look at myself in the mirror. But the plain fact, too, is you look

---

for others. Louie would try to screw you more on prices, would hold out on paying the price you agreed on if you gave him the goods first, which sometimes the thief has to do. Sam was better that way but he would finagle, too. Don't let him bullshit you there. But Louie would be more likely to fuck you than Sam." Rocky notes: "Louie would dime [snitch] but mostly on black guys who were really dummies. They wouldn't figure out in a million years who fingered them. I take that back—a couple of them did cause Louie got stabbed by two colored guys at Highpoint Prison, two guys that Louie had snitched on. Face it though, that's a big reason Louie stayed out of jail so long—twenty, thirty years he operated—by snitching." Mickey adds: "It was known on the street Louie was a snitch, not all the way now, but if the police squeezed him. Some thieves still went to him 'cause he always had the cash, especially after the Vietnam War when the drugs got big. Now the better thieves were shying away from Louie, wouldn't bother with him on account of the snitching, even though Louie was trustworthy with them. They would go to Sam or they had their private buyers."

down the road, you can't be snitching all the time and stay in business. If the word gets out you're that kind of a snitch, you can't make the connections. Even a little snitching will hurt you with the better thief, with the better class of people.[20] ◄

The notion of being solid also entails honesty in living up to agreements, paying one's debts, and, in general, not ripping off one's associates. This does not preclude, however, considerable finagling and "getting over" on the part of the fence—after all, trading in stolen goods takes place within both an underworld and a business setting where hustling and sharp trading are taken for granted. Honesty here also means honesty in dealings within one's own group. Sam's integrity did not prevent him from cheating on or stealing from citizens or businessmen. (To do otherwise, not to take advantage of certain opportunities is to be a sucker.)

► It was known that my word was good, but that doesn't mean I didn't clip some of the people I dealt with. That has nothing to do with being solid. See, it depends on who you are clipping. Take Hirsch, he and his mother were very big antique dealers and importers. I did a lot of business with them, legit and illegit. But I did arrange for a burglary of their shop which was a very large haul, and I was clipping them at the docks, like on the grandfather clocks. The way this happened is, I'm in their shop, talking to Norm. And I asked where Sarah was, his mother. "Oh, she's in Europe this month buying more of those grandfather clocks, and other items." So, my mind clicked, that I'd have the guys I knew that worked on the docks watch for her crates to come in. Break them, and clip a few. Off-and-on, then, when Sarah made a trip, I'd post the guys at the docks.

Now, if it was someone like Angelo or Ciletti or Grasso, I wouldn't clip them that way. You don't do it to your own kind. Know what I mean? But otherwise, yes, I would take what is being handed to me and many times handed on a silver platter. ◄

---

20. Jesse comments that Sam is trustworthy but is too trusting of others:
"You could trust him in any shape or form. But he was careless, he trusts too many people. And that sometimes gets in the way of his being trusted, know what I mean. That's his biggest mistake in his whole life. If it wouldn't be for that, he could still be operating in the city. You mark my words, even to this day, some guy will come up, somebody he really doesn't know that well, will come up and say, 'Hey, Sam, I got a load of shit,' he'll buy. Or, 'I know a spot.' He'll go. You can bet on it.

But there are very few people you can really trust. Know what I mean? Very god damn few. But there were some fences you could lay your faith in. The foundry guy, Angelo, a few others. Some others, no. Louie? Jesus Christ, no. Rosen, the jeweler guy? I'd trust his old man, 'cause me and Sam peddled jewelry to him, but not the kid. Fuck no. This depends, too, on how protected the guy is. Is he gonna get jammed up? Take this lawyer, holy fuck, he is so protected, there is really no worriment on anybody's part. And he does things right. It's a whole lot easier to trust someone like that."

Well-Connected

The talents and qualifications discussed up to this point are the wellspring of the fence's ability to be well-connected, the *sine qua non* of a successful trade in stolen goods. In the sense that success breeds more success, there is, as well, a self-building side to having connections, in that knowing the right people and having a reputation for having connections itself leads to the making of even more contacts.

▶ A fence has to have the contacts — that is the biggest thing. I came a very long way. Where Louie or Angelo already have contacts from having ties, I had to start from scratch. Once I got a few spokes in the wheel, got the spider web going, that was all I needed. ◀

Taken together, a mix of interactional, social, perceptual, and organizational talents are needed to survive and to succeed as a dealer in stolen goods.[21] Some fences must also possess technical or craftsman-like skills pertinent to their particular trade. The fullest complement of these skills, obviously, is not required of every fence, and some talents may be required more of some dealerships than others, and the fullest complement of the qualifications described above may not be required of every fence. The successful dealer in jewelry, for example, must be able to do different things than the successful dealer in securities, automobiles, or furs. On the other hand, the specialist fence who only deals in stolen goods which match his legitimate trade does not have to do the vast number of things required of the generalist dealer.

▶ It isn't easy to be a fence, not by a long shot. This will depend on the kind of dealer one is — what he needs to know, how much he has to be on his toes in different ways. In my eye, any fence has to be world-wise, has to have the heart and be trusted by those he's dealing with. That and he has to make his own openings, be a good schemer, which can only come about if he's world-wise and has the heart. The street knowledge and the eye for the easy dollar must be there. He has to have the confidence in himself, that he can get over on others, and other ones have to have the confidence in him. To have the personality is a must, that he can mix with different people and gain their confidence. ◀

In sum, the talents required of the fence are partly the stock in trade of seasoned criminals, and also of successful businessmen and salespersons.

---

21. Klockars (1974: 77) offers this assessment of the talents and attributes of the modern day fence. "Ability, energy, ingenuity, and certain persuasive skills are absolute prerequisites . . . sociological forces alone are simply not strong enough to carry someone without such talents into the role. To be sure, talents are plastic attributes subject to growth and development in the course of a career, but the distinctive feature of becoming a professional fence that makes certain talents prerequisite is that errors of judgment, lack of effort, or failed persuasion, especially early on in one's career, can end it."

Some of the skills are at least partly common to all members of society, but they are systematized, sharpened, and refined by the "dealer" who consciously uses them. It is the combination of skills, and the degree to which they are finely honed, that makes up the fence's "working personality" and is his distinctive stock in trade.

The fence's talents are subject to growth and development, so that increasing mastery improves performance, produces higher earnings, and draws the practitioner to fencing as a way of life. Fencing becomes a more attractive and enjoyable activity as the rewards become more possible or likely, and the costs more easily managed.

What these rewards are, is better addressed after first detailing Sam's "retirement" from fencing: the events and circumstances that led to his arrest and conviction on charges of receiving stolen property. Thus, the next chapter describes "Sam's fall," after which, the meaning and rewards of his fencing involvement are examined.

Chapter 10

Sam Takes a Fall

Whatever his talents and resourcefulness, the fence's immunity, his "license to operate," is seldom, if ever, an absolute one. The cooperative or symbiotic alliance that Sam enjoyed with law enforcers was a fragile one, as he reluctantly discovered.

Sam's arrest and subsequent conviction on charges of receiving stolen property in the late nineteen-seventies was the culmination of a long-standing investigation by the state police, also targeted at Louie, who too was convicted on receiving charges during this same time period. Both Sam and Louie's arrests were partly a consequence of enterprising police work, and partly a matter of fortuitous circumstance. Once arrested, moreover, the publicity surrounding the case helped to move it through the courts and hampered both Sam and Louie's chances of "beating the rap."

The event setting all this in motion was the arrest of two run-of-the-mill burglars, cousins of Dorothy Ford, who confessed to a series of house burglaries involving the theft of antiques, and also admitted to selling the antiques to Dorothy. Under the pressure of intensive questioning and in exchange for charges being dropped against her, Dorothy admitted to buying the stolen antiques and confirmed police suspicion that she was selling them to Sam. Dorothy further disclosed that she had, on several occasions, accompanied him to Woody's Auction House in Southfield, one of his outlets for stolen antiques. For the state police, this is crucial information; they now know the whereabouts of one of Sam's major outlets.

▶ Dorothy Ford snitched, even blew the whistle on where I was taking the stuff. This hurt 'cause knowing one of my main outlets gave the state police a better shot at me. It turns out the state police here contact the police in Southstate to be on the watch, and now the two police forces are working together. And my store was being watched more closely—Kuhn and Martin, two state cops, were in the coffee shop across the street all the time it seemed. They would often do that but it picked up a lot at this time. When they saw Reggie and Rocky come and go, they were figuring it had to do with a couple of burglaries that just happened. They had a list of what was taken and notified the police in Southstate that I might be coming, to have them check what I was bringing. As soon as I left Woody's, they came in with a search warrant and grabbed some of the antique pieces. The stuff matched up—it was the good antiques from a couple of homes that nailed me 'cause the people could identify them.

This is kinda funny, but my ass could of been in much more trouble than it was, 'cause on the trip back from Woody's I was carrying seventy-nine very warm guns to peddle to Louie. But I spotted a tail on me, so I shoot for the back roads and lost the tail. I just had a feeling something was up, so I unloaded the guns and anything else that might be warm in this old railroad car which I sometimes used for storing warm stuff. The next morning I come to my store and there were cops all over the place. They made a big thing of arresting me, pictures in the paper of me standing spread-eagle and being searched. It was a lotta bullshit.

That same day the cops pick up Reggie and Rocky and are really giving them the third degree—that they had fingerprints, that somebody seen Rocky's van at one of the burglaries, and that the other one was snitching. See, they separated one from the other, and would show each one what was supposed to be a signed confession from the other.

The police had themselves a good patsy in Reggie 'cause he starts blabbering—snitches on Rocky, that he done the burglaries with him. And snitches on me, too, that they were selling the stuff to me. But it doesn't end there. The state police pump Reggie about Louie and, it turns out, a few days before he had sold Louie a bunch of warm guns. Reggie fingers him, too. Next thing, Louie's place is searched and the cops find the guns. So, Louie gets busted, too.

I have to hand it to the state cops, really to Kuhn and Martin, the two detectives. They were very clever about the whole thing. They pulled some real shit, too, like the phony signed confessions. They even had it figured out to have a magistrate outside the city handle the preliminary hearing, so the case wouldn't get kicked out right away. They were taking no chances.

But, still, the case should have never gone to trial, on account of Reggie should have been taken care of. Louie got soft and didn't carry out his end. See, what happened is, we had Rocky's van blown up, as a warning. And Rocky never did talk. But Reggie was still talking, and Louie was supposed to get him out of the way 'cause he had the contacts for doing that. But Louie's reputation was bigger than the man, and he didn't have it done. At one time Louie would've had it done—just bing, bing. Louie had gotten soft. And even if it came to a jury convicting him, Louie was figuring he wouldn't have to do time.[1] ◄

Trial and Sentencing

Amidst the considerable publicity surrounding the trials of Sam and Louie and at the urging of the state police, the local district attorney, Mark Cummings, withdrew from the cases because of his alleged links to Louie, and a special prosecutor was appointed.

The prosecution evidence against Sam included the following. (1) The recovery of stolen property—antiques identified by the rightful owners as having been stolen from their residences. (2) The testimony of a thief, Reggie Rhoads, that he and another burglar, Rocky Lozier, had stolen the antiques and had sold them to Sam Goodman. (3) The testimony of Woodrow Bundley that he had purchased the antiques from Sam. (Woody of course was not on trial, but if he was, his defense would be that he was unaware and did not know the antiques were stolen.) (4) The jury conviction of Rocky Lozier on charges of burglary a couple of weeks before Sam's trial—and the use of Rocky Lozier as a witness testifying that he had been found guilty of theft of the antiques in question. (5) The testimony of the state police that Sam ran a secondhand discount store, that Reggie and Rocky were frequently observed entering and leaving Sam's store and, in fact, were so observed the weekend of the burglaries, and that Sam had reasonable cause to believe that the antiques they were selling were stolen; that is, that Rocky and Reggie could not possibly have been the legitimate owners of such a large supply of high-quality antiques.

Through his lawyer, Sam admitted to buying the antiques from Reggie Rhoads and reselling them to Woody but he also maintained that he did not know the antiques were stolen, that buying antiques from the walk-in traffic is an established aspect of his secondhand trade. Sam's defense, ultimately, was that Reggie Rhoads should not be believed because he is a thief and that his testimony should have been further discounted because he was offered a deal by the prosecution. The prosecution, in turn, advanced that no deal had been made with Rhoads; in questioning Rhoads testified to this.

Sam's claims were somewhat weakened by his precaution of not taking the stand and testifying on his own behalf, since this may have allowed the prosecutor to inquire about Sam's past (e.g., his prior criminal record) and thereby sway the jury towards his "suspect" character.

---

1. Sam's account of the events, culminating in his arrest and conviction square fairly closely with the accounts of several state police involved in the investigation. One trooper noted: "Gunning for those two [Sam and Louie] all this time, then to have it break the way it did. I'd like to think we're plain good, but you got to get lucky, too. It was one bingo after another. Once the 'old gal' [Dorothy Ford] started talking, the pieces fell together like you wouldn't believe."

▶ When Reggie opened his mouth on the stand, I could've blown his head away. See, it was doubtful up to the end that he would testify, 'cause he was getting shaky. But the state police had themselves a good patsy. And they did have the stolen antiques and Woody's testimony that he did buy the stuff from me. And Rocky had already been convicted of the burglaries, in a jury trial, 'cause Reggie was testifying against Rocky, too. The special prosecutor made Rocky take the stand and testify to that effect—that he'd already been found guilty. Rocky held up, never did snitch, but this hurt me 'cause the jury could put two-and-two together.[2]

Looking back, I should've taken the stand, but that was a risk, 'cause the prosecutor could bring up my record, that I had done time, and even ask general questions about my business. In my lawyer's eye, the jury would really turn against me if all that shit was brought up. See the prosecutor can't bring up your prior record unless you take the stand as your own witness, then he can. It still happens, though, that the good prosecutor can slip in other shit about you that lets the jury know you ain't no angel walking on water.

The jury was mostly working people, the ordinary Joe Blow who shopped in my kind of shop. In my eye, the kind of guy who probably bought warm stuff at one time or anther. But the gig was up. They finds me guilty and the judge hits me with a three to six. I should've appealed, 'cause really the jury took the word of an asshole thief. [But] I said "fuck it, do my time and get it over with." ◀

---

2. By his own admission, however, Rocky came close to snitching on Sam. Rocky explains, "This was my first time through this kind of thing—the cocksuckers [the state police] buffaloed me. So I admitted doing the burglary, and they got a signed statement from me. Then they pushed me to testify against Sam. Fuck, that's when I knew I had been taken—they weren't gonna cut a deal with me unless they got Sam. There was no way I would do that—so my story was that Reggie took care of getting rid of the stuff, that I didn't know where he took the stuff. Then later my lawyer advises me to deny the burglaries, that the state police had tricked me into a confession. So when my lawyer put me on the stand my testimony was I didn't have nothing to do with the burglaries, didn't know a thing about them. But they still had my signed statement. It didn't take the jury long to find me guilty. And all this time the state police and special prosecutor are pressuring me to testify against Sam—and Louie, too—but I wouldn't talk. It's against my nature to do that. And face it, there's a risk in doing that—there was a reason for the fucking van going up in smoke. I'm no dummy." Another burglar who knew both Rocky and Reggie, as well as Sam, comments: "Rocky didn't talk at the end but it was touch and go for awhile there, that he would. Reggie caved in all the way. He had done time before, so his old man was telling him, 'you're gonna lose your girl and go to jail for a long time, if you don't testify against Sam and Louie.' Then Louie was offering the state police a deal to burn Reggie. But it backfired 'cause the state police took this right back to Reggie, that Louie was gonna fuck him, so Reggie ain't got no choice but to testify. The state police were beating Louie to the punch."

One week after Sam's conviction, in a separate jury trial, Louie was also found guilty of receiving stolen property. The case against Louie was stronger than that against Sam—since Louie was caught in possession of stolen property (i.e., guns) that did not match his legitimate business identity. Thus, Louie could neither challenge the credibility of the thief's testimony, nor claim that he did not know the property was stolen. Otherwise, the elements leading to Louie's conviction parallel those in Sam's case—the testimony of Reggie Rhoads of selling stolen guns to Louie; the recovery of the stolen guns and Louie's possession of them; and the identification of the guns by the rightful owners.

▶ Louie was deader than me 'cause he wasn't covered on the guns. Me, I was covered on the antiques 'cause I'm an antique dealer. Louie's advantage was he didn't have a criminal record—some arrests, but no convictions—but there was other shit that the prosecutor could bring up if Louie took the stand. It's doubtful whether any of the jury didn't hear of Louie anyway. Louie was very well known and the papers were blowing this up something fierce. Even in my case, this was true on account of the papers. It took a long time to find a jury to hear our cases. But my jury could have gone either way. Whereas Louie's was more open-and-shut. In my eye, once it got that far along, Louie knew he would be found guilty. But he didn't think he would get that harsh a sentence. That's why he appealed, 'cause he thought he could pay off once things settled down. Then, he got popped a second time, for buying these big recreational vehicles from a couple of fucking kids. Imagine that. So Louie got himself another three to six, is ending up doing a lot of time. ◀

Factors Contributing To Sam's "Fall"

Sam and Louie's convictions point to a combination of elements which apparently are necessary to successfully prosecute large-scale dealers in stolen goods: the recovery of stolen property; the identification of property by its rightful owners; the testimony of thieves regarding the fence's possession or control of the property; and perhaps the documentation or at least the suggestibility of the suspect character of the fence. But successful prosecution is also inseparable from the ability and willingness of the authorities to move forward in charging and prosecuting cases against fences, including perhaps the need for some orchestrated visibility or publicity surrounding both the trial and the sentencing. The significance of Sam's case lies not only in the factors that led to discovery or proof of his fencing involvement but also in the factors that brought the case against him to its final dispostion.

The Case Against Sam

It is sometimes claimed that the police are disinclined to use thief-informants in building a case against a fence, that the testimony of the thief is

not credible because he is a "thief," and because he has been bribed by
the police or prosecution (e.g., by a promise of leniency) to testify. Indeed, this was a major part of Sam's defense—that he had bought the
goods in question but did not know they were stolen at the time he purchased them. The matter then became one of whom the judge and jury
would believe.

At first, it may appear that a jury would decide in the fence's favor; after
all, the fence appears to be a respectable businessman. What happened in
Sam's case, however, suggests that juries are quite inclined to believe the
testimony of thief-informants against a fence, providing that the prosecution has prepared an adequate case to begin with. Other evidence suggests that what happened to Sam is not uncommon. There has been, for
example, a string of convictions of fences in both Midstate and in other
eastern states during the past decade and a half, with the elements com-
prising these convictions paralleling the prosecution's cases against Sam
and Louie. The problem of convicting fences may stem less from reluctant
jurors, as traditionally believed, than from reluctant "authorities" who
may be less than eager to bring the fence to trial in the first place.

The credibility of the thief's testimony, furthermore, is likely to be enhanced by the fence's suspect character since many have prior criminal
records or, at least, run quasi-legitimate businesses. (This is evidenced in
Sam's refusal to take the stand in his own defense—because it entailed
the risk of the prosecution bringing up his criminal past.) Moreover, stolen property recovered by the police which does not match his customary
product line is itself strong evidence of criminal intent. This explains
Sam's relief at not being caught with stolen guns on his return trip from
Southstate, the evening prior to his arrest. And it explains why the case
against Louie was more open-and-shut than that against Sam—because
Louie was not covered on the stolen guns he had purchased from Reggie
(while Sam was covered on the stolen antiques.)

Irrespective of the context and the circumstances surrounding Sam's
arrest and conviction, the state police and special prosecutor can be credited with developing a strong case against him (and also against Louie).[3]

---

3. Steelbeams, who attended both Sam and Louie's trials, comments: "The evidence against Sam was solid, very solid. They had the antiques and that which was
stolen. Had the people saying, 'Yeh, this came out of my house.' Reggie was testifying against Sam. Don't forget, too, Rocky had been found guilty already. The
jury knew that. The special lawyer they brought in to prosecute Sam and Louie
was a cocksucker but he was fucking sharp—would stick in little pins and needles
to let the jury know about Sam's record and about Louie, too, that he was part of
the Mafia. Shit like that, which the jury was eating up. The state police and the
prosecutor had it very well planned—weren't taking no chances that somebody
would fuck them up."

Jesse, who attended Sam's trial adds: "They had a lotta stuff that was brought
back from Southstate, and this was linked to Sam. A fucking lot of stuff. Had the
auctioneer, Woody, on the stand, saying: 'This I took off Sam's truck.' And Sam's
record was worked in. Without a shadow of a doubt it was. Holy fuck, your lawyer

The coordination of law enforcement agencies, the skillful use of the informant role, the nullification of the complicity of local officials, all jelled to
ensure that the case against Sam not only met the requirements of the receiving law but that it was, in fact, processed to its final disposition in trial
court: the case reached the jury which rendered a guilty verdict, and the
sentencing judge imposed a stiff sentence (i.e., imprisonment).

▶ Even up to the end, I was figuring the judge would go easy. If not
right away, that I'd let things cool down, then appeal and get the sentence knocked down. Even more so Louie was figuring this, 'cause
he didn't really have a criminal record. But he got socked worse then
me. ◀

Sam's Link To Louie

Sam's association with Louie had a kind of spillover effect which contributed to his arrest and subsequent incarceration. First, because the state
police "hated Louie with a passion," they increased their surveillance of
Sam as a way of keeping tabs on Louie. Second, the added publicity that
came with Louie's arrest led to the assignment of a special prosecutor
and, in general, diminished Sam's chances of having the case against him
"fixed". Third, Louie's position in the local underworld was on the decline. In a sense, the local gang allowed Sam to sink along with Louie.
The local gang more or less watched in silence, relief, and some relish, as
the law did what the gang lacked both the will and the muscle to do:
"knock Louie down to size." In distancing itself from Louie, in effect, the
gang also distanced itself from Sam and was reluctant to intervene in his
behalf.

▶ The state police hated Louie with a passion. 'Cause he made fools
out of them a couple of times and he was always putting them down,
like calling them "goons." That hurt me 'cause the heat on Louie was
bringing heat on me. Now, Louie at one time had some connections
with the state police, years ago. Then, Louie got too cocky, his
mouth got too big, and the state police hated his ass. They really
wanted Louie bad. That, and once the thing hit the papers, everybody ran for cover. They were afraid of getting nailed themselves
'cause the state police and the crime commission were pushing hard,
very hard. The other thing was, once Louie started sinking, the local
gang was glad to see him out of the way. Louie had made too many
enemies, on account of he was too greedy and could be a snitch, too.
   Louie wanted to be a big shot, a big, big shot. That was Louie's
downfall—wanting to be in the limelight, playing up the Mafia shit,

---

can object in court—but after something is said—it don't fucking matter. It's out
in the open."

and bad-mouthing the cops. Louie's worst enemy was Louie. Louie's mouth got him where he is today.[4] ◀

Law of Averages

Still, the state police had an intense interest in Sam that went far beyond any vendetta against Louie. Sam had emerged as a major dealer in the area and was increasingly bold and wide-open in his fencing activities. Not only did Sam's name frequently come up in burglary and larceny investigations, but a growing number of individuals of varying degrees of trustworthiness were doing business with Sam and could supply incriminating evidence against him. By Sam's admission, he became overconfident in his license to steal, taking greater and greater risks so that the law of averages was almost bound to catch up with him.

▶ I was getting too careless. Thought I had a license to steal. Carried it too far, you might say. I was buying from anybody and everybody. And I trusted too many people. Too many people knew my business. Like Dorothy, I never should have taken her along to Woody's. That was my undoing, very careless on my part.[5]

---

4. Jesse comments:

"I think what hurt Sam is because Louie was not liked around here. The state police hated him with a passion, without doubt. They were after Louie a hell of lot more than they were after Sam. Holy fuck, a hell of a lot more. The good lawyers didn't like Louie either 'cause he would hold out, wouldn't come up with the bread. And he was always jumping from this lawyer to another. You don't do business like that.

I warned Sam about that so many times, 'cause Louie I never cared for. I will never understand how he had the reputation he had. He wasn't what he was supposed to be. Where everyone got the idea he was the Mafia—he knew Mafia people but he wasn't Mafia. Holy fuck, there are others who are really big, I mean to tell you. Now don't get me wrong. Louie did know some people, like he knew some of the magistrates and them very well. I just never could swallow him, maybe that's it. Louie had a name he shouldn't had. He screwed a lot of people, made a lot of enemies. I'd say Sam got most of his time on account of Louie."

5. Mickey comments: "When I knew Sam, he was buying from anyone, damn near anyone coming in the store. If he had the money and it was something good, he'd for sure buy. He wasn't very leery, put it that way."

Steelbeams claims that he specifically warned Sam about Reggie Rhoades: "I says to Sam: 'I can't say about Rocky but you're gonna get busted if you keep fucking with Rhoads—the guy's no fucking good. If he takes a fall. He's gonna give you up to save his own ass, sure as shit.'"

Jesse notes: "I told Sam many times, you're gonna get nailed if you keep fucking with those goddamn kids and if you keep buying from off the street. Stick to your own kind."

A member of the local clique adds: "I'd stop by to see Sam and all these young guys hanging around the store. I said, 'Sam, quit screwing with these motherfuckers. Sure as Christ, they're going to put you away.'"

It got harder and harder to walk away from a deal 'cause I got too greedy. I wanted the last dollar. And being noticed was part of it—people knowing who I was, coming to me for deals, being in the center of things. The other thing was, I thought I couldn't be touched. I still shake my head that I got popped. But I did leave the door open for the state police.[6] ◀

Overlapping Law Enforcement Agencies

Sam's arrest and conviction also intertwines with the increasing role of the state police, and that of the state crime commission, in the internal law enforcement of American City. This involvement was part of a broader trend in the state as a whole—beginning in the late sixties and coming to fruition in the seventies—of the growth in availability of competing law enforcement agencies and the decline of local police autonomy.

In comparison with the local police, the state police tend to be more oriented toward and more capable of combating sophisticated and organized kinds of criminal enterprise—such as burglary rings, drug networks and fencing operations. First, the state police are likely to have greater resources for coordinating policing efforts with other enforcement agencies which may span city, county, and even state boundaries. This is important, because the theft of property and its distribution is oftentimes not restricted to the jurisdictional boundaries of a single police agency, particularly when large-scale fences like Sam are involved. Second, because their rewards and enforcement priorities are more oriented towards making arrests of "big cases" rather than simply toward making many arrests, the state police are likely to have greater incentive than the local police for investigating professional and organized criminals. In particular, the state police are more likely to bargain or deal with underlings who effectively inform against more significant figures. The use of informants in this way, moreover, is itself part of a significant trend in law enforcement in recent years—the cultivation of informants as a principal police

---

6. Jesse comments: "I was down there one time and the freaking state cops come in, are going through the whole place looking for guns. Another time, holy fuck, I'm there and they come in looking for coins. This one time is funnier than hell 'cause the police come barging in—really I believe the motherfuckers had Sam set up 'cause Sam had just bought from this guy. The one cop is telling Sam to keep Muffin away, else he'd freaking blow Muffin away. Now, they never found what they were looking for. But you better believe the state police were sitting on him. He was getting too hot." Rocky adds: "Kuhn and Martin were after Sam all the time. Watched him constantly. And everyday they'd see the same people walking in and out. To them, it was a matter of time before there was a slip-up." Chubbie notes: "Mostly it was the one state cop, Kuhn, who'd come in Sam's store and spot check. Maybe write a few things down. Sam and he would joke with each other, but Kuhn meant business. Maybe ten, twelve times I seen the state police come in with a search warrant to check the place for this or that."

strategy, including the increasing use of low-level informants to snitch on higher-ups.

The more active role of the state police in local enforcement matters coincides with the formation of the state crime commission. As in the case of the state police, members of the commission and its investigative officers are not as likely to be swayed by the local crime élite, nor to be captured by local political machines. Rather, they tend to be civil servants who usually do not have political ambitions (e.g., unlike the local district attorney). Political issues are not irrelevant, but the connections between members of the Commission and local legal officials with whom they are dealing are long and complicated. It is simply more difficult to co-opt them.

What happened in American City reveals the complex structure of contemporary law enforcement in most U.S. cities and the changes in this structure over the past couple of decades (e.g., the involvement in local police matters by organized crime strike forces or drug enforcement). With the more active role of outside police forces and investigative agencies, corruption of local officials no longer provides the comprehensive protection that it perhaps did in previous eras: overlapping and fractured police authority prevents a single department or officer from being able to issue an absolute license for an illegal operator. The change here is not just that police authority has become fragmented, but that it has become less sensitive to local political authority.[7]

▶ In some ways I was pretty well protected but not like, say Angelo or Phil, or even Louie. That Louie buried a lot of people saved his ass in more than one tight spot. And when Cummings was the D.A., Louie had free rein 'cause Cummings was really his candidate. But Louie

---

7. The FBI, of course, has always been somewhat involved in the investigation of fencing activities—an involvement that has intensified in recent years—but its role remains restricted, as Agent Bogart explains:

"For the FBI to get involved it has to be one of two things: either the theft of an interstate shipment—could be a dime's worth or fifty thousand dollars worth, the amount doesn't matter—or the interstate transportation of stolen property over $5,000. Those are two different things. Say you stole a $100 carton of clothes that was going in interstate commerce, that's a federal violation. But if you burgled or stole something in another state that was, say, $4,800, and brought it across state lines, then no federal violation. It has to be over $5,000. So if you stole jewelry worth $10,000 in one state and took it to another state, that's a federal violation. So, the FBI was very restricted, and fences like Vincent would be cautious of buying if they thought we'd get involved.

Now, there has been some change in the last five years or so. The FBI has put more men and resources into it, not just going after the fencing but organized crime, too. And the technology of surveillance is a whole lot better today. And the informant system is much more a part of enforcement today, is much more developed in just the last few years. So Vincent would find it much harder to operate today, once he was targeted, then 10 to 15 years ago."

wasn't tied up the way Angelo and Phil were. No way. At one time maybe, but Louie made a lot of enemies that hurt him in the end.

See, Angelo and Phil had the local cops, the magistrates, and the D.A., too. Even when Cummings was in, he wouldn't buck Angelo. Another thing, the good lawyers would take my case if I got jammed up, but they won't go to bat for me, pull out all the stops, the same way they would for Angelo. He is connected something fierce. And Angelo is smooth, very smooth. I really believe he could buy off the trial judges if it came down to that. It's a fact that he has some connections in the state police. That I do know.

Myself, I had very few worries from the local police or the local D.A., very few. This I believe: that if the fucking state cops had kept their noses out, I'd still be operating in American City.[8] ◄

Climate of Reform in American City

Finally, Sam's arrest took place within a climate of reform (as part of the upcoming mayoral election) and amid charges of official corruption in American City, spurred on by the politic release of findings by the state crime commission which for several years running had been investigating official corruption and organized crime activities. The commission's interests extended beyond Sam and Louie, both of whom, once arrested, were seen as possible avenues for apprehending an assortment of Mafia figures, local businessmen, and corrupt officials.

---

8. Agent Bogart emphatically comments:

"*The* big problem in stopping your bigger fences is local law enforcement. From the point of view of the FBI, our concern was: Who can you trust? Who can you trust? I'm not saying all the cops in Mid-City are corrupt. Some would be honest. But what can they do? They're assigned to certain areas of the city or they are given assignments which limit the kinds of information and the kinds of crime activities they deal with. We found it hard, very hard, to work with the local police because you can't trust them. Whether it's always intentional or not, they can foul up or knock out an investigation so easily.

The main fences in Mid-City could operate without any problem, because we were actually the only ones who were interested in knocking them off. Mid-City was off limits for the state police. It would be very rare that they would get involved in local enforcement matters because the Mid-City police did not want the state police around. There is no way that Vincent could of lasted as long as he did, as wide-open as he was, if the state police had been involved in Mid-City. No way.

See the FBI is limited, first, by having jurisdiction only over certain kinds of fencing activities [see note 7]. Second, the FBI usually has to work with local law enforcement, with local police and local judges. Many times you can't trust them. They can make it very difficult to run a successful investigation. If we gave them information that we had on Vincent, say, Vincent would know about it too. So many times we played cat-and-mouse with the local police. Not lying to them but more holding back on what we were doing."

▶ It was a bad time to take a "fall" 'cause corruption in city hall and in the police department was a hot potato. An election year and the papers played it up big. That, and the crime commission was releasing reports about the Mafia and organized crime in American City. It was splashed all over—the magistrates and the D.A. didn't have any leeway. Take the trial judge, Larry Hale. I believe if the bread was right and you had the connections, you could deal with him. But there was too much heat all the way around and you couldn't maneuver. See, Louie was about as well connected as anybody, and he had the bread to make a helluva big payoff; but even he couldn't swing it.

Even after I was in prison, the crime commission was offering me deals: "Help us out with Angelo" 'cause they were figuring that Angelo was an outlet for the cigarettes and liquor, and that I knew about the gambling. And all along they were pushing me to give them information on Phil, Duggan, Melvie, Lorenzo. Charlie, too, 'cause they figured he was linked up with Angelo. And they wanted Duggan and the chief something fierce 'cause they were a real thorn. The crime commission wanted to close American City down, were after the really big fish.

But it didn't work out that way. The place has changed some but the same names and a few new ones keep coming up. Angelo is more behind the scenes but still has his fingers into things. He is very smooth. Phil has pretty much taken over where Louie and me left off, but some little dealers have picked up the slack, too. Skip Henderson and his dad have gotten bigger, too. Are operating in Birdville, a little town outside of American City, a secondhand place and a small foundry. They were operating before but were pretty small. Off and on I did some business with them. Some of the ones I dealt with are dealing with the Hendersons now. The way it was run down to me was that in some ways its better now, 'cause Louie is out of the way. ◀

Chapter 11

Rewards of Fencing

In It For The Money

▶ What do you mean, why did I do it? Because it was good money. I did it for the easy dollar. What you can buy cheap will have a bigger cut in it for you.[1] ◀

One important reason for Sam enjoying fencing is, understandably, the money. Sam is a businessman, and whether he trades legitimately or illegitimately, he is in business to make a profit. Stolen goods can be purchased more cheaply than legitimate goods so that Sam stands a chance of making a greater profit. Furthermore, with the kind of business that he runs (antiques, secondhand goods), Sam may earn his profit with less travail when buying stolen rather than legitimate merchandise.

▶ Say there's an ad in the paper, somebody wanting to sell eight pieces of wicker furniture. I'm gonna buy it legit, right? So I makes a call, then I drives out and checks it over. The guy wants so much but I don't want to pay that. So we haggle over price. Maybe we don't come to terms, so I got to call him back or make another trip out. That is a lot of time, a lot of bullshit, really. Here's the thing: if I run to the auctions, watch the ads in the paper of private sales, and that, I can buy pretty cheaply. But I got my time, the trip, and having to deal with some Joe Blow who is trying to jew me. Fuck it. You don't always make more on the warm stuff, many times you don't, but there's less hassle and haggling. ◀

As an incentive for fencing stolen goods, money is important to Sam for more than just its potential for acquiring material possessions. As with the rest of us, Sam places great importance on the symbolic value of money for satisfying all sorts of diverse needs in our society. Thus, when Sam in-

---

1. A representative comment from police and prison officials who know Sam is as follows: "Sam's problem is, he's greedy. Can't walk away from an easy buck. Otherwise, he's a helluva guy. Can't help but like him."

terprets his fencing involvement as money-motivated, he means several things. First, he enjoys what money can buy—the goods and services that can be bought with it. Second, he enjoys the process of making money—the feelings of satisfaction and well-being that come from turning a fast dollar. Third, Sam enjoys the peer recognition that comes both from having and making money, since money is associated with achievement and recognition or, conversely, of failure.[2]

It is not surprising that at first glance Sam ascribes the overriding (and sometimes the sole) motivation for his fencing involvement to the desire for money. After all, with know-how and connections, fencing stolen goods can be very lucrative. And in our culture, the desire to make money is a highly acceptable and rational explanation both to oneself and to others of why one does what one does, especially when asked to explain involvement in a high-risk enterprise, be it legal or illegal. Nonetheless, at other times, and on closer inspection, Sam is also attracted to fencing by the social or non-economic rewards that inhere in expertise, prestige, power, a positive self-image, and a number of other job conditions he defines as desirable.

"Being Somebody"

Within the criminal community—where status is determined by one's skills, racket or hustle, financial success, reputation for being solid, and connections—being a large-scale dealer in stolen goods brings with it a certain amount of prestige and power. Fences are viewed as skillful, well-connected, and as making good money. They are also seen as having a respectable hustle or a preferred kind of criminal business in that fencing is dependable, yields a good profit, allows for considerable independence and control, and is reasonably legitimate because it is built around a regular business. Furthermore, while not all fences are pillars of integrity, Sam takes special pride in being somebody who is solid, and more generally, is recognized as "good people."

First, as a fence, Sam occupies a strategic position in the underworld. He is an important person to know, in the obvious sense that he is a mid-

---

2. An associate of Sam's notes: "Sam made a lot, spent a lot. He was a high-liver. Was a big spender when he went out, say, at a bar, buy everybody a drink. He was that way. Gambled a lot, one helluva a lot. I used to watch the games, played a few times, too, 'cause I was invited. It was too big for me 'cause I had seven kids. I couldn't afford that shit but I was welcome. There was dice and poker, and a professional dealer. Sam would win sometimes but he was pretty loose with the money, wasn't one to quit when he was ahead. He'd play all night." Rocky notes: "If Sam wanted a woman, not that he would pay her, but he would give her a gift or whatever, show her a good time and anybody that was along, too. If you went out with him, everything was on him, and he never quit early. He wasn't scared to spend money." Jesse comments: "Sam don't think nothing about a buck. I mean Sam can go through money, gees, like Sherman going through Georgia."

dleman for the trafficking in stolen goods, but also because he is a source of contacts and a conduit of information on underworld activities. As Sam's fencing operation shifted into high gear, he found himself increasingly in demand—by thieves coming to peddle stolen wares, merchants wanting to purchase merchandise at below-wholesale prices, and store customers hoping to find what they need at bargain prices. Sam may play down the significance of how burglars and other thieves view him, but he enjoys the recognition and adulation he receives from many of them. For a few, Sam acts as an "old head" offering advice on theft techniques and the underworld code.

▶ The whole thing was being noticed. That everybody knew me, knew who I was. People would come in the store, "Where's Sam? When's he coming back?" Just being recognized on the street, or going into a place to have coffee. Stopping at Casey's after the races on Fridays, buying drinks for the house—which was a way of keeping the thieves in my pocket but it was being a big shot, too. It's human nature to want that recognition, not so much that you're the center of attention, now, but that they look up to you, respect you for what you are. Take the thieves asking for advice, really they are looking up to you.[3] ◀

Second, fencing for Sam is a step up from burglary, even a step up from being a "good burglar."

▶ It changed for me, when I got into dealing, put it that way. I was making more money, some more, anyway. But mainly I wasn't crawling in windows anymore, where I could get shot or whatever else. See, a thief is a thief, and the fence has higher status, more recognition, than a thief. It's a step up. Even your good thief is still a thief, although they can be very respected.

I considered myself a notch above even the good burglar. On a scale of one to ten, the fence is pretty high, especially if he's solid. Now, I wouldn't be as high as Angelo or Little Nicky 'cause they were in the rackets something big and had ties, but your fence is pretty high. ◀

---

3. Jesse comments: "To tell the fucking truth, Sam likes that when he gets looked up to. To them damn kids, he was big stuff. Ate that shit up. And the better the thief, the more he was that way. Take Steelbeams, Bowie, and them, it was important to Sam they looked up to him. Why, Jesus Christ, I will never know. In Sam's mind, they were good burglars but, holy fuck, they were not really that good. If they ever wanted to pull a safe with me, they can go fuck it."

Rocky recounts the following incident: "We had this safe from this church, a big fucking safe. Couldn't get it open, so we lugged it out, hauled it to this old garage. Got Sam to come and open it. He kept telling us: 'Won't be a fucking thing in it. It's a church safe, motherfuckers are always empty.' He got it opened in less than five minutes, and sure as shit, the goddamn thing was empty. But Sam was in heaven, fucking heaven. It was a real kick for him to open it, all the more 'cause we couldn't."

Third, to the extent that fencing is an outgrowth (and perhaps a culmination) of prior illegal and quasi-legitimate involvements, becoming a successful dealer not only is a "promotion" of sorts but also may bring about
changes in the "kind of crowd that one hangs with." Being a fence meant
that Sam belonged to a more élite class of underworld members, that he
associated with more important people, and that he was a "heavy" in the
local community. More than anything, perhaps, Sam cherished being
identified with and rubbing shoulders with the local gang as well as being
a member of the gambling club.

The gambling group meets almost weekly and is both a play and a business group. It is a place to go and relax, a place to have fun, and a refuge
from the hard work of criminal enterprise. It also combines at least a little
business with pleasure, in particular, by being a source of information or a
place where members can find out something about each other's activities
or inactivities. Mainly, however, the club does not so much consciously
facilitate crime as it emphasizes the satisfying and rewarding payoffs associated with illicit livelihoods. The club provides a setting where members
can "play" successful and self-assured criminals, displaying little difficulty
and even less ambivalence in accepting that identity.

▶ I enjoyed the gambling. That I can honestly say. It was relaxation
and a chance to find out about what is happening in town. But the
whole thing was being noticed, too. That I was a pretty big person
around town. A big shot, you might say. There's a recognition that
comes from rubbing shoulders with Angelo, Little Nicky, and them.
You're aware of that. See, I came up without nothing. Everything I
got I worked for, got on my own. It was more or less important to me
to be hanging with the better class of people.[4]

You're in with a different class of people when you're fencing, in
with businessmen and that. A really different class of people. When
you're into burglary, you're with guys that horse around, have fun,
drink beer, go nightclubbing. Guys that mostly don't work.

I considered myself higher than the thieves. They sold to me,
some hung in my store. I might buy them dinner or drinks at Casey's.
But as far as social, no. There were a couple I was friends with, but
that was it. I wouldn't travel in their crowd. I was traveling with a
different crowd. Don't get me wrong, there are some burglars out
there that are good people, but it's different. Whole different crowd.

With the fencing, your dealers are higher class. They're really

---

4. Jesse notes: "I think Sam liked having a reputation. Some guys want to be
known. Even more so Louie, he really sucked on that, that 'Louie ran American
City.' Which was mostly bullshit. Jesus Christ, the cops called Louie a 'kingpin.'
Gave him that name. Would you fucking believe, Louie ate that shit up. Myself,
you try to keep things as quiet and normal as possible. Take the lawyer, who handles the coins and that, he stays in the background. Even Angelo, all the shit he is
into, does it quietly so his name doesn't come up that often. Now that is hard for a
lot of them to do. Like Sam, it is his nature that he likes to be known. He probably
would like to be known as a kingpin, I would estimate the cocksucker would."

businessmen and are into a higher racket. You're playing cards, maybe going to Vegas or Atlantic City, or you go out for dinner at a better class of place, have steak, mixed drinks. It's a whole different league. ◄

Also, as a legitimate general merchandise dealer, Sam can, and indeed does, lay claim to the status of businessman, a fact which is indistinguishable from his sense of well-being and his place in the broader society. Sam not only recognizes the legitimacy and stable social identity that attaches to anyone who falls into the general classification of businessman, but also appreciates that what he does as a businessman-fence differs only minutely from that of legitimate members of his trade; that is, fencing itself is a business and requires valued attributes, such as hard work, marketing skills, and the ability to manage money. That Sam associates with and is on friendly terms with many legitimate businessmen, he interprets as further evidence of his acceptance in the local business community.

► I look at it this way, I was a businessman. That's the way I saw myself. That's the way others treated me. Even those that didn't do business with me in the hot stuff, respected me, accepted me for what I was, and I respected them. I would have coffee and that with them. They might stop at my store, I might stop at theirs. ◄

Finally, an added sense of respectability and of being somebody derive from Sam's business in still another way. As a merchant who offers merchandise at "bargain" prices and who is sometimes generous in other ways, Sam can play the role of "Robin Hood." (As described in the next chapter, both the Robin Hood role and Sam's friendly association with local businessmen also form a major part of Sam's rationale.)

► I did a lot of good, helped a lot of people. I had the best prices in town which helped a lot of poor people. They came to me like I was the last one on earth. There were many of them that put me up on a pedestal like you wouldn't believe, 'cause I gave them easy credit and everything. Same with some of the local merchants 'cause buying from me helped them get over the hump. And the Red Cross and Hope Rescue would come to me to help out this or that family. This was a very good feeling. Like I was the last one on earth they could turn to. ◄

Excitement: Enjoying the Action

In comparison with most conventional occupations and daily routines, there is an element of excitement and sometimes even drama in being a dealer in stolen goods. The "action itself" of wheeling and dealing or "of being where the action is" represent one set of attractions for fences like Sam. Even the actual buying and selling of stolen goods represents a source of action and, although it may come to be viewed as a routine activity, there will be occasional deals that are so challenging or lucrative as to generate a sense of excitement. Likewise, while concerns about the police can be annoying—the sporadic searches and questioning, the episodic periods of surveillance—they tend to make life more dramatic for the fence than it is for persons engaged in legitimate business. Really good deals and fear of detection, while probably more exciting to the new-comer, can generate some drama even for an "old head" like Sam.

In a sense, fencing is a kind of "adventurous deviance" in which the un-certainty, the anxiety, the risks involved are an intrinsic source of plea-sure. When kept at a manageable level, the risks may be viewed as excite-ment, challenge, or fun—as more or less pleasantly fearful, pleasantly anxious, pleasantly uncertain, pleasantly risky.

▶ Fencing is hard work, don't get me wrong, but I like the excitement of it. It was never boring, always something happening. That, and having to be on your toes all the time, 'cause you can get burned bad if you're not careful. It's not like a high but in a way it is. There's a thrill there. See, there's a risk in fencing—with the cops, with whether you can you get rid of what you buy, is your back covered? To me, that risk was tension, but it was enjoyment, too. In different ways, there is a challenge in fencing that in truth I could say I liked.[5] ◀

In other respects, running a fencing business is for Sam a kind of "com-petitive play," a way of matching wits with others. One kind of play is to buy stolen goods cheaply, to sell them for a nice profit, and to have de-feated the law and its agents in the process.

▶ It would tickle me pink. Say, the state cops were watching my store. I might get in one of my trucks, take off and they was following me, but see I wasn't carrying anything warm. I would take them on a big fox and goose chase, drive out into the country and everything.

Or the different times the police searched my store, never found anything. I wouldn't rub it in to them, but it tickled me pink. See, by the time they hit me with a search, the stuff was long gone.[6] ◀

---

5. Jesse comments: "Burglary, and I estimate fencing is like that, gives you an excitement. Life is dull as hell if you don't have nothing like that. It's a challenge, I'd have to say that. It really fucking is. Sometimes on a burglary the closer they were, the harder they were, the more exciting. To see if you could really get away with it. That may sound freaking dumb, but that is how it really is. Understand now, you didn't do it just for that, you done it for the money. The only thing that really comes close is nutzin' around with a good sexy woman, a real good piece of nooky."

6. Agent Bogart comments: "Vincent liked the dollar, but he didn't need the money. I would think that in many ways he was in it for the kicks." Jesse adds: "The freaking lawyer, Jesus Christ, and the foundry guy, too, they was both roll-ing in money. But I guess the more you got, the more you want to have. You en-joy making the fucking pile bigger. But they is getting a kick out of it, too, of getting away with something they shouldn't be doing. The lawyer for sure I would

Another kind of play is to beat the system in a more general sense, to gain control and to manipulate one's environment, such as by covering one's back, by arranging sales outlets, or in general, by establishing the contacts for buying and selling stolen goods.

▶ Beating the police is one thing, but you got to be beating the system all the way down the line. It's like a big chess game, really, 'cause you always got to think ahead about covering your back, keeping the thieves in your pocket, and making your contacts for unloading. ◀

A third kind of rewarding play occurs when Sam competes directly with trade partners, for example, when he negotiates with thieves or buyers over prices. Hard bargaining and sharp trading in dealing with one's "economic foes" confirms a professional, businesslike self-conception. Sam enjoys "getting over" on thieves and out-hustling other dealers, exercises in which the give-and-take is typically friendly, but his biggest kick comes from beating somebody "who wanted to be more than he was."

▶ Just the dealing part itself. How should I say it? You enjoy that. Making the thief think you don't want what he's peddling when you do. With the other dealers, you would try like hell to beat him, and they're doing the same to you. Then, afterwards, you kid each other. See, it's mostly friendly.
I don't know if I enjoyed beating people; it wasn't that so much. Now, if it was someone that thought he was a big shot, wanted to be more than he was, I meant to beat him bad. I can truthfully say, I got a bang out of that. ◀

A fourth kind of competitive play is a type of confidence game in which Sam takes advantage of either the dishonesty or the gullibility of the "victim." This usually involves selling run-of-the-mill merchandise at inflated prices: (a) by allowing a merchant to believe the goods were stolen but are of high quality, or (b) by concocting a story for a customer about the origins or authenticity of a particular item of merchandise. In both instances, Sam plays on his reputation as someone who handles stolen goods and also on the cupidity, if not the stupidity, of the victim.

▶ I really got a bang out of this. Say I got a load of rugs that were seconds, which I bought dirt cheap, but bought them strictly legit. What I might do is call another dealer, or a place that handled rugs, let them know that some rugs had come my way, that they looked very good and that I was interested in dumping them, if I could get the right price. Let them read between the lines that they're warm.

---

say got a fucking kick out of it. Now, maybe the money did look good to him 'cause a lot of these lawyers will have a woman on the side, or get caught up in gambling something fierce. And some of your younger lawyers are into dope, heavy into dope, don't forget that. So they need the extra bread. But they enjoy it, too. There is a thrill there to get away with something. That is human nature."

Many times, the guy would jump so fast that he would pay more than he'd have to if he bought them legit.

The other thing is, a lot of your public wants a story. See, some of them surmised I was dealing in warm stuff, and I would play on that. Make up a story about how so-and-so was peddling this or that piece, and I decided to take a shot at it, that the guy was in a hurry and he didn't even know what he had. Then I'd show them a piece, say, maybe an old chair that would pass for an antique, how I found out later that the chair is very valuable, that it belonged to this or that person, had come out of a well-known home. Many times they would pay a big price just for a piece of junk. All the time, I'm laughing like hell cause it's really funny how the public can be fooled that way. Your public wants a story, and I would give them that.[7] ◄

Another source of excitement for Sam comes from involvement in action situations. Not only is Sam's store an action spot, but his position as a fence facilitated entry into the gambling club, gave him special acceptance at bars and other hangouts, and also provided him with the money to seek excitement in women or in gambling.

► There was always something happening at my shop. Never a dull moment. Casey's, on Friday nights after the car races, would really be hopping. I would stop there for a sandwich or maybe have a drink, and everybody knew me, knew who I was. But the gambling was my main enjoyment. It wasn't just the gambling, but sometimes the gang would bring in girls and that, too. And Louie and I would go to Vegas or into Atlantic City to gamble, to have a good time.[8] ◄

---

7. Jesse comments: "Sam gotta always think he's pulling something. I think that's the only way he's happy in life. That he's doing somebody in." Steelbeams adds: "This is hard to believe but some Sunday mornings, before he'd go to his shop, Sam would drive around town, hit all the Hope Rescue Mission boxes. Check to see what people threw away. Like an old radio, TV, and that. He'd fiddle with it, get it working, sell it for $5, $10 in his store. Once in awhile he'd come across a good antique piece somebody threw away, but otherwise, it wasn't the money. What the fuck would he make from this? No, it was just the idea of pulling something. He got a bang out of it."

8. Chubbie comments: "It wasn't a big part of the gambling clique but girls were brought in sometimes, 'cause different ones that stopped by Sam's store would joke each other about what happened. One they laughed most about, was Helen Shutt, would give blow job's 'cause she had a small pussy and could only screw guys with little dicks. Something happened to her once, had an operation and that, ended up with a small pussy. They used to joke a lot about her." Jesse notes, with respect to "goings on" in Sam's store, that: "This wasn't a regular thing, no way. But a nice looking broad come in off the street, Sam was known to make a play. Knock off the price a little on something, to get a little nooky. Hell, yes, who wouldn't." Tommy reports the following incident: "This was really something. I couldn't believe it. A really attractive girl. She came in on a Friday evening, at closing time. Me and Sam is talking, she really caught my eye. Stacked.

Finally, "being somebody" is itself a form of action. Whether it is flashing a roll of bills in paying a thief, buying drinks for the crowd at Casey's pub, playing cards or shooting dice with the gambling group, conducting a buying spree at one of the local auctions, or hobnobbing with Louie, Charlie, or other big shots in American City, being somebody is a means of self-expression and generates an element of excitement for Sam. He is accorded prestige not only because he has successfully accumulated possessions, but also because he displays the here and now value of dramatically making the scene—by "blowing money," for example.

▶ I made a lot of money, but I blew a lot, too. But I blew it the way I wanted. I had two Caddies, one for me and one for my wife [i.e., Becky], three trucks, a house, and everything.[9] I could buy what I wanted, go where I wanted. I can truthfully say I liked being a big shot. Like going to Casey's and buying drinks for the house. Or the gambling, if I wanted to shoot for it, the money would be there on the table. ◀

Sam's display before his peers is not entirely a matter of seeking status. Since by definition his criminal entrepreneurship is secret, the fence must somehow communicate his successes and competence to others if he wishes to develop and sustain the contacts he needs to continue operating. Nevertheless, Sam's tendency to flaunt his success was greater in the early phases of his fencing involvement, for with time he came to appreciate the advantages of remaining in the background.

▶ It was more in the beginning that I was trying to be a big shot. Later on I handled it better. I wasn't out front as much, was more content

Sam and me is kidding with her. Sam says, 'How about an orgy.' Goddam, she went for it. Sam says, 'Take her upstairs.' I says, 'Sam, I don't even know her.' 'Go ahead, go ahead,' he says. So I goes. Unbutton her blouse, big tits fall out, body out of this world. Finally, I come down, says to Sam, 'You go up, I can't handle that anymore.' So he goes up. In the meantime, Charlie Ciletti comes in. I tells him what's happening: 'Hey, there's an orgy going on.' By then his tongue is hanging out. He goes up. I goes up. Sam goes back up. Then I couldn't go back up no more 'cause it was too soon. I went home, I was so tired. And wouldn't you know it, that night after I went home after all that banging, my old lady wanted it. No way, I said I'm too sick. I can't move."

9. Jesse comments: "Sam is exaggerating here. You got to watch him for that. The fucking caddies he had weren't new, no way. Had a couple of beat up trucks. What the fuck, the house was Becky's. He might a helped out with some bills, paid his way, but, holy fuck he is blowing himself up there." Steelbeams notes: "The one caddie was half old, the other was pretty new, was in good shape. Two trucks weren't so old but were pretty beaten up. Had a red pickup and an eighteen footer, that were pretty new. Sam kept them nice, was particular about them. Can't say about the house but do believe that was in Becky's name 'cause she was working and that. But Sam spent a lot of money on her and those kids of hers. That I do know."

to stay in the background. But you have to be noticed too, make people aware; once I got rolling that wasn't as necessary. ◄

Accomplishment: Sense of Mastery Over One's Life

Sam's success as a fence fostered in him a strong sense of being in charge of his own activities and behaviors, a satisfaction with his ability to take care of himself and to deal effectively with stress and decision-making. There is, on the one hand, the sense of mastery that comes from performing well at a demanding job, taking charge and acting decisively to tackle both the routine and happenstance problems that arise in a fencing business. There is also a broader sense of effectiveness at surviving as a fence over the long haul, a feat which also intertwines with Sam's success as a legitimate businessman (albeit, as Sam fully understands, a success at least partly based on illegal gains). No matter how it is achieved, success is still *success*—and solving the social and economic realities of a dealership in stolen property is hardly a minor achievement.

▶ There's a satisfaction in knowing you can do it, knowing you can handle whatever comes up. See, it was up to me, depended on me, rested on my shoulders to deal with this or that. The fencing is much more satisfying than just having a legit business which is pretty cut and dried. You have to really be on your toes with the fencing, much more on top of things. Not that the legit side wasn't satisfying but in a different way. 'Cause I was building up my store, investing what I was making from the fencing. I thought it was good business to do that. Made me feel like I was progressing.

The fencing gave me a sense of myself, of knowing what I was capable of doing. I always felt I had business ability, a knack for the business end of things. Now I knew it. The fencing gave me a different outlook on life, on myself. I always felt I had leadership qualities. The fencing proved that to me.

There's a feeling of confidence I have of going into an area and outdoing the next guy. Whether it's the fencing or strictly with the legit, I feel I can do whatever needs to be done. 'Cause the fencing taught me how to make things happen, that to make it go I had to stay on top of things and get others to work with me. ◄

Interest and Expertise

There are, as well, a number of job conditions associated with fencing that Sam defines as desirable. First, he attaches a kind of intrinsic or creative enjoyment to "the dealin', the coverin', and the gettin' over." When one has a skill (or a set of skills), finely honed and polished, one uses it and enjoys it. Like the surgeon, the auto mechanic, or the salesman who uses his training, Sam enjoys and takes considerable pride in his ability to "doctor" merchandise, to capitalize on his reputation as a fence by selling perfectly legitimate goods as if they were stolen, or to engage in sharp trading with a thief or another dealer. Moreover, because fencing offers considerable job variety, it elicits a kind of all-around test of one's talents or mettle. For Sam, fencing is a source of self-expression, a kind of creative functioning as a whole rather than as a segmental person.

▶ I don't know how to say it, but fencing involved all of me in a way that burglary and the legit business didn't. Fencing made me use all of my abilities, tested me for what I was made of. I liked that. ◀

Independence

Second, not only is fencing interesting and challenging, but it allows one to make decisions about one's own working and other behaviors. Sam enjoys both the autonomy and the responsibility of running a fencing business—of being self-employed, of being his own boss, and of not having to work within the structured and dull atmosphere of routine employment.

Association—Friendship

Lastly, Sam's fencing involvement is also a *social* undertaking: it not only serves as the medium for the formation and ranking of social relationships in general, but it serves as the source of the majority of the satisfying relationships that he has. While dealing itself is an enjoyable activity, it is made even more so because it sustains a network of both business and social relations.

This associational side of fencing has many elements. They include customers who provide an opportunity for sociability and friendship where there is a tie-in between good relations and the completion of sales, the dual satisfaction of real enjoyment in his salesmanship together with awareness of its financial return.

▶ I got a kick out of the people that came in my shop, all different kinds and from all walks of life. Many times they're looking for a bargain and think they're real hustlers. It would be funny as hell 'cause you could really take them over the coals if you wanted to. And I always had lots of regulars, especially the poorer people 'cause they could buy cheap and the better-off ones checked over the antiques. I would rap with them, find out about their families and that. It was all very friendly and good for business, too. Very few people walked away without buying something. ◀

Another social element of fencing includes congenial relations with employees, local businessmen, and the assorted group of hangers-on and semi-retired thieves who stop by or simply hang out at Sam's store. While Sam may sometimes complain about some of the regulars who always seem to be in his store, he generally enjoys their company and the recognition that comes from their personal following.

But probably most enjoyable and satisfying to Sam are the feelings of camaraderie and the business affiliation he experiences with some of the dealers, such as Louie, Woody or Scottie. In similar fashion, Sam's associations with some members of the local clique combine business with pleasure and also give him access to the fast life that is an established feature of this upper segment of the underworld. With them Sam partakes in a kind of shared thrill of breaking the law, and in the excitement, perhaps, of having unlimited amounts of money to spend.

Taken together, the rewards of dealing and the satisfying relationships and mutual obligations to thieves, to buyers, and to other dealers increasingly involve Sam in the social and business activities of dealing. His life and identity are extensively shaped by fencing and his continued well-being, both financial and social are heavily dependent on it. Fencing is both a business and a way of life, and Sam's enjoyment of it is a process, built up by favorable definitions of the experience that he acquired from others and from the action itself. Once acclimated to the dealing lifestyle and community, and pushed on by both the guarantee of a good income and by resulting patterns of association and friendship, Sam acquires a strong taste for fencing, which becomes increasingly pleasant, desired, and sought after. This taste is multifaceted and includes attainment of success and recognition, the application of skills, the feelings of growth and the control over one's life, and involvement in one's work.

Exit from Fencing: Meaning and Impact For Sam

Sam's arrest and imprisonment for criminal receiving also allows him to measure what he forfeited as a consequence of his forced exit from fencing. Income? Prestige? Interest? Probably his major loss is a financial one: it is income which provided the overriding drive and rationale for his dealership. Sam is faced with the realization that he is unable to make as much money in legitimate business as in fencing, and that his lifestyle requires more money than his legitimate business can pay for.

▶ I'll tell you what you miss. The money, mainly. What money can get for you, of people knowing you have the money. That, and being able to get what you want. If I wanted something, or I wanted to gamble big, the money was there. I miss that. ◀

Second, Sam forfeits his acquired knowledge, skills, and connections for successful dealing. He had spent considerable time and energy cultivating contacts and "getting an education;" he had also made expenditures on equipment, travel, and legal services. Because of these personal and deliberate investments, Sam almost comes to feel that fencing owes him something, a debt that can be realized only through greater participation. (The following quote from Sam implies as much.)

▶ I was more or less at my peak when I got popped. I had my education, had the contacts, and then poof, that is all gone. What I would like to do is, maybe, break someone in, like Steelbeams, 'cause he's got a good head on him and is solid. See, I've got the knowledge of prices and how to hustle, the worldwiseness, you might say. And my contacts—they ain't what they used to be—but they are still pretty good. I could have Steelbeams, say, deal with the thieves—that way I keep a layer in between. I would handle the selling end and help him out with the prices and that. Really, I can't afford to take another fall, 'cause I'd end up drawing social security in prison. And the hassles that come with the fencing, and the long hours, I can do without. ◀

Third, Sam's exit from fencing entails a loss of identity, a shift in organization of life roles, and a transition in the way he thinks and feels. Through the experience of dealing, Sam became deeply embedded in the social and business life of fencing and developed motivations, ties, and identifications with the criminal world, with the occupation of running an illegal business, and with his professional associates. For smoothly efficient and successful deals to occur, trust was extended, alliances formed, and secrecy and safety ensured. This created a kind of commitment to the overall norms and values indigenous to thieves, to other dealers, and to the larger criminal community. The police were a common enemy, kinship was felt with one's associates and trade partners, and binding principles of honor (at least in the ideal) operated. Sam looked on dealing as a career—as both a way of making a living and as an accomplishment—and derived much of his self-image and identity from this part of his life.

Fourth, exiting also meant giving up the *fun* elements that were associated with many aspects of planning and executing deals, as well as access to the hedonistic lifestyle (e.g., gambling, casual sex) which pervaded the higher-level echelon of the underworld in American City. Socially, moreover, Sam forfeited the interactional enjoyment generated through patterns of association and relationships with others in the dealing world.

Fifth, Sam's exit from fencing meant for him the loss of a fairly powerful and prestigious position within the criminal community, together with the ego gratification that came from recognition by others and from the power he could wield over others by trading or by refusing to trade with them. Even more broadly, it meant the loss of the power to withhold or provide friendly advice, extend a recommendation in the right place, or offer assistance of one kind or another. It also meant giving up the enhanced status in legitimate society that Sam had achieved as a businessman-fence.

Lastly, while exiting involved the loss of being somebody in a multifaceted and deeply personal way, perhaps the most painful side of this had to do with Sam's reputation as "good people". Being somebody who is solid is difficult, if not impossible, to transfer to a conventional world role.

All things considered, fencing expressed values that were very important to Sam and enabled him to demonstrate his own mettle and moxie.
On the one hand, fencing tapped into values embodied in American culture: material success, acquisitiveness, competition, and freedom of action, or independence. On the other hand, fencing expressed values and
beliefs that derive specifically from Sam's working-class background (reinforced both by his prison experience and involvement in the theft subculture): streetwise savvy—the ability to outfox and outcon the opponent,
and to outsmart the law; an acceptance of involvement in trouble-making
activity as something which confers prestige, if handled successfully, or
incompetence, if not; a concern with demonstrating physical or mental
toughness and one's ability to take care of oneself; a search for fun and excitement rather than safety and passivity; and strong concern about personal freedom and autonomy. Indeed, in contrast to what so often appears
to be the case with modern man, *alienation* from his work is clearly not
one of Sam's problems.

▶ What did I give up when I got popped? I gave up my life, virtually
everything you might say. Think about it. There's the money. Fencing can make you a very good dollar if you can handle yourself and
know what you're doing. But I miss the action, too, that something
was always going on. The good times with the local gang, just rubbing shoulders with them. Of being known as "good people" by the
thieves and different ones. Really, I gave up being a big shot which in
truth I can say I miss. Fencing gave me a sense of knowing who I was
and a confidence in myself. Tested all my abilities, you might say.
That, and I just miss the satisfaction that comes from being a dealer.

Satisfaction and recognition. It was good money and, like you
asked, prestige in being noticed. But there was a satisfaction there,
just enjoying the action of it and happy with myself, that I was progressing by building up my legit business and the fencing, too. Satisfaction in dealing with people. It made me a smarter person. Gave
me an understanding of things. A different outlook on life. It taught
me to be able to relate to different kinds of people. I always felt I had
leadership qualities. The fencing showed me I could do that, gave
me more confidence in myself, what I was capable of doing. Showed
me I had the business ability. That I was my own boss, that what
happened depended on me, that it rested on my shoulders. If I had
to start life all over, I would be a fence. 'Cause it was really beautiful. [10] ◀

---

10. Jesse muses: "Will Sam fall back into the fencing? I look at it this way.
Once a crook, always a crook. Sam ain't happy unless he's pulling something. If
the risk ain't that high, if the opportunity is there, he'll go for it. Without a
doubt."

Paying The Price

Fencing can be rewarding and enjoyable, nonetheless, it can also wear on a person. First, there is the problem of respectability, which public fences like Sam face, as well as the tensions associated with actual or potential legal complications. Second, there is the fatigue and burn-out that comes from having to constantly out-hustle others, and to contend with the risks inherent in hobnobbing with thieves and other underworld figures. Third, fences like Sam must be prepared to work long hours with few, if any, days off, particularly since they have little control over the timing of thefts and may also have to transport stolen merchandise quickly. Fourth, fencing can play havoc with the fence's personal and family life, since the time and energy required leaves little time for family involvement and the like. Finally, in comparison with legitimate work, fencing does not offer much in the way of job security (to Sam's discovery and dismay).

▶ It can be a bitch, too, can get to you. I used to go up to the park area that overlooked the city, and sit there for hours, just to relax, get rid of the tension, get away from everybody. It can be very, very fast. Always something going on. Somebody calling you, can you handle this or that, meet me at such and such. It's long days, lotta hours. You never know when you'll get a call. Can be three o'clock in the morning: 'Hey, I got such and such.' I was always on the go, always on the run. It's very hard work that way. And having to be on your toes all the time, to out-hustle your thieves and other dealers that are pretty sharp. Different hassles that come up, with the police, say. It can get to you. That's one reason I would stop at Casey's or go up to the park, to relax. The gambling helped there, too, 'cause that was relaxation. In some ways it was too fast. You don't have time for yourself or for your family. It was tough on Becky and the kids on account of they never knew if I'd be around or not. On the spur of the moment, I might load up the family in the van and take off for the day. Get out in the country and have a picnic.

The other thing is knowing the "law of averages" can catch up with you. That something unforeseen can happen, or that you get careless. There are a lot of snitches out there, and fucking crybabies, too. I don't mean your good thieves or your better dealers, now. 'Cause I would rather deal with a good thief than your businessman, any day. Really, there are a lot of assholes out there. All these things can get to you. ◀

Obviously, the rewards of fencing cannot be considered independently of the potential costs, so that the meaning of a dealing career may not be the same for other fences as it is for Sam. The everyday life and background of individual dealers, together with their conception of the part their fencing careers have played in their lives, will affect the reward-cost balance.

Buying stolen property is illegal, immoral, and oftentimes disapproved of. The social controls against becoming a dealer in stolen goods include not only fear of material deprivations and punishments which might result from being discovered, but also apprehension about the deleterious consequences of such a discovery on one's attempts to maintain a consistent self-image, to sustain valued relationships, and to preserve current and future statuses and activities. Some prospective dealers must consider many different side effects; others need consider only a few. Some would-be fences strongly fear the threat of arrest or incarceration and may be anxious about the effects on their reputations should they be discovered by family, friends, or neighbors; others worry little about getting caught by the police or about others discovering their fencing involvement.

While any dealer would prefer to keep his fencing secret, he is unlikely to enjoy handsome profits or earn a good living from it if he only occasionally buys stolen goods from thieves or, if over his entire career, he deals with only a small number of regular thieves. But if he expands his trade and really gets into business, not only many thieves, but eventually the police, will find out.

Becoming known to the police is likely to be an unsettling experience for several reasons. First, it may mean becoming a prime suspect for burglary and larceny investigations—when the police become aware of a property theft and have no evidence leading to particular suspects, the fence may be one of the first persons approached. This, in turn, may lead to being investigated, searched, fingerprinted, having to appear in court, and perhaps even jailed. And becoming publicly known in this fashion will influence the way in which the fence becomes fully known to all his other audiences—not only to his legitimate customers—but also to those who live and work near him who may be concerned about the stigma or objectionable moral evaluation implied by an arrest or conviction.

How damaging the effects of discovery and official labeling are, will partly depend on the dealer's circumstances. The discovery that a lawyer is buying stolen merchandise from thieves who are his clients will likely result in loss of at least some kinds of legal work, if not censure and disbarment. A jeweler or art dealer, for example, may find that certain customers or institutions would withdraw their patronage from the kind of person who would buy and sell stolen jewels or art works. The mere observation of police or thieves at his place of business may so threaten the credibility of the business merchant that customers withdraw their trade because they believe his advice or work cannot be relied upon.

Because Sam is self-employed in a relatively unregulated business, the stigma of an arrest or conviction is less damaging than it might be for someone in a more conventional employment or business. (The same holds for Louie who ran a bail-bond business or Phil who ran a salvage yard operation.) Also, because of Sam's past (e.g., burglary involvement, imprisonment), police contact is not as unsettling as it might be to another merchant; nor is Sam very troubled by the stigmatizing effects on friends and family of his dealing in stolen goods.

Indeed, for Sam and for successful dealers like him, an arrest or conviction may be a benefit, taken as evidence within the criminal community that his relationship with the police is not overly cozy but that "he is one of us." Furthermore, if he performs well before the police or in court and is able to escape deserved penalties, the fence may earn a reputation within law enforcement circles for toughness, for being well-connected, or both. That is, pinning a conviction on him may mean a great deal of work with a low probability of reward.

In sum, the potential costs of discovery and the stigmatizing effects of being a "public" dealer in stolen goods will be greater in some situations and for some individuals than for others. For those more strongly tied to conventional society, either by upbringing, by reputation, or by business circumstances, the material and monetary rewards achieved through fencing stolen goods may not be sufficient to offset the fear of arrest or conviction and the possible loss of friends and personal ties. These side effects will influence one's choice about whether to pursue or sustain a fencing career, just as factors such as skills and bonhomie with the underworld influence one's chances of being selected as a fence.

One's biography and current circumstances may dovetail with the rewards of fencing in still another way. Where one's primary ties to respectable society are strong and where one has been conventionally socialized, the individual may face a *moral problem* at the prospect of engaging in illegal and disapproved behavior. The costs here will include one's ability both to disavow or define away conventional norms as evaluative criteria for one's behavior and to manage the putdown of a criminal status. The prospective dealer who is unable to rationalize his guilt and is unable to reconcile his wish for a positive self-image with his actual career in crime, will be inclined to relinquish the fencing behavior, to retreat to conventional society and conform.

These ethical costs apply very little, if at all, to Sam. Fencing does not pose a moral problem for him. Nor does Sam accept the stigma that some associate with the designation "fence." That Sam's movement into fencing came naturally and painlessly, is described in the next chapter.

Chapter 12

Rationale: The Fence and Society

The only time professional criminals need offer an account of their lives is when they come into contact with curious or critical members of legitimate society who know of their criminal involvement—as Sam did in the preparation of this document.[1] Seasoned criminals like Sam do not need to justify "theft as a way of life;" it is taken for granted and those involved come to accept the idea that they are thieves, hustlers, racketeers, fences, etc., because these are the activities in which they are engaged. Most do not experience much difficulty coming to terms with self-respectability although they may occasionally feel a sense of marginality and estrangement from the society in which they live. Their involvement in illegal or quasi- legal activities and associations with similarly situated persons generally leaves little time or energy for extensive self-reflection or for considering alternatives.

▶ It's not something you really think much about, the fact that you're doing wrong in society's eye. May cross your mind, but you don't dwell on it. I don't feel that much different from the way most people in the straight world feel about theirselves. 'Cause everybody's got

---

1. The theoretical writings that this chapter follows include: Buffalo and Rodgers, 1971; Burke, 1945; Lupsha, 1981; Mills, 1940; Scott and Lyman, 1968; and Sykes and Matza, 1957. Two major themes of these writings are strongly manifest in Sam's account of his life and behavior: that people have a powerful urge to explain themselves, and that man is better at justifying himself than at behaving himself. That Sam recognizes as much, is evident from this quip, which he made shortly after he had read a draft of the book: "Yeh, I liked that chapter 12, [it] was really good. It had me believing I didn't do that much wrong. I always figured there was some saint in me, now I know. [laughter] What you write there is true, 'cause who is guilty and who isn't. But I'm no saint, not all the way anyway! [more laughter]"

his thing, has got skeletons in his closet. I don't feel bad for what I
done. I feel bad for the *way* I done it. The fact I got caught. ◄

Whether an afterthought or an abiding philosophy, Sam's rationale is a
complex set of attitudes and beliefs rooted, first of all, in American ideology that offers many loopholes to the moral axiom that "honesty is the best
policy." Second, his rationale is rooted in the theft subculture in which
seasoned thieves and established members of the underworld see themselves as separate from the amateur offender, the violent criminal, and
the sex offender; and in which criminal activities are defined as paralleling
the dishonest practices of businessmen and corrupt legal authorities.
Third, Sam's rationale is specifically flavored and shaped by the fence role
and by themes in the society-at-large that support the traffic in stolen
property.

Evaluation of Fencing: "It Ain't That Bad"

In this, the first part of how he sees and justifies his fencing involvement,
Sam offers an offense-specific defense of his criminal career by focusing on
the particularly benign aspects of his occupation and by interpreting what
he does in the most favorable light. Next, Sam switches to a general evaluation of his character, after which, he further disarms the critic with his
evaluation of the old saying, "if there were no fences, there would be no
thieves."[2]

The Fence Isn't A "Thief"

By the time the fence sees a stolen item, the crime has been committed.
Nothing can change that. The thief is a thief. But the fence is in a position
to make the best of a bad situation, to put to good use that which has been
taken from the respectable. There is a profit, of course, but that is what
business is about.

▶ A thief is out there stealing, breaking into people's places, and he
would have a tendency of hurting somebody if he was caught, or try
to struggle to get away. A fence would not do that. A fence is just
buying what the thief brings, he is not the one crawling in windows. ◄

By saying, "I don't crawl in windows," Sam magnifies a common distinction between theft and receiving. Either directly or by implication

---

2. Sam's rationale was elicited not only by prodding and moral questioning but
by observation of his comments and responses to varying persons, situations, and
events during the many hours of interaction I had with him. In form and content
Sam's rationale parallels that of Vincent Swaggi, so that I have organized it along
the lines of Klockars' treatment of Vincent's "apologia pro vita" in chapter 6 of *The
Professional Fence*.

Sam means, first, that he does not actually take the merchandise from its rightful owners. Second, Sam means that the distaste and fear which the concept "thief" connotes to some people should not, and does not, properly apply to him. Like the driver or employee thief, the fence does not enter homes or stores to remove property; there is no danger of violence in his presence. The "thief" is lazy, a shadowy figure, somewhat unstable and unpredictable in his behavior; the fence is hard-working and industrious, a businessman who walks public streets openly and may perform public tasks as well.

It can be argued, of course, that Sam is a thief. First, his activities fit the common-law definition of theft: he does "take the goods of another without permission" and does "deprive that person of his rightful property." That Sam recognizes as much is at least implied by his boast in the bloom period of his fencing career about having a "license to steal." Second, Sam at one time was a full-time thief. Third, Sam still does on occasion organize, and even participate in, burglary and truck hijacking.

Sam dismisses these objections as irrelevant to the main theme of his argument. In regard to the first objection, Sam observes that the law itself makes distinctions between theft and receiving, that the police and other legal authorities are much more concerned with thieves than with receivers, and that, if the law was strictly enforced, a good many otherwise law-abiding citizens would qualify as "thieves." Sam claims that, in reality, his behavior is not unlike that of average citizens who buy stolen property but would be outraged at the thought of committing robbery, burglary, or larceny themselves. Moreover, not only the law but his customers, his friends, and his neighbors know there are differences between thieves and receivers, and so does Sam.

In answer to objection number two, Sam maintains that his career in burglary is a matter of his *past* biography for which he, in fact, has served time in prison, thus paying his debt to society. Sam is *now* a fence, has been one for quite some time, and feels he ought to be judged by his present, not his past, social identity.

▶ Are you asking about the burglary or the fencing? When I was into burglary, I was a thief. When I became a fence I gave that up. I wasn't a thief no more. ◀

Third, Sam argues that he is not a "thief" in spite of the burglaries he's committed after becoming a fence—because these are occasional events, a sideline to his major line of criminal work. Like the truck driver, the dockworker, or the store employee, Sam does not steal regularly. Furthermore, Sam defines his burglary as something not typical of the fence role or of what most fences do, but as uniquely personal, a spin-off of the experience and contacts he acquired in an earlier burglary career.

▶ Now I did do a few burglaries and truck thefts. But this was just a sideline. Say, Louie had a contact with a truck driver and wanted to clip a load of merchandise. I might handle it—maybe call Steel-

beams and that crew would do it, or maybe I would do it myself with
Steelbeams. It was the same way, if I had good information on a safe
or on good antiques in a house. I sometimes clipped the place myself, say, with Steelbeams. That way there was more profit for me.
And I enjoyed just pulling a job once in a while. There was a certain
kick there, a little thrill you might say, of opening a safe and seeing if
you can still do it.

But this is not part of being a fence. Not at all. Most of your fences
wouldn't have the experience and the contacts for doing the burglary. Would be out of their league. Take like Louie, he might have
the information on a place to be clipped, but he wouldn't have the
know-how and couldn't get the good thieves to clip with him. 'Cause
I had been a burlar, I knew what to do and the thieves had the
confidence in me, too. ◄

Besides the differences between thieves and fences, Sam claims that
there are also differences between fences and the general run of the criminal population. That the fence straddles the boundary between the
legitimate and illegitimate worlds—indeed, that his success depends on
getting insiders to cooperate with outsiders through him—gives Sam
considerable leeway in separating himself from stereotypical underworld
types, such as drug addicts and robbers, kidnappers and rapists, murderers and mobsters. Fencing is not so bad, Sam reasons, because there are
other possible behaviors and ways of making a living that are far worse.

▶ The fence is no angel, but he's no devil either. Think about it. He's
not mugging old ladies, he's not pushing drugs on kids, he's not
burning down buildings. The fence doesn't force himself on anybody, doesn't take advantage of them that way. He's not into the dirt
either, like the baby porn shit, doesn't lower himself that way. ◄

Lastly, to further magnify the differences between thieves and receivers, Sam maintains that there are also differences between thieves and
drivers, and between thieves and average citizens who buy stolen goods
—with the fence, in Sam's view, being more like the driver or the average citizen than the thief.

▶ A thief is going out knowing he is going to rob somebody, knowing
this beforehand. And most of your thieves don't work, whereas your
truckdriver is an ordinary working man. A person working on a dock
or driving a truck sees an easy way to pick up an extra couple dollars.
So, he clips a little, more or less to have extra beer money or to buy
something for his kids.

Now, those drivers and dockworkers that were stealing regular
and are stealing large things, those I would call a thief because they
know what they're doing. But a driver who may once in awhile bring
something in, I would not consider a thief. That's my belief.

Another thing, the line between a thief and a fence is broader than
the line between the fence and the public. The difference between

me and the public is I done it on a bigger scale. Where your average Joe Citizen would go in a barroom or come to my shop and buy a cheap radio or TV, they'd be looking for bargains, I'd be after truck-loads. They're doing it to save money. I done it to make money. That's the only difference 'cause, see, they're guilty of receiving, too. ◀

Effects of Fencing on Victims are Trivial

Part of Sam's judgment that fencing is not a very serious crime is that it causes little significant injury since the victims are usually individuals or places of business that can afford the loss and can recover most of their loss from insurance payments or through tax write-offs. The fact that these individuals and organizations continue to thrive and to announce large net profits is further evidence to Sam of the inconsequential character of his fencing. He also finds it easy to minimize the general effects that theft produces on pricing. It costs everyone surely, in higher mark-ups and in-surance rates, but the effects are indirect rather than direct, and are spread across many individuals. And these higher costs are hardly trace-able to Sam, since many others are also receiving stolen merchandise and because it is shrinkage (e.g. damaged or lost merchandise) as much as theft that produces higher prices.

▶ I don't feel I hurt any little people 'cause most of the stuff did come out of business places and big places, which were insurance write-offs and which they will many times mark it double what it was. In a roundabout way, yes, the individual is going to pay for it, like with the higher transport and that. I would not feel bad about this. It's the same as, say, chiseling on income tax. You cheat Uncle Sam, but that's not the same as cheating this here person. ◀

That there are no real victims of his fencing activities Sam also extends to those among his customers who he may defraud in one way or another, as when he sells perfectly legitimate merchandise at inflated prices, as if it were stolen. Sam reasons that the greedy individual, or perhaps a naive and easily duped one, is fair game for those who are sharper, quicker wit-ted, or more worldly. The person who is conned by Sam into believing he is buying goods at "just-for-you prices" is a deserving victim and deserves to be taken advantage of. Sam's frequent comment that the "public wants a story" rings like the admonition "There's a sucker born every minute," which has been an ingrained part of our cultural heritage. One of the most American things about American crime is that we are all at liberty to be suckers or swindlers.

▶ The public wants a story. They want to think they're getting some-thing for nothing, a special deal. Many times, now, I've sold what was really junk for a good price 'cause they thought it was stolen. This is really a funny one: Amos Feathers bought a lotta antiques from me, what he thought was antiques. Very educated man, was brilliant, very brilliant, but he was kooky in some ways—believed in devils and was a real religious nut. He was easy to get over on. One time I got two old chairs from the Salvation Army, for like ten bucks a piece. I scratched on them the name of William Church, who was governor of Midstate in the 1890s. Then I put "Death Chair" on one and "Life Chair" on the other, and stained over it. I told Amos this long story about where the chairs came from, the legend behind them, and how the governor kept them in his bedroom. He fell for it, could hardly pay me the money fast enough. Two junky chairs and I got like $600 a piece for them. It's amazing how dumb people are, how easily they can be fooled. ◄

Sam admits, however, that not all victims are so deserving of what happens to them. He handles this by observing that, at least in some instances, he has returned stolen property to its rightful owners, although he admits that, in practice, he does so only when the property is not of great value. The reality for him is his own decency, and the comparatively trivial effect of his fencing activities on victims.

▶ I do feel bad about some of the stuff that came out of private homes 'cause it could be a keepsake piece. Now, I did do this already, like a place was robbed that had 17 guns. One was a German Luger which the guy got while in Germany in World War II, off a dead German officer. This was really a keepsake to him. I ended up with the gun, and I was in a bar, a club, when he was complaining about it. He don't give a damn about the other guns, but that German Luger he'd like to have. I went by his place one night, out in the country, wiped the gun clean and put it in his mailbox. Couple nights later he came in the bar and was talking about the gun. Whoever done it he really appreciated it. It made me feel good knowing he felt good.

But it was funny to hear him talk about it. I got a kick out of it. To hear him, it was some kind of gun. Worth so much. I felt like telling him, he's a goddamn liar. It was a piece of junk. Same way with other people. They build up their story to make it look good in front of others. Like it might have been a .22 or a horseshit pistol, but they tell it like it was an antique 30/30. ◄

Fencing Is Akin To Any Legitimate Business

All things considered, moreover, in Sam's estimation not only is fencing not as bad as some other behaviors, but it is not much different from many legitimate activities. To begin with, fencing is reasonably respectable simply because it is built around a legitimate business. Thus Sam is able, on the one hand, to at least give the impression that he is not "really bad" even though what he does is illegal. And he is able to lay claim to the status of businessman and draw from it both a sense of his well-being and of his place in the broader society. Sam also appreciates that, with the exception of the fact that the fence buys and sells stolen goods, his day-to-day behavior is not especially different from that of his legitimate businessman counterpart. Sam is in his store every day of the week. He buys and sells things, waits on customers, transports merchandise, and advertises in the yellow pages. That is, fencing itself is a business; the apparatus and behavior of the fence parallel closely that of the legitimate merchant.

▶ Not as a fence, not as a hustler, not as a thief. I didn't think of myself any of those ways. A "dealer," yes. But more as a businessman 'cause my legit business always done good. ◀

Equally important, Sam appreciates that dishonesty is a relative, not absolute, quality and that the occupation or business does not exist which does not employ some degree of fraud and deceit in attempting to manipulate the client. Sam can give many examples, say, the funeral director who plays on the bereaved family in order to merchandise his services, but his favorite is probably the building contractor or security agent who recommends a costly, but mostly ineffective, security system as "protection" against burglary-theft.

▶ Every business has its hustle. You ever watch the preachers on TV? Now, that is a good racket, making a fistful of money playing on old ladies and people on their deathbed. They are the ones that ought to be locked up. Your fence really isn't much more crooked than your average businessman, who are many times very shady. It's very hard to do well in business unless you chisel or clip in one way or other. ◀

Sam recognizes that these practitioners usually have little exposure to persons in underworld activities as a whole, so that their less-than-honest practices are apt to be regarded as "legitimate" or as less frequent than those of a dealer in stolen property. Still, the practices represent what Sam believes are widespread violations of the spirit, if not the letter, of the law and enable him to interpret fencing as not really stepping outside the moral boundaries of the society as a whole.

Fencing Thrives Because Of A Hospitable Environment

That the trade in stolen goods requires the knowing participation of otherwise law-abiding citizens affects the way Sam sees his own behavior. More than most people, he witnesses extensive violations of the law against receiving. He sees members of respectable society, including the police and other public officials, coming to him for bargains that they know are suspect. In addition, he is solicited by otherwise legitimate businessmen interested in buying something that they deal in—should he come across it. This widespread trafficking with him is frequent evidence of willful, guilt-free violation of the receiving law, and constitutes an important vindication of the possibly shady character of what he does. These "good" people believe that stolen items make good business. Matters of conscience in no way interfere with their pursuit of a bargain. Furthermore, the legitimate citizen or the businessman who doesn't buy from Sam may maintain friendly relations with him, apparently not sufficiently offended by his activities to ignore him. Sam's customers and his legitimate associates simplify his explanation of why fencing isn't that bad after all.

▶ I'm not saying everyone who gets the chance will buy stolen goods, 'cause there were some who knew I was a dealer and would never buy from me. Like Gene Eastwood—ran the biggest furniture place in town, very expensive furniture—he and I would stop at each other's shop, just to chat, rap about the furniture business. He was legit all the way, strictly legit. I accepted him for what he was, and he accepted me.

But there aren't many Eugenes out there. Tell me this, who wouldn't buy stolen goods if the good opportunity was there. This I believe: Say, you're selling $300 watches for $50. Of ninety-five people, no more than three, at most, would walk away. As long as they're sure they won't get caught and that it's really a bargain, the ninety-two will buy.

Even those I didn't do business with, it was friendly between us. They knew who I was and accepted that. Take Mrs. Ruth, was into arts, crafts, and that. Very knowledgeable, very respected lady. I would go to her for advice, to identify a particular antique, say, a chandelier 'cause it's hard to know a chandelier's age and what it's worth. She'd always tell me: "Sam, if I'm not in the shop, come over to the house." I was always welcome. ◀

Receiving Would Take Place Without Sam

The willingness of many people to buy stolen goods, along with the continuous rise of new fences to replace old ones, is evidence to Sam of how insignificant his own fencing involvement is in the larger trafficking in stolen goods. On grounds that a person's culpability for participation in deviant or illegal acts disappears, or is at least minimized, if the acts are likely to occur anyway, Sam reasons that the consequences, if any, of his private refusal to buy are small.

Whether someone else would buy the merchandise if Sam refused is debatable. The vast majority of merchandise in which Sam trades could be handled by other fences, sold at auctions, or even peddled to friends and neighbors. This will depend on the character of the merchandise—Sam is a general and convenient outlet and is able to dispose of some merchandise which other fences would have difficulty selling (e.g., valuable antiques). And particular thieves or drivers may have great difficulty locating another fence to sell to if Sam refused to buy. Sam elects at this point, however, to interpret these situations as exceptions to his general argument that the buying of stolen goods would thrive without his involvement. There will always be fences or other criminal receivers, and the industrious thief can always find an outlet for his stolen wares—Sam's fencing doesn't change that.

▶ Say, I turned a thief away—many times he will have other outlets, especially the good thief. So I should walk away [from a deal] so some guy up the street can make an easy dollar? Now the shit-ass thief or the truck drivers, maybe not. But I didn't deal that much with the shit-ass thieves anyway. Or say I quit the fencing, packed it in. There would always be another one to take my place. The stealing may slow down for a bit, but not for long. Any gap is always filled in.

It is funny, but you and I would never realize how many people are out there buying stolen goods. The thief can always peddle somewhere. It's amazing. Not fences like me, necessarily, but still buying stolen goods. Really, compared to what goes on, my buying is like a drop in a bucket. ◀

As in judging the morality of receiving stolen property, Sam's eye for the loophole and his ability to puff up some things and to discount others works to his advantage in rendering a favorable accounting of his character and moral worth. His name of balance between good acts and bad, his appreciation of the "evil" in every man's registry, and his commonsense perception of the vague standards by which most of us evaluate men, allow Sam considerable leeway in support of his claim that, all things considered, he's a pretty decent guy.

"I Do A Lot Of Good"

▶ I done wrong in some ways, I know that. But I do know I done a lot of good, too. Anybody that came in my store that was on the level, got a fair shake from me. I'd see a needy person, anybody that came in with nothing, I took care of. I done the poor people of American City a whole lot of good, not just because of the good deals I gave them but in other ways, too. Take Donnie that lived across the street from me. Needed a refrigerator, but he was broke. I told him, "Take it buddy, pay me when you get the money."

I'm no Robin Hood, but I don't feel as though I took bread out of anybody's mouth. No. I do feel as though I put a lot of bread *in* people's mouths. My shop was like no other shop in town. I feel personally I had the best shop in town, the cheapest prices and the most choice of merchandise—and everybody that came got a square deal. You could shop around and come down to my shop and if I see you needed it, you could get it a whole lot cheaper from me than from anyone else.

In my eye I helped a lot of your smaller store people against your big stores like a K-Mart or a Sears. Think about it, many times on TVs, appliances, cassette recorders, lawnmowers, and that, a K-Mart can sell at retail what the little guy is paying wholesale. K-Mart may even take a loss on an item, to get people in the store. Think about that. Your smaller operator can get fucked over pretty easy by the big places. My selling to them can be a help that way. ◀

Besides suggesting that he helps distribute wealth in an affluent society and besides pointing to the good things he has done for people which his role does not require him to do, Sam singles out with special emphasis the assistance he has given to the Red Cross and to other charitable organizations.

▶ The Red Cross always came to me, and they trusted me so much that if there was a fire, say, people got burned out, they would send the people to me to furnish the house, and all I had to do was send them the bill. They never even looked at the furniture. That's how they trusted me. This was strictly aboveboard, now. I treated them fair, more than fair. Gave the stuff away for nothing, you might say.

Or, say, it was Christmas time, this or that club or church group wanted to help out some families, they would come to me for the furniture and for household supplies. It was known that I had a soft heart. ◀

But Sam, himself, considers his generosity and goodwill toward children the most convincing evidence of just how decent a guy he is.

▶ I was always tops with kids. Why, I don't know. Maybe 'cause adults know what they're doing but a kid is never really bad that way. I gave a lot of stuff to kids. I might buy four, five big boxes of toys. Kids come in my shop, dirty kids, Puerto Rican kids, whatever. I'd give them toys.

I would hire some of them to wash windows, clean up the parking lot, do odd jobs. It was more trouble than it was worth. Made a bigger mess than anything. But I felt it was good for them, gave them a chance to work and to make a few bucks.

In my neighborhood I would load up the whole bunch on my truck, go out for ice cream or take them to a ball game. Same with Becky's kids. I was a father to them.[3]

Another thing, if a mother came into my shop, say, she had a couple of kids, and I saw they needed something—they had the run of the store. I was a pushover that way. The same with a couple of fe-

---

3. A neighbor of Sam's comments: "Whenever he'd see kids, I don't care who they were, he was good to them. Mine, anybody's kids, he would go out and buy. In the summer he'd come by in his truck, pick up all the kids in the neighborhood, maybe fifteen, twenty kids, take them to town, go for ice cream. Shit like that. Especially good with kids. That I can say." Rocky notes: "I'm not saying Sam didn't care for Becky 'cause he did, but he stayed with her 'cause of the kids, too. I think he felt sorry for them, that if he didn't get them things, they'd be doing without. Now Becky was good to him, never gave him any hassles, and all that. He did what he did, came and went when he wanted, you might say, no backtalk from Becky. But this made Sam feel good, 'cause he was like a Dad to her kids. The little girl especially Sam was close to." Jesse comments: "He was a goddamn sucker for that woman. Threw away a lot of money on that. I could never understand what he saw in her."

male shoplifters that were peddling to me. Rosie Pieper was one, had three kids she was supporting. A tiny woman, a very good shoplifter. I always paid her top dollar 'cause she was doing it for her kids, not for some doper or some asshole.[4] ◀

Sam is also a kind and responsible employer, as is evidenced in his hiring of Clyde. The fact, however, that Clyde is a valuable employee suggests that Sam's generosity is at least sometimes self-serving.

▶ I took Clyde in off the streets. He was a bum, you might say. I gave him a place to live and paid him a good wage. Anyone that worked for me, I dealt with fairly, helped them out in little ways. Now, Clyde was a good worker, had a good head on his shoulders. That I can truthfully say. He more or less ran the store which freed me for other things. ◀

In other cases, the roles of "good fence" and "decent guy" are, in part congruent, raising questions of self-interest for Sam in acts of apparent generosity.

▶ This has happened more than once, now. Say Davey Lachs was in jail for burglary and his parents came to me 'cause Davey could get paroled if he had a job lined up. Would I help Davey find a job? So I'd sign the papers getting Davey out. What I'd do is hire him for a week or so, then he had to find another job. I was doing it for the parents, too, 'cause many times their hearts are broken to have their sons in jail. Now, Davey did bring me some pretty good stuff, but still, I didn't have to go to bat for him that way. ◀

That Sam may benefit as much (or more) as the recipients of his largesse is acknowledged by Sam and easily accepted. He accepts the gratitude and appreciation of those he helps whether or not he makes money off them, but if motives of making money and doing charity can be combined, so much the better.

▶ It is my nature to lend a hand if someone's in a jam. But this is good business, too. In the long run, chances are it will pay off. You never

---

4. Chubbie notes: "Sam was generous to people, was not a good businessman that way. It was hard for him to turn somebody away. In all truth, some of these mothers, like on welfare, played on that. Especially if they came in with kids, he could be taken that way. Now, if a woman all dressed up and showing off her money came in, if she hassled Sam too much on price, he had a short fuse. One time this woman, high faluttin' type, wanted this chair Sam had upholstered— matched her dining set—but she keeps haggling Sam on price. I'll never forget this 'cause Sam let her have it. 'Lady,' he said, 'You want this chair? You can have this chair!' Carries it outside, right in front of the store, breaks the chair in pieces on the sidewalk, swinging and kicking and smashing it. So Sam says to her: 'This chair means so much to you, you can have it for nothing.' The woman's eye's about popped out, thought she was gonna have a fucking heart attack right there. Sam was something else, I mean to tell you."

know when your paths might cross down the road. A lotta businessmen and shopowners don't think that way—they're greedy, want the
dollar right away, or they don't wanta be bothered with those kinds
of people. Really, they're too dumb to know they are hurting theirselves. ◄

Sam Is Liked And Respected

Sam is a "public" criminal; almost everyone he knows is aware that he is a
fence. His friends and acquaintances include both upperworld and underworld types, not only thieves and drivers, but police, customers, and
businessmen. Some people turn to him for help when they are in a jam
and don't know what to do. He is popular with children, and it should be
added, is somewhat of a ladies' man.[5] That all these people maintain
friendly relations with him is seen by Sam as a reflection of his own worth.

▶ You could not get the people of American City to say I was no good.
There would be many different ones that would recommend me for
anything. I treated people right, dealt with them at their level, no
big front like I was somebody. My word was good and they got a fair
shake. ◄

Sam also knows he possesses qualities admired by others—ambition,
drive, ingenuity, and independence; and he is less of a parasite on society
than many others.

▶ I personally feel this, not necessarily that people looked up to me,
no, but they respected me for what I was. That I built up a business
from scratch, that I always fended for myself. It is not my nature to
be taking a handout.
    Think about it, though, who isn't getting a handout or a free ride in
one way or another. I don't mean just your poor people that come in
my shop on "Mammy Whammy" day [the Friday, twice a month,
when welfare checks are issued.] It's the big shots, too, who are
getting the tax breaks, and the farmers who in many ways are being
supported by the government. Or take your college professors who
take the taxpayers' money to write books about people like

---

5. Bernice, Jesse's wife, comments: "He was a ladies man, for sure. There's
something about him, he knew just what to say and how to say it. He does. No
shit. I mean I knew him, so that's why he couldn't pull nothing with me. But, oh
man, he had a line. He's an interesting man." Steelbeams notes: "Sam liked his
women. He wasn't much to look at but they liked his personality 'cause he was
joking around all the time." Jesse adds "If it was a woman he was after, that son-of-
a-bitch could make himself cry in front of her. No shit. He never shed three tears
in his whole goddamn life, yet this one woman tells me that Sam just cried, had
tears in his eyes. It's hard to believe but he can pull the godamnest things to do
somebody in."

me—who's to say: are you [in a half-serious, half tongue-in-cheek reference to the author] clipping the public, too? ◄

Finally, Sam considers his criminality and his exemplary behavior on the same balance sheet when judging his own character. He is not only loyal to criminal cohorts, but unlike some of his criminal associates, he also has a sense of civic responsibility.[6]

▶ Louie was a greedy bastard. Not just with the fencing, but Louie was a slum landlord, and he would fuck over the Puerto Ricans who many times could hardly speak English. Louie only looked out for himself. If the Red Cross came to Louie, he would throw dirt in their face or chisel them blind. ◄

Only Non-Sinners Can Cast First Stone

It takes a great act of faith, in Sam's view, to believe that human beings voluntarily conform to law solely or even mainly because they have learned from their cultures to believe in its moral rightness. Rather, people refrain from illegal activities in order to avoid jeopardizing relationships that are mutually beneficial or in order to avoid the imposition of punitive sanctions by those with power and authority.

Throughout Sam's rationale, moreover, there is an implicit distinction between two kinds of moral norms—one having to do with standards of conduct that are believed to be "right," "just," or "ideal" forms of behavior; the other with standards of conduct that are deemed the "real patterns," i.e., what people actually do, irrespective of what they are ideally supposed to do, or what they themselves believe they should do. By emphasizing the contradiction between moral codes for the world as it is and as it should be, and by observing that others in society frequently fail to live up to society's ideal norms, Sam favorably compares his own behavior to that of others whom he sees as deviant as himself, if not more so.

▶ I truly believe that everybody has some degree of larceny in them. Everybody is out for the easy dollar. The exceptions to this are very, very few. The line is so narrow between the do-gooders and the ones that receive, it's so narrow you can barely run a thread between them. And the do-gooders, how should I say it, are not more moral. They're leery. Whereas I went through a lot of risk and I wasn't afraid of taking a chance. The average person would be afraid, leery of his old lady finding out, or maybe his kids and the people he knows, and scared of the cops, too.

---

6. Another neighbor of Sam's notes: "What he done was wrong, I know that. But other ones in this town have done a lot more that are still walking free. Sam was good to people, good to his friends. I don't think he really did that much that hurt anybody." Chubbie adds: "Sam was well liked. He was honest with people. Treated people fair."

I know I done wrong. I will say that. But this I truthfully believe: that, in their own way, everybody has their racket and many times what they're doing is much worse than what I was doing. If they ain't receiving, they are chiseling in some other way. There is a weak side and good side to everyone, same as me.

To me this is funny—but if the average person knew how much larceny goes on, the shit that people will pull, say, if they're in a pinch, there would be even more larceny in the hearts of people. Whole lot more.

This is not my thinking now, but there is the old saying about throwing the first stone if you haven't sinned. Remember? *Only* if you haven't sinned, then can you throw. I don't feel that many stones will be falling on me. ◄

The moral hypocrisy that Sam attributes to conventional society may represent a cynical view of the world, but his justification is a well-established one in society at large: "There are others just as bad, if not worse, than me." In effect, Sam asks: "How am I different from anyone else." It is corrupt cops and public officials, however, who are the strongest living witness to Sam's view of the world and also confirm his own moral decency.

► I know officials that was on the take. I know local cops, state cops. I know lawyers, district magistrates, clerks, that was on the take. I know of businessmen that were into one thing or another, shady you know. But the cops I knew through my life was the worst. They were more wrong than me because they want to put on a front for the public, yet they would patronize me.

Now, I don't blame the cops for what they done, 'cause they have to make a living, too. But the crooked cop that puts on a false front, wants to blow himself up in the public's eye and put himself up on a pedestal, that I couldn't stand. Take this one cop in American City, Willard Pike, would fix parking tickets and that for half the city. But he picked up his own brother for drunk driving and wouldn't give him a break 'cause he wanted to blow himself up as a good cop. What a creep.

The same way with this one state trooper, Kenny Krug. It was always blown up in the paper about what a great cop he was. Yet he could be bought off. Ran around giving talks at the church clubs, see him on TV blabbing about the judges being soft on criminals, and that. He wanted to come across as a goody-goody cop, yet when it came to taking money, his hand was very open. ◄

In sum, by offering positive anecdotes about his own generosity, by defining the average citizen as having larceny in his heart, and by finding others—thieves, corrupt police, and unscrupulous fences—more morally bankrupt than himself, Sam can lay claim to his own good character (namely, that in spite of everything he has done, he is a pretty decent fellow). This claim is reinforced by Sam's judgment that he is not a "thief," that comparatively few people are hurt by his fencing activities, and that matters of conscience seldom keep respectable people from buying stolen items from him.

Because of the way Sam organizes his rationale, it is difficult to criticize what he says. His eye for the loophole and his ability to easily shift the moral grounds for establishing responsibility work as well in interpreting his fencing involvement in the most favorable way as they do in displaying evidence of his good character. That Sam also adheres to deeply ingrained "American" values—competition, material success, individual action, freedom, hard work, acquisitiveness, and loyalty—further allows him to display his faith in a moral order not notably different from that which most of us accept. There is a good bit of the American dream in his fencing career—taking advantage of the opportunity to make money where [in America] there is too much wealth and corruption, and where there are so many larcenous people who are seen as morally no better than the receiver of stolen goods. Within this framework, fencing is not only a matter of morality but of merit.

If No Fences Then No Thieves: "Who is Responsible?"

The final, and most riveting, fragment of Sam's rationale—in many ways a culmination of what has already been described—is revealed in his evaluation of the old adage: "If there were no receivers, there would be no thieves." This saying has for centuries been the rallying cry of commentators, jurists, and criminologists pressing for legal and social reforms aimed at the criminal receiver. Supposedly, fences encourage thieves by rewarding them for their stealing and by advising them about how to steal successfully. Simply by their continued existence and availability, fences tend to assure the continued existence of a population of thieves.[7]

---

7. The saying "if no receivers no thieves" was first quoted by Patrick Colquhoun (*A Treatise on the Police of the Metropolis*, 1795:289) in his pioneering studies of receivers in late eighteenth-century England. Since then, many commentators have exactly repeated the saying, while others have said the same thing in more colorful language. In 1872, the crime fighter Edward Crapsey used a military metaphor suggesting that without the receiver "the rogues would be an army without arms." In 1887, Matthew Davenport proposed that the thief without the receiver would "resemble a merchant in the desert who could not exchange his goods for the necessities of life." In an April 1926 *New York Herald-Tribune* article entitled "Swift Punishment of Crafty 'Fences' seen as key to War on Theft," John Harrington argued that "the real instigator" of thievery is the fence who "is the invisible master of the show, pulling the strings which move the puppets of crime." More recently, Robert Earl Barnes, a repentant thief, in self-serving testimony before a congressional committee investigating fencing, explained that without the fence "a thief who steals merchandise is like bread without yeast, no good," and added in later testimony that "punishing thieves rather than fences is

An Illusory World

Sam concedes that there is some truth in the saying, but generally dismisses it as "goofy"—first, because it portrays a world which never did and never will exist; and second, because it contrives a lopsided answer to the question of "who is responsible?"

▶ What do you mean, "if no receivers no thieves," 'cause there are many people, in the law's eye now, who are guilty of receiving? If you mean people like Louie and me, then I'd say "No"—that stopping us wouldn't make much difference. If you got rid of all receiving—so the thief had no place to peddle the stuff—it would be more true. But how can that be, 'cause the world doesn't operate that way. There are so many people who will buy hot stuff. I would say today that most of your good jewelry goes to private buyers, say, a lawyer the thief knows, more so than through regular fences. And many times the thief can peddle stuff at a flea market or an auction and the people buying don't even know it is stolen.

I don't feel that my being a fence contributed much to the burglaries and that in American City. Instead of selling to Louie, maybe, or going to a fence outside of town, they were coming to me. That would be about it. I think if anything it would've helped with cutting down on the robberies and the muggings, where the thief goes after cash, 'cause now he has an outlet for merchandise.

To me, the saying is just that: a saying. Probably made up by the do-gooders and the cops wanting to blow themselves up. What world are they talking about? Not this one. Here's the thing—you will always have thieves, same as you will always have fences, the same as you will always have people guilty of receiving, and the same as you will always have do-gooders and corrupt cops. I don't think that can be changed. ◀

What Sam argues, is that eliminating fences like himself would have minimal effects on overall levels of property theft, since many thieves and drivers do not use a fence in this sense at all. In the hypothetical eventuality that *all* criminal receivers were to disappear, many thieves would also disappear. But there would still be left plenty of thieves, such as the thief who steals money, credit cards, or checks which he passes himself, or goods for his own consumption. Other thieves would manage to pawn

---

like cutting off the end of the worm. The small part lays there, while the large portion crawls off, and within a few days heals itself and once again is complete." Subsequently, in her 1970s work, *The Fence: A New Look At Property Theft*, Marilyn Walsh has deified this "old view" of the fence's role in property theft: "The thief is little more than an instrument of the fence—a highly visible but relatively minor cog in a gigantic distribution circuit. The fence, then, is the controlling influence over both the thief and his theft activities. As such, the fence of stolen goods emerges as the *prime mover* (emphasis mine) in property theft" (Walsh, 1977: 175).

their takings to lay receivers or to ordinary shopkeepers who either do not know that the goods are stolen or, if they do, do not make a business of dealing in stolen merchandise. Still other thieves would sell their stolen wares cheaply in a tavern, on the street, at a flea market, or at work; or they may sell stolen goods to their friends and neighbors or to other thieves or police, perhaps, stealing on order. At any rate, as Sam sees it, the utter disappearance of receivers is a hypothetical eventuality, not a real one.[8]

The Fence Doesn't Cause The Goods To Be Stolen

▶ Listen to this: A big thing in Midstate right now is whether to legalize the video poker machines and whether to bring in casino gambling. A couple of years ago the big stink was over bingo, like in the churches and fire halls. What difference will it make, if the poker machines are locked up and the churches give up the bingo games— would that stop people from gambling? ◀

In the same way that video poker machines and gambling casinos assure the continued existence of a population of gamblers, Sam acknowledges that fences are part of the machinery that sustains and encourages theft. One can state categorically that, if there were absolutely no gambling devices, no places to gamble, there would be no compulsive or intemperate gamblers. But with a logic that is probably familiar to many casino owners, bingo enthusiasts, and bookmakers, Sam argues: "I don't make anybody steal."

According to Sam, the motives for theft are relatively simple: people steal for money or for excitement. Stealing is the main livelihood of some thieves while for others the illegal earnings provide drugs, gambling, women, and "high living" in general. Drivers and warehouse thieves, on the other hand, use the money from what they pilfer and then sell to add a little extra to the family income or for "beer money" or for "getting a little nooky [sex] on the side."

Sam is a one-time burglar: it is preposterous to suggest to him that it is he, rather than the thieves and drivers, who is responsible for theft. Nor is Sam swayed by the contention that he and other fences encourage thieves by approving of their stealing or by advising them how to steal successfully. Sam contends that most fences offer little in the way of advice and support to thieves, and those that do, not only do so infrequently, but mainly provide it for only a handful of select thieves.

---

8. Klockars (1974:166) makes a similar point: "It is reasonable to suppose that in the hypothetical eventuality that all receivers, criminal and noncriminal, were to disappear, many thieves would continue to exist by shifting their stealing to non-receiver-dependent lines. In brief, if there were no receivers, there would still be all sorts of thieves, and possibly more thieves of sorts we don't like than we have now."

▶ I didn't help that many thieves, now. I think the same goes with other fences. Most of the time, you're just buying what they bring, nothing more. When I was into burglary, there wasn't any fence coaching me or putting up the money and that. A lot of that is bull-shit. A thief is doing his thing, and the fence is doing his.

Now, it is only natural that a thief is curious and will ask questions, say, about antiques—and you explain to him what you are looking for, and what's a good piece and what ain't. And fences learn from thieves, sometimes. It goes both ways. It is a fact, too, that I did show Rocky and a couple of other burglars how to open a safe, 'cause they came to me for help. But this was a fallback to my being a burglar, not on account of my being a fence.[9] ◀

Moreover, Sam's sense of his own life history is one of individual responsibility. He can see how some of his experiences and contacts encouraged his criminal career. But to blame anyone else for what he's done or what he does today would strike Sam as unmasculine, and mark him as a weak person. And if according to law and in the public's mind a thief is deemed responsible for his stealing behavior, than how is the fence also responsible?

▶ I could point to this or that which made me be a burglar or a fence. You see this in prison. Guys whining, crying it wasn't their fault. The

---

9. Rocky describes what happened: "I'm bullshitting with Sam about when him and Jesse hit safes, so he says: 'Tell you what, I'll take you to this safe, let you prac-tice on it.' Showed me how to punch it. Explained how to peel it, if it won't punch. Then one night I tells Reggie, we're gonna grab this safe. So we hit a fire station, found the safe and it opened easy like you wouldn't believe. Next day I sees Sam, tells him what happened. He says: 'You're crazy, you didn't do that.' I said, 'You wait and read the paper.' That same day it was in the fucking paper. Sam says: 'You cocksucker you, you did do it. And you did okay.' 'Cause there was like $1400 in it." Rocky then adds: "So, I did learn from Sam but not because he was a fence. I sold to Louie, too, but I didn't learn shit from him. With Sam, it was natural you'd talk about things. He'd say: 'If you ever get picked up [by the po-lice], don't say a damn word. Tell them you don't know nothing, wanna call your lawyer.' Or, he'd say: 'You got to watch the areas you go into, for pulling jobs. Make sure nobody sees your car, be fucking sure they don't see your face.' Shit like that." Another burglar recounts: "Sam broke me in on safes. How to open them. My buddy and me would carry the box out, contact Sam and he'd open it, for a rakeoff of like fifteen percent. And he was doing it for a favor, too, 'cause we was bringing him a lotta stuff. Once I got the hang of it, then we didn't have him come no more. Didn't need him. More money for us." Jesse comments: "If the truth comes out, I fucking wonder how many guys learnt from Sam how to crack a safe. For a fact I know he taught Bowie 'cause when I first met Bowie he didn't know nothing about safes. Years later I bumps into him, he knows all about safes. 'Where in the fuck did you learn this shit,' I says. 'From Sam,' he says. Now you can bet your fucking ass there are others, that Rocky and some of those fucking kids learnt from Sam. He'd want to impress them, get a kick out of showing them."

counselors are playing 'head' games with them and they are playing 'head' games with the counselors, and with themselves. What I did, I did because I wanted to. Nobody got me to steal, nobody made me be a fence.

This I believe: A thief is a 'thief.' He's gonna steal 'cause that's what he knows how to do. And the thief will give up stealing only when he wants to, when he gets tired of crawling in windows. A fence can't change that.

This is bullshit, blaming the fence for what the thief does. Tell me this: why did I do all that time in the penitentiary for the burglary. I didn't hear no judge say, 'Sammy, you can go free 'cause your fence made you do it.' ◄

With this same line of reasoning, while Sam may hold many thieves in low regard, seeing them as stupid and even as easily led, he does not regard them as puppets of the fence as they are sometimes characterized. The exception, possibly, is very young or juvenile thieves, but Sam doesn't buy from them. Adult thieves steal freely and of their own volition. While a particular thief may be more dependent upon a particular fence than the fence is upon the thief, both are dependent upon each other. What exists are mutually beneficial relations between autonomous thieves and autonomous fences.

▶ The fence usually has the upper hand, but the thief is no patsy. It would be different, say, if the fence is just dealing with kids—'cause they can be more easily led—but who's to say, 'cause some of these kids are thieves all the way.

Really, the thief and the fence need each other, and each one is doing his thing. It can just as easy be said, that 'if there were no thieves there would be no fences,' know what I mean? ◄

Public-Police Involvement in a Criminal System

Sam's counterclaim—that it is thieves who in fact keep fences like Sam in business—is just the tip of the iceberg in a logic by which he turns upside down the moral premise or reasoning which undergirds the decree that the continued existence of fences assures a population of thieves. What about those elements, he asks, that assure the production of new fences, to wit, not only thieves but also businessmen and private citizens who willingly buy stolen goods from suspect characters "no questions asked," along with legal authorities who in the first place allow these suspect characters to practice their trade?

▶ Who is guilty and who isn't? I am fencing, right? I quit crawling in windows, have somebody else crawl in the windows for me, you might say. But still the thief is doing his own thing and is bringing the stuff to me.

But where does it stop? To me, the people who buy are as guilty as the ones who steal. Listen to this. The public and your ordinary businessman is buying from me, knowing or surmising the stuff is hot. I get popped for fencing and the lawyer takes my money that I made fencing to defend me. He's receiving money that I made from receiving stolen goods. The DA's brother and the cops are shopping at my store, patronizing me, looking for bargains and asking me to keep my eyes open for something they needed. Where does it end? ◀

The fact that the fence's success rests so much on what others from respectable society are willing to do both for and with him helps the fence reconcile his wish for a positive self-image with his actual career in crime and is, in the final analysis, the heart and soul of the fence's rationale. Thus, Sam's reflection:

▶ I'm not saying I done no wrong. Not saying that. I'm not saying the good I done makes undone the wrong. But the line is very thin, who's guilty and who ain't. ◀

Importantly, Sam concludes his rationale, admitting to his own, and to any fence's, contribution to property theft. But employing a concept of responsible for his stealing, then Sam is not), Sam forcefully plays hardball with our own contribution to the nature of things. Why, Sam muses, should receiving be a moral problem for him, when it isn't one for the people around him? Simply stated, the fence is responsible for encouraging theft but it is also painfully evident that:
If there were

- No thieves and drivers
- No bargain-hunting private citizens
- No unscrupulous businessmen
- No corrupt police or legal authorities

. . . there would be no fences.

Chapter 13

In Perspective: The Making
of a Fence

More than anything the focus of this document has been on the process of becoming and being a fence: buying and selling stolen property profitably and continuing to do so without getting caught.[1] From the vantage point of the prospective dealer, this process entails both *being willing* and *being able*, i.e., it hinges on whether dealing in stolen goods is subjectively acceptable to an individual as well as objectively possible.

Both are necessary conditions, and may complement one another. A willingness to buy may lead to the search for skills and opportunities, and the available opportunities may increase the desire to buy. Like their legitimate counterparts, those who pursue illegitimate careers gravitate to those activities which are easily available, are within their skills, provide a satisfactory return, and carry the fewest risks. Simply put, one is more willing to do what, in fact, one is able to do.

Being Willing: Is Fencing Subjectively Acceptable?

Whether one is *willing* to deal in stolen goods depends on the extent to which the activity is seen as immoral, as inexpedient, or both. For the average citizen or merchant—because of upbringing, of ties to conventional society, or of risks to a legitimate career or business—the attractions of fencing stolen goods are offset either by moral concerns over engaging in illegal and disapproved behavior, by worries about discovery and getting caught by the police, or by fears of exploitation and violence associated with an illicit setting. Sam puts it this way:

---

1. This chapter is framed in the theoretical tradition of Howard Becker's work *Outsiders* (1963), especially his seminal piece "On Becoming A Marijuana User" in which Becker describes the conditions or contingencies for both becoming and being a regular user of marijuana. Also helpful was chapter 7, "The Sociology of Vincent's Place," in Klockars's *The Professional Fence*.

▶ It's a must the fence have larceny in him ["larceny in his heart"], maybe even a bigger dose than what most people will have. 'Cause, really, the fence is a thief—you're stealing but you don't call it that. Myself, if the chance is there to "clip" or "get over on" someone, I'm not worrying if it's crooked or not. Another thing, the average person is leery: afraid of his old lady finding out, or maybe his kids and the people he knows. And scared of the cops *and* the thieves, too. Myself, I ain't got the heart I once had, but I went through a lot of risk and am not afraid to take chances. ◀

Being Able: Is Fencing Objectively Possible?

Whether one is *able* to deal in stolen goods involves overcoming the economic and legal obstacles of running an illegal business. On the economic side, the would-be fence must confront and solve the problems that present themselves to any business: capital, supply, demand, and distribution. On the legal side, he must cope with the dangers posed by control agents and the potential disruption of his fencing business.

Managing the economic and legal realities of running a fencing business are the "job" demands facing any prospective dealer in stolen property. Both Sam's account and the other literature on fences suggest that, no matter how varied and diverse the criminal careers of successful fences are, they embody solutions to *five* demands or interrelated conditions. These conditions must be more or less continuously and simultaneously met, but for descriptive purposes each is considered separately here.

Condition #1: Upfront Cash

The absence of the strong arm of the law to enforce agreements, the need for secrecy, and, frequently, the thief's need for money—all contribute to a general rule in fence-thief dealings: the fence pays on the spot. Thus, much more so than in legitimate commerce, running a fencing business requires upfront cash, or at least the capacity to raise cash quickly.

How much upfront cash is needed will vary by type of dealership in stolen goods. Moreover, the amount of cash needed can vary considerably from one time to another owing to the unpredictability of the trade in stolen goods—fencing can be busy one week, dead the next. The fence's preferences obviously influence the thief's stealing behavior, but the fence controls neither when the thief steals, nor what is stolen.

Condition #2: Knowledge of Dealing: Learning The Ropes

Individuals who become dealers in stolen goods are subjected to learning experiences along five themes. These types of learning, furthermore, occur more or less concurrently and continuously throughout the fence's career. First, there is the sharpening of one's "larceny sense"—the learning of attitudes and techniques conducive to general forms of theft and fraud. Second, there is learning how to "buy right"—to buy and sell stolen property profitably while maintaining the patronage of both sellers and buyers. Third, there is learning how to "cover one's back"—to buy and sell regularly and routinely without getting caught. Fourth, there is learning how to make and sustain the contacts for establishing a successful fencing business—that is, the necessary contacts with thieves, with buyers, and with complicitous legal officials. Fifth, quite broadly and intertwining with the other learning experiences, there is learning how to "wheel and deal"—to exploit one's environment, to *make* one's opportunities rather than simply buying and selling stolen merchandise when the opportunity presents itself.

Condition #3: Connections With Suppliers Of Stolen Goods

Many people in society occasionally find themselves being approached to buy stolen property. Persons engaged in certain occupations, for example, those of pawnbroker, jeweler, secondhand dealer, salvage yard operator, and auctioneer, particularly lend themselves to these invitations because of the similarity between the types of property commonly stolen and those routinely handled in their occupations. Other persons, for example, bartenders, bondsmen, criminal lawyers, policemen, gamblers, and drug dealers, are also likely to be invited to buy stolen property owing to the types of people they routinely meet.

The fence differs from such persons in that he must generate and sustain a steady clientele of suppliers in order to buy stolen property regularly and routinely. Creating a steady stream of willing sellers may not be difficult if the prospective dealer is willing to buy from the "bottom-barrel" thief or the thief with a low level of sophistication. But building up a clientele of thieves who steal merchandise of good value and who are also relatively safe to do business with (e.g., they don't engender hassles with the police) is a quite different matter. In this regard, the fence's suppliers of stolen goods may include not only burglars, shoplifters and other criminal types but truck drivers, warehouse workers, shipping clerks, or salesmen.

Condition #4: Connections With Buyers Of Stolen Property

What the fence offers the thief—the opportunity to convert his stolen property into money rapidly, and the option to save him the time and labor of locating an outlet for his stolen wares—rests ultimately on the fence's ability to sell the property he has bought. While it is commonplace to emphasize how the thief depends on the fence (e.g., "if no receivers then no thieves"), the fence is in precisely the same position as the thief in regard to his dependence on a market for stolen goods. That is, the fence must have ready access to markets that are effectively closed to many thieves. By virtue of his legitimate holdings, the fence may be in these markets already. But many, if not most, fences rely on outlets other than their legitimate business for disposing of the stolen merchandise they purchase. Thus, in what is probably a more difficult and complicated matter than making connections with thieves and suppliers, the prospective dealer needs to establish contacts with store merchants or other secondary purchasers as markets for selling the stolen property he has bought.

Condition #5: Complicity of Law Enforcers

By buying and selling stolen property on a regular and sustained basis, the fence becomes a public figure with a reputation as a fence not only among thieves but among the police. He must, then, contend with the prospect of aggressive enforcement efforts being focused on him.

This problem can be handled in one of two ways. The fence may corrupt the authorities with favors, e.g. good deals on merchandise or cash payments, with the latter paid directly by the fence or made through the services of a well-connected attorney. Or the fence may play the role of informer, and supply criminal intelligence to the authorities in exchange for being permitted to operate. He may aid in the recovery of stolen property that police are under special pressure to recover, and he may facilitate the arrest of thieves or other criminals.[2]

Inseparable as it is from official complicity of one kind or another, the fence's immunity also springs from the legal difficulties of proving the crime of receiving stolen merchandise. Some fences rely heavily on official protection, but all employ procedures aimed at frustrating attempts to prove illegal conduct by making their fencing activities indistinguishable from those of the legitimate business world. Besides using a legitimate business to mask an illegal trade, many fences are experienced men, with financial and legal resources that enable them to thwart successful prosecution should it be initiated.

Particular dealerships may require different solutions to the economic and social realities of running a fencing business. Some fences may need only a modest amount of upfront cash because they deal with seasoned thieves who are willing to give them short-term credit or leeway to raise the money. Also, some fences may have extensive legitimate holdings or may deal in only one or two product lines, so that they have less need to develop outside markets for disposing of the stolen property they buy. And fences who deal with a handful of carefully selected thieves may manage to keep their fencing involvement more or less secret, and thus will have less need for complicity with law enforcement than the fence who

---

2. Fencing, of course, is not the only kind of criminal enterprise that often relies on official corruption. From the observations of many law enforcement officials as well as from the findings of many sociological studies of crime, apparently it is a virtual "iron law" that official complicity of one kind or another is a necessary condition for many kinds of lucrative criminal enterprise.

deals with a wide array of general thieves who, not only are likely to be arrested by the police, but if arrested, may inform against the fence.

Being able to deal successfully in stolen merchandise carries with it not only the reward of money but also the satisfaction inherent in salesmanship, expertise, challenge, and associated status. To deal successfully also implies something about the fence's abilities, such as interpersonal and manipulatory skills and business acumen. But, as has been described, fences like Sam succeed not only because of their talents and entrepreneurial initiative, but as much, or more so, because of the relationships and social networks they form both in the underworld and in legitimate society. The fence's success depends not only on what he himself is able to do, but on what others are willing to do for and with him. These others, Sam explains, include not just "thieves" but "law-abiding citizens," too.

▶ The thieves *made* me a fence, and the different ones that bought from me. The local businessman and the public, too, 'cause they would shop at my store and buy what they could surmise was warm. The local gang was very important 'cause they threw a lot of openings my way, and that was more or less a sign to others that they could deal with me. The cops helped, too. You got to have their cooperation.

The line is thin, very thin, between the public and the fence. Where your average Joe Blow would go in a barroom or come to my shop and buy a cheap radio or TV, I'd be after truckloads. They'd be looking for bargains, I done it to make money. Who is guilty and who isn't? I don't think that many stones will be falling on me. ◀

Sam's reasoning on how he, and presumably other fences, are "made" is less an indictment than a substitute for indicting, an induction that gives himself and other fences an easy conscience about behavior that is, for them, fun and profitable. The substance of his argument is not so easily put aside, however. The fence's role in the overall flow of stolen property from thieves to eventual consumers is obviously an important one. But so is that of other agents in the traffic in stolen property: thieves, occasional dealers, or those to whom the fence sells. Then there is the role of police and other authorities for whom the fence may issue his services. All things considered, Sam points out, the sins of the "dealer" are not terribly serious.

Appendix

Images of the Fence's Role in Property Theft

Nothing can be more just than the old observation, "that if there were no Receivers there would be no Thieves."—Deprive a thief of a sale and ready market for his goods and he is undone. [Patrick Colquhoun, A Treatise on the Police of the Metropolis, 1795:289*]*

Already an "old observation" when Colquhoun first quoted it in his pioneering study of receivers in eighteenth-century London, the saying "if no fences no thieves" has been a bedrock of the socio-legal writings about fences that have been heavily colored by the writer's interest in social and legal reforms that would better take into account-from the writer's point of view-the fence's role in property theft.[1] Colquhoun himself was quite explicit: his intent was to instruct both the citizenry and the authorities that:

▶ In contemplating the characters of all these different classes of delinquents, there can be little hesitation in pronouncing the Receivers to be the most mischievous of the whole lot; inasmuch as without the aid they afford, in purchasing and concealing every species of property stolen or fraudulently obtained, Thieves, Robbers, and Swindlers, as has already been frequently observed, must quit the trade, as unproductive and hazardous in the extreme. (Patrick Colquhoun, *A Treatise on the Police of the Metropolis*, 1795:289) ◀

And Colquhoun's purpose was a call to action, an admonishment that the strong arm of the law better take into account the role of the receiver in property theft:

▶ Let the strong arm of the law, and the vigor and energy of the Police be directed in a particular manner against Receivers; and the chief

---

1. See chapter 12 (*n.*7) for a discussion of differing ways of "repeating" the old saying "if no receivers no thieves."

part of those robberies and burglaries, which are so much dreaded, on account of the acts of violence which attend them, would absolutely cease to exist:—and the resource for plunder being thus narrowed in so great a degree, robberies on the highway would alone seldom answer the purpose of the adventurer; where the risk would be so exceedingly multiplied, while the advantages were in the same proportion diminished;—the result therefore would be, that in the suppression of the Receivers, the encouragement to be Thieves and Robbers would be taken away: and the present Depredators upon the Public must either return to honest labour as useful members of the State, or submit to be starved. [Patrick Colquhoun, *A Treatise on the Police of the Metropolis*, 1795:289–290] ◄

It is Colquhoun's view, and that of many writers both before and since him, that the fence is the main species of "bad guy," the principal if not the sole culprit of property theft. This conception of the fence, coupled with the reformist agenda of many jurists and commentators, helps explain the literary legacy of the eighteenth-century fence, Jonathan Wild. (Already briefly discussed in chapter 1). Far more than any fence in history, Wild is a model for the saying "if no receivers than no thieves." Whether, the model of the fence that Wild provides is much bigger, more important, and more representative than it ought to be—is another matter.

Jonathan Wild

The remarkable Jonathan Wild is, without doubt, the most powerful and prominent fence in history.[2] Wild dominated the London underworld from roughly 1714 until his hanging in 1725 and, according to Daniel Defoe, employed some seven thousand thieves. Wild's career captured the imagination of pamphleteers of his age who peddled "biographies" of him before and after his death, while historians have recorded Wild's exploits in numerous monographs. Even today, some two-and-half centuries after his death, it is common practice for writers to describe Wild's fencing career as a backdrop to their discussion of contemporary fencing activities.[3]

Wild was born about the year 1682 in Wolverhampton, Staffordshire. Little is known about his life before 1710, when at age twenty-five, he came to London and shortly thereafter was arrested and thrown into the Wood Street Compter, a debtor's prison, for monies owed to several creditors. During his stay in prison, Wild observed corrupt jailers and

---

2. For more detail about Wild's life and criminal career, see Howson, 1970; Klockars, 1974; and Pringle, 1958.

3. The Pennsylvania Crime Commission, for instance, includes a section about Wild's criminal career in its report, entitled: *A Decade of Organized Crime, 1980 Report*, as evidence of the fence's power and his role in property theft.

magistrates and cultivated the friendship of a great many thieves from whom he learned much about their way of life and occupation. Wild himself says of his incarceration that he was "let into the secrets of criminals under confinement; of which afterwards he availed himself." [George Borrow, *Celebrated Trials*, 1928:517]

Within a year after his release from prison in 1912, Wild had hooked up with Mary Milliner, a prostitute who became his mistress and who further introduced him to the London street scene.

▶ Like many of her colleagues on the game, Mary was, in the crooks' slang of that time, a "buttock-and-file." The first word meant whore and the second pick-pocket, and the reason for the hyphens is that she did both jobs at the same time. Most whores did their business standing in the street, and a girl with a light touch was in a good position to pick her customer's pockets when he was likely to be somewhat off his guard. The main danger was that he would discover the theft before she had time to get away, so most girls liked to have a boy-friend lurking in the shadows. He was called a twang. Wild went out as Mary's twang. [Patrick Pringle, *The Thief-Takers*, 1958:21] ◀

Wild and Mary eventually opened up a small brandy shop, from which Wild built up a small but thriving business disposing of watches, snuff boxes, and other goods brought to him by thieves. It was at this location, also, that Wild met and became a junior partner with the notorious City Marshall, Charles Hitchen, who was then the city's principal thief-taker —someone who aids in the capture of thieves or provides evidence to convict them—and largest dealer in stolen personal property. From Hitchen, Wild learned much about the intracacies of trading in stolen goods, including the requirement that the safest way to be a successful receiver was to be a thief-taker too. (See discussion of thief-taking below.)

The partnership between Hitchens and Wild lasted about a year. Then Wild struck out on his own in 1714 with the advertisement quoted below:

▶ Lost on Friday evening 19th March last, out of a Compting House in Derham Court in Great Trinity Lane, near Bread Street, a Wast Book and a Day Book; they are of no use to anyone but the Owner, being posted into a Ledger to the Day they were lost. Whoever will bring them to Mr. Jonathan Wild over-against Cripplegate Church, shall have a Guinea Reward and no Questions asked. [Quoted in Gerald Howson, *Thief-Taker General*, 1971, 66] ◀

Such advertisements were common in the London papers of Wild's time and were used by any number of entrepreneurs to build up a "lost property business"—a subterfuge by which they established contacts with thieves and, in effect, fenced stolen goods by selling them back to their original owners and collecting rewards. Wild placed hundreds of similar advertisements during the next few years on behalf of victims of theft. Each described the property which had been "lost" (stolen), offered a reward, and explained where the property could be returned, "no questions asked." The advertisements served several purposes: they diverted suspicion from Wild as a possible confederate of thieves; they brought him new thieves who could be recruited to work for him, if, in fact, he did not know who had stolen the goods; and, they kept the name of Jonathan Wild before the reading public as a man who could successfully recover stolen property.

Wild made a fortune by opening an office for the "recovery of lost property" and built it into the greatest criminal organization in history. In later years, Wild branched out from recovering "lost" property to owning a cargo ship, the *Captain Roger Johnson*, which transported personal property stolen from English gentlemen and ladies to their counterparts in Europe, and returned to smuggle goods back into England. At the peak of his power in 1724, he ruled the London underworld and knew more about what was happening in it than all of the law enforcement bodies in Great Britain combined. Wild's career ended on the gallows in 1725, his downfall caused by the combination of "bad press," (a withering public image) and the enterprising efforts of various law enforcers to convict him by whatever means could be arranged.[4]

Thief-Taking

What Wild accomplished, far more than anyone before or since, was to use thief-taking to achieve a near monopoly on receiving stolen goods. Besides his own extraordinary talents, Wild was able to do this because of the weak state-control apparatus that existed in sixteenth and seventeenth century London. The "law" was no match for the strength of sanctuaries and criminal structures that were emerging out of the industrial and commercial transformation of the times. There was no professional police force, and formal agencies of social control were largely unpaid, overworked, divided, geographically contained, and without coordination and support. The watch and ward, the constabulary, and city marshalls were seldom capable of surveying, detecting, and stopping crime. Amateur volunteer police were reluctant to enter criminal areas. Instead, the state relied on private intermediaries to enforce the law and adopted strategies of spying, informing for profit, and pardons to control crime.

---

4. The immediate event leading to Wild's declining public image was his arrest (thief-taking) of Jack Sheppard, a likable outlaw who enjoyed a small folk-hero's reputation for once breaking into prison to rescue his mistress. This reputation ballooned after his arrest by Wild when he managed to miraculously escape by freeing himself from leg irons and handcuffs, and then breaking through six iron doors. For ten days, Sheppard roamed the streets of London until he was finally arrested, drunk, in a gin shop. Upon his return to prison, he was the most celebrated man in England. The daily press reported what he had to say, visitors flocked to see him in his cell, and Defoe took his life story. What Sheppard did, mainly, was rail against Jonathan Wild. Almost overnight, Wild's public reputation withered.

Attempts to regulate crime in this context gave birth to the private enterprise of thief-taking. Informers and thief-catchers, recruited from the criminal world, were sent back to survey criminal activities and provide police intelligence. By the time of Wild, the thief-taking business had been boosted by the introduction of the general warrant, which authorized arrest on suspicion of crime, and by the passage of the Highwayman Act of 1962 which offered a reward to anyone who captured a thief and provided evidence leading to his conviction. In addition, a royal pardon, along with the reward, was to be given to anyone who informed on at least two other thieves and secured their convictions.

Fences, in particular, benefitted from a technicality of the law which, in effect, forced apprehended thieves to confess, inform, and return stolen articles or face an expensive and unpleasant stay in prison. Like other receivers, the thief-takers returned stolen property to the rightful owners. But at the center of market merchandising and intimately acquainted with criminal structures, they also easily served as police agents. They culled, protected, and betrayed specific groups of criminals. And as intermediaries fulfilling two roles—market merchandiser and state-endorsed enforcement officer—they amassed considerable power.

The case of Moll Cutpurse, who acquired some control over the organization of thieving in London in the early 1600s, is exemplary. As described by the crime historian John McCullan, her influence as a receiver and thief-taker was institutionalized:

▶ Her informers and accomplices advised her about robbers and pickpockets, and advertised her reputation. She cultivated specific crimes, instigating a lucrative trade in stealing and returning shopbooks and account ledgers that had specific value only to business owners. She established a market in high-value items such as personal jewels, rings, and watches. Her influence in the underworld stemmed from her power as defender of the public interest. After a theft, she guaranteed the recovery of the stolen property. Her role as an insurance broker was tacitly acknowledged by state officials. Commercial interests, government, and the public at large recognized her authority, and the open trade in pardons and rewards linked the judiciary to private retrieval and thief-taking schemes. [John McCullen, "Criminal Organization in Sixteenth and Seventeenth Century London. 1982:319] ◀

Wild's Legacy

Jonathan Wild is by far the most significant figure in the history of fencing for several reasons. First, the image of the fence that Wild portrays perfectly fits the needs of those pressing for changes in the law on criminal receiving and in public policy directed at the dealer in stolen goods. Wild's exploits and their literary embellishment over time (which have made him an even greater super-crook than he was in real life) help to dramatize the skillful, rational techniques of the dealer in stolen goods.

Second, the secret to Wild's success—a system which attracts both thieves and customers and satisfies the law as well—still stands as an archetype for those who follow him. What Wild exemplifies is the legitimate and illegitimate bases of which the operations of all fences are variations. This does not mean that fences after Wild study what he did or adapt his methods to their own contemporary circumstances. Indeed, because of weak policing and the system of thief-taking, Wild's age is the pre-eminent period for fences, many of whom amassed far more power than is possible by modern-day fences. Rather, it means that Wild underscores the significance of dressing an illegal traffic in the paraphernalia of lawful enterprise and of satisfying the needs of various groups. These needs, Klockars writes, exist today just as they did in Wild's age:

▶ Thieves still have property to sell and still seek the best price they can obtain for it. The courts and the police are under continuous pressure to solve those crimes which the public conscience finds offensive; and although there is no longer a quota of hangings per month, the most commonly used measure of police performance is the rate at which crimes are "cleared" by arrest. People who have their property stolen are now often covered by theft insurance, so that needs are not what they were in Wild's day; but the attraction of a "bargain" serves to replace those who fed his system with an equally willing group. [Klockars, 1974:28] ◀

Third, Wild represents the watershed of an historical shift in theft and the trade in stolen goods. He began his career on the eve of the industrial revolution, the economic and social effects of which profoundly changed not only the nature of property theft (and the trade in stolen goods) but also the growth of the law on crimes against property. Indeed, at the time of his hanging in 1725, the business of fencing as we know it today was just beginning to emerge as a major enterprise of the London underworld, with Wild serving as a transition point in the history of criminal receiving: from recovering stolen property and collecting rewards from original owners to buying stolen property for purposes of resale.

Industrial Revolution: From Returning To Redistributing Stolen Property

The unprecedented economic and demographic growth of the late seventeenth and eighteenth century Europe dramatically changed the nature, the abundance, and the distribution of property. The growth of large-scale production and the marketing of goods on a wide national basis made possible the rise of large-scale fencing operations which are now institutionalized in industrial societies.

Fencing as we know it, was less practicable in Wild's society, although he obviously saw the possibilities, as evidenced by his interest in shipping. In Wild's age, the amount of movable property available for theft, and the opportunities to dispose of this property except by personal consumption or by restoring it to the original owner, were limited. Personal property still tended to be concentrated in the upper classes and to be of a distinct and highly individualized nature—snuff boxes, diaries, watches, and jewelry. It made much more sense, therefore, for the fence to act as a third party or middleman who would return stolen goods to their owners on behalf of a large number of thieves. Wild, of course, did a great business in this line, exploiting the thieves and milking the victims.

Unlike Wild, today's fence operates in a world of mass-produced and mass-owned consumer goods for which there is little chance of traceability or recognition by the owner. Rather than "recover" property in order to exchange it for the owner's reward, fences now buy stolen property to resell it, often at a distance or after a time has elapsed, for a handsome profit. The development of this specialized role of the receiver was an escalating feature of the eighteenth-century underworld that also coincides with the appearance of the cant expression "fence" in the slang of thieves (see chapter 1).

Set against these changes in thievery and the rise in large-scale dealing in stolen goods, the existing legal sanctions against theft and criminal receiving were also undergoing change, albeit more slowly and in patchwork fashion. More broadly, in fact, the modern criminal justice system and contemporary criminal law are an invention of late eighteenth century society (England). Jerome Hall, the preeminent authority on the origins of property theft law, writes in *Theft, Law, and Society* (1952):

▶ Growth [of the criminal law] in the eighteenth century is so accelerated that it protrudes conspicuously from the pattern of the whole course of the criminal law . . . for it is in this century that one comes upon the law of receiving stolen property, larceny by trick, obtaining goods by false pretenses and embezzlement. Here for the first time the modern lawyer finds himself in contact with a body of substantive criminal law which he feels is essentially his own [Hall, 1952:34]. ◀

The Law On Criminal Receiving

In its most primitive form, the legal language of receiving was an outgrowth of English common law aimed at the "harbouring of stolen cattle," the most important crime against property in medieval England. Then, the thrust of the law gradually shifted to "concealing of an outlaw" or "assisting an accused brother," as suggested by the following comment from Pike, in reference to fourteenth-century receivers. "The common receiver is by no means a creation of our great modern cities, but has descended to us from the days when Europe was in a state of brigandage and when the guilds assisted an accused brother to obtain an acquittal." (Pike, 1876:285)

Indeed, for many centuries English common law was directed at the receiver of "bad men" rather than at the receiver of stolen goods. To assist a fleeing felon made a man guilty of being an accessory after the fact to that felon's crime. "He who knowingly receives robbers, who is termed a receiver of bad men, and neglects to give them up to justice, shall be punished." (Quoted in Hall, 1952:53)

This does not mean that buying stolen property could not have gotten one hanged, but it would have been for being an accessory and for sheltering thieves. Furthermore, since the receiver was only considered to be an accessory, English law would not punish him more severely than his principal, and not at all, if the thief escaped conviction. Thus, the receiver could not be brought to trial unless the thief had first been captured and then convicted.

This situation prevailed until 1692, when the first English law on receiving was passed, making the buying of stolen property a felony but only if the thief was convicted first. This law is significant, first, because it removed the obstacle of having to prove that the receiver aided or concealed the thief. Second, the law's language is the prototype of subsequent receiving statutes and legal vocabulary and also reveals how wide open the trade in stolen goods was in the seventeenth century.

► And forasmuch as thieves and robbers are much encouraged to commit such offences, because a great number of persons make it their trade and business to deal in the buying of stolen goods; be it therefore enacted by the authority aforesaid, that if any person or persons shall buy or receive any goods or chattel that shall be feloniously taken or stolen from any other person, knowing the same to be stolen, he or they shall be taken and deemed as accessory or accessories to such felony after the fact. [Hall, 1952:54; Colquhoun, 1795: 294] ◄

The law's requirement that the thief be convicted first, however, made successful prosecution of the receiver exceedingly difficult:

► The receiver, who is generally the employer and patron of the thief, very often escaped with impunity; for if he could keep the thief out of the way, he, the receiver, could not be tried, and therefore went unpunished. [Quoted in Hall, 1952:55] ◄

Thus the 1692 law was amended in 1706 to abolish the requirement that the thief be convicted first, but the prosecution was still limited to only charging the receiver with a misdemeanor (punishable by a fine or whipping) rather than a felony (punishable by transportation to the colonies or death). During the remainder of the eighteenth century, it was established procedure that "the receiver be prosecuted for misdemeanor only if the thief could not be taken; that if the thief could be apprehended, the prosecution must be for felony as accessory" (Hall, 1952:56).

The next major shift in English law toward a legal distinction between thief and receiver was in 1782, when it was enacted "that a principal felon may be admitted as a witness against his accessory, under this Act of Parliament." From then on, the thief could testify against the receiver.

Then, in 1827, receiving stolen property was finally treated as a separate substantive offense. The law made provision for the independent trial of the receiver, whose offense was made a felony regardless of whether or not the thief was arrested first. This 1827 English statute is the prototype of subsequent American law. "A person receiving stolen property knowing the same to be stolen was deemed guilty of a felony and could be indicted and convicted either as an accessory after the fact or for a substantive felony." (Hall, 1952:57)

Fence's Relationship To Theft: Supporter or Instigator of Thieves?

Coinciding with the legal revisions in the receiving law, commentators were placing greater and greater stress on the role of the fence in the larger theft industry; there was a growing charge that the fence, rather than the thief, was the principal felon. The fence was depicted not only as someone who supported theft by providing an outlet for the thief's stolen goods, but also as someone who instigated and even organized thefts.

The image of the fence as *supporter* of thieves can be traced to the time when the receiver befriended "bad men" or helped conceal their "garbage" (stolen goods). In this view, the fence's role in property theft is relatively passive. Thieves are dependent on him in the sense that he assists them by providing a market for their stolen goods. He is a functional part of the larger system of theft but not its main protagonist.

By the early part of the nineteenth century, the image of the fence as supportive of thieves gave way to that of the fence as playing a more active and central role in property theft. Because the fence does other things besides passively purchasing stolen goods—not only marketing the goods but also initiating, planning, and organizing the stealing behavior of thieves—he is seen as the *instigator* of the theft. This position was summarized by William Neale writing on juvenile delinquency in Manchester in 1840.

▶ The juvenile delinquent is in great measure in the power of the proprietor of the lodging-house, the spirit shop, or that in which property is received—who for indemnification of the lodging, food and liquor, or money given in advance, stimulates him to fresh plunder, the great proportion of which is appropriated to themselves. [W. Neale, *Juvenile Delinquency in Manchester*, 1840:48] ◀

This view of the fence as an *instigator* of thievery is both reflected and reinforced in the literary portrait of Fagin in Charles Dickens's *Oliver Twist*, a work which has contributed greatly to the folklore on fencing. While Dicken's purpose is to show the wretchedness of underworld existence, sandwiched between the lines of an involved plot, he has a good deal to say about the role of the fence vis-à-vis the thief. The fence (e.g.

Fagin) is portrayed as both the tutor and protector of the thief and as the greedy extorter of the lion's share of his profits. Perhaps the most enduring facet of Fagin's character, apart from his greed, is his role as corrupter of youth.

By the 20th century, the image of the fence as instigator and even organizer of theft is firmly established in the writings on the trade in stolen goods, particularly on the part of those commentators and jurists pressing for legal reforms to better deal with the criminal receiver. To them the receiver is not simply a tool of his supplier, nor does he passively offer protection and services; rather, he is seen as actively training, recruiting, organizing, and controlling thieves. The fence is now pictured as the main protagonist in property theft while the thief is little more than his instrumental employee.

In an April 1926 *New York Herald-Tribune* article entitled "Swift Punishment of Crafty 'Fences' Seen as Key to War on Theft," John Walker Harrington argued that "the real instigator" of thievery is the fence who "is the invisible master of the show, pulling the strings which move the puppets of crime." Harrington also insisted that the old-time Fagin character was "put to shame by the modern ilk."

▶ It was the old theory of the law that the receiver of stolen goods was merely the tool of the bolder thief. Indeed, this idea seems to have obtained until the beginning of the last century . . . Certainly, according to all recent developments in the history of crime, the fence is the worse criminal than the hold-up man or the burglar. [Harrington, 1926:3] ◀

Two years later in 1928, the Prison Committee of the Association of Grand Jurors of New York, in its survey of the receiving laws of the forty-eight states and Alaska, described the receiver as follows: "He not only furnishes the incentive to crime by providing a market, but he organizes and directs criminals, and very often finances them." (Association of Grand Jurors, 1928:4)

In his preface to this grand jury study, entitled *Criminal Receivers in the United States*. Thomas Rice proposed that:

▶ Only in the last few years in the whole history of crime, which is as old as civilization, has the seriousness of receiving stolen goods been recognized . . . the layman, the lawyer, the legislator and, above all, the judge . . . have little understood the status of the fence as a promoter of theft. [Association of Grand Jurors, 1928:xii] ◀

Another account, said to be by a fence (Joseph Grizzard), the most notorious receiver of stolen jewelry in England in the early 1900s, claims that:

▶ Your up-to-date fence is usually an organizer of crime, a capitalist who provides the money without which nothing worthwhile can be done . . . He usually remains well in the background, the man with the purse, the man who knows too much for any of his trusted confederates to betray him . . . It would be nearer the mark to call them salaried employees who receive in addition a commission whenever they do a good stroke of business. [John Gregory (ed.), *Crime From the Inside*, 1932:209] ◄

In more recent writings, the up-to-date fence who "remains well in the background" has been tagged as a "master fence"—he deals with thieves and purchasers indirectly, sometimes through agents by telephone, and seldom buys unless a resale has been arranged. Writing in the 1976 *Michigan Law Review*, Robert Blakey and Michael Goldsmith state:

► The master fence . . . serves as a middleman . . . and is distinguished by his ability to insulate himself from the actual theft and subsequent redistribution. He operates as a broker, buying and selling stolen goods valued in the hundreds of thousands of dollars that are always the product of largescale theft, yet rarely, if ever, seeing or touching any of it. [Blakey and Goldsmith, *Criminal Distribution of Stolen Property: The Need for Law Reform*, 1976:1535] ◄

Probably the treatise making the strongest claim for the fence as the less visible yet "Mr. Big" of property theft is the early 1970s study by Marilyn Walsh, *The Fence: A New Look at Property Theft*. In pressing for a new look at property crime which will place greater emphasis on the fence than on the thief, Walsh offers this assessment of the fence's role:

► The thief is little more than an instrument of the fence—a highly visible but relatively minor cog in a gigantic distribution circuit. The fence, then, is the controlling influence over both the thief and his theft activities. As such, the fence of stolen goods emerges as the prime mover in property theft. [Walsh, 1976:175] ◄

Not all students of the fence agree with this conception of your up-to-date fence. Mary McIntosh, in the *British Journal of Criminology*, points out that when reputed cases of the fence as Mr. Big are investigated more closely, "it usually turns out that police and journalistic myth-making have constructed an organization where none exists." ["Thieves and Fences: Markets and Power in Professional Crime," 1976:260]

McIntosh cites the case of Joseph Grizzard (mentioned above) as an example of such myth-making, particularly as Grizzard has been portrayed in the writings of Christmas Humphreys. Known as "Kenny" or "Cammi," Grizzard was a celebrated fence who met his downfall after the Great Pearl Robbery of 1913 and is often said to have been an organizer and instigator of thieves. Humphreys wrote that the burglar Lockett was alleged to be the ringleader of a gang of daring thieves but that, in reality, he was merely the "able lieutenant of the clever Grizzard" (Humphreys, *The Great Pearl Robbery of 1913*, 1929:19). To prove this, Humphreys cites police observations of Lockett, Grizzard, and others meeting each other and talking in various places. On the strength of this sort of evidence, he referred to thieves as Grizzard's "tools."

▶ Yet, a thief who was in Parkhurst Prison with Grizzard wrote later: Grizzard . . . was not the mastermind. He did not plan and organize the robbery. In fact he knew nothing of the matter until after its accomplishment. Kenny was a fence pure and simple, and like the majority of buyers of stolen property, was excessively greedy, grasping and avaricious . . . I flatly contradict any statement to the effect that he was the master mind which organized any of the big jewel thefts of recent years for which he is credited. He may have been indirectly responsible for the successful perpetration of a great many robberies carried out upon a grand scale, by financing the real operators. [McIntosh, p. 260; from George Gordon, *Crooks in the Underworld*, 1929:185] ◀

McIntosh's view is that thieves are much more autonomous than the view which suggests there is a mastermind or prime mover exercising control. In the case of Moll Cutpurse, for example, as a patron of crime she provided shape and discipline to thieving gangs and expanded the frontiers of theft. But her authority was seldom that of a boss. Furthermore, wide areas of thieving remained outside her influence because criminal competitors, other fences, informers, and prison officials ran parallel rackets. She and her intermediaries seldom had advance knowledge of crimes; they contacted the thieves after the event.

Even in the case of the redoubtable Jonathan Wild, there is little evidence that he was an organizer of thefts or that he was the "master mind" of thieves. Nor is there evidence, except what was produced at his trial, for the claim that Wild was frequently a confederate who robbed along with known felons; and of the many robberies from which he is known to have profited, there were hardly any in which he did not contact the thieves after the event rather than before. Thus, there is little to support the idea, concludes McIntosh, of a criminal conspiracy involving fences controlling thieves.

The evidence regarding what in recent years are referred to as "master" fences is even more ambiguous. On closer inspection, many of them turn out to be small-time brokers in stolen property or "regular" fences who occasionally arrange a transaction in which they do not come in contact with the stolen goods. In some cases, for example, the "master fence" has turned out to be a "street man," someone rather like a numbers' writer, who frequents certain areas and buys stolen property as an agent for a fence.

Classes of Fences: "Occasional" and "Professional" Receivers

The shift from a "passive" to a more "active" conception of the fence's role in property theft is accompanied by a movement in the literature toward distinguishing different classes of receivers. Thus, already by the late sixteenth century some commentators were beginning to distinguish between the lesser forms of receiver and the other, more important, dealers in stolen goods. In a tract on "cony-catching" written in 1592, Robert Greene differentiates between bawds and brokers.

▶ Now, these lifts [thief] have their special receivers of their stolen goods, which are of two sundry parties: either some notorious bawd, in whose houses they lie, and they keep company in tapping-houses, and have young thugs in their house, which are consorts to these lifts, and love them so dear that they never leave them till they come to the gallows; or else, they be brokers, a kind of idle sort of lewd levers, as pernicious as the lift, for they receive at their hands whatsoever garbage is conveyed, be it linen, wollen, plate, jewels. [Greene, p. 171] ◀

By the late eighteenth and early nineteenth century, with the growth of fencing operations accompanying industrialization, it was commonplace for students of fencing to distinguish among receivers according to scale of operations and criminal intent. Colquhoun, who provided the outstanding interpretation of the trade in stolen goods at the beginning of the nineteenth century, divided receivers into twelve different classes along with their estimated numbers.

1st.	Opulent Receivers who trade on a large Scale	20
2d.	Interior Receivers who deal with Lumpers, & c.	25
3d.	Copemen in connection with Revenue Officers	20
4th.	Dealers in Old Iron, and Old Ships' Stores, & c.	55
5th.	Small Grocers and Chandlers	55
6th.	Publicans	35
7th.	Twine and Rope Spinners	20
8th.	Female Receivers	50
9th.	Covetous Receivers	60
10th.	Careless Receivers	150
11th.	Receivers on the Banks of the Thames, and Medway below Deptford	40
12th.	Jew Receivers and others who travel with Carts	20
	Total	550

(Patrick Colquhoun, *A Treatise on the Commerce and Police of the River Thames,* 1800:197)

According to Colquhoun, though small in number, the individuals of the first class are the most important traders in stolen goods:

▶ Of all others, (they) are the most noxious and destructive to Commercial property . . . These availing themselves of the pecuniary resources they possess, give existence and vigour to depredation, upon a large scale, by solicitations and facilities, without which they could not have been committed; and when under the embarrassment of detection, avail themselves of pecuniary resources, in calling forth the talents of Counsel and the whole chicane of the law, to enable them to elude the punishment due to their crimes; in which the friends of

Morality and Justice have to lament that they are too often successful, producing thereby incalculable injuries to the Community at
large. [Colquhoun, 1800:192] ◄

After Colquhoun, other commentators also distinguish between the
"lesser" or "occasional receivers," who were "by no means the pillars of
the trade," and what were increasingly being designated as "the professional receiver," or the "fence-master," who is at "the top of the guilty
profession." (Anonymous, 1865) This distinction was further developed in
America at about this time by Edward Crapsey, a journalist with extensive familiarity with the New York underworld. Writing in *The Glaxey* in
1872, Crapsey confirms Colquhoun's original observation that there were
many who occasionally dealt in stolen goods, saying that they "practically
were fences and yet do not exclusively devote themselves to the pursuit."
Crapsey's major concern, however, is with "professional fences" who are
ready at any time to buy anything that promises a profit and who work stolen goods back into legitimate trade through contacts with legitimate
businessmen.

Hall's "Professional Dealer"

The culmination of the trend toward distinguishing the "lesser" from the
"more important" receivers is the publication of *Theft, Law, and Society*
(first published in 1935), in which Jerome Hall developed a simple typology, distinguishing his "professional receiver" dealer from both the "lay
receiver," who knowingly bought stolen property for his own consumption, and the "occasional receiver," who bought stolen property for resale
but only infrequently. In the remainder of his discussion, Hall embel-
lishes the concept of professional dealer by distinguishing him from other
criminal receivers on a number of criteria.[5]

► The behavior of the professional criminal receiver is persistent and
complex. His activities are entirely different from those of the lay or
the occasional receiver. [He] deals in stolen merchandise and is apt
to be in possession of a large amount of such commodities. [He] operates a business and can no more stop his criminal activities for any
length of time than a legitimate businessman or manufacturer can
shut his doors for indefinite and irregular periods. [He] acts as a
bridge over which many millions of dollars' worth of illegally acquired goods pass annually from criminals to merchants and on to the
consuming public. [He] is difficult to convict . . . is equipped both
mentally and financially to take full advantage of the weaknesses in
the administrative machine, should prosecution be initiated. [He is]
for the prospective thief a reliable market, known in advance to be
available . . . [Hall, 1952:155–159] ◄

---

5. As noted in chapter 1, Hall's intent with his typology of receivers was to
press for law reform that would better take into account the "professional dealer."

Klockars's Elaboration of Hall

Hall's conception of the "professional dealer" is elaborated on by Carl Klockars in *The Professional Fence* (1974:172), where he proposes that three criteria best distinguish the fence from other traders in stolen goods.[6]

▶ First, the fence must be a dealer in stolen property; that is a buyer and a seller with direct contact with thieves (sellers) and customers (buyers).

Second, the fence . . . must buy and sell stolen property regularly and profitably, and have done so for a considerable period of time, perhaps years.

Third, the fence must be public: he must acquire a reputation as a successful dealer in stolen property among law breakers, law enforcers, and others acquainted with the criminal community. ◀

Klockars then goes on to explain why "for reasons of convenience" he decides to attach the adjective "professional" to Vincent Swaggi, whose career Klockars is chronicling:

▶ I have chosen to add the adjective "professional" to stress certain characteristics which already inhere in the definition of fence: career, occupation, certain skills, and ability. In "professional fence," the word "professional" denotes nothing that is not already inherent in the concept of fence, but in a way that is harmless, suggests that certain features of the fence are more distinctive than others. [Klockars, 1974:172]

Misuse of Concept of "Professional" Fence

The concept of professional fence as described by Hall and as defined by Klockars has much to recommend it. The problem, however, is that more than one meaning of "professional" exists in the literature, so that the concept lacks uniform usage. Indeed—and with Hall frequently cited as the authority source—some writers label as "professional" virtually any receiver who buys and sells stolen goods, without regard for the scale of his receiving activities or his relationship to thieves.

An example is Marilyn Walsh's 1970's work on fencing mentioned earlier. Based on her examination of police records in a northeastern city of about 125,000, Walsh reports identifying 115 *professional* fences. It is Walsh's claim that she is reporting on "professional" fences because she has:

▶ Adopted the guidelines of Jerome Hall in distinguishing between the "lay" and the "professional" receiver. The lay receiver acquires

---

6. See chapter 1 for discussion of the origins of the cant expression "fence" in thieves slang, which signifies the development of this specialized role of criminal receiver.

stolen property for personal consumption. The professional receiver acquires stolen property for purpose of resale. [Marilyn Walsh, *A New Look at Property Theft*, 1976:5] ◀

With this statement, Walsh misconstrues Hall's guidelines so directly and simply that the reader is likely to miss it. By defining the professional fence as anyone who acquires stolen property for purpose of resale, Walsh converts Hall's consumption-resale distinction into the distinguishing feature of the professional fence. Recall, however, how emphatic Hall is, that buying stolen goods for purposes of resale does not, in and of itself, make one a professional fence. The occasional receiver, says Hall, also buys for resale but his behavior is much less "persistent and complex" than that of the professional dealer. And following up on Colquhoun's stipulation that the fence is a "ready-made market for thieves," Hall holds that the professional dealer's relationship to thieves is a direct one: "for the prospective thief, he is a reliable market, known in advance to be available."

Walsh adduces her sample of "at least 115 professional fences" from police activity reports, that frequently are based on hearsay information about someone who is alleged to have bought or is presently buying stolen goods, with little or no effort directed at verifying the accuracy of the information.[7] A close reading of her report reveals that the sample includes: part-time and perhaps even a few one-time receivers; persons acting as agents of a thief to dispose of what he has stolen (e.g., Walsh re-

---

7. The following are specific examples from police activity reports of "fences" in Walsh's sample (see her testimony before 1973 *Hearings in Congress*, Part 3, pp. 770 passim):

"Received info from informer that of all the cabbies fencing hot stuff, Mr. X is doing the most business. It is reported that he pays $20 for stereo players taken from cars while others are only paying $15. Further stated that he keeps stuff in trunk of the cab.

We dug up an old pigeon . . . and he said that junkies are taking a lot of TVs to Mr. B's furniture store.

Information from tipster that X is responsible for the burglaries on the north side and is peddling all the loot to Mr. C. Information also that Cs antique store is presently closed and he's operating at home.

Received information from informant that several hound men on West Side are committing house jobs. They take the jewelry and other loot to Mr. Y. who is an attendant at the ____ bowling alley everyday at 1 p.m.

Information that G & H are buying lots of boosted clothes from junkies. The junkies are told to save the price tags on the garments and are paid around 1/3 the price.

Mr. S. who owns a jewelry manufacturing company is alleged to be fencing for some of our better burglars. He supposedly has nationwide customers and contacts.

Went to jail and talked with ____. He said recent daytime burglaries are being set up by Mr. L. He tells the junkies to go from door to door and if someone answers to attempt to sell them a *Reader's Digest*."

ports on several women who hold or help dispose of property stolen by an important male in their lives (father, son, or boyfriend); and retail merchants who buy stolen merchandise from true fences and then resell the merchandise to eventual consumers. In effect, Walsh's sample of "fences" is an imprecise bag of assorted types of criminal receivers. How many, if any, of the fences in her study fit the conception of fence employed by Hall or Klockars is unknown.

Concept of "Professional" Fence as Attention-Grabber

Hall's use of "professional" fence is part of a larger trend in the crime literature as a whole, already in full swing by the late nineteenth and early twentieth centuries, in which the language of the "professions" is borrowed to describe specific patterns of criminality or a particular subset of the criminal population. The usual analogy is that professional crime compares to other crime as conventional professions (e.g., law, medicine) compare to other legitimate occupations (e.g., carpenter, truck driver).[8]

Unfortunately, depending on the interests and purposes of the writer, the term professional has become hopelessly compromised by its use as a synonym for virtually any thief, any receiver of stolen goods, or any criminal. For some writers, the notion professional criminal is used restrictively—he is characterized by the pursuit of theft as a livelihood and as a way of life, by relatively complex skills, by high prestige and recognition by other criminals, and by loyalty to the underworld code of ethics. For other writers and law enforcement officials, however, the label "professional" is attached to any offender who commits crime on a regular basis or

---

8. The concept of professional crime was introduced to the social science literature in 1937 with the publication of Edwin Sutherland's *The Professional Thief, by a Professional Thief*. Sutherland's use of the term referred mainly to nonviolent forms of criminal activity pursued with a high degree of skill in order to maximize financial gain and minimize the possibility of arrest or incarceration. The professional thief made a regular business of stealing, was the graduate of a developmental process that included the acquisition of specialized attitudes, knowledge, skills, and experience, and identified himself with an exclusive criminal fraternity that extended friendship, understanding, security, and respect.

The term professional thief was not Sutherland's own creation, however. William Harrison's *Description of England* (1577) observed the unity of generalized thieves as members of a "profession." In 1800 Colquhoun noted that "professed thieves" were members of a fraternity who could buy their freedom by bribing witnesses. Crapsey, the New York journalist who had extensive contacts with the underworld during the 1860's and 1870's, described specific pickpockets, shoplifters, etc., as "professional thieves" who depended exclusively on theft for a livelihood and who were generally immune from punishment. And Inspector Thomas Byrnes' 1895 publication of *Professional Criminals of America* describes 609 professional criminals that Brynes was familiar with. According to Sutherland, however, Byrnes's offenders are mostly *habitual* and not professional thieves as in the designation used by Sutherland.

who makes a living from crime (even though he may barely eek out a subsistence in so doing). By this criterion, any habitual or career criminal, however petty or amateur, and regardless of skill level or status in the underworld, would be called a professional. Such a definition would include every type of criminal from junkies, who steal anything they can to buy dope, to Mafia chieftains.[9] Still other writers attach the adjective "professional" to offenders who, on closer inspection, turn out not only to lack skill and status in the underworld but to be part-time offenders.

Invented by criminologists, law enforcers, commentators, and the media to describe what they believe (or want others to believe) is a special subset of the criminal population, the term "professional criminal" has an aura that accounts for its popularity and frequent misuse.[10] For the law

---

9. An example of loose usage of "professional thief" is, again, provided in Walsh's fencing study in which she reports interviewing a "very professional burglar," named Greg, about theft and fencing for purposes of supplementing her analysis of police files. From bits and pieces of information in her report, one learns the following about Greg: (1) He is about twenty years old when he is arrested. Later, he becomes an informant for the local police/prosecutor and agrees to testify against his thief associates. It is within this context that the prosecutor provided Greg to Walsh as a source of information on theft and fencing. (2) Greg claims to have taken a gemology course at a nearby university, after which he provided expert counsel to fellow burglars about jewelry they had stolen. (3) Greg described an incident when he did not have a ready outlet for stolen furs, tried to sell the furs to local fences who, Greg claims, entered into a pricing conspiracy against him, after which he decided to search for a buyer outside the city. Eventually Greg found a buyer, but on returning to the city is beaten up by thugs acting on behalf of local fences and the money he made on the furs is taken from him. (4) In another instance, Greg reports being intimidated by a "local enforcer" and forced to sell an expensive bracelet at an extremely low price to a local syndicate person.

Whether these represent real events, or jail tales or are products of Greg's imagination is one issue. Whether someone who is young, is a snitch, lacks contacts with reliable fences, is intimidated by local thugs, qualifies him as a professional criminal is another matter.

10. Is the word "professional" used by and among professional thieves? Peter Letkemann in *Criminal As Work* (1973), in one of the most comprehensive studies of seasoned criminals, writes: "Although used by both layman and academics, the category 'professional criminal' was seldom used by my subjects; even well-known rounders did not refer to themselves as professionals. When I enquired about the concept they were unable to identify anyone as professional. One must conclude, therefore, that the concept of the 'professional criminal' lacks objective reference." (1973:26)

But what about first person writings in which thieves supposedly use the adjective professional to refer to themselves or to colleagues. The answer, I believe, is suggested in correspondence with Robert Prus. In his book, *Road Hustlers* (1977), a study of élite card and dice cheats, Prus provides first person accounts in which his hustlers apparently speak, for example, as follows: "Another important difference between professionals and nonprofessionals . . . I don't like working

enforcer, the arrest and conviction of a "professional" criminal declares his own superior professional skills in a way that a bungling amateur simply could not. If nothing else, this enhanced status ascribed to some criminals by the police provides grist for the mills of sensational journalism, helping to further reify the concept in the mind of the public. For the crime writer, the value of doing research or writing a report on "professional" crime is one thing, quite another when the product is that of ordinary offenders. For jurists and commentators with correctional interests, the image of the skilled, rational, professional criminal tends to give the greatest possible leverage in pressing for social and legal reforms. Thus, even though Hall used the term restrictively, it was his unconcealed interest in reform that prompted him to choose the label professional in the first instance, as Klockars points out:

▶ In choosing "professional" [Hall] found an image suitable to his task [of giving] the law a new image of the conduct it was designed to control and the criminal it had to contend with . . . that substantively and administratively the law was lamentably inadequate to the task of controlling the skilled, professional, criminal dealer in stolen property. [Klockars, 1974:169–170] ◀

As the image of the fence as "professional" is a useful attention-grabber for those pressing for legal and social reforms, so also, in recent years some writers have found attractive the portrayal of the fence as a *"respectable businessman."* Neither the citizenry nor its law enforcers view the fence as a very serious menace to society, it is argued, both because the fence wraps himself in the legitimacy and the respectability which Ameri-

---

with these nonprofessional hustlers . . . when you see a professional crew working." (1977:26ff *passim*)

In personal communication, however, Prus clarifies: "No, they didn't use the word professional or nonprofessional—I inserted this in the text for the reader's convenience. The 'professionals' I interviewed referred to themselves as hustlers or as good hustlers."

From interviews with a mix of burglars, armed robbers, drug dealers, etc., in the northeast and southeast of the United States, I agree with Letkemann's conclusion that the expression "professional criminal" lacks objective reference within the underworld. I have encountered a few young burglars and armed robbers who occasionally used professional as a self-designation. However, when I inquired of others who knew them, they reacted derisively to such claims.

That professional is not part of the lexicon of the underworld does not mean that thieves and other criminals never use the expression. Thieves are aware of the word's meaning in the larger society, and may use it as a shorthand way of communicating with members of straight society. Rather than struggling to explain to an "outsider" the difference between an amateur or "common thief" and a "good thief," it may be convenient to say: "He's an old pro," or "he's a real professional." Also, criminals are aware of the status enhancing side of the label, and it is not surprising that some of them, especially if appropriately coached, are willing to call themselves "professional" or apparently aspire to this status when writing their autobiographies.

can society bestows on anyone who runs a business, and because he appears to be no different from the "ordinary" businessman.

Fence's Character: Underworld Figure or Respectable Businessman?

Various images of the fence's character are presented in the literature, ranging from the portrayal of him as a wholly *underworld* figure to that of a *respected* businessman. The criteria for linking the fence with one image or the other are more implicit than explicit but mainly have to do with the fence's background or prior criminality, his affinity with the underworld, and his reputation in legitimate society or in the business community.

In the popular literature and particularly in folklore, the fence is often portrayed as a grimy man of the underworld who oftentimes happens to be a Jew. Thus, Fagin in Dickens's *Oliver Twist* is described as a "crafty old Jew, a receiver of stolen goods." He is a wretched creature, a shadowy person who lurks in the underworld and imposes an even grimier existence on those dregs of society over whom he exerts control.

Another popular image of the fence is that of the pawnbroker or the itinerant merchant who peddles stolen goods to customers on the street or, in more modern times, the flea market vendor. The pawnbroker, in particular, has been suspect and as early as the seventeenth century in Western Europe was frequently linked to the trade in stolen goods. Patrick Colquhoun, writing in 1795, refers to that class of "Swindling Pawnbrokers . . . [who] are uniformly receivers of stolen property; and under the cover of their license do much mischief to the Public." He suggested that a uniform licensing system be adopted with the requirement that a "certificate of character" be produced for those who wished to enter the trade. Indeed, the suspicion that pawnbrokers and itinerant merchants (and later on dealers in jewelry and secondhand goods) were allied with the trade in stolen goods led the English Parliament during the 18th and 19th centuries to pass a series of laws aimed at regulating these occupations. The statutes that were passed were the forerunners of licensing procedures for pawnbrokers, peddlers, and so forth which are now found in nearly every British and American city.

In comparison with the Fagin or the seedy pawnbroker image, however, firsthand studies of individual fences, as well as the more comprehensive surveys of criminal receivers (e.g., Colquhoun, Crapsey, Hall) portray the fence not so much as a lurking creature of the underworld as someone who has a strong affinity with it and who may also have extensive ties to legitimate society. The observations, in particular, of those who have studied the lives of fences and the information about fences in the biographies and autobiographies of thieves, attest to the prior theft and hustling activities as well as underworld affinity of many fences. According to these sources, fences disproportionately come from either the ranks of ex-thieves and one-time hustlers (although the tendency of fences to be ex-thieves has diminished somewhat over the past century), or from families or friendship networks already linked to illegal or quasi-legitimate activities. In recent years, for example, the role of organized crime syndicates in the traffic in stolen goods has been observed frequently. On the basis of testimony presented before the 1973 U.S. Congress, *Hearings on Fencing*, Blakey and Goldsmith write:

▶ In recent years, organized crime syndicates have expanded their fencing operations to exploit the growing demand of consumers and businesses for stolen goods. This expansion has been made possible by the ability of organized crime to marshal its tremendous resources to solve the complex financial and logistical problems that are inherent in large-scale theft and fencing activity. The syndicate's connections with master and professional fences, and the influence it exerts over many legitimate businesses, have enabled it to develop a redistribution system capable of funneling stolen goods through interstate commerce with great ease. [Blakey and Goldsmith, "Criminal Redistribution of Stolen Property," 1976:1539] ◀

The firsthand studies and the general surveys also document the considerable participation of fences in quasi-legitimate businesses and occupations. A representative view is Hall's observation that the business of dealing in stolen goods is:

▶ Closely interrelated with those of auctioneer, pawnbrokers, and dealers in second-hand goods who provide large outlets for the sale of stolen goods. These businesses are "regulated," but in such a perfunctory manner that they continue to be active in both the receipt and the disposal of stolen property. There is very little regulation of transient vendors of jewelry or of smelters and refiners of precious metals. [Hall, 1952:162–163] ◀

There is an emerging mid-20th century view, however, which challenges the traditional image of the fence as being of dubious character and nefarious background. Some writers portray the typical fence as a "respectable" businessman of gentlemanly background. Fences are depicted as remarkably similar in character, background, and status to other members of the local business community. Apparently, dealing in stolen goods is a career line open to most merchants and businessmen.

The strongest statement of this "white collar" image of the fence comes again from Walsh who reports that the majority of fences in her study are "very ordinary men" and "most [are] respected businessmen." As with her description of "professional" fences, Walsh's choice of adjectives and the evidence upon which she arrives at her conclusions requires close scrutiny.

▶ [The typical fence] was neither pawnbroker nor street peddler. He wasn't a retired thief. He wasn't even confined to the poorer parts of town. Instead he was a 45 to 55 year old, white, male businessman.

As such, he looked strikingly similar to most managers and administrators in wholesale and retail trades . . . and even more strikingly dissimilar to his partner in crime—the thief. In short, the fence was demographically a very ordinary man. [Walsh, 1977 p. 15] ◀

And Walsh goes on to add that many fences are not only businessmen but "businessmen of the most respected type," using the following as her definition of respectability: "A respected businessman is one who presides over a well-known, successful enterprise [while] a marginal businessman presides over business ranging from less successful to barely surviving in nature."

There are a number of difficulties with Walsh's interpretation. First, Walsh attaches great significance to the observation that in comparison with the thief, fences are older, have a business or occupation, and have less involvement with the wheels of justice. Unquestionably she is right; indeed, these and other thief-fence differences have long been recognized in the literature. But whether the differences and the attributes (e.g., age) which Walsh uses for the comparison have anything to do with respectability is another matter. An alternative interpretation is simply that the accumulation of experience and connections needed to be a fence are greater than those needed to be a burglar.

Second, Walsh provides a peculiar, if not misleading, definition of "respected." Her standard of respectability is linked to the size and financial success of the fence's business enterprise rather than to his background or to his reputation in the legitimate business community. By Walsh's definition, even Mafia chieftains who run visibly successful legitimate businesses are "respectable."

Third, bits and pieces of information in the Walsh study also suggest a picture of the fence at odds with the one she paints. Most of the fences in her study, in fact, had arrest records in the police jurisdiction where the study was conducted. (How many of the remainder had police contact which went unrecorded or had arrest records elsewhere is unknown.) In addition, a substantial number of the fences were managers or proprietors of quasi-legitimate establishments or were known to be involved in other illegal activities.

Fourth, these shortcomings are compounded by Walsh's imprecise definition of "fence" (reviewed earlier). The part-time dealer or the merchant who once in a while buys and sells stolen goods can be expected to have less official contact with the police, less in the way of a prior criminal history, and less affinity with the underworld than a true fence (i.e., as defined, for example, by Hall or by Klockars). The imprecise definition also helps explain Walsh's discovery of a whopping 115 "professional fences" in a semi-metropolitan outpost (population of about 200,000) in the upper regions of New York State.

This questioning of Walsh's portrayal of the fence as a respectable businessman, nonetheless, neither overlooks the fact that fencing itself is a business activity, nor that most fences are engaged in a legitimate business at the same time that they are carrying on an illegal trade in stolen goods. Hall writes:

▶ As long ago as the beginning of the eighteenth century, i.e., since Jonathan Wild, the professional receiver was recognized for what he was—a criminal businessman . . . The criminal receiver is an established participant in the economic life of society, whose behavior has been institutionalized over a span of more than two centuries in Anglo-American experience . . . They are frequently specialists in their chosen fields, able to evaluate merchandise expertly and to compete generally on the basis of their special skills. [Hall, 1952:155, 157] ◀

Klockars adds to this:

▶ The fence is a businessman. He buys and sells merchandise in order to make a profit. Some of his merchandise is stolen, some of it is not. There is only one advantage to trading in stolen goods; one can buy them cheaper than legitimate goods and thus make a greater profit. [Klockars, 1974:77] ◀

But on other grounds and, perhaps, for other purposes, the fence is hardly the former boy scout or the clean businessman that Walsh implies. If "fence" is defined along the lines suggested by Hall or Klockars, what evidence is available strongly suggests that most fences are characterized by one or more of the following: (1) prior criminal contact or background in criminal or quasi-legal activities, such as theft, hustling, or the rackets in general; (2) operation of a quasi-legitimate business such as a second-hand discount store, a salvage yard, an auction house, a foundry, or a bail bonding business; (3) affinity with the underworld, such as ongoing business and leisure associations with established members of the underworld. The significance of the fence having affinity with the underworld and not only within the realm of seemingly honest business is in terms of his acquiring the skills and contacts necessary to run a fencing business.[11]

Fence's Relationship to Theft Reconsidered

Walsh's description of the fence as both a "professional" and a "respectable businessman" is the most recent phase of a centuries-old trend aimed at giving legal authorities a more weighty image of the conduct they are to control and the criminal they have to contend with. In dramatizing the ra-

---

11. That the fence is not your average businessman does not overlook the greed of many legitimate merchants. One of the major outlets, after all, for stolen goods handled by fences is that of legitimate businessmen who are willing to buy suspect merchandise if it assures them of a higher profit. But running a fencing business is another matter. The chances of an everyday merchant becoming a dealer in stolen goods, should he so desire, may be as remote as are the chances of the typical ex-con becoming a legitimate businessman.

tional, calculating, economically motivated behavior of the professional businessman-fence, Walsh's intent is to dislodge what she labels as the "conventional view of theft with its emphasis on the thief rather than the fence" and to replace it with a "new look" at property theft. This new look places primary emphasis on the role of the fence, and is needed, Walsh says, because, "Even when the conventional view of theft does its best it doesn't do very much. It ignores most of the iceberg in favour of focusing on its most visible part; and rather than slaying dragons, it feints at their images." (Walsh, 1977:175)

Stuart Henry refers to this trend in imagery as "the stereotype of the fence as the 'Mr. Big' of property crime," as the main species of "bad guy." This imagery has been strengthened in recent years, Henry maintains, by transforming the fence from an underworld supporter of theft to a businessman-dealer who organizes, and is the brains behind, theft.

▶ The dominant figure in the emerging scenario is the "professional businessman-fence." If apparently legitimate businessmen with "good education" and gentlemanly background were involved (as fences), then they fitted neither into the underworld, being too clever for it, nor into the majority of the population, being too dishonest for it. Their natural place was at the top: the key figures in the property theft business. [Stuart Henry, *The Hidden Economy*, 1978:70] ◀

It is Henry's view—and one already hinted at in scattered places in the literature survey—that this conception of the fence's role in property theft is bigger and more important than it ought to be, and that the involvement of other participants in an illegal trade is overlooked. Henry proposes that this conception, resting as it does on the old saying "if no fences no thieves," assumes that thieves are not autonomous or "free" in their stealing behaviors, and that the police and the public have little or nothing to do with the maintenance of a criminal system.

But, while the thief is supposed to be dependent on the fence, he is, at the same time, assumed to engage in his theft activity independently of him, so that an inherent paradox exists. "If the thief is independently motivated to theft, that is in some sense *a priori* a 'thief,' then he will steal irrespectively of whether or not receivers exist." (Henry, 177:126)

Furthermore, emphasizing that the thief depends on and could not exist without the fence ignores the fact that the fence is in precisely the same position as the thief: he is dependent on outlets or a market for stolen goods. Frequently, this problem is resolved by the involvement of merchants who are tempted to purchase stolen goods at cheap prices in order that they may sell at a higher profit. Public demand for stolen goods also helps maintain the fence. Budget-conscious consumers are often willing to buy stolen goods, "no questions asked," and need little encouragement when presented with "bargain" prices. In addition, when they are victims of theft, members of the general public are frequently willing to forego prosecution once their stolen goods have been restored to them or they have received compensation. In a similar way, insurance companies and private detective agencies protect the fence from public or legal reaction to the theft, either by diluting the rightful owner's desire to pursue those responsible by providing compensation, or by cooperating with him for the return of stolen property.

Equally important, in Henry's view, the saying ignores that official complicity of some kind is apparently required if the prospective fence hopes to buy and sell stolen goods regularly and over a period of time. Sometimes the official protection a fence enjoys is an outgrowth of the corruption of law enforcement and justice on a large scale. Present-day fences connected to Mafia syndicates, for example, apparently extend to the traffic in stolen property the corruption of legal authorities achieved by way of general racketeering activities. Other times, the basis of the police-fence link is more direct:[12]

▶ Because of their respective positions, both have access to resources desired by the other. The fence is able to give information about thefts, for he knows who commits them as well as where the goods are likely to be; he can also set up a thief, arranging for the police to be present; he is often able to secure the return of stolen goods as a result of his knowledge and contacts; and finally, he is able to offer the police 'bargains' or gifts of stolen goods . . . In return for all this, police can warn the fence of impending investigations or of the danger of purchasing certain goods. They can provide protection by not pursuing their enquiries should their investigations lead to him. ("On The Fence," *British Journal of Law and Society*, 1977:132) ◀

All things considered, therefore, Henry judges that the saying "if no receivers, no thieves" rests on pretending that real crimes are committed by "real" criminals, not by ordinary people and certainly not by oneself. The recognition may be too hard to fathom, he says, "that honest people are not so honest after all . . . and harder still to recognize our own contribution to the nature of such things."

This review of Henry's assessment, along with the literature survey that preceded it, spotlights what has been a preeminent issue in the sociolegal writings on the traffic in stolen property: the fence's role in the overall flow of stolen property from thieves to eventual consumers, and whether or not enforcement efforts should be more rationally directed at him than at other agents in the traffic in stolen property; thieves, occasional receivers, those to whom the fence sells, or complicitous authorities. This issue is a complicated one and has provided a continuous backdrop for a good deal of the prodding and questioning that developed into the present document's description of a modern-day dealer in stolen goods and the world in which he conducts his business.

---

12. See chapter 7 for historical examples of this police-fence link.

Bibliography

Adler, Patricia, and Adler, Peter. The Irony of Secrecy in the Drug World. *Urban Life*, 8:447–465, 1980.
_____. Relationships Between Dealers: The Social Organization of Illicit Drug Transactions. *Social Science Review*, 67:270–278, 1983.
Albini, Joseph. *The American Mafia: Genesis of a Legend*. New York: Appleton-Century-Crofts, 1971.
Applebaum, Herbert, ed. *Work in Market and Industrial Societies*. Albany: State University of New York Press, 1984.
Asbury, Herbert. *The Gangs of New York: An Informal History of the Underworld*. New York: G.P. Putnam's Sons, 1928.
Association of Grand Jurors of New York County. *The Criminal Receiver of Stolen Goods—Source of Organized Crime and Creator of Criminals*. Report of the Prison Committee. New York: Putnam, 1928.
Barnes, Robert Earl. The Fence: Crime's Real Profiteer. *Reader's Digest*, 155: 152–154, 1973.
Becker, Howard. *Outsiders: Studies in the Sociology of Deviance*. New York: Free Press, 1963.
Black, Jack. *You Can't Win*. New York: Macmillan Co., 1926.
Blakey, Robert, and Goldsmith, Michael. Criminal Redistribution of Stolen Property: The Need for Law Reform. *Michigan Law Review*, 74:1511–1613, 1976.
Blau, P. Structural Effects. *American Sociological Review*, 25:178–193, 1960.
Borrow, George. *Celebrated Trials, Vol. 2*. New York: Payson and Clarke, 1928.
Bryant, Clifton, ed. *Deviant Behavior: Occupational and Organizational Bases*. Chicago: Rand McNally, 1974.
Buffalo, M.D., and Rogers, Joseph. Behavioral Norms, Moral Norms, and Attachment: Problems of Deviance and Conformity. *Social Problems*, 19:101–113, 1971.
Cameron, Mary Owen. *The Booster and the Snitch: Department Store Shoplifting*. New York: Macmillan, 1964.
Caplovitz, David. *The Merchants of Harlem*. Beverly Hills: Sage Publications, 1973.
Chesney, Kellow. *The Anti-Society: An Account of the Victorian Underworld*. Boston: Gambit, 1970.
Clinard, Marshall. *The Black Market*. New York: Rinehart & Co., 1952.
Colquhoun, P. *A Treatise on the Commerce and Police of the River Thames*. London: Printed for Joseph Mawman, 1800.

———. (A Magistrate) *A Treatise on the Police of the Metropolis*. London: Printed by H. Fry for C. Dilly in the Poultry, 1796.

Crapsey, Edward. *The Nether Side of New York*. New York: Sheldon and Co., 1872.

Crissman, Lawrence W. On Networks. *Cornell Journal of Social Relations*, e:72–81, 1964.

Defoe, Daniel. *The King of the Pirates, Including the Life and Actions of Jonathan Wild*. New York: The Jenson Society, 1901.

Dickens, Charles. *Oliver Twist*. London: Oxford University Press, 1949.

Dubin, Robert, ed. *Handbook of Work, Organization, and Society*. Chicago: Rand McNally, 1976.

Elliott, Ian D. Theft and Related Problems: England, Australia, and the U.S.A. Compared. *International and Comparative Law Quarterly*, 26:110–149, 1977.

Emerson, E. Frank. They can get it for you better than wholesale. *New York Magazine*, Nov. 22:34–37, 1971.

Fielding, Henry. *History of the Life of the Late Jonathan Wild. The Complete Works of Henry Fielding*. New York: Barnes and Noble, 1967, Vol. 2.

Fisher, Claude; Jackson, Robert; Strieve, C. Ann; Guson, Kathleen; and McCallister Jones, Lynne. *Networks and Places: Social Relations in the Urban Setting*. New York: The Free Press, 1977.

Foster, George M. Godparents and Social Networks in Tzintzuntzan. *Southwestern Journal of Anthropology*, 25:261, 278, 1969.

Friedman, E.A., and Havighurst, J. Work and Retirement. Nosow, Sigmund and Form, William, eds. *Man, Work, and Society*. New York: Basic Books, 1962, pp. 41–55.

Fuller, Ronald. *The Beggars' Brotherhood*. London: George Allen and Unwin, 1936.

Gay, John. *The Beggar's Opera*. Lincoln: University of Nebraska Press, Regents' Restoration Drama Series, 1969.

Granovetter, Mark. *Getting a Job: A Study of Contacts and Careers*. Cambridge: Harvard University Press, 1974.

Green, R. 1592: The Second Part of Cony-Catching. Judges, A., ed. *The Elizabethan Underworld*. London: Routledge and Kegan Paul, 1965, pp. 149–179.

Hall, Jerome. *Theft, Law, and Society*, 2d ed. Indianapolis: Bobbs-Merrill Co., 1952.

Hall, Richard. *Organizations: Structure and Process*. Englewood Cliffs: Prentice-Hall, 1972.

Harrington, J.W. Swift Punishment of Crafty Fences Seen As Key to War on Theft. *New York Herald-Tribune*, April 11:3, 1926.

Harrison, William. *The Description of England*. London: North Shropshire Society, 1876. George Edelton, ed. Ithaca: Cornell University Press, 1968.

Hayward, Arthur, ed. *Lives of the Most Remarkable Criminals*. London: George Routledge and Sons, 1927, Vol. 1.

Henry, Stuart. On the Fence. *The British Journal of Law and Society*, 4:124–133, 1977.

Henry, Stuart. *The Hidden Economy*. London: Martin Robertson & Co., 1978.

Hill, Matthew Davenport. *Suggestions for the Repression of Crime*. London: John W. Parker and Sons, 1837.

Hitchen, Charles. *The Regulator: or A Discovery of the Thieves, Thief Takers, and Locks, alias Receivers of Stolen Goods, in and about the City of London*. London: Printed for T. Warner at the Black Boy in Pater-Noster Row, 1718.

Howson, Gerald. *Thief-Taker General*. New York: St. Martin's Press, 1971.

Humphreys, Christmas. *The Great Pearl Robbery of 1913*. London: William Heinemann, 1929.

Hutton, Luke. 1596: The Black Dogs of Newgate. Judges, Arthur V., ed. *The Elizabethan Underworld*. London: Routledge and Sons, 1965, pp. 265–291.

Ianni, Francis. *Black Mafia*. New York: Simon & Schuster, 1974.

Inciardi, James A. *Careers in Crime*. Skokie: Rand McNally, 1975.

Kanter, Rosabeth. *Men and Women of the Corporation*. New York: Basic Books, 1977.

Katz, Fred. Occupational Contact Networks. Nosow, Sigmund and Form, William, eds. *Man, Work, and Society*. New York: Basic Books, 1962, pp. 317–321.

Keenan, R. Kenneth, and Peterson, Lorrain. On Fencing. Report prepared for the National Institute of Law Enforcement and Criminal Justice, Law Enforcement Assistance Administration, August 1973. Mimeographed.

Klockars, Carl. *The Professional Fence*. New York: Free Press, 1974.

———. Jonathan Wild and the Modern Sting. Inciardi, James and Charles Faupel, eds. *History and Crime: Implications for Criminal Justice Policy*, ed. Beverly Hills: Sage, 1980, pp. 225–260.

Lawler III, Edward. *Motivation in Work Organizations*. Monterey: Brooks/Cole, 1973.

Letkemann, Peter. *Crime as Work*. Englewood Cliffs: Prentice-Hall, 1973.

Life and Death of Mary Frith, commonly called Moll Cutpurse. London, British Museum, 1612. Author Unknown.

Lupsha, Peter. American Values and Organized Crime: Suckers and Wiseguys. Girgus, Sam B., ed. *Myth, Ideology, and Popular Culture*. Albuquerque: University of New Mexico Press. 1981, pp. 144–154.

Mainwaring, George. *Observations on the Present State of the Police*. London, 1822.

McIntosh, Mary. *The Organization of Crime*. London: Anchor Press, 1975.

McIntosh, Mary. Thieves and Fences: Markets and Power in Professional Crime. *British Journal of Criminology*, 16:257–266, 1976.

McMullan, John. Criminal Organization in Sixteenth and Seventeenth Century London. *Social Problems*, 29:311–323, 1982.

McMullan, John. *The Canting Crew: London's Criminal Underworld, 1550–1700*. New Brunswick: Rutgers University Press, 1984.

Miller, Gale. *Odd Jobs: The World of Deviant Work*. Englewood Cliffs: Prentice-Hall, 1978.

Moore, Mark. *Buy and Bust*. Lexington: Lexington Books, 1977.

Neale, William. *Juvenile Delinquency in Manchester: Its Causes and History*. Manchester, 1940.

Nosow, Sigmund, and Form, William, eds. *Man, Work, and Society*. New York: Basic Books, 1962.

Note: Constitutionality of Presumptions on Receiving Stolen Property. Turning the Thumbscrew in Michigan and Other States. *Wayne Law Review*, 21:1437–1454, 1975.

Note: Property Theft Enforcement and the Criminal Secondary Purchaser of Stolen Goods. *Yale Law Journal*, 89:1225–1241, 1980.

Partridge, E. *Dictionary of the Underworld*. London: Routledge and Kegan Paul, 1968.

Pike, Luke Owen. *A History of Crime in England, Vol. 1. 2d Series*. London: Smith, Elder and Co., 1876.

Pringle, Patrick. *Hue and Cry*. Great Britain: William Morrow and Co., n.d.

Prus, Robert C., and Irini, Styllianoss. *Hookers, Rounders, and Desk Clerks: The Social Organization of the Hotel Community*. Toronto: Gage, 1980.

Prus, Robert, and Sharper, C.R.D. *Road Hustler*. Toronto: Gage, 1977.

Raub, Richard. Effect of Antifencing Operations on Encouraging Crime. *Criminal Justice Review*, 9:78–83, 1984.

Rice, T.S. Preface to Prison Committee of the Association of Grand Jurors of New York County. *Criminal Receivers in the United States*. New York: G.P. Putnam's Sons, 1928, pp. iii–xiii.

Roselius, T., and Benton, D. Marketing Theory and the Fencing of Stolen Goods. *Denver Law Journal*, 50:177–205, 1973.

Roselius, Ted; Hoel, R.; Benton, Douglas; Howard, M.; Sciglimpaglia, D. *The Design of Anti-Fencing Strategies*. Fort Collins: Colorado State University Press, 1975.

Roumasset, James, and Hadreas, John. Addicts, Fences, and the Market for Stolen Goods. *Public Finance Quarterly*, 5:247–572, 1977.

Shaffer, Ron; Klose, Kevin; and Lewis, Alfred E. *Surprise! Surprise!* New York: Viking, 1977.

Sharma, K.N. Resource Networks and Resource Groups in the Social Structure. *Eastern Anthropologist*, 11:13–28, 1969.

Shover, Neal. Structures and Careers in Burglary. *Journal of Criminal Law, Criminology, and Police Science*, 63:540–549, 1972.

Stanton, William J. *Fundamentals of Marketing*. 3rd ed. New York: McGraw-Hill, 1971.

Steffensmeier, Darrell. Organization Properties and Sex-Segregation in the Underworld: Building a Sociological Theory of Sex Differences in Crime. *Social Forces*, 61:1010–1032, 1983.

Steffensmeier, Darrell, and Terry, Robert. Institutional Sexism in the Underworld: Male Criminals and Their Use/Misuse of Women as Crime Partners. *Sociological Inquiry*, forthcoming.

Sutherland, Edwin H. *The Professional Thief*. Chicago: University of Chicago Press, 1937.

U.S. Congress, Senate. *Criminal Redistribution Systems and Their Economic Impact on Small Business: Hearings Before the Select Committee on Small Business*. 93rd Cong., 1st Sess., May 1 and 2, Criminal Redistribution (Fencing) Systems, Pt. 1., Washington, D.C.: Government Printing Office, 1973.

————— 93rd Cong., 1st Sess., May 1 and 2, Criminal Redistribution (Fencing) Systems, Pt. 2., Washington, D.C.: Government Printing Office, 1973.

————— 93rd Cong., 2nd Sess., April 30 and May 2, Criminal Redistribution (Fencing) of Goods Stolen From Legitimate Business Activities and Their Effect on Commerce, Pt. 3., Washington, D.C.: Government Printing Office, 1974.

————— *Professional Motor Vehicle Theft And Chop Shops: Hearings Before the Permanent Subcommittee On Investigations of the Committee On Governmental Affairs*. 96th Cong., 1st Sess., Nov. 27–30 and Dec. 4, 1979, Washington D.C.: Government Printing Office, 1980.

————— Select Committee on Small Business. *The Impact of Crime on Small Business, Part VI Criminal Redistribution (Fencing) Systems*. Sen. Rep. No. 1318, 93rd Cong., 2nd Sess., Washington, D.C.: Government Printing Office, 1974.

————— Permanent Subcommittee on Investigations of the Committee on Government Operations: *Hearings On Organized Crime: Stolen Securities*. 92nd Cong., 1st Sess., Washington, D.C.: Government Printing Office, 1971.

U.S. Department of Justice, Criminal Conspiracies Division, 1978: *Taking the Offensive*. Washington, D.C.: Government Printing Office.

U.S. Department of Justice, Criminal Conspiracies Division, 1979: *What Happened*. Washington, D.C.: Government Printing Office.

Vincent, Teresa. *My Life In The Mafia*. Greenwich: Fawcett, 1973.

Vroom, Vincent. *Work and Motivation*. New York: Wiley, 1964.

Walsh, Marilyn E. *The Fence: A New Look at the World of Property Theft*. Westport: Greenwood Press, 1977.

Weiner, Kenneth A.; Stephens, Christine K.; and Besachuk, Donna L. Making Inroads into Property Crime: An Analysis of the Detroit Antifencing Program. *Journal of Police Science and Administration*, 11:311–327, 1983.

Weiner, Tim. *Philadelphia Inquirer*, November 2, 1984.

White, Harrison. *Chains of Opportunity*. Cambridge: Harvard University Press, 1970.

Whyte, William. Street Corner Society. Chicago: University of Chicago Press, 1955.

Wilken, Paul. Entrepreneurship: A Comparative and Historical Study. Ablex Publishing Corporation, 1979.

Zuckerman, Harriett. *Scientific Elite: Nobel Laureates in the United States*. New York: Free Press, 1977.

Index